T

velopment

Prof

Brian Foss
of London

Understanding Child Development

**Psychological perspectives in an
interdisciplinary field of inquiry**

Sara Meadows

First published in 1986 by Unwin Hyman Ltd
Third impression 1989

Reprinted 1992 and 1995
by Routledge
11 New Fetter Lane, London EC4P 4EE

Simultaneously published in the USA and Canada
by Routledge
29 West 35th Street, New York, NY 10001

Printed and bound in Great Britain by
Butler and Tanner Ltd, Frome and London

British Library Cataloguing in Publication Data

A catalogue record for this book is available from the British Library.

ISBN 0–415–08436–9

Contents

Acknowledgements

The author and publishers would like to thank the copyright holders below for permission to reproduce the following material:

Figure 2 from *Advances in Child Development and Behaviour*, vol. 17, 1982, reproduced by permission of Academic Press; **Figures 3, 4, 5 and 7** from M. M. Haith and J. J. Campos (eds.), vol. 2 of the *Handbook of Child Development*, 1983, reproduced by permission of John Wiley & Sons, Inc. Publishers; **Figure 9** from R. Kail, *The development of memory in children*, 1979, **Figure 13** from R. Mayer, 'Mathematical ability', in R. J. Sternberg (ed.), *Human abilities: an information-processing approach*, 1985, both reproduced by permission of W. H. Freeman; **Figure 11**, **Table 3** and accompanying text, and **Figure 12** from B. Kroll and G. Wells (eds.), *Explorations in the development of writing*, 1983, reproduced by permission of John Wiley and Sons Limited; **Figure 14** © 1972 by the American Psychological Association, reprinted by permission of the authors; **Figure 15** and **Table 4** by permission of British Psychological Society and the authors; **Figure 17** © 1980 by the American Psychological Association, reprinted by permission of the author; **Figures 18 and 19** by permission of The Controller of Her Majesty's Stationery Office; Longman Group Ltd for pages 155–6 of Houlbrooke, *The English Family 1450–1700*; **Plate 1** © Bodleian Library, Oxford; **Plate 2** © Henri Cartier-Bresson; **Plates 3, 4, 6, 7 and 15** © G. A. Clark; **Plates 8 and 11** © John Bignell; **Plate 9** by courtesy of the Board of Trustees of the Victoria and Albert Museum; and **Plate 12** © O. P. Marzaroli.

Preface

My concern in this book is to discuss the course of child development. I regard understanding child development as uniquely important both for its practical implications for minimizing unhappiness and maximizing goodness and fulfilment, and for its intrinsic intellectual interest. All of us have been children and most of us will be parents: understanding child development may ameliorate the human condition. All of us know a lot about child development; few of us could make exact statements about why a particular child or children in general should have developed in this familiar or that unfamiliar way: understanding child development is a riveting intellectual problem. I shall not propose either child-rearing panaceas or stunning new basic theories. My more modest aim is to look at work which is either current or fairly recent and some older very influential work; and to consider how it may begin to be fitted together into a good theoretical framework. There will be a lot of pointing out what we don't know, but also, I hope, some pointing out exciting new questions, answers and ways of working.

I am a psychologist whose recent teaching has been work with experienced school teachers doing higher degrees that included courses on developmental psychology. My research career began with an esoteric theoretical problem studied using experiment and factor analysis, and moved to work which was much more concerned with a tangle of 'real life' issues and with the methodological problems involved in undertaking rigorous but uninterrupted measurement and observation of the life of the child. These experiences have shaped my view of what the psychology of child development is and could be, and hence the approach I have taken to writing this book. It is about my current understanding of what child development is and why it happens as it does: it

is not an encyclopaedia of experiments or an instruction manual of child-rearing techniques. I have tried to give references to the research which substantiate my assertions so that readers can evaluate them for themselves, as limitations of space, and the need to keep the argument going, made it impossible to give much more detail on the material I have used. Readers may draw recommendations from these pages about what to do and what to avoid when dealing with children: I have not intended that they should do so, and I take no responsibility for the results! Nor do I claim that my current understanding of child development is correct, complete, or what I will myself believe forever. I am merely presenting a frame of reference which I think is worth trying, and material to fill it out which seems to make a useful fit. I am not presenting a completely worked out and documented theory.

It is not a new theoretical frame, nor is there much dramatic new evidence. Experts in any of the fields I discuss will find nothing in my discussion that they have not known about for a long time, and may, I fear, be exasperated by my simplifications and omissions. I hope that they will accept my account as an approximation to what the non-expert might usefully think about, before and during the reading of the more detailed and advanced material I have tried to cite. I have tried to bring together areas that have been worked on separately because I believe we are far enough advanced in our understanding of child development to try out what an overall picture might be like. I also believe that such a trying-out may, even if no coherent picture emerges, provide some insights drawn from areas outside the expert's normal range of reference which will enrich further work in the area of detailed study. There are signs of this happening, for example in growing links between areas of developmental psychology, and in two-way traffic between researchers working on adults and researchers working on children.

Prefaces are places for stating why one has done what one has, and also for acknowledging the help one has had in doing it. I want first to offer my general thanks to the international community of developmental psychologists who, although they produce far more than I can keep up with, even allowing for the repetitive, the bad and the boring, have generated enough ideas and put forward sufficient data to fill my professional life and, more importantly, to move us further towards understanding child development. Nearer home, I owe an enormous amount to talking with friends, colleagues, teachers and students over the last eighteen years, and I am most grateful for this. While writing this book, I was most generously provided with unpublished material by members of the Thomas Coram Research Unit, the Child Health and Education Study (Director Professor Neville Butler), the MRC National Survey of Health and Development, the South London Under Fives Project, and others. I used libraries in London and in Bristol which may have by their excellence misled me about the availability of material: the librarians of the School of Education of the University of Bristol were particularly helpful and clever despite being seriously overworked; they were paragons of patience and efficiency and I

have learned a great deal from them. My secretary, Maureen Harvey, shares all these virtues, and deserves the highest praise. Among the friends who read and criticized parts of the text were Elizabeth Robinson, Maggie Mills, Sandy Acker, Peter Robinson, Brian Foss, Claire L'Enfant, Steve Whittaker, John Conroy, and John Cowley: Philip Meadows helped with indexing. Mike Smith of the History of Art Department, University of Bristol, and the staff of the Victoria and Albert Museum, the Ashmolean, and the British Museum helped with the pictures. My thanks to them all.

When I was 9, my best friend in the junior school and I ganged up on another little girl, and if I remember correctly I hit her, though I hope not with the hammer I think I remember. Certainly she then had to be placated so that we should not be reported to the teacher, and in the course of doing this I used as a bribe the promise to dedicate a book to her when I grew up and was an author. While this is not the sort of book we then expected, it has benefited from my experience of children from my own childhood on, and I do therefore feel it is appropriate to redeem my promise now. I was wrong to make it, but it is right to acknowledge the contribution of the young Margaret and the young Sara and many half-forgotten others to whatever progress I have made towards understanding child development.

Note on reading

Although I have tried to make this text intelligible and sound enough to 'do' alone for readers who do not wish to take things further, I am very anxious that readers should go on from this book to the more detailed information that lies behind what I have said here. I have therefore tried to give sufficient reference for this to be done; as far as possible I have referred to review papers which are worth reading in themselves and also provide citations of further sources. Limitations of space in many cases preclude citing the original research papers: I hope readers will track these down through the review sources given. Among the criteria which guided me in choosing references were their importance, intelligibility, accessibility (a serious problem as libraries' costs rise and purchases fall) and how well they represented their field. A few 'non-psychology' books are included, mainly because they provide insights and enjoyment complementary to that gained from the 'standard works'.

Note on pictures

The pictures in this book are there for three reasons. First, to provide agreeable resting places in the text. Second, because each can be related to one or more important issues in developmental psychology (for example, the Cartier-Bresson photograph of children in Seville reflects the relation of play to the ecosystem, in this case showing enjoyable play and classic 'play faces' in a city ravaged by civil war). Third, each has aesthetic merit or historic interest, possibly on a minor scale.

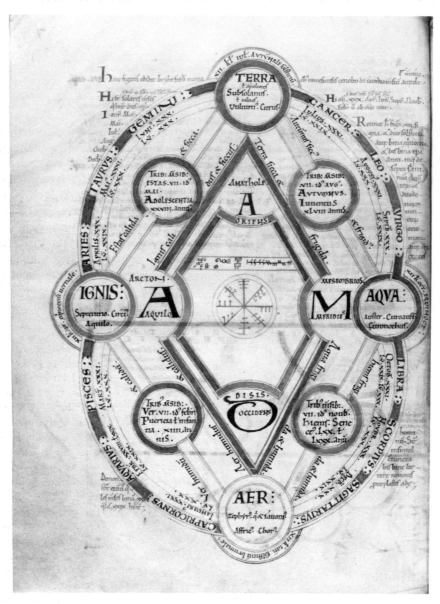

Plate 1 An illuminated diagram from a Natural Science textbook compiled by the monk Byrhtferth at Ramsey Abbey between about 1080 and 1090. It is used as illustration here because in its picture of the place of Man in the universe it links the four ages (boyhood and infancy, adolescence, young manhood, and old age) to the influence of the signs of the Zodiac, the four seasons, the four points of the compass, the four elements of earth, air, fire and water, and the four humours (hot, cold, wet and dry). It might thus be seen as an early model of the developmental psychology of personality. Childhood and infancy (bottom left dark circle), ages 0–14, lie between air and fire, west and north, Capricorn and Pisces, and are wet and hot; adolescence (top left), ages 14–28, between fire and earth, north and east, Aries and Gemini, and is hot and dry. (Young manhood lasts, readers will be glad to learn, until 48, and old age to 70 or 80.) Which of the four humours dominated the body had implications for medical treatment and for 'personality' (see Chapter 5), and may have influenced concepts of education and child-rearing.

1 Introducing the study of child development

Conceptual issues

Before we embark on either description or explanation of the course of 'child development', let alone before we consider what efforts we might make to change its course, I must stress that neither 'child' nor 'development' could be said to be simple unproblematic concepts; in particular they are inextricable from beliefs about how to bring up children. There are many variations between cultures on what they believe children 'naturally' are and how they should behave (Laboratory of Comparative Human Cognition 1983).* There are also historical changes within societies. The study of the history of western childhood is only just beginning and its picture is controversial. Philippe Ariès' pioneering study (Ariès 1962) argued that strong concern and affection for children, and a belief that childhood was an intrinsically valuable period, were historically recent developments associated with the rise of the affluent household in the sixteenth and seventeenth centuries. Previously, he claimed, there was no concept of 'childhood': children were regarded with indifference by their parents or as inferior miniature adults to be strictly reared and severely punished. De Mause (1976) put forward an even blacker model of maltreatment and cruelty to children – infanticide, beatings, sexual abuse and a casual acceptance of high mortality through infection, accident or child-rearing practices such as wet-nursing or using opiates to quieten a crying child. Ariès and De Mause have both been accused of selecting their data without much concern for their representativeness, and of interpreting dubious 'facts' in unjustified ways (Pollock 1983; Houlbrooke

1984). As more evidence is examined, the picture of what was happening to the 'crowds and crowds of little children [who] are strangely absent from the written record' (Laslett 1971) becomes clearer and more complex. Houlbrooke (1984, p. 155–6) summarizes the relationships between parents and young children (in the English family between 1450 and 1700) in a picture which resembles what emerges from the mainly nineteenth century diaries reviewed by Pollock (1983) and the autobiographies from a later period collected by Burnett (1982).

The Middle Ages passed on an ideal picture of the relationship between parents and their offspring. Children were welcome gifts from God. Parental love was the most deeply rooted of all human instincts, and showed itself especially in the mother's tender and loving care of the helpless baby. But it was futile to grieve in the face of infant deaths. Rather should the truly Christian mother be glad that God had taken her child to himself. The child which died before seven, the age of reason, was normally incapable of mortal sin and assured of paradise. Yet the child inherited original sin, which began to manifest itself even in infantile greed and rage, and the inborn propensity grew with intelligence. So it was the duty of the solicitous parent to correct his child with the rod. Successful parenthood largely depended upon the ability to curb one's natural inclinations, and those who did not want their children to become soft, truculent and good-for-nothing were wise to put them out in late childhood to undergo further discipline and training at the hands of strangers.

Much of the inherited picture survived throughout this period, but it changed in important respects. The Protestant reformers took over an emphasis on original sin and the parents' corrective responsibility. They also laid greater emphasis on the parents' part in early and thorough religious education. The humanists, on the other hand, believing as they did in the child's capacity for good and the moral neutrality of

* Full references quoted in text appear in the Bibliography on pp. 212–37.

13

its impulses, sought to protect innocence and prevent deterioration rather than to correct inborn vices. To show natural parental affection seemed less dangerous than hitherto. Humanist readiness to give expression to natural pleasures and sorrows made more acceptable the display of delight in children in letters and of a qualified grief at their loss in memorial inscriptions. From the sixteenth century onwards there was a greater variety of patterns of upbringing. Yet the fusion of Christian and humanist ideas encouraged a 'middle way' in upbringing, between the extremes of severity and indulgence. It enhanced the complexity of the task of nurture, and consequently of fine judgement on the part of those who undertook it.

Actual experience and practice often stood in contrast with ideals. Children were not always welcome. Some birth control was practised, and the danger of infanticide was widely recognized. Yet despite the ease with which infanticidal practices could be masked within families, parish registers suggest that infant and child mortality were relatively low and very largely explicable in terms of environment and disease. There is much direct evidence of the reality of loving care in some families and of parental grief in face of the loss of children. Women of the upper classes did not generally suckle their own children, though humanist and Protestant propaganda may have persuaded a minority to do so. But this did not preclude care and solicitude in the choice and supervision of wet-nurses. Differences between the life patterns of socio-economic groups had many other effects on the child's prospects. The offspring of the urban poor, rapidly growing in numbers during this period, always had the poorest chances of surviving infancy. It was the poorer groups in society who had to exploit their children's labour in the struggle for survival at the earliest point. Only fathers and mothers who enjoyed the advantages conferred by economic means, education and a certain amount of leisure were able to approach the ideal of intensive parenthood set out in the literature of counsel, carefully polishing their children's manners, inculcating the principles of religion and laying the foundations of literacy. Such instruction for life as most children had from their parents was probably gained in byre and field, at spinning-wheel and oven. But the quality of parenthood was not of course determined by material circumstances alone, very important though these were. The unquantifiable and still only partially understood elements of individual character were

crucial in this period as they still are today (Houlbrooke 1984, pp. 155–6).

The relationship between what is believed about children, what is prescribed as appropriate child-rearing, and what is actually done, is not clear. However different basic theories carry different practical implications. For example, if children are seen as firmly predestined from birth (because of innate qualities such as different levels of intelligence) to be intellectuals or technicians or general workers, the most efficient way of educating them may be to provide separate training in the appropriate roles. Such a system was recommended by Plato in *The Republic* and might be identified in the tripartite secondary school system set up in Britain under the 1944 Education Act. The research problems will centre on how to make the initial diagnosis of the child's nature (various psychometricians – Burt, for example – were involved in this) and on how to run the education. If, on the other hand, children are seen as changed and shaped by their experience, with little or nothing in the way of predestined characteristics, initial diagnosis is irrelevant, and child-rearing and education are just a matter of providing the right experience. Advocates of this view judge the 'rightness' of experience according to a variety of criteria: for Skinner in *Walden Two* and for the inhabitants of Huxley's *Brave New World*, the main criterion is fitting happily into and serving society, and a major means to this end is pervasive and skilful conditioning. Huxley, unlike Skinner hostile to Utopias, incorporates in his techniques of child-rearing and social control elements of genetic selection (and genetic engineering) and chemical control of development and behaviour both before and after birth: he also suggests that for the highly creative and innovative intellectual even this all-enveloping system might not work. Skinner has not seemed to be troubled by such libertarian qualms, arguing that an effective system which would make all development smooth and happy would be preferable to the ineffective conflict-filled systems and the unhappy results which he believes exist now.

Similar disagreements exist about the nature of human nature. Assuming that the infant is nearer to what is 'natural' than the adult (a dangerous assumption which I shall seek to question later), infant 'nature' has been said to be innately good, better than adults'. Rousseau argued for an education of maximum freedom so that the child's innate goodness should not be spoiled or his creativity, spontaneity and ability to love curtailed. I say 'his' deliberately, since Rousseau saw women as inferior and fit only to be trained to serve males: the history of his own children is unclear, but he claimed in his autobiography to have sent them as babies to orphanages. Despite this personal bad example, the progressive educational movement took up Rousseau's ideas and this model of the child has dominated early childhood education. Non-interventionist ideas may also be seen in Piaget's accounts of learning, teaching and cognitive development.

An alternative view of child nature was the older one of natural badness, Original Sin, unsocialized egocentricity, etc. This view emphasized children's unpleasant characteristics and prescribed strict, punitive and intrusive childrearing and education: these took some extraordinarily harsh forms (see de Mause 1976; but also Pollock 1983). It is hard to find a contemporary example, though Sir Truby King's prescriptions in the 1930s of conditioning babies to a rigid four-hour feeding schedule perhaps comes near. Many psychologists have had in mind, however, views of children as inferior to adults, being, for example, egocentric, dominated by animal instincts, irrational and so forth, and needing to grow out of, or be trained out of, these undesirable faults.

The 'biological' and 'social' 'causes' of development

Underlying all the debate outlined so far are a knot of difficult issues. The core one is the question of the relationship between 'biological' and 'social' factors in human life, especially human development, since development is often said to be about how the 'biological' infant turns into the 'social' adult. How to think of this crucial question is a very complex problem, bedevilled by the tradition of separating and opposing 'biology' and 'society', 'heredity' and 'environment', 'nature' and 'nurture'. Once opposed, one pole is valued highly and the other denigrated, and, since neither can alone provide a satisfactory explanation of all human development, there is a history of see-sawings between polar extremes. This is all the more unsatisfactory because 'biological' and 'social' are not at all clearly separable. Biological facts, such as the physical consequences of possessing a functioning Y chromosome, are acted on by society, which classifies its members as 'male' or 'female'. Social preferences have always been among the forces admitted as working for 'natural selection'; social changes, such as industrialization, have biological consequences, such as changes in what causes illness or death. Even at the level of the genes, exactly how their instructions work may be strongly influenced by the environment. Hofer (1981) gives an example:

the amount of dark fur on the feet and nose of Siamese cats depends on the ambient temperature in which they were reared as kittens, the skin on the extremities being normally cooler than other skin areas. The expression of this genetic predisposition depends on the temperature of the skin during a critical period of postnatal development. Raised in an incubator, Siamese cats turn out uniformly light, and if in an icebox, uniformly dark (Hofer 1981, p. 10).

Thus even if there is a genetic difference between two individuals, exactly what its influence is will depend on the environment. If every relevant aspect of their environment has been identical, differences between them can be attributed to how their genes expressed themselves *in that environment*. Reared in a different environment, again exactly the same for both individuals, the genetic difference may express itself differently and the differences between the two individuals' behaviour be completely changed. Imagine, for example, that one of the two has genes which predispose that individual to highly aggressive behaviour and the other does not. Both are reared in a society which encourages aggression, like Margaret Mead's Arapesh or ancient Sparta.

15

The former will find this a congenial society, will be very aggressive indeed and will be regarded as a satisfactory or even admirable citizen. The latter will find it uncongenial, will be less aggressive and less well-regarded, and may have a lesser sense of self-esteem and social acceptability. Alternatively, suppose that both are reared in a society which discourages aggression, as Mead said the Mundugumor did. Success and public approval will come to the genetically less aggressive person; dissatisfaction, low social acceptability and neurosis will come to the other, who is being required by society to suppress genetically 'natural' behaviour. Heredity and environment will interact to produce differences not only in aggression, the only part of behaviour where there is a genetic difference, but in other areas of behaviour and thinking which are related to social experience, such as self-esteem, social role, and acceptance of social values.

This is quite obviously a gross simplification of the sort of interaction between genetic programming and experience that really happens in development. In particular, we would be rash to assume that any given environment is 'identical' or works 'identically' for two individuals, or indeed two groups. If the environment does differ, it may be these differences as much as any genetic ones which cause differences in behaviour. To take aggression as an example a second time, it is possible that there is a genetically caused difference in aggression between males and females. In many species, our own among them, males are more aggressive in more situations than females are. However it is quite clear that at least in the human species there are systematic and pervasive differences in the ways that males and females are treated, from birth on, which overlay any genetic difference. By and large, males are treated as stronger, more independent, braver than females, and their aggression is accepted or even encouraged: females are treated as softer and weaker, more dependent, more in need of protection, and aggression or even self-assertion is discouraged except occasionally, in private, or when very indirectly expressed.

I have written here as though environments impinged on passive individuals, but this, of course, is not the case. Individuals' behaviour, idiosyncratic as a result of genetic programming and past experience, will elicit reactions from the outside social world which correlate with those idiosyncracies. The child who has, for example, a genetically caused articulation problem, such as a cleft palate, may be less rewarding to listen to, less encouraged to talk, less rewarded for social interaction, more introverted, more reclusive and lower in self-esteem than the child whose conversation has been more accessible to listeners. There may be deliberate selection of one environment rather than another; there may be selective attention to particular aspects of environments. It has been suggested that much of development is a process of negotiation or transaction between the child and the surrounding adults or other important social facts of life. This metaphor too has its dangers, but we will use it at times.

The implication of the interweaving in development of 'biological' and 'social' is that theory and research must deal with them together. Neither can be reduced to the other. Which is more important in explaining a particular phenomenon will vary, will be dependent both on the phenomenon and on the sort of explanation sought. It has often been seen as a reason for studying children that they are nearer the 'natural', 'biological' state than the adult who has become a member of the 'social' world. This is a misleading belief in important ways (Gottlieb 1983). The feral child, the isolated monkey of Harlow's experiments, surviving without any social contact, is not more 'natural' than the child or monkey growing up in a family or other social group. Harlow's experiments show that social experience is necessary for much social behaviour such as successful mating; similarly, physical experience such as movement is necessary for much of the development of physical structures, as well as behaviour (Hofer 1981).

Scarr and Kidd (1983), in a useful review of 'developmental behaviour genetics', discuss the relationship between human biology and culture. They point out that there have been no important changes in brain capacity during the last 30,000 to 100,000 years, though changes in the internal organization of the brain are possible. Culture has reduced some selective pressures, for example the effects of climate which we can cope with by using artefacts such as clothes rather than by having to grow thicker fur. It has also imposed selective pressures, for example to be able to learn to use cultural artefacts and to live in groups. The possibility of complex learning is seen as one of the most important of evolutionary changes. Much of our genetic material is very similar to that of other primates: what makes us different is not the instructions for making proteins which our genes carry but the *regulation* of protein manufacture, in particular the prolongation of infantile characteristics or 'neoteny' which I discuss in the section on play at the end of this chapter. The evolution of brain development has selected not for a specific and limited brilliance, but for generalized adaptability, including adaptability to culture.

It seems likely in fact that much genetic programming for behaviour in human beings is relatively unspecific (Scarr and Kidd 1983). Some animals, such as insects, do have rigid programming of behaviour, but are only suited to relatively stable environments. If the animal is to encounter an unpredictable environment, one with a variety of possible events and even experiences never before encountered by any member of the species, it may do better if its genes have programmed into it a flexible repertoire of alternative tactics for coping with events, and an ability to learn from its interactions with the environment. Learning by proxy, by observing other individuals or by being taught by them, may be a particularly useful strategy. This sort of animal will need experience in order to cope with all the learning and development of behaviour that it must do. It will have a relatively long learning period – 'childhood' – and many characteristics designed to elicit and make use of learning opportunities. Although it may well have genetic programmes for certain behaviours, or genetically set goals, these are likely to be modified by experience: that is the same function may be

served first by a genetically programmed sequence of behaviour which later is superseded by a learned one. It also may have alternative routes to the same final state: not all individuals will learn exactly the same sequence.

Appropriate genetic information is necessary, but it is not at all clear that it should be regarded as in any sense more fundamental, the most essential cause where other contributions are relatively trivial. Rather the 'state of nature' is more probably for human beings to be brought up with other human beings: a long evolutionary history and a cultural history which is shorter in terms of years, but very much faster (probably) in producing change, have combined to make this possible. It should also be noted that 'natural' and 'best' are not synonyms: for a clear discussion of the philosophical pitfalls of equating the two see Radcliffe Richards (1982, pp. 67–80).

The belief that it is sensible to concentrate on one ultimate essential cause of development can be extremely strong. It is a belief allied to reductionism, the attempt to explain the subject matter of the social sciences in terms of the subject matter of the biological sciences, or the subject matter of biological sciences in terms of the physical sciences; and also to historicism, a belief in tracing events back to the first in a sequence which is then identified as the ultimate and most important cause of the final event in the sequence. Attributing complex behaviour, such as acts of aggression, to genetic programming or separation from mother during infancy is both reductionist and historicist. The danger of such attribution is that it overlooks other possible contributing causes which may be just as important. It increases the possibility that nothing will be done to intervene to break the sequence, as it is argued that people who had had the very early experience which 'causes' aggression much later will inevitably be particularly violent, so that it is too late to prevent it. Historicism can thus lead to a very determinist view of development and extremes of optimism or pessimism. It is clear, as we shall see, that in many areas early experience may have particularly marked effects so that an important cause of behaviour may be traced back through a sequence of several years. Nevertheless it is rarely the case that early events like separation from mother or even physical deprivation *invariably* lead to inexorable late results. Early disadvantage quite often but not by any means always leads to late disadvantage. Early privilege quite often (slightly more often) but not by any means always leads to late privilege (see, for example, Jencks *et al.* 1972). If there is continuity it may be because the early experience all by itself has such bad (or good) effects that nothing which happens afterwards can restore normal development, as is clearly the case in much early physical and perceptual development where, for example, rearing kittens without normal visual input at particular periods in the first few weeks of their lives will leave the cells in their visual cortex fewer in number, unusually specified and unresponsive (see Chapter 2). This sort of effect cannot, so far as we know, be reversed, so the animals are blind for ever after. In human psychological development, however, it seems more likely that there is continuity of the effects of an early experience because it sets in train other later experiences which have similar effects. Thus an embryo may have inherited a high genetic potential for intelligence from its intelligent parents; but intelligent parents are more likely to provide their child with good antenatal conditions, a trouble-free birth, suitable stimulation of language and cognitive development, a good school, support for school activities, a good diet etc., while the child's interacting genetic potential for high intelligence and good early experience are likely to provoke stimulation, support and high expectation from parents, teachers, siblings and others. Similarly it is well documented (Rutter and Madge 1976, Rutter 1985a,b,c) that disadvantage all too often does not come singly, but in battalions. Epidemiological studies suggest that single isolated events predict later psychosocial disorders very poorly, but that if there are multiple difficulties, especially difficulties which last for a long period of time, the likelihood of later problems such as persistent juvenile delinquency or psychiatric illness is much increased. On the other hand, if there are changes in the environment (such as adoption produces) there are likely to be changes in development. For example, although in three large American studies the IQ scores at adolescence of adopted children are positively correlated with the IQs of their biological parents, as theories which ascribe intelligence to genetic influence would predict, they are also higher than would be expected from their biological parents', raised towards the higher IQs of the adoptive parents (see Scarr and Weinberg 1983). A smaller British study of late adoption (Tizard 1977) described children who had had the same emotionally bleak orphanage rearing for the first few years of their lives and were, at the age of 4, socially, emotionally and intellectually retarded. Those who were then adopted into well-off families who made great efforts to give them the best possible life improved; those who were returned to their natural parent, to families which were much less rich in resources and were ambivalent about the return of the child, tended to deteriorate. Environmental changes for the better give opportunities for changes for the better in development; changes for the worse do the reverse.

Continuity and discontinuity in development

It is important to emphasize that 'continuity' in development is not a simple concept or simple to measure. As I discuss in the context of temperament (p. 144), it may not be clear what behaviour is 'continuous' with what precursor. Kagan (1984), for example, found in his longitudinal study that boys who were very timid and withdrawn at ages 3 to 8 had as adults chosen secure jobs with large employers rather than choosing risky entrepreneurial occupations. Aggressive boys were likely to be bullying adolescents (see also Olweus 1979; and p. 153 this volume). However, the detail of behaviour in a timid child just starting school and a young man in his twenties will involve many differences as well as some similarities: the young man will presumably have given up thumb-sucking, if not a general unwillingness to take risks. Unless we have a very good understanding of behaviour at several different levels of analysis we may not look at the right things when trying to assess continuity.

More importantly still, 'continuity' should mean links over time not just a lack of change. In other words, we need a fine-grained step-by-step analysis of what led to what, which will mean the inclusion of many relevant variables and an assessment of how inevitable or how weak the links between steps were. We need to examine how the 'same' behaviour functions for the child at different points in his or her life. We also need to know how long the continuity lasts, and whether it becomes unchangeable or can be broken by a change in circumstances. Preferably we would also have a theory of the underlying causes of continuities or discontinuities and a system of social or educational intervention or support which worked against bad effects and for good ones.

At this point I will sketch an example which will be returned to throughout the rest of this book (it is near the centre of my professional preoccupations). We know from a great many pieces of research that there is an association, perhaps a continuity, between growing up in a disadvantaged home and showing behaviour problems as a child and into early adulthood (for reviews of the literature, see, for example, Rutter and Madge 1976; Rutter 1985a). Does the family environment cause the child's problems, or are there alternative explanations such as a 'born to fail' child or the effects of other parts of the social system? What characteristics of the environment are effective, for worse or better? What characteristics of the child create, elicit, aggravate or tone down their effect? Are the effects short-term or long-term, reversible or permanent? What are the mechanisms of continuities or discontinuities?

Tentative answers to these questions would be roughly as follows: they are fully treated later in this book, particularly in the last chapter. At present there are many gaps in the evidence which prevent a full understanding. Family environments do affect their members and may cause them to have problems, and so too do other environments such as schools. There are however also 'genetic' influences which make problems more or less likely, for example susceptibility to alchohol, an impulsive temperament or a low IQ, and some individuals would probably function badly in most environments. Children affect their families as well as being affected by them; and both children's and families' problems may be associated with some extraneous variable or event, such as social disadvantage or war. Nevertheless, despite the validity of these alternative possibilities, family environments can cause problems in their children.

Among the general characteristics of families which are strongly associated with problematic outcomes for the children there are a few which have turned up repeatedly, particularly in studies of persistent delinquency and psychiatric disorder. Discordant and disorderly family relationships, parent and peers who model maladaptive behaviour, lack of effective and warm prevention and control of misbehaviour and disputes, inability to deal with crises without extreme stress or helpless collapse, low intelligence, high socioeconomic disadvantage, appear, when they occur, to make people function miserably and to make life choices which increase their problems. I shall try to present some detailed studies of relevant processes in my discussion of the development of cognition, personality and social relationships. An important and incisive paper by Rutter (1985a) reviews family and school influences on the development of socially maladjusted behaviour.

'Stages' in development

'Stage' models of development are relevant to the concept of continuity and discontinuity in development. 'Stages' differ in type from theory to theory. Some are purely idealizations, used by the writer to evoke particular images in the reader, and do not refer clearly to anything definite or measurable in behaviour. Erikson's evocative stages of psychosexual development (1950) are an example of this sort of usage. Some 'stages' do refer to measurable behaviour. 'Stages' here are synonymous with particular behaviours in an age-related process of change; the 'crawling stage' might be separated out in the gradual change in ways of being mobile that we all go through. Descriptive stages like this can be rather arbitrary and they can be used tautologously – 'he's being difficult because he's in the 2-year-old obstructive stage', for example. The better descriptive stage models include analysis of the structure and interrelation of the behaviours which make up a stage: if it is to be worth separating out from the flow of development, a stage's behaviours should presumably cohere throughout the field of relevance and be relatively separate from the adjacent stages. Piaget's own stages of cognitive development do have such underlying models of their structure, though as we shall see in Chapter 2, there are many problems with his account: all too many of the attempts to extend 'Piagetian' stages into moral and social cognition fall down badly on this. Goldman and Goldman (1982) for example, had interesting discussions with a large number of children on their ideas about sex and various associated issues, but do very little to justify their forcing of these data into 'Piagetian' stages. We are not therefore able to judge whether children's thinking in this area really goes through an orderly sequence of wide-ranging and separate stages as the analysis and presentation propose.

Even if they do contain a decent description of the internal organization of a stage and of how it differs from other stages, descriptive stage models often do not account for movement from one stage to the next. If they are to *explain* development, stage models must do this (as must models which do not draw discontinuities in the course of development). Again, Piaget's is the main stage model to try. Explanatory stage models must specify the behaviours subject to age changes which make up the stages: they must propose variables which are responsible for the changes between stages and the organization of each stage: they must provide ways of measuring these variables independent of the behavioural changes they are supposed to produce. Unless this last condition is satisfied, stages risk being tautologous – 'she's sucking her thumb because she's in the oral stage' describes behaviour and

has an elaborate model of the causal processes behind the behaviour, but there are no measures of the oral stage independent of behaviours like thumb-sucking and the sentence is descriptive not explanatory.

Judgements of the merit of stage theories vary (see, for example, Piaget 1970; Brainerd 1978). My own feeling is that they can be useful shorthand but that precisely this speed and simplicity makes them potentially dangerous. Unless the conditions I have outlined in the last paragraph are fulfilled, 'stages' tend to segment development in ways which may not be justified, to simplify the complexity of behaviour by overlooking the ways in which it varies from situation to situation, and to give an inadequate account of transition and continuities. I hope the remainder of this book will illustrate how much has to be integrated into a developmental model before stage analyses can be sound.

The ecology of child development

There is little doubt that the environment children grow up in is a source of influences on their development. Work on defining the 'ecology' of child development is a burgeoning field. There is a strong awareness of how complex 'environment' is. It is not just a collection of dyadic relations; in particular it is not a collection of mother–child relations. While the ways in which people interact even in large groups and institutional settings may bear some resemblance to the way a baby interacts with its mother, the differences will be obvious, and they need a different explanation. The view taken by Bronfenbrenner, that social experience is 'as a set of nested structures, each inside the next, like a set of Russian dolls' (Garbarino, 1982, p. 21), is to be preferred. Bronfenbrenner's 'set' forms a framework for discussing child development, which is relevant in more than just the social sphere.

Bronfenbrenner (1979, pp. 21–8) emphasizes that for human beings the environment is much more than just 'the immediate, concrete setting containing the living creature', though this may possibly have been an adequate way to think of it when studying animal behaviour. He asserts that

the ecology of human development involves the scientific study of the progressive, mutual accommodation between an active, growing human being and the changing properties of the immediate settings in which the developing person lives, as this process is affected by relations between these settings, and by the larger contexts in which the settings are embedded (p. 21).

The 'ecological environment' of an individual consists of micro-, meso-, exo-, and macrosystems.

A micro-system is a pattern of activities, roles and interpersonal relations experienced by the developing person in a given setting with particular physical and material characteristics (p. 22).

The baby's life at home with its family is one example; the baby's microsystem is the pattern of feeding, sleeping, bathing, playing, etc., of relations with parents, siblings, visitors, etc. (and between these individuals, of 'playing the role' of baby in a family playing other roles). As people get older, their range of microsystems increases: settings like playgroup, school, church, club, work place and so forth involve a different range of activities, roles and interpersonal relations

A meso-system comprises the interrelations among two or more settings in which the developing person actively participates (such as, for a child, the relations among home, school and neighbourhood peer group; for an adult, among family, work, and social life) (p. 25).

The nature of the links between an individual's microsystems is what is involved here. Strong and varied links between microsystems – such as other people who participate actively in both settings, communication between settings, knowledge and attitudes being applicable to both – are seen as being an advantage to the people involved. A weak mesosystem, minimal links between home and school, for example, may place the child at risk.

The last two systems are more removed from the child.

An exosystem refers to one or more settings that do not involve the developing person as an active participant, but in which events occur that affect, or are affected by, what happens in the setting containing the developing person (p. 25).

The macro-system refers to consistencies in the form and content of lower-order systems (micro-, meso-, and exo-) that exist, or could exist, at the level of the subculture or the culture as a whole, along with any belief systems or ideology underlying such consistencies (p. 26).

Thus exosystems are settings which affect the child but in which he or she takes no part, for example the parents' work or their friendship networks, or local government decisions about schools, housing, playgrounds etc. Macrosystems reflect lifestyles and belief systems which are in contrast in different societies and which affect the smaller-scale systems in which individuals move. A belief in social competition rather than social co-operation, or in democracy rather than autocracy would be examples. So would the degree of priority given to the needs of children.

Bronfenbrenner goes on to emphasize that life contains many transitions between ecological settings, which are a function of biological changes such as increased maturity and of altered environmental circumstances, and that these transitions are both consequences of developmental processes and instigators of further change. He then defines human development as follows:

Human development is the process through which the growing person acquires a more extended, differentiated and valid conception of the ecological environment, and becomes motivated and able to engage in activities that reveal the properties of, sustain or restructure that environment at levels of similar or greater complexity in form and content (p. 27).

This is a definition which we will consider further in the remainder of this book. The rest of

Plate 2   Seville, 1933

this chapter is on 'Play', a topic which does not fall neatly into the categories which organize the rest of the book, but illustrates some of the issues about the nature of children and of development which I have discussed.

Play

Children, like many other young mammals, spend a considerable amount of time and energy playing. This activity has been evaluated by adults in a wide range of different ways. One view has been that although children's play may be enjoyable to the participants and charming to fond parents observing it, it is essentially frivolous, a pastime with no intrinsic consequences, which is grown out of without it having made much impact on development. At one extreme this view was stiffened by a sterner judgement that frivolities should be discouraged in favour of useful activities, that children should play less and work or pray more. It has almost certainly been a fairly recent development to take a contrary view and see play as making important contributions to the child's development, to consider it to be an important way of learning things that the adult will need to know. This view has had a period of considerable dominance in psychological and educational theory: the paradoxical slogan 'play is the child's work' has been implicit or even explicit in many early childhood curricula.

It seems to be common practice in our society to draw a distinction between 'work' and 'play'. Parents do this, so do teachers: so do children, who come home from infant school and tell their inquiring parent that they 'just played', though the teacher no doubt defined their activities in the classroom as educationally important and as work. The work/play distinction is conflated with the distinction between having to work and being free to do what one wishes, and 'play' is seen as voluntary and not obligatory. Voluntary activity is seen as free, absorbing, spontaneous, enjoyable, not serious and done for oneself not for other people (see p. 85 for discussion of similar approaches to study). Given a model of motivation which rests on the assumption that an organism will not expend energy on activities such as play which are neither obligatory nor obviously useful in terms of drive reduction or immediate profit, it becomes a problem to explain why anyone should play. I will discuss here some general theories of play and the validity of the assertions that have been made about its nature and functions: because 'play' will be seen to have many different forms and functions, detailed accounts of their contributions to development will be found in the appropriate sections of the following chapters. Thus the contribution of play to cognitive development is examined in Chapter 2: social play in school playgrounds in the section on peer relations in Chapter 6.

Defining play

I have already implied that judgements of what is 'play' may be subjective and hard to agree on. Building a wall is likely to look like play if a 2-year-old does it with wooden blocks, and to look like work if an adult does it with bricks to earn a living or improve the look of the garden or even to acquire and practice a new skill; though the effort, involvement and pleasure at the finished product may be equivalent in each case. Dressing up in fancy clothes and pretending to be someone else is certainly 'play' in the nursery classroom's Wendy house, and in a more subtle form it might still be so in the stalls at the National Youth Theatre: but on the other side of the footlights, or in the stalls at Covent Garden, is it 'play'? A casual knocking-about of tennis balls with tennis rackets in a suburban street is 'play': the Wimbledon championship matches barely are, however much we may extol 'amateurism'.

However, there are certain characteristics which we may see in prototype instances of play, though more marginal instances may lack most of them. Garvey (1977) provides one useful list. First, play is essentially enjoyable and associated with positive affect. Second, it is an activity done for its own sake, rewarding in itself, and not dependent on extrinsic motivation or the achievement of goals outside the play. Third, it is spontaneous and voluntary, chosen and generated by the player not by outside authority. Fourth, it requires active involvement on the part of the player. Fifth, and very important, it is contrasted with 'non-play' by being in a sense set aside from 'real life': it is not intended literally, is not meant to be taken at face value. Play involves actions done out of their normal pattern, perhaps fragmented, rearranged or repeated, carried out as the player chooses not organized in ways specified by the achievement of an outside goal. It is 'framed' by special signals that this is 'play', not literally what it appears to be, not leading to the usual consequences, not to be reacted to by other people as if it were real fighting, real boasting, real going shopping. Sutton-Smith (1979) proposes that it is a sort of performance, not a solitary act but a communicative act directed at real or imagined others, even if the 'others' are aspects of oneself. This contrast with 'non-play' allows play to be 'buffered' from its normal consequences so that possibilities can be tried out without responsibility for what happens: 'It's all right, I'm only playing.'

While these 'defining characteristics' are certainly worth thinking about, cumulatively they lead to a misleading idealization of play. It has been said to be free, outside ordinary life, not serious, not literal, not for profit: absorbing, spontaneous, voluntary, due to intrinsic motivation: refreshing, flexible, egalitarian and showing positive affect. It is thus heavily contrasted with the serious aspects of life, such as earning a living, passing examinations, getting promotion or an overdraft, fighting, feeding, etc., which are seen as lacking these essential qualities. While the general tendency may be for instances of play to deserve these pleasant adjectives, to *require* them as constituents which must be present if something is to be called 'play' is to pile up a very large number of problem instances. Exactly what is meant by the free/voluntary/spontaneous cluster, for example? As Sluckin (1981) has observed, much of what goes on in the school playground is strongly constrained and coerced by other children (and to a much lesser extent by adult supervisors also): 'freedom' here (as elsewhere) is a nebulous concept. The playground

again provides many examples of 'play' behaviour characterized by negative affect, by fights and tears and jibes rather than by smiles and affectionate hugs, and of play which is most certainly not egalitarian. Indeed 'we were only playing' is often used in an attempt to excuse too much damage being done.

Play is not necessarily always functional, either. Fagen (1981) points out that animals take risks and incur injuries in play, and this is all too evident in human beings. Sutton-Smith and Kelly-Byrne (1984, pp. 314–16) give some rather shocking examples of their students' 'deep play': to their examples of dangerous play arising from adolescent bravado, one could easily add many other instances including the statistics of injuries to young children from more innocent playground activities. Play certainly becomes less common if the individual is in adverse circumstances, ill, hungry, frightened or under stress (Smith 1984, Gould 1977), which might suggest that it can involve a degree of additional stress to be avoided when times are hard. Play, like any other behaviour, can contain negative aspects within a generally relaxed and positive ambience.

A final characteristic found in many instances of play is the special quality or state of being which Csiksentmihalyi (1979) calls 'flow'. 'Flow' involves a blissful involvement in what one is doing, a loss of self-consciousness, being carried away by the activity but simultaneously participating fully in it and not being out of control. This sort of experience can be found in many activities which are not 'play' – academic work, when it goes well, is an example, so might aesthetic experiences and sexual activities be – and many instances of 'play' would be devoid of 'flow', but there is obvious overlap between the two. Considering children's activities in terms of 'flow' might also usefully decrease the idealization of play and the artificial play/work distinction which has impeded useful analysis and provision for so long.

An alternative to defining play by constructing lists of its essential characteristics, such as I have just discussed, is to construct taxonomies of different types of play behaviour. An early example is Piaget's threefold scheme (Piaget 1962): practice play, which involves repetition of actions with elaboration of means being more important than the ends served, symbolic play involving the manipulation of symbols, and games with rules. Hutt (1979) distinguishes exploration and problem solving from play which is symbolic or rule-governed. Other taxonomies have been devised, including some which specify the materials of play (Garvey 1977) or its social interactions (Parten 1932). Some of my own work (Meadows and Cashdan 1983) rated 'play' behaviour, like other behaviour, on dimensions such as social participation, degree of child's involvement, number of operations, themes or skills involved, extent to which materials were used, and apparent goals of the child, which did not reduce tidily to separate types of play. Approaches such as these are useful in that they stay close to observable behaviour and stress the variability intrinsic to the concept of play.

It should be noted, finally, that 'play' needs to be studied in the context of its ecological environment. As we will see, it is an important part of the microsystems of a young child in the family and of children together in school, street or playground; it is affected by the exosystems which, for example, decide to provide or not to provide playing fields, amusement arcades or cable television; it is allowed, curtailed or channelled by the macrosystem which insists that children must contribute to the economics of their family from a very early age or not until they are in their late teens, or encourages football in little boys and discourages it in girls, or fosters conceptions of children's innocence which push their sexual or scatological interests underground. What play is, and what it does, will not be understood without consideration of its ecology.

Theories of the causes of play

Play is found in the young of many species. Because of this possible biological impetus to play, one strand of interest in theories of why play happens is the consideration of evolution and biological function. Classic theories (for a review see Millar 1968 or Garvey 1977) described play as

being 'for' getting rid of surplus energy, or 'for' practising skills which will be needed later in life. An early evolutionary theory of play, famous, picturesque, influential and total nonsense, was G. Stanley Hall's recapitulation model. There was at the time (the turn of the century) a belief that a species' evolutionary history was recapitulated in the development of the individual, that ontogeny recapitulated phylogeny. (Some apparently supporting evidence came from embryology; for example, the embryo was seen at one stage to have gill slits like a fish, and later looked rather like a monkey. Freud's theory of psychosexual stages is also recapitulatory.) Hall proposed that the successive stages of children's play recapitulated the behaviour of their evolutionary ancestors. Babies enjoyed splashing about in the bath because their distant ancestors had been aquatic creatures splashing about in the primeval slime. The pre-school child climbed, jumped, swung as monkey-like ancestors had done. The hide-and-seek games and gangs of older children recapitulated the hunter–gatherer activities of early man. Team games recapitulated tribal conflicts, stamp collecting the ascendancy of capitalism. This model is historically crude, selective in the play it accounts for, and strongly resembles Kipling's *Just-So Stories*. It is in any case rooted in a theory now known to be fallacious, since ontogeny does not recapitulate phylogeny (Gould 1977). Hall's theory seems, however, to have rooted itself in common-sense theories of play: adults' general comments on children's play and professionals' evaluations of 'natural' materials like the sand and water found in many pre-school curricula often bear a recapitulatory resonance.

More recently, advances in evolutionary biology have produced more sophisticated and better founded accounts of play. Recapitulation theories, which identified a series of adult ancestral forms in the immature baby and child who develops beyond them, have been replaced by models which see human development as retarded, not as speeded-up and extended. Instead of being like adult moneys when we are children, and developing beyond where the monkey stopped to be super-adult humans, we retain

Table 1 *Retardation in humans compared with other primates*

	Rhesus macaque	Gibbon	Chimpanzee	Gorilla	Human
Gestation	24 weeks	30	34	37	40
Complete hair covering	During gestation		onset during gestation, completed after birth		Never completed
Ossification centres in wrist at birth	All	2–3	2	—	None
First teeth (months)	0.6–5.9	1.2–?	2.7–12.3	3.0–13.0	6.0–24.0
Second teeth (years)	1.6–6.8	?–8.5	2.9–10.2	3.0–10.5	6.0–20.0
Growing period (years)	7	9	11	11	20
Life span (years)	25	33	35	35	70

many of the infant characteristics we (and monkeys) had as infants, for far longer than the monkeys do. Information from Gould (1977) illustrates this (Table 1).

This retardation in development reflects an evolutionary trend which has been pervasive among large mammals: instead of having large litters of young which although born helpless develop rapidly to independence, they have reacted to selection pressures and produced smaller litters of slow developers, a long gestation and a long period of the offsprings' dependence on adults. The human pattern is an extreme version of this, and it includes a prolongation of infantile physical characteristics. To quote Gould (1977, p. 371):

In practically all human systems, postnatal growth either continues long past the age of cessation in other primates, or the onset of characteristic forms and phenomena is delayed to later times. The brain of a human baby continues to grow along the fetal curve; the eruption of teeth is delayed; maturation is postponed; body growth continues longer than in any other primate; even senility and death occur much later.

Gould sees retardation as of adaptive significance in human evolution because it allowed the retention of juvenile physical characteristics for longer than was otherwise possible ('neoteny'); a psychologically important example is skull shape and hence brain size (Gould 1977, pp. 376–99). Retardation made both possible and necessary some distinctively human characteristics – particular body shapes, sizes and co–ordinations, more elaborately developed brains, longer and better learning of a more open potential range of behaviour and ideas, longer and more elaborate parenting, more complex social relationships – which have interacted synergistically so that human development is more plastic and less preset than that of other animals. We will return to some of the implications of this at intervals throughout this book: I will argue here that the causes and functions of play can be fitted neatly into the neoteny framework.

Recent evolutionary accounts of play (e.g. Burghardt 1984; Byers 1984) use more sophisticated concepts of how evolutionary processes work together (see, for example, Gould and Lewontin 1979). They make the important point that the functions which play in the young of a particular species now serves are not necessarily at all the same as the functions which similar behaviour served back in their evolutionary history. It will be difficult to clarify the evolutionary functions of play avoiding the *Just-So Stories* which amuse but have no scientific foundation. However, the core is a recognition of the young animal as being born immature and very able to learn, needing to live with its conspecifics and to learn many complex skilled behaviours, and possessing energy and curiosity and social affiliativeness enough to do this. Play is a result of these characteristics and a facilitator of development.

Some possible functions of play

Arousal modulation
One proposed function of play (Berlyne 1960; Shultz 1979) is to modulate arousal. If there is not enough environmental stimulation to induce a moderate level of arousal in the child, he or she will play to increase arousal level. If arousal level is high, if the child is anxious or over-excited, play that is stimulus-seeking will cease and the child may turn to play which is calming and reduces arousal level. Undertaking a new behaviour will be arousing, and may, if it is too much so, be mildly aversive, but anticipating or achieving control over this novelty will reduce arousal to the optimum and be pleasant.

Obviously this theory of arousal is a very general one which could apply to any sort of activity. The model is particularly appropriate for play, however, in so far as it is a largely voluntary activity. The child has opportunities in play to modulate his or her own arousal level autonomously, indeed to 'play' at arousal modulation by seeking over-stimulation and coping with it. The 'getting over-excited' in play, to which children often succumb, is perhaps the converse of this function of play: arousal must not get too far off balance if what Csikszentmihalyi (1979) calls 'flow' is to be preserved.

Practising adult activities
Kittens play at chasing and catching mock prey. Colts race each other round their pastures. Little girls play at making tea, washing up and putting their dolls to bed. Adults, watching, see all this as practising adult skills which the young will need when they grow up. Play is said to be 'for' devel-

oping behaviours and rehearsing roles which will be necessary for individual success and for the survival and propagation of the species: it is thus an important component of socialization, biologically programmed.

Is this explanation and function true? The answer is yes and no. Human beings even more than other mammals have to learn complex sequences and patterns of behaviour which are not genetically programmed. As I discussed, evolutionary theories note the contribution that play can make to this learning because it is voluntary, flexible, and sanction free. The existence of play does serve the development of immensely complicated adult skills such as food gathering, keeping with the herd, and parenting, but play is not 'for' these things. The most prominent candidate for genetically programmed preparation-for-adult-skills play is rough-and-tumble play (Humphreys and Smith 1984), which is clearly culturally influenced in who does it, and differs in many ways from the adult fighting for which it is supposed to be a preparation. Children are very subject to adult pressures, both implicit and explicit, to play 'properly', and it is these that shape the content of their play, not an evolutionary plan. Thus play is rarely simply practising adult activities, though it does allow the practice of behaviour and roles which are not irrelevant to adult life.

Allowing behavioural recombination
Play activities tend to occur most in the early stages of the behaviour systems involved. They serve the mastery of complex behaviour which requires both practice and the integration of the behaviour into other systems and knowledge. After the kitten's play pouncing, pouncing behaviour is used by the cat, more skilfully and better integrated into the whole stalk–pounce–catch routine. But because play is 'framed', non-literal, and concentrates on means not ends, it allows the recombination of pieces of behaviour, ideas and consequences in innovative or repetitive ways. The child has good opportunities in play for varying what are the normal conditions of reality, breaking set, introducing new

considerations and choices, and so coming to control in action and understanding the rules of individual or social behaviour. It is important to stress that play may do this but does not always do so: some play is rigid and inflexible. Further, behavioural and conceptual recombinations may be sought deliberately and non-playfully, as in certain teaching programmes for cognitive development (see Chapter 3).

Emotional and social functions of play

A variety of emotional functions have been proposed for play, notably by Freud and his followers. They include wish fulfilment, anxiety reduction, and mastering a traumatic event. Clinically these functions seem very possible. Play which could serve them seems to be displaced in time from the height of the emotional crisis, which could be congruent with the arousal theory discussed above. Whether play *does* reduce anxiety or induce catharsis has been hard to assess, and no conclusions are possible on present evidence (Rubin, Fein and Vandenberg 1983).

Play is often engaged in with other people. It therefore offers opportunities of learning about other people, adopting different social roles, establishing group structures, etc. As I discuss in the chapter on social development, even very young children seek social interaction and play with other children, and those who lack play and social experience as children tend to have social difficulties as adults. It must not be concluded from this, however, that children's social play is uniformly beneficial or that the solitary child is necessarily in developmental danger.

The development of play behaviours

Whether play contributes to the development of the individual is a question to which we will return later. The development of the child is certainly involved in the changing patterns of play which we can observe from infancy to adulthood. Garvey (1977) describes how new skills, experience and knowledge become 'the resource or materials' for play. Infants play with motion and in interaction with their caretakers, play with objects develops then play with language, with

social materials and peers and eventually play with rules. Those 'resources and materials' for play which were available early do not necessarily become redundant as new ones are acquired: instead they are combined in progressively more complex ways to suit the child's purpose.

As Piaget (1962) has described, infants play with the movements they can make and the results of these movements. Such play seems to be enjoyable for its own sake, but no doubt also contributes to the child's control and co-ordination of movements and to his or her physical awareness, through kinesthetic feedback. Movements are also commonly part of parent–infant games, for example games of clapping hands or riding the parent's knee. I discuss the social structure of these games in Chapter 6; early on the adult is responsible for the maintenance of the movement game, as also of course for the recitation that often accompanies it, but as the infant learns the routine of the game he or she comes to take a more active part. Traditional rhymes provide not only opportunities for contrasting movement, but also linguistic and social information, as in this rhyme dating back several hundred years:

> This is the way the ladies ride,
> Nimble, nimble, nimble, nimble,
> This is the way the gentlemen ride,
> A gallop, a trot, a gallop, a trot;
> This is the way the farmers ride,
> Jiggety jog, jiggety jog;
> And when they come to a hedge – they jump over!
> And when they come to a slippery space –
> They scramble, scramble, scramble,
>   Tumble-down Dick!
>
> (Baring-Gould and Baring-Gould 1962)

Infants come to play with objects in a more and more complex fashion. Initial object play is often said to be 'indiscriminate' in that infants assimilate objects to their repertory of behaviours like grasping, shaking and mouthing without much adjustment to the object's particular characteristics (Kagan *et al.* 1978; Rosenblatt 1977). From the latter part of the first year onwards, play with objects becomes more likely to involve the use of more than one object, to show response to the characteristics and the normal function of the objects, and to begin to involve pretence, for example that a doll can 'drink' from an empty cup. Pretend play increases rapidly at about the same time as language development is taking off: several theorists have seen them as two facets of the child's new insight into the possibility of representational behaviour (see, for example, Rubin, Fein and Vandenberg 1983).

Given the opportunity, children enjoy play with materials that allow them to make constructions. Building with bricks, fitting bits of meccano together, glueing bits of paper to cardboard boxes, and the slightly different activities of painting and completing jigsaws, all allow the child to set a goal and then achieve it. They also can fit into, indeed be done in order to serve, social and pretend play. These are favourite activities from the pre-school years onwards, often producing especially long bouts of concentration (Sylva *et al.* 1980; Meadows and Cashdan in press).

As they come to spend more time with agemates, children come more and more to play with peers (see Chapter 6). Early play *with* peers is very much dependent on the ability of at least one participant, and preferably all, to sustain a sequence of interaction. During their pre-school years children develop more efficient ways of recruiting, incorporating and directing peers in joint play (e.g. Asher and Gottman 1981), but some adjustments to another's presence and activity are made even in 'parallel play', especially if the children playing side by side are reasonably familiar with each other. Early social play with peers is facilitated, as early adult–infant play was, by social routines. Garvey (1974, 1977) provides many examples of ritualized exchanges of language. For example:

X's turn	*Y's turn*
1 Hello, my name is Mr Donkey	Hello, my name is Mr Elephant
Hello, my name is Mr Tiger	Hello, my name is Mr Lion

2 I have to go to work	You're already at work
No I'm not	
I have to go to school	You're already at school
No I'm not	

The 'scripts' of 'Playing house' or 'Superhero' (Paley 1984) also provide a supporting structure for young children's social play. Much of such play is excruciatingly banal and stereotyped to the adult eye and ear, and many commentators have been worried by its sexist and aggressive components, but it seems to be very resistant to adult attempts to induce a new role play of egalitarian sweetness and light (e.g. Best 1983; Paley 1984). Script play no doubt reflects children's social knowledge, which so far as sex role goes tends to involve relatively rigid stereotypes during the infant and junior school years (see p. 197). Scripts can become more elaborate as children get older, often deriving from the stories they read. Alison Lurie's novel *Only Children* (Lurie 1980) contains notable examples of such fantasies.

Play with rules, where the play depends on an externally fixed set of regulations, is usually seen as a late emergence in the development of children's play, though it could be related to the structured social routines of adult–infant play. The participants in games with rules have to recognize, accept and conform to constraints imposed on their activity. They have to take turns, for example, accept losing, not cheat, etc. Especially in Piaget's account (Piaget 1962), play with rules centres on co-operating in order to compete. (Competition is of course not a salient characteristic of adult–infant routines.) Games with a competitive element and a rule-governed structure may involve movement, language (see Opie and Opie 1967, 1969, 1985), objects, social interaction and even scripts. They are probably the most conspicuous activity in many junior school playgrounds, and in very sophisticated forms such as football persist into many adult lives.

There are marked variations between children

in the ways that they play. Individual differences in temperament and perhaps intelligence (Rubin, Fein and Vandenberg 1983) are one source of variation: the ecology of the play setting is another (Smith and Connolly 1981): the materials available for play are also important (e.g. Meadows and Cashdan, in press; Fein 1981). Probably the most important source of variations in play is, however, culture. Schwartzman (1978) provides an excellent review.

On the importance of play

I began this section by saying that after a period when adults saw play as being frivolous and inconsequential, we have had a period in which play has been seen as an important contributor to the child's development. It is important to note that there is little conclusive evidence for the case that play is of unique importance. Experimental studies (see Smith 1984, Rubin, Fein and Vandenberg 1983; and pp. 65–6) do not show for certain that more play causes better problem solving, language, imagination or social adjustment. Children deprived of play who show impaired development have almost always been deprived of other things as well, indeed rather severe deprivation is needed to stop play. Lack of more suitable play facilities contributes to the sort of delinquency that is antisocial play. It is probably the case that the benefits of play could accrue from other non-play activities, that it is not altogether essential in development.

Nevertheless, play cannot be written off as useless. In the first place, it is a source of enjoyment and pleasure and may hence make a positive contribution to the child's emotional well-being. It is a potential source of feelings of competence and achievement and so a contributor to the child's self-esteem and feelings of self-efficacy. It is part of the child's social worlds of peers and of adults. The contribution of adults to children's play, through encouragement, support and resource provision, should not be underestimated even if children do have a private world secluded from their parents and teachers. Play provides opportunities for trying out skills and investigating the world. It may also be used to assess the child's development, and through some therapies to enhance it. The proverbial wisdom of 'All work and no play makes Jack a dull boy' has considerable truth in it.

Plate 3

Plate 4

2 Perceiving and understanding

Cognitive development

Studying cognitive development, we are concerned with 'the child as knower'; with someone who thinks, understands, learns, remembers, and so forth. There is still no clear, complete and valid account of what adults do when they think, understand, etc., despite hard work by philosophers over thousands of years, more recently by psychologists, and very recently by computer scientists and neurophysiologists. Accounting for cognitive development additionally involves describing *what* develops, that is, noting what changes between different ages and explaining *how* these changes come about. Quite obviously these are extraordinarily formidable questions. We cannot yet answer them; but currently psychologists who have learned from Piaget's partly correct and partly incorrect answer are putting together an exciting new account.

I will outline and discuss Piaget's achievements first, and then proceed to the post-Piagetian picture of what and how thinking develops. Good introductions to Piagetian theory are provided by Brainerd (1978) and Brown and Desforges (1979); for fuller accounts of Piaget's work see Flavell (1963, 1977), Vuyk (1981) and Gelman and Baillargeon (1983).

Piagetian theory

An anecdote which Piaget used many times gives a good picture of the Piagetian child. A boy aged 5 was playing with his collection of pebbles. He laid them out in a line and counted them along the line from left to right: there were ten. Then he counted them from right to left, and 'to his great astonishment' the total was, again, ten. He put them in a circle and counted them first clockwise and then counterclockwise: 'full of enthusiasm' he discovered that there were always ten, that the sum of objects was the same whatever order they were counted in. He grew up to be a professional mathematician, attributing his choice of career to this experience at 5. It had been an excitement and a delight to achieve a new cognitive control in the world by putting the pebbles in order, comparing that order with another pre-existing order, the string of numerals from one to ten, and so create a property of the collection, their sum of ten, which did not exist independent of the counter's activity.

Cognition as adaptation

Piaget's theory of the development of thinking has at its centre the child actively trying to make sense of the world, just as any organism must try to adapt to its environment. According to the theory, 'making sense of', at whatever intellectual level, is a special case of the adaptive processes which pervade all biological existence and evolution. It proceeds through the twin 'functional invariants' of assimilation and accommodation. 'Assimilation' is the relating of new information to pre-existing structures of understanding, and 'accommodation' is the development of old structures into new ones at the behest of new external information or problems. The two occur together, though one may dominate the other, and their functioning gives rise to a series of 'structures' of cognition, that is, cognition is organized into systems of rules, categories, procedures and so forth which eventually amount to unified organizations of logical operations. Cognitive development proceeds through the steady functioning of assimilation, accommodation and organization, which together give rise to a succession of increasingly complex, differentiated, integrated and flexible sets of ways of understanding the world. There are such successions of qualitatively different structures in a number of different areas of content, such as conservation, perspective-taking, causality and number concepts: there is also, more importantly, the succession of such stages in the global area of cognition-in-general, in so far as the structures of thinking apply across different contents. Piaget's model insists on the general application of cognitive structures: there are only minor differences in a child's level of thinking in different areas or different materials, and differences between children only in rate of progress through the invariant order of stages. The emphasis is thus on cognitive structures and logical operations which are universal and abstract: inferred from behaviour, not immediately observable.

Thus the Piagetian child is an active thinker who continually strives to understand the world in a coherent way. Trying to understand, constructing a world-model, adapting to the demands of the environment, are constant in development and do not change. Insistence that knowing and thinking are active not passive ways of coping with the world is Piaget's first important contribution. The model of assimilatory and accommodatory processes for taking in information, that is relating what one discovers for the first time to what one knows already, would also seem to be an important one, indeed many psychologists believe that a model without assimilation and accommodation would be quite implausible, though they need much more precise specification (see, for example, Gelman and Baillargeon 1983; Meadows 1983; Siegler 1983). From birth (or even earlier) to death we are processing new information and fitting it to our old knowledge, thus transforming old knowledge into a new improved version.

As far as what *does* develop during cognitive development is concerned, Piaget suggested that there was a move during childhood from thinking that was fragmented, partial and closely tied to experience, to thinking that was at least capable of being logical, abstract and very flexible, by adolescence. We will see that there is good reason to doubt both whether young children are as unsystematic and illogical as Piaget supposed, and whether older children and adolescents (and

indeed adults) are as logical. The role of education will turn out to be rather important in understanding cognitive change.

Causes of cognitive development

Piaget's model (see, for example, Piaget and Inhelder 1969, pp. 154–7) of *how* cognitive development proceeds was complex. He lists four factors, which are of rather different types and not clearly interrelated. The first relevant factor was organic growth, particularly the maturation of the central nervous system. It is quite obvious that a properly functioning brain is normally necessary for adequate cognition and that the immaturity of infants' brains (brain development, most rapid before birth, proceeds rapidly for the first year or two after birth and continues to some extent for much longer) makes them both unlike adults and capable of becoming like them. Very recent research is beginning to inform us both about brain development and about the brain's role in cognition (pp. 58–9). At present theories of cognition flourish without much neurophysiological base, but eventually, one might hope, we will know enough to link the different levels. Kinsbourne (1980) addresses the problem.

Piaget's second factor explaining *how* cognition developed was 'the role of exercise and of acquired experience in the actions performed upon objects', including both direct physical experience, e.g. the weight of pebbles, and indirect reflective experience of logico-mathematical rules and relations, e.g. the total number in a collection of pebbles. Again, some such necessary factor is incontrovertible, even if it is not entirely clear what and how much experience is needed. The restrictions of experience suffered by some very severely deprived children (Skuse 1984) or by children who are congenitally paralysed, blind or deaf, do not necessarily lead to deficient cognitive development though there may be abnormalities and problems. It has often been inferred from Piaget's account of the role of experience in cognitive development that young children can only learn by active involvement, not through observation or being taught: we will see that a definition of 'experience' that restricts it to 'hands-on' experience is too restrictive.

Other sorts of experience are implicated in Piaget's third factor, 'social interaction and transmission'. This was the least developed part of Piaget's model, but has received a great deal of attention in recent years. We will discuss it later, and see that the social ecology is of great importance to cognitive development – and to its diagnosis by experimenters.

Equilibration

Piaget's final factor, equilibration, was invoked to co-ordinate the diverse contributions of maturation and physical, social and logico-mathematical experiences. It was a central concept in his theory, most important in accounting for *how* development occurred. Briefly, he postulated that organisms needed to maintain a stable internal equilibrium within the changes and uncertainties of the outside world. Body temperature in warm-blooded animals is a good example of the sort of process involved: the feedback systems of thermostatically controlled central heating are also analogous. In equilibrated systems, of which cognition is supposed to be one, the changes and demands of the outside world produce small 'perturbations' or 'conflicts' in the system which automatically adjusts itself to cope with them and return either to the original steady state or in the case of cognition to a new and better equilibrium. There is a strong need for equilibrium: 'durable disequilibria constitute pathological organic or mental states' (Piaget 1968, p. 102).

The concept of equilibration explains *how* cognitive development occurs in terms of a 'need' for a coherently organized and consistent way of thinking. This 'equilibrium' is gradually constructed as partially adequate ways of thinking conflict with the data provided by the external world, or with their own inconsistent processes and results, and have to be improved. 'Equilibration' implies that there should be a considerable degree of organization and coherence in cognition. It also implies that conflict between ideas or models or ways of doing things will be a major source of progress. Piaget's account of it also involved an insistence that the series of stages of equilibrated ways of thinking which he described was universal. Before the formal operational thought that is the pinnacle of human cognition can be achieved, every human being must go in the same order through the sensori-motor sub-stages, the period of pre-operational thought and then concrete operations.

Because 'equilibration', 'assimilation', 'accommodation' and 'organization' are complex and abstract concepts, providing behavioural examples is difficult. I offer a fictional one, designed to highlight three points I want to make about the equilibration model, but not, I hope, a caricature of what Piaget intended. At the outset, the protagonist of the example is a moderately experienced cook. He or she has successfully cooked carrots and potatoes, carrots by boiling them, grating them raw for salads, and making carrot soup, potatoes by boiling, roasting, frying, mashing and making chips. The initial state of knowledge of ways of cooking carrots and potatoes could be represented as a matrix, thus:

Method	Carrots	Potatoes
Boiling	√	√
Chipping	not tried	√
Frying	not tried	√
Grating/salad	√	not tried
Mashing	not tried	√
Roasting	not tried	√
Soup	√	not tried

The cook now meets parsnips for the first time. The new vegetable is *assimilated* to the carrot repertory, perhaps on the basis of similarity of shape and texture. Parsnips boil very well, make a rather bland soup, and although they taste quite pleasant raw are not a visually attractive ingredient in salad. The cook also assimilates parsnips to the potato repertoire: parsnips are disastrous chipped or fried, mash well and are delicious roasted. The knowledge matrix after assimilation of parsnips would have one further column, thus:

35

Method	Parsnips
Boiling	√
Chipping	No
Frying	No
Grating/salad	maybe
Mashing	√
Roasting	√
Soup	maybe

Assimilation is always accompanied by accommodation, however. The schema 'vegetables you can mash' is augmented with parsnips, for example, and the importance of butter is emphasized. The cook may accommodate further by extending the mashing schema to carrots, and hence to the full range of vegetable purées. Since roast potatoes and roast parsnips are successful, the schema 'roasting' may be tried out on carrots, with success. A fully equilibrated knowledge system for cooking carrots, potatoes and parsnips might look something like this:

Method	Carrots	Potatoes	Parsnips
Boiling	√	√	√
Chipping	No	√	No
Frying	No	√	No
Grating/salad	√	No	maybe
Mashing	√	√	√
Roasting	√	√	√
Soup	√	maybe	maybe

This sort of procedure is obviously infinitely extendable. The same basic principles of assimilation, accommodation and organization leading to a thorough equilibrated knowledge structure will apply whatever new vegetable the cook encounters – turnips, celeriac, Jerusalem artichokes, and so forth.

The three points I want to raise from this example are as follows. The first is the question of what criteria of content guide assimilation. Why are parsnips assimilated to the carrot and potato schemas, and not to the schemas for cooking aubergines or cauliflowers, or indeed to schemas for playing chess or cleaning cars? I suggested similarities, of shape, texture and, implicitly, being root vegetables. Nutritionists, aware of the chemical constituents of the vegetables, or cookery-book writers, aware of the long history of 'cuisine', might have other suggestions to make. There is no Piagetian answer, and indeed not much of an answer elsewhere, as we know very little of how people's conceptual systems are organized.

The second point to be raised is how thorough and how wide ranging we should expect people's equilibrated knowledge systems to be. Are all gaps in knowledge really investigated or thought through, and are all internal contradictions really faced and resolved? Is there one unified system of knowledge in which cooking is a small but integral component? Is 'cooking knowledge', even, systematic and integrated? Piaget's work implies the answer 'yes' to these questions: what evidence there is suggests local organization with a lot of inconsistencies remaining (Boden 1982).

My third point is about where knowledge comes from. Cooking illustrates it particularly well. A truly Piagetian cook would arrive at his or her knowledge of ways of cooking vegetables from assimilating new objects to the pre-existing repertoire of techniques and accommodating the old repertoire to the new objects, as I have described. Most of the cooking I know of consists of doing things because other people have done them successfully, copying parents or friends, following the instructions given in a recipe book or on the packet. Even though some cooks may vary recipes to fit their taste, pocket, time or available ingredients better than the original, the origin of the 'knowledge' is heavily social, and as I suggested in the last paragraph, what is done, and probably what is known, may be fragmented rather than unified. Piaget underemphasized, I think, the role of apprenticeship to more knowledgeable others in the construction of 'knowledge', and the possibility that much of what we know is what anthropologists call 'bricolage', or *ad hoc* 'works adequately but not perfectly' ragbags. We will return to these points later.

Problems with the Piagetian model

Predictions can be derived from the equilibration model and examined. Is there a 'need' for thinking to be consistent and free of contradictions? Does conflict between different ideas lead to their resolution into a better idea? Is there one universal series of stages of thinking? There has been much debate over exactly what the philosophical implications of these predictions are and what would be relevant behavioural evidence (Rotman 1977; Boden 1982; Meadows 1983). The issue is very complicated indeed. Performance on tasks is less consistent than Piaget's competence model would appear to propose, the competence model has problems predicting particular performance, conflict leads to progress only sometimes, and equilibration is not an adequate explanation of development (Bryant 1982; Gelman and Baillargcon 1983; Flavell 1982; Sternberg 1984). Here as elsewhere in Piaget's theory there have been problems in translating his abstract fundamental mechanisms into terms of measurable behaviour, and all too often the behavioural evidence has not supported the existence of the abstract mechanisms.

Probably the best known aspects of Piaget's theory are the sequence of major stages and the accounts of children's behaviour when given problems of conservation, classification, perspective-taking, etc. It is, however, precisely these that are now seen as of relatively less value, and Piaget himself developed other theoretical areas at the end of his life (Vuyk 1981). Although there quite obviously is a shift from sensori-motor action-dominated cognition to reflective abstract quasi-logical cognition as development proceeds, there is little experimental evidence to suggest that it follows the picture of discrete, integrated, general stages that Piaget proposed. I have discussed the difficulties of stage theories in Chapter 1; in general the evidence on 'stages' in cognition suggests first, that cognitive performace is often inconsistent, varying across tasks, materials and brief periods of time (see, for example, Brown and Desforges 1979; Miller 1982), and second, that correlations between tasks which are said to require and be indicative of the same cognitive structure are no higher than correlations between tasks whose basic structures are quite different (e.g. Meadows 1975; Klausmeier and Sipple 1982). Flavell (1982) argues that we need to think carefully about what sort of homogeneity and what sort of heterogeneity we expect in cognitive development. Theorists who have clung to Piaget's stage model have suggested that transitions between stages may be longer and the differences thus less clear-cut than was originally proposed (e.g. Beilin 1980); it may be more useful to abandon the notion of general stage structures for the moment, and pay more attention to the variety of cognitive processes used in different areas and at different times. It is this sort of approach which seems to be proving fertile at the moment. (Freeman and Cox 1985 suggest it for the study of children's drawings also.)

Piaget's accounts of children's behaviour have turned out to be problematic in related ways. No one disputes the brilliance and ingenuity of his questioning, or that young children do indeed give the bizarre answers he recorded on what have become standard tests of 'concrete operations', though when his theory first made an impact on English language psychology in the 1950s a great deal of effort was put into replications of his experiments to see whether what he had observed really happened. What is now disputed, and quite often refuted, is his account of young children's failure in terms of the inadequacy of their logic (and indeed of older children's success in terms of their more adequate logic). Other explanations have been proposed for many of the failures which occur. One particularly illuminating example is the case of the 'transitive inference'.

Transitive inferences

Piaget took over transitive inference problems from his early work on Binet's intelligence tests. They involve the combination of two pieces of relational information to infer a third relation. Binet's test items were of the form 'Suzanne is taller than Emilie. Suzanne is shorter than Claudine. Who is the tallest?' Piaget's easier task (Inhelder and Piaget 1958) involved three sticks of just noticeably different lengths and the spoken and/or demonstrated information that 'A is longer than B. B is longer than C.' The 'transitive inference' question was 'Which is the longest, A or C?' Children over the age of about 7 would be quite sure that A had to be longer than C; children under 7 said they did not know, that they would have to compare A and C directly. In related tests they also had difficulty with measuring tasks and with seriation. Piaget attributed young children's failure on the task to their inability to integrate two pieces of information and make the required inference, and older children's success to doing precisely that.

Peter Bryant and Tom Trabasso suggested that both success and failure might have different explanations, and in a series of experiments demonstrated both what such explanations might be and a number of other rather important points for the diagnosis of cognition. Bryant and Trabasso (1971) argued, among other things, that failure to know the relation between A and C might be due not to an inability to infer that given A>B and B>C then necessarily A>C, but to simply not remembering one or both of A>B and B>C. They also argued that success might be due to having attached the label 'long' to A and the label 'short' to C. In their experiments they ruled out both these possibilities by training children on the longer/shorter relation of all adjacent pairs of the series A>B>C>D>E (and testing their memory of these pairs), and questioning them on the crucial relationship between B and D, which had never been seen together and which had each been 'longer' and 'shorter' equally often. Children as young as 4 were successful on the B>D comparison if they remembered B>C and C>D: and in further experiments they were also successful on comparisons they had only been told about, not seen for themselves. Memory difficulties are quite clearly implicated in 'transitive inference' failure – though not necessarily in all cases or as the only cause of failure. Memory is a result as well as a cause of what is known.

Further work by Trabasso and his colleagues (Trabasso 1975; Riley 1976) suggests that the making of a transitive inference is not necessarily what children (or adults) generally do when faced with a 'transitive inference' problem. It would seem that it is normal procedure to construct a mental picture of an ordered array of the objects concerned, particularly if they bear physical relations of height, size, weight, etc., but also if they are related in degree of characteristics such as 'niceness', and to scan it and 'read off' the answer to the question. Here, as in other instances which we will come to later, it is not that children fail to be logical while adults succeed, but that both children and adults may sometimes use non-logical procedures to solve 'logical' problems.

Logic as a model for cognitive development

This possibility is particularly interesting because philosophers and psychologists from Aristotle to Piaget have tended to assume that there was a close relationship between logic and reasoning, even that the rules of logic were the laws of reasoning. Developments over the last hundred years, as new forms of logic were invented and as psychology grew away from its philosophical roots, have left this relationship looking rather different from what was assumed (Braine and Rumain 1983, Wason and Johnson-Laird 1972). It is not clear whether reasoning is itself non-logical but logic is the normative standard for evaluating the validity of reasoning, which the transitive inference data might suggest, or whether reasoning is logical but error-ridden, a more Piagetian position.

The development of children's handling of logical problems is obviously relevant here. Braine and Rumain (1983), summarizing a substantial amount of work on propositional logic and some on predicate logic, suggest that there is a considerable resemblance between the reasoning of children entering school and that of older children and adults. Some logical problems are handled correctly even by very young children, and these are easy for older people too, while some other logical problems are handled incorrectly or inefficiently by most people young or old.

A classic logical problem is of the combining of pieces of information and testing the validity of inferences from them. For example, we have a statement of the form 'If p, then q' which we assume to be true ('If it rains, then we get wet'). This is followed by another statement, which tells us whether one of p, not–p, q or not–q, is the case at the moment, and from this we have to draw a conclusion about what else about p, not–p, q or not–q we can be sure is also the case. Any reader who does not know the answers may like to try the problems set out as Figure 1, remembering that 'If p, then q' must be taken as unquestionably true.

Children as young as 6 can draw the correct inference in the *modus ponens* problem, 'If p, then q:p, therefore q'; children and adults alike commonly draw incorrect conclusions on problems such as 'if p, then q: not p, therefore ?' or 'if p, then q:q, therefore ?' let alone on more complex inferences involving chains of reasoning. Analysis of errors in terms of the logical structures of problems, the language and various context effects, has suggested that logical reasoning involves utilizing a previously learned 'inference schema' to reach a valid conclusion.

Braine and Rumain (1983), summarizing the evidence, suggest that some inference schemas are learned very early, possibly through normal language learning, some only late and through special training. Using them involves getting the starting information into the form of a suitable schema and working through the schema, resisting errors from misinterpretation of language or context or response bias, and neither importing extraneous information nor forgetting what is relevant. All these errors are common in children and adults. Language may give rise to particularly severe problems in young children because the language-processing needed in logic tasks requires purer analysis than they are used to. In understanding a normal sentence (see Chapter 4) listeners process the words but also use other information available about the speaker, the world, the subject matter and the conversation, a much-practised and very skilled comprehending of language-in-context. In understanding a sentence in a logical problem listeners *must not* do this; instead they must concentrate on the words and segregate the information they give. What is important is what is *said*, not how it is said, what might be intended, what was said previously or what is generally known. Logical problems require slow careful analysis at a high level of verbal

If p, then q		If it rains, then we get wet	
p, therefore ?	It is raining, therefore ?	q	we get wet
not p, therefore ?	It is not raining, therefore ?	?	no conclusion possible (we don't get wet from being rained on, but we may not be wet or we may be wet from some other source such as swimming)
q, therefore ?	We are getting wet, therefore ?	?	no conclusion possible (we may be getting wet from rain or from some other source such as having buckets of water thrown at us)
not q, therefore ?	We are not getting wet, therefore	not p	it is not raining

Figure 1

skill, a sort of analysis which is rare culturally and associated with scholarly or highly literate pursuits. Young children, used to employing context and general knowledge to understand language, employ them too in logic problems.

There are other aspects of the 'ecology' of logic tests which have to be considered. One common error in propositional logic is to accept a conclusion as valid when the problem is formally undecidable. In the conditional syllogism 'if p, then q: not p, therefore ?' it is a common error to complete it by saying 'not p, therefore not q' ('If it rains, then we get wet: it is not raining, therefore we do not get wet'). People faced with undecidable problems like this tend to come to an invalid conclusion, to be unwilling to say that one can't tell whether q or not–q is the case. There may be various reasons for this, including expectations that 'logic' leads to clear conclusions and that testers do not ask questions which have no answers, and unwillingness to admit to the tester (an authority figure) that one 'can't tell' which in other situations is an admission of ignorance. Similarly, understanding what *has* to be the case and what merely *may possibly* be the case is important. Logical necessity, incompatibility and entailment are crucial notions which are relevant to various issues in the areas of language and logic. Children's understanding of these problems develops gradually (Russell 1978, 1982).

It would appear then that although some aspects of logical reasoning appear very early in children's development, possibly being derived from ordinary language use, there is a distinction between formal reasoning, based on analytic processing, and ordinary everyday reasoning which is often based on intelligent guesses about plausibility. Guessing, importing information, using common sense, are strategies often brought to bear on formal reasoning tasks. 'Disembedded' formal reasoning appears to be rare except in highly educated groups but is probably quite easily taught (see Donaldson 1978). It is not, on the whole, likely to be perfectly representative of ordinary everyday cognition: a model which encompasses a wider range of task variables and thinker characteristics is necessary. It seems clear that 'ordinary cognition' is inseparable from 'knowledge'. While current research does pay more attention to differences between tasks and between thinkers, as we shall see, there are as yet no satisfactory high level models which integrate findings from different areas and approaches.

Information-processing approaches

A major contribution to the study of cognitive development has been made by 'information-processing' approaches. Work in this tradition emphasizes precise analysis of how information is recognized, coded, stored and retrieved, and because computer simulation techniques are often used the 'structures' and 'processes' involved in handling information are relatively tightly specified and testable. Information-processing studies typically present people with a problem and examine what information they select, how they store and organize it, what models or hypotheses are involved, and what cognitive processes they use to reach a solution.

Capacity, processes and knowledge

Pascual-Leone (1970) and Case (1978, 1984, 1985) have proposed neo-Piagetian models of cognitive development couched in information-processing terms. They propose that what develops is, on the one hand, a series of distinct executive strategies for solving problems, and, on the other, the size of 'working memory' or the amount of mental 'space' available for information-processing strategies to work in. It is certainly the case that the number of things a person can do at one time increases as they grow older or more expert in a task, and that overloading working capacity interferes with performance and may disrupt it (e.g. Baddeley 1976). As we shall see when we discuss metacognition and study skills, even quite young learners can recognize the need to avoid distraction. It is not clear, however, whether the developmental increase in the functioning of memory and information-processing is due to an increase in the capacity of working memory or 'M-space'. Pascual-Leone proposes that M-space gets bigger with age and development, that is it becomes able to handle more strategies or programmes or schemes at the same time. The person's repertoire of strategies, etc., also increases with age and development: each strategy may also develop so that, for example, it becomes slicker and more automatic. Pascual-Leone claims that changes in strategies only account for improvement within a stage of cognitive development: changes *between* stages are due to increases in M-space.

It is a serious problem however to distinguish between changes in strategies and changes in M-space either in terms of behaviour or in theoretical terms, because they necessarily interact. Children's performance on a cognitive task will be a function of the strategy used, the demands which that strategy makes on M-space and the size of M-space itself. We know that the first two of these develop with age: attempts to measure the size of M-space have to hold strategy and strategy demands constant if they are to distinguish between changes in the size of M-space and changes in the way a stably-sized space is used. Let us suppose that the transitive inference task requires four units of processing space: one each to store A>B and B>C, one to store the information that 'longer than' is a transitive relationship as opposed to one such as loving which is not ('Tybalt loves Juliet' and 'Juliet loves Romeo' do not combine transitively into 'Tybalt loves Romeo'), and one to make the inference. Children may come to be able to deal with the transitive inference task by achieving an M-space of four units. They may also come to be able to do it by having their inferential strategy use up less space, for example by learning the relative sizes of A and B and of B and C so well that they require only half as much storage space. Or they could be able to deal with the task by using a non-inferential strategy – such as reading off from a visual image – which needs less M-space. Only very precise analysis of tasks, of learner activities and of the interdependencies between knowledge, strategies and processing can explain the contributions to cognitive development of growth in processing capacity, growth in the information archives, greater sophistication of pro-

cessing, greater sophistication of the catalogue and cross-references of the archives, and interaction among all these. At the moment the 'best guess' seems to be that the first of these is the least important in cognitive development, indeed that the limits of information processing change little though there are enormous changes in what goes on within them (Brown, Bransford, Ferrara and Campione 1983). Case's recent developments of his model take this line and include experimental evidence which supports it (Case 1984, 1985), though Sternberg (1983, 1984) still argues for an increase in total capacity.

Information-processing approaches to cognitive development assume that 'people are in essence limited capacity manipulators of symbols' (Siegler 1983, p. 129). Over the course of development the processes which people use to 'manipulate symbols' become more complex, more accessible, more exhaustive, more flexible and faster, in ways which may be analogous to the changes which happen in the move from being a novice to being an expert. There are also developmental changes in symbol storage as more knowledge is acquired and as it is organized differently. We will look at some aspects of how children organize their knowledge later. Recent information-processing work is giving more attention to 'knowledge-rich domains' such as mathematics. Early work used artificial domains because they did not call on subjects' prior knowledge and thus complicate the picture with uncontrollable variation between subjects. It is not clear how 'knowledge' and 'processes' interact, not even when the knowledge is knowledge about processes (see Chapter 3, section on metacognition). Prior knowledge has been shown to influence recall, increasing the frequency of 'intrusion errors' where recall includes information which is correct and relevant but comes from what was known before the experimental presentation of the material to be learned. More prior knowledge may sometimes produce more efficient processing, perhaps because it reduces memory load to deal with overlearned information, or perhaps because the connections between items are more accessible, or perhaps because the important characteristics of the input are more obvious and their irrelevant aspects can be more easily set aside. Knowledge of the task and of one's own abilities are particularly important aspects of performance (see Chapter 3, section on metacognition).

Mechanisms of cognitive development

It is not yet clear in what ways children's cognition comes to develop from immature cognitive processes to more mature ones. Answers to questions of the 'mechanisms' of cognitive development are still very tentative indeed; all that is clear is that it must be 'mechanisms', plural (Sternberg 1984). Kail and Bisanz (1982) outline the general features which will characterize information-processing models of cognitive development as they emerge over the next few years. First, they will be concerned with how information is given internal representation in the organism. While it is agreed that much information is represented in symbolic form, there is much debate about what symbolic systems are used, and when (see, for example, Cohen 1983 for an introductory account of this debate). The

problem of how external stimulation is turned into internal representation is also still a serious one. Developmental theories will have to describe what features of complex stimuli are processed by children of different ages. Changes would seem likely to be related to the development of the ways in which concepts are linked in children's knowledge (see p. 139 below). Information processing theories assume that concepts are linked in a network of associations. In the course of development the network comes to include more elements; superordinate conceptual links between them become stronger and more important than perceptual ones, and processing can involve larger units of information. Kail and Bisanz (1982, p. 60) illustrate this with the knowledge-of-fruit structures of two children (Figure 2).

For the younger child, both apples and peaches are characterized as fruit (an is a relation) but their perceptual characteristics (is round, has a stone or seeds) are stronger, and the child would say that apples and peaches are alike because they are both round. For the older child, in contrast, apples and peaches are more strongly

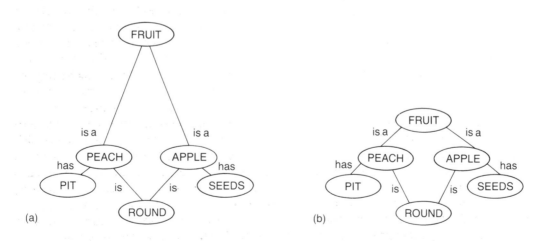

(a)

(b)

Figure 2 Portions of the knowledge base concerning fruits. (a) The knowledge of a 5-year-old, for whom peaches and apples are alike primarily because they are both round. (b) The knowledge of an 8-year-old, for whom peaches and apples are similar primarily because they are both fruits.

Source: From Kail and Bisanz (1982), p. 60.

linked to the superordinate category of fruit than they are to their perceptual characteristics; the is a relation is more important.

The organization of knowledge in real cases is likely to be far more complex and hard to discover and describe. A pioneering but methodologically flawed study by Chi and Koeske 1983 seeks to map a 4-year-old's knowledge about dinosaurs. Repertory grid techniques hold promise but are difficult to use with children (Ravenette 1975; Fransella 1976).

The second aspect of information-processing models of cognitive development which Kail and Bisanz (1982) discuss is their account of changes in the cognitive processes which generate, transform or manipulate representations of knowledge. They anticipate that research in this area will identify a very large number of ·complex procedures specific to particular tasks, domains or persons but a relatively small set of elementary procedures underlying them. I discuss some of the specific cases below. The general developmental change is, they suggest, towards an increasing use of rules which are *sufficient*, that is they apply correctly to all cases and do not need supplements or exceptions, rather than rules which are only partially correct and apply successfully only in a limited range of tasks or settings. Siegler's analysis of the balance task (Siegler 1981, 1983, 1984) is one example; the history of science provides many others, such as the replacement of Newton's model of gravity by Einstein's. There is a similar developmental shift towards using more *efficient* processing, to using procedures which are more powerful and require less role repetition and 'unskilled labour'. Such procedures need fewer resources of attention and effort to run successfully, at least once they are established (see Chapter 3); using them thus frees attentional resources for other bits of processing. Finally, development in cognitive processes may be an increase in the speed of the processes used rather than in what the processes themselves consist of.

How might such changes come about? How do we manage a development, continued over many years, which gives us an increasingly full and flexible conceptual structure, increasingly efficient and sufficient cognitive processes, and an increasing availability of attentional resources? Even if we reduce the scale of the change by allowing, on the one hand, that very young children are cleverer than some theorists had supposed, and, on the other, that adults' cognition is often enough inefficient, insufficient and an unsystematic sort of 'bricolage' or botching together, rather than brilliant craftsmanship, the phenomenon of cognitive development is worth admiration. What sort of system would allow such changes?

The explanatory framework Kail and Bisanz (1982) propose has two general components. The first is increases in attentional resources, which I discussed above. They see increases through growth in the total resources available (cf. Pascual-Leone) as being compatible with increases without total growth, due to better automatization and chunking of information (cf. Case), though as we saw it may be hard to distinguish between them. Their second general component is a set of processes which modify the knowledge base. During conceptual development new elements and characteristics are added to the knowledge base, that is there are new 'nodes' in the associative network. Some old nodes are deleted, and there are new or changed links between nodes. Among the modifying processes are addition/deletion processes and processes for strengthening or weakening links. There are also important processes for determining that change is needed. They suggest that these involve the detection of inconsistencies, that is there are processes which compare processes with other processes or with goals or external events. An obvious example is what happens inside a child in a conservation test, when judgement on the basis of the changed appearance of the array is inconsistent with judgement based on the knowledge that nothing has been added or taken away. A need to resolve inconsistency is, of course, at the core of the Piagetian notion of 'equilibration'. Inconsistency detection is not, however, the only monitoring process Kail and Bisanz include in their account. Another analysis involves detecting regularities which recur and demand resources. If there is repeated use of the same sequence of processes, or if the activation of one node in the concept network always involves the activation of the same set of representations, it may make fewer demands on resources to modify the knowledge base and set the recurrent regularities up as a sort of package which can be called up *en bloc*. Detection of regularities may also be useful in detecting redundancies and so streamlining processes. It may also show up occasions when different processes have the same result, thereby enhancing the possibility of higher-order organization of processes, and perhaps also increasing one's confidence in the correctness of the result the processes have reached (Bryant 1982).

Monitoring processes are seen as being heavy on resources, however. Thus there may not be any developmental change, even though an inconsistency or a recurrent regularity has been detected, unless sufficient attentional resources are available. If total resources available do increase with growth, growth may make the use of monitoring processes possible where they could not be implemented before. Resources also become available through the automatization of content in the knowledge base. Automatization is to be associated with repeated use of processes and with the strengthening of links between conceptual nodes and hence should, I would suppose, be positively related to the detection of regularities and consistencies. As I read their account, it would not seem to be as closely related to the detection of inconsistencies and conflict, so it is possible that in Kail and Bisanz's model, development through confirmation, practice, positive feedback and more polished and efficient performance of established processes may be easier than development through detecting inconsistencies and conflicts, and enforced change in processes or knowledge organization. This reading goes against the Piagetian emphasis on conflict-led equilibration, which I argued against at the beginning of this section; it accounts quite nicely, however, for various observations, such as people's difficulty in giving up a practised but insufficient strategy for a better one (e.g. Brown

et al. 1983), Bryant's arguments about conflict and confirmation in conservation (Bryant 1982) and the difficulty of negative instances in concept formation and scientific problem solving (e.g. Bruner, Goodnow and Austin 1956; Wason and Johnson-Laird 1972).

The final point Kail and Bisanz make about their knowledge modification processes is that they interact with the resources available, and each modifies the other. Changes in the knowledge base alter the ways in which the cognitive system investigates or interprets its environment, which in turn alters the internal and external feedback monitored by the regularity and inconsistency detectors – a formulation very reminiscent of the Accommodation and Assimilation model, though perhaps potentially at a more specific level. Thus changes in the knowledge base may allow the system to identify inconsistencies and regularities which were previously undetectable – an account of the phenomenon of sudden insight, perhaps?

I have dealt with the Kail and Bisanz model at some length because it seems to me to be an unusually intelligible account of what sort of account the mechanisms of cognitive development may be expected from the information-processing approach. It is not the only model in the field; Sternberg (1984) contains six more, with Flavell's comments on each. It does have some notable omissions or underemphases which need some further elaboration. One of these is the area of the accessibility and difficulty of cognitive processes, which is likely to be of particular interest to people concerned with individual differences but will also have to be dealt with by models of general cognition. Another, which I shall discuss at more length (Chapter 3), is the currently lively area of executive control, metacognition and strategic thought. The underemphasis is surprising, since information processing in computers is one main source of the 'executive control' metaphor. It is quite clear that in cognitive development thinking becomes more strategic and more controlled by the thinker, as we will see in areas such as attending, remembering, text processing and problem solving discussed in

Chapter 3. Children also know more about cognition as they get older, and this too is a flourishing area of research. Models of 'cognition' will have to account for 'metacognition', though the interaction of the two is unlikely to be simple: it is quite clear that one can know but not do, and do without knowing, as well as the two consistent positions of know and do, not know and not do.

I have described three different models of cognition, the Piagetian, what one might call 'the logicians' account', and information processing. The second of these is not a contender as an account of how we reason in general; rather, logical problems seem to be a restricted domain where general processes have to be used in rather specialised ways. Piaget's model remains an immense intellectual achievement, worthy of great admiration. Some of its features now seem to be rather seriously dubious (c.g. automatic equilibration, the groupings model), and some need to be given a much more specific form (e.g. Assimilation and Accommodation): some, like the tendency to play down the possibility of development through social interaction and being taught, have distorted our view of children's thinking and education and need to be reversed. The information-processing approach has not yet achieved a satisfactory model of cognitive development. It has produced some very interesting accounts of processes and rules involved in solving a number of problems, some of which were derived from Piaget's tasks (see, for example, Klahr and Wallace 1976), and I would expect there to be considerable progress in the next few years on higher-order modelling of general cognitive systems. However, there are certain reasons for caution rather than optimism about this approach. One important problem is the difficulty of observing thinking: there is a tendency for some work in this area to base its model on data which are only very distantly related to the observable behaviour of real children. This was a problem for Piaget too, of course, and it still needs to be guarded against. It is, of course, a perfectly valid choice to concentrate on providing a model of idealized competence rather than actual performance; competence models may be interesting

in themselves, and may illuminate performance. What they do omit, perhaps inevitably, is, of course, much consideration of the context of cognition. Questions of why cognition proceeds as it does, how it is shaped and constrained and fostered in development, how biology and social experience are involved, seem very important to me, and hard to deal with in the traditional information-processing terms – computers do not have much in the way of ecology. Some philosophers argue anyhow that the computer metaphor is seriously inadequate in that it sets aside as negligible the roles of consciousness, experience and intention (Searle 1984; Russell 1984). I can do no more here than refer back to the second sentence of this chapter – 'there is still no clear, complete and valid account of what adults do when they think, understand, etc.' and add that there is none for children either, let alone an account of the change from child to adult. It is, however, the case that we are increasing our understanding in some more limited ways, as I shall go on to discuss.

Infants' perception and cognition

I must preface my brief account of perception and cognition in infancy with two remarks to guide the reader throughout the rest of the discussion. The first is that I am not myself involved in research on infants: I have thus had to rely on the work of others to an even greater extent in this section than elsewhere. The second is that the degree of controversy in infant perception and cognition seems to be higher than in most other research areas: there is profound disagreement not just about ideas or interpretations but about behavioural facts. Do infants imitate facial expressions, babble more if given contingent reinforcement, search for an object that has moved out of sight? Yes, say researchers on one side: no, we cannot replicate this finding, say researchers on another. Non-replications such as these are not always attributable to methodological changes or age differences, or even to experimenter bias: some remain mysterious, and the experts as yet cannot resolve them. A non-expert, I have not tried to

Plate 5

do more than point out issues and indicate useful sources. Most of the material and evaluation in this section derives from the second volume of the *Handbook of Child Psychology* (Haith and Campos 1983). I will begin by discussing what is known of the infant's perceptual capabilities (visual, auditory and olfactory, and some aspects of brain development) and then proceed to the cognitive development that ensues. Throughout I would wish to emphasize that ultimately we should link development at anatomical/physiological levels with development at behavioural levels, and explain developmental changes with reference to their functions as part of the evolutionary 'push' and the environmental 'pull'. Our present understanding being distinctly limited, however, we will have to be cautious about the nature of these links, and particularly about their causes and directions.

Seeing and hearing

The 'hardware' of vision

Banks and Salapatek (1983) review infant visual perception. Human infants are born with eyes that are moderately mature in anatomical and physiological terms, more mature than cats, for example, and less mature than macaque monkeys (Figure 3). As in adults, light passes through cornea, lens and the body of the eye to the retina at the back of the eye. One layer of the retina is of light-sensitive cells, the 'rods' and 'cones': when light reaches these receptors, signals are sent via the other layers of retina to the optic nerve and thence to successive parts of the brain. Compared to adults', the infant's eyes are relatively short from front to back, there is less possibility of adjusting the focal distance of their lenses, and there are immaturities in the retina. In particular,

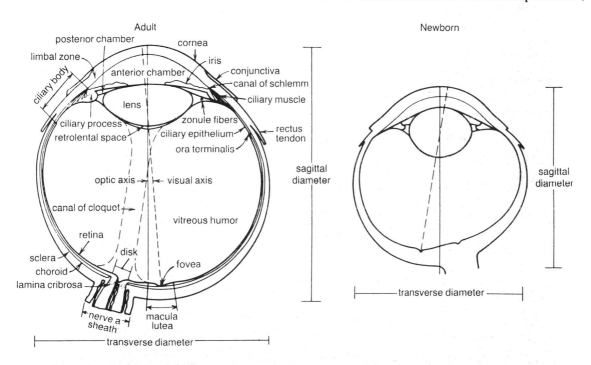

Figure 3   Cross-sectional drawings of the adult and newborn eye. The adult eye (a) is a horizontal section of the right eye. Important structures are labelled. The visual axis is represented by the broken line and the optic axis by the solid line. The newborn eye (b) is also a horizontal section of the right eye. It is drawn to scale to represent its size relative to the adult eye.

Source: From Banks and Salapatek (1983).

in the adult eye there is a central area, the fovea, which differs in cell type and in sensitivity from the rest of the retina. In this area visual acuity is better than in the periphery; as we are all aware, we normally see objects more clearly when they are in the centre of our visual field than when we use our peripheral vision. The newborn baby has a much less differentiated fovea, and therefore probably does not see shapes and contours as clearly, or discriminate them as finely, as adults can using their foveal vision. The retina develops quite rapidly after birth and is anatomically mature by about the end of the first year.

Babies' vision gets more acute quite rapidly as developments in the retina (and better control of the lens) are accompanied by developments in various parts of the brain. In 'the next major structure in the ascending visual pathway' (Banks and Salapatek 1983) (see Figure 4), the lateral geniculate nucleus, which is essentially a relay station between eye and cortex, there are postnatal anatomical changes, as the neurons grow, and functional changes, as response to stimulation becomes less sluggish and less easily fatiguable, and as visual acuity increases in the cells serving the developing fovea, the nerve pathways connecting structures slowly grow a sheath of myelin, which allows better transmission of signals. In the visual cortex itself, structural development, which began before birth, continues for

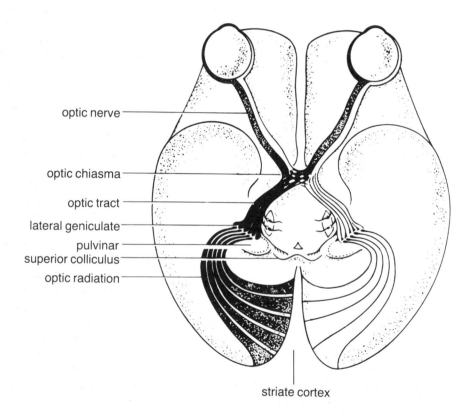

optic nerve

optic chiasma

optic tract

lateral geniculate

pulvinar
superior colliculus

optic radiation

striate cortex

Figure 4 Major pathways from the eyes to the central nervous system. Fibres of the optic nerve from the temporal halves of each retina remain on the same side of the head; that is, they project to the ipsilateral hemisphere of the brain. Fibres originating from the nasal halves of each retina cross at the optic chiasma and then project to the contralateral hemisphere. The lateral geniculate nuclei are part of the thalamus. The superior colliculi are part of the mid brain. The striate cortices are part of the cerebral cortex.

Source: From Banks and Salapatek (1983), p. 446.

a considerable period after it. Evidence from studies of kittens shows that although capabilities often appear before they are needed, and some structural organization emerges without needing experience, much later-appearing organization and visual capability is guided by visual experience: neither cats nor monkeys (nor, possibly, humans) develop the normal population of cortical cells which deal with visual input in terms of binocularity unless they have had experience of both eyes seeing together. Again, animals raised in environments dominated by lines at a particular orientation develop a disproportionate number of brain cells sensitive to that orientation (Banks and Salapatek 1983, pp. 458–9).

The 'mechanisms' of vision

Eyes are often compared to cameras, but there are significant differences in how they work. For example, prolonged stimulation leads to fatigue: if an eye is immobilized so that light falls on the retinal receptors for a prolonged period, they cease to respond to it until the input light changes. Further, the central foveal area of the retina is more sensitive than the periphery. These characteristics mean that in order to see something clearly we have to move our eyes: in one sort of way to move the retinal image enough to stop it fading, and in another sort of way to get the image on the fovea rather than the outer parts of the retina where our acuity is less. Furthermore, since we have two eyes, we have to co-ordinate them and their movements: *and* compensate for movements of our heads and bodies: *and* for any movements of what we are looking at. Adults manage to do all this with only occasional difficulties: how do these skills develop?

The saccadic eye movement system of rapid changes in fixation, which relocates targets first seen in peripheral vision on to the more sensitive fovea, is functional at birth, provided the peripheral target is not too far off the centre. The effective visual field which will elicit saccades, so that the eye moves and the target comes to the centre of the retina, grows postnatally, and so does the accuracy and speed of the eye movement. Eye movements which compensate for the observer's movements are made via various re-

flexes in adults. Some of these reflexes are present in newborns, including blind infants, but not until about 3 months of age are they well co-ordinated with other movements, or accurate. Eye movements which follow a moving object are also possible at birth though they are jerky like saccades. Smooth visual pursuit appears first when the target object is moving slowly, but by about 12 weeks infants can track even fairly rapid movements quite smoothly.

Human eyes, like cameras, can only be focused for one viewing distance at a time. Objects at this distance are in sharp focus, objects nearer or further away are blurred. Adult eyes adjust automatically and accurately, largely by changing the curvature of the lens (accommodation). Newborn infants do not do this with any accuracy; like a pinhole camera they have a fairly good depth of focus but at longer and shorter target distances than this range they see less clearly and do not accommodate well. There is a rapid improvement in accommodation over the first three months of postnatal life.

Infants able to support themselves sitting or standing use visual feedback as information not just about the movement of other objects but also about their own movements. If we move forward, particularly if we fall forward, things initially near the centre of our visual field move outwards towards its edge and things initially near the periphery move outwards out of sight. Conversely, if we see a centrifugal visual field, we may feel we are falling forward (a feeling Stanley Kubrick used in his film *2001*). Experiments with babies (e.g. Butterworth and Hicks 1977) showed that they felt like this when the room wall in front of them moved forward, and adjusted their posture appropriately, swaying or even falling in the direction of the room's motion. We do not yet know how much experience of one's own motion is necessary for this.

Looking at objects and patterns

I have outlined the basic anatomy, physiology and mechanisms of the infant's visual system: we have seen that even very young infants can detect and look at objects, but that only postnatal development allows babies to see as clearly as adults do. As far as acuity is concerned, to begin with babies have difficulty detecting stimulus differences which convey detailed information about patterns. The rapid development of the fovea is one area of improvement, but beyond that there are probably difficulties due to limitations in the nervous system's ability to process the retinal image. There is extensive evidence that visual acuity improves dramatically over the first year of life: neonates seem only to attend to large objects, apparently not discriminating their details, while older babies notice fine detail much more readily.

A most useful paradigm has been developed for investigating infants' ability to discriminate between patterns: pioneered by Fantz, it is the visual preference paradigm. Two patterns are presented simultaneously to the infant and he or she is observed to determine whether the two objects are looked at for different lengths of time. Provided controls for position preferences, etc. have been properly implemented, if one object is looked at significantly longer than the other the infant must have discriminated some difference between them, and may perhaps be said to prefer the one looked at more (if we assume that infants are not given to mortifying themselves by looking more at objects which are liked less). Indices like smiles may also be used. The habituation paradigm is also used for investigating visual discriminations: habituation indicates that the pattern is seen as being the same, dishabituation that a difference is discriminated.

There is now an extensive literature on infants' preferences in patterns (though little on older children's or adults'). Other things being equal, infants tend to prefer red and blue to green and yellow, some pattern to no pattern, curved lines over straight ones, concentric patterns over non-concentric ones, symmetry to asymmetry, and so on. Some of these 'preferences' are no doubt due to 'hardware' and 'mechanics' properties of the visual system: some have been explained in terms of a general preference in the infant for 'complexity'. While such an explanation has intuitive appeal, it has proved hard to define and measure 'complexity' (Banks and Salapatek 1983, pp. 497–506). It is clear that predictions work best,

however, when based on a model of preference which combines the infant's perceptual/cognitive state and the stimulus characteristics: infants of different ages, with different capabilities and different knowledge prefer different patterns (Kagan *et al.* 1978).

In one instance of pattern preference, evolutionary adaptiveness and ecosystem demands both seem to be potential explanations and contributors. Infants look at, and smile at, faces. There is controversy over how they process the complex information that a face provides (Harris 1979, 1983) though detailed observation has shown agreement on exactly what they attend to. Under about 2 months old, infants looking at a face look most at areas of high contrast such as its outside border. Next they attend most to features, particularly the eyes, and may differentiate between artificial faces in terms of 'eyedness' (Kagan *et al.* 1978). Then a face comes to be attended to as a whole, and infants develop ideas about the relative familiarity or novelty of faces (Fagan 1976). A preference for faces which leads to more looking at them would both give the infant more opportunities for social learning and increase his or her attractiveness to caretakers (see Chapter 6). Parents commonly say that they begin to regard their baby as 'a real person' once mutual gaze and smiling has begun. Infants who do not look at your face, and anyone whose facial expression does not respond to yours, are unattractive or even aversive stimuli. On the whole, infants find blank faces less attractive than responsive ones, as adults do.

Infants' scanning

Eye movements are necessary for seeing. As we look at a scene, saccadic eye movements continually move the fovea from fixation to fixation, from one feature to another. Observation of where these fixations fall, usually by photographing reflections on the cornea relative to the pupil, indicate what features are being looked at in what order. Although adults can certainly get information from peripheral vision, and infants may do too, studies of foveal scanning do illuminate how information is gathered from the stimulus. Banks and Salapatek (1983) review their development (pp. 507–15).

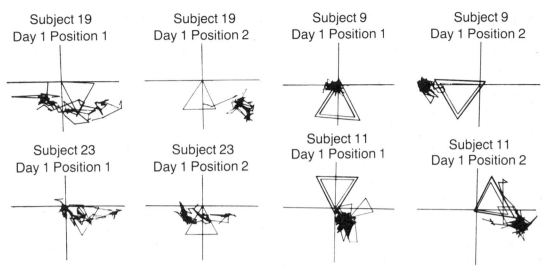

Figure 5 Scanning patterns of newborns. The left portion shows scanning patterns when newborns were presented a homogeneous field. Each dot represents eye position at one time sample. The lines connecting the dots simply connect eye positions at adjacent time samples. The vertices of the triangles represent infra-red marker light positions. Thus, the triangles shown were actually not present during these trials. The right portion of this figure shows scanning patterns when newborns were presented a solid black triangle on an otherwise homogeneous field. The outer triangle on each record represents the triangle's contours. The vertices of the inner triangles represent the marker light positions.

Source: From Banks and Salapatek (1983), p. 511.

Given a simple vertical or horizontal line or edge to look at, newborn infants fixate more in the region of the contour than in the rest of the visual field, particularly if it is a vertical contour. This is probably because it is easier to make horizontal eye movements across a vertical contour, as infants do, than vertical eye movements across a horizontal one. Given a figure to look at, newborns tend to fixate a point which has a high degree of contrast (Figure 5).

In the left-hand side of the figure, newborns were looking at what to them was a uniform visual field, and they made no consistent fixations. In the right-hand side, the newborns looked at a solid black triangle on an otherwise uniform field, and fixated one corner of the triangle. Older infants began to scan more widely, for example along the edges of the triangle, but not randomly. Their scanning came to be concentrated on areas of maximum information, as that of adults is. There is an increasing degree of

perceptual organization. Cognition has become inextricably mixed with perception.

Auditory perception
I will describe the development of hearing more briefly than I did the development of vision. Discussion of infants' speech perception may be found in the chapter on language development. Aslin, Pisoni and Jusczyk (1983) review auditory development in infancy and were the main source for this section. They point out that despite much recent relevant research, many basic questions about the development of auditory function remain unanswered, and indeed our understanding of hearing in adults is much less complete than our understanding of vision.

So far as the outer ear is concerned, the main difference between the adult's ear and the infant's is that the latter is smaller in size throughout. This may lead to the infant hearing best sounds which are at a slightly different frequency

51

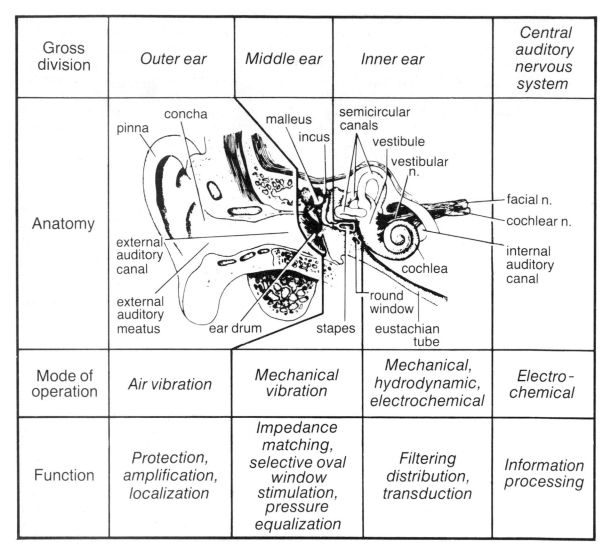

Gross division	Outer ear	Middle ear	Inner ear	Central auditory nervous system
Anatomy				
Mode of operation	Air vibration	Mechanical vibration	Mechanical, hydrodynamic, electrochemical	Electro-chemical
Function	Protection, amplification, localization	Impedance matching, selective oval window stimulation, pressure equalization	Filtering distribution, transduction	Information processing

Figure 6 Cross-section of the human ear showing the three major divisions (outer, middle and inner ear), their mode of operation, and their presumed function.

Source: From Aslin, Pisoni and Jusczyk (1983), p. 586.

range from the sounds the adult hears best, sensitivity possibly being shifted towards higher frequencies. Because sound sources are localized using differences in the times at which the sound reaches left and right ear, the fact that the infant has a smaller head between his or her ears than the adult means that the time difference is smaller and infants may therefore have more difficulty localizing sounds. Bower (1974) points out that because their heads are growing the inter-ear distance of infants is changing and they will need to adjust to this continuing change when localizing sound.

The functioning of the middle ear and the inner ear is complex and not perfectly understood. Much of middle ear structure seems to be adult-like at birth, but its smaller size may shift sensitivity towards higher frequencies. Anatomical comparisons between adult and infant inner ear structures might also lead to predictions of sensitivity to high frequencies developing before sensitivity to low frequencies, but research studies have not yet tested these predictions. What functional differences there are is very unclear: certainly infants and children from 5 months old onwards are better at detecting high frequency sounds such as bats' squeaks than people with ageing ears but this may be because the latter have lost their sensitivity. Infant insensitivity to low sounds has not been demonstrated.

The complexity of brain involvement in hearing is very great. Research on cats and rats done in the last decade or so suggests that there are big postnatal developments of many different sorts in these animals. There is little evidence on the functional development of the auditory brain in humans, so we do not know whether postnatal changes in sensitivity and responsiveness to sounds are due to an improvement in perception or in neural connections and interactions.

Pregnant women have long since reported that sudden loud noises led to sudden movements of the foetus in the womb. Recently, convincing evidence has been presented that the foetus moved because it heard the noise, not merely as a response to its mother's reaction to the noise (Aslin *et al.* 1983, pp. 602–3). The infant *in utero* can hear noises from outside, particularly perhaps loud noises at low frequency, and the ambient noise in the womb turns out to be fairly loud (85 decibels or so). Recodings of these ambient rhythmic noises have, of course, been quite a commercial success as lullabies, marketed as soothing noises to be provided to the baby who has lost them by being born.

From at least a few weeks before birth, then, infants can hear, but the threshold of stimulation needed to produce a noticeable reaction is higher than adults need. Newborn infants can do some crude localization of sound sources, orienting reliably to sounds at 90 degrees left or right of their midline, but their reactions are slow, and they do have problems controlling their head movements. Older infants, 1 to 3 months old,

may turn their heads less towards a sound source, but after this period orientation to the sound picks up again. Babies can fairly easily be conditioned to turn their heads to one side in response to a sound, particularly for a reward of a pleasant sight or food, as in the classic work by Papousek (1967). Animal evidence suggests that binaural experience is necessary for sound localization, much as binocular vision seems to be necessary for normal visual development.

Summary

So far as the best-studied senses, vision and hearing, are concerned, it is a simplification but not a falsification to say that even newborn babies have a capacity to function which is not very different from that of an adult. Developments in the brain, and growth of knowledge, account for most of the developmental changes in perception: developments in the peripheral organs or perception seem to be less important.

Development in other sensory modalities

I have briefly described the development of vision and hearing in the two previous sections. There has been much less work on the other senses; indeed they are much less emphasized by people generally. Not being able to see or hear is regarded as a significant handicap, but having no sense of smell or taste is not felt to be more than a trivial disadvantage. While it is certainly true that human beings make much less conspicuous use of smell, taste and touch than of vision and hearing, it would be wrong to assume that these other senses are unimportant, or that they play no part in the development of behaviour.

Very little can be said at present about the development of taste and of touch. Some discrimination between sweet and salty taste is found at birth or even *in utero* (Crook 1978), and babies are said to discriminate between breast milk from different mothers (Macfarlane 1976). It has been suggested that there are developmental shifts in liking and disliking the taste of later foodstuffs, reputedly that young children positively enjoy the cod liver oil which adults find disgusting. How clear such changes are, and how they come about, is not known. Sensitivity to touch is present from birth: infants needing to be nursed in incubators thrive much better lying on a soft fleecy surface than on a smooth hard surface (Harlow's infant monkeys also preferred a soft surrogate mother to a hard one which fed them). Skin-to-skin contact with the mother directly after birth has been claimed to be an important contributor to mother–infant bonding (Klaus and Kennell 1976), but there is reason to doubt its necessity (Sluckin, Herbert and Sluckin 1983; and Chapter 6, this volume).

Recent work has begun to illuminate the developmental importance of the sense of smell. There is not a great deal of evidence from humans, although Macfarlane (1976) showed some time ago that neonates can discriminate between the smell of their mother's breast milk and that of another mother. Work on mice however indicates that their maturation rate is affected by their olfactory experience. Specifically, female mice exposed to the odours of natural secretions from male mice reach puberty earlier than average (and may possibly, though there is some controversy about this, be larger in size), while female mice exposed to smells from adult females mature sexually more slowly than average (for a review see Johns 1980). Behaviour and morphology too are shifted, towards the norm for male mice in females exposed to male secretions, and in the female direction for mice exposed to female secretions.

Prenatal exposure to hormones also affects behaviour. Female mice who were adjacent to males *in utero* (mouse foetuses are lined up like peas in pods) tend to behave more like male mice, and male mice who were between females *in utero* behave more like females. There may have been a similar result in humans in the cases where female foetuses were exposed to high levels of androgen prenatally. In childhood and adolescence these girls were said to be 'tomboyish' in their behaviour and 'masculine' in their outlook (Money and Ehrhardt 1972). Their parents' knowledge of the congenital syndrome which caused excessive productions of androgens and its 'likely effects' complicates the picture so that conclusions are very hard to draw (see

Huston 1983; and the section on sex differences in Chapter 5, this volume). The evidence on whether mothers who were treated with oestrogens or progesterone when they threatened to miscarry early in pregnancy have 'feminized' offspring is also not clear (Ehrhardt and Meyer-Bahlburg 1981). Measures of 'sex-typed' behaviour and attitudes in humans are problematic, and sex differences due to social and cultural factors could be argued to be far more important than any hormonal base. These difficulties would appear not to be so great in mice: the mother mouse (or foster mother) probably does not treat her infants differently on the basis of the hormones they were exposed to prenatally. It is hard to interpret the differences in mice's behaviour, growth rate and anatomy as the result of cultural influences!

So far as the development of olfaction is concerned, then, there seems to be an interesting possibility that some naturally occurring substances may affect development through the olfactory pathways. Further research is needed.

The last sense I want to mention is the kinaesthetic sense, which tells us about the body's movement and position. Receptors in muscles, tendons, joints and elsewhere send messages about their activity to the cortex; we perceive the relationship between these messages in a pattern over time which depends on the size, direction and speed of body and limb movements, as well as on the resistance to movement that we encounter. We do not know a great deal about how kinaesthetic perception develops. Messages from muscles, etc., are emitted automatically, but what they are understood to mean depends on experience. Infants, for example, spend quite a long time watching their hands and learning to correlate visual and kinaesthetic information. Deliberate skilled movement requires the use of kinaesthetic feedback; children who are clumsy and poorly co-ordinated often seem to have particularly poor awareness of their posture and movement (Laszlo and Bairstow 1985). Kinaesthetic awareness, and skilled precise motor action, take practice as a major contributor to their development.

Some aspects of brain development in infancy

I emphasize again my assumption that mind and behaviour depend on brain and body, that without the latter the former would not exist. Nevertheless, there are real problems in relating brain and behaviour, which are particularly sharp in the study of development. In most of the cases where we find a change in brain and a change in behaviour which coincide in time, we may wish to infer a causal link between them, but there is rarely evidence to test the inference of causality. The central empirical problem is how much and for how long do the two causal chains below occur.

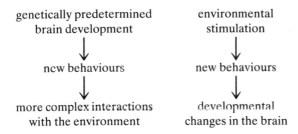

The answer is probably different at different stages of maturation: for example, foetal development before thirty-six post-menstrual weeks, about four weeks before term birth, is not much affected by sensory input, because of limitations in foetal sensory receptors and transmission to the cortex. Subsequently, development shifts towards a predominance of environmental factors in behavioural and cognitive development: genetic programming does not explain a great deal of the variance in behaviour such as reading, chess playing or ability to run marathons. Even if there is neurological dysfunction or damage, such as cerebral palsy, cognitive skills can develop in a strikingly normal way, given a favourable environment. Recovery from brain damage at birth is very much positively correlated with how good an environment is provided for the infant and young child (Shaffer 1985).

Brains consist of millions of nerve cells, intricately interconnected, and making up various structures which are involved in functions ranging from controlling the breathing, sleeping and waking of the organism to abstruse cognitive, linguistic, affective and spiritual activities. Much of the development of cells and structures originates prenatally, and throughout early life the brain is nearer its mature state than any other part of the body (Tanner 1978). There is however substantial postnatal development of many anatomical, neurophysiological and functional features of the brain. Parmelee and Sigman (1983) review recent work: I will sketch the extent of the work and indicate some interesting developmental findings.

Brains contain two sorts of cells, the neurons or nerve cells, which transmit impulses, and the neuroglia, which form a support system for the neurons both by forming a guide for their development and by supplying substances needed for the manufacture of nerve fibres and their insulation and of neurotransmitters. A neuron has a nucleus and surrounding cell body, like any other cell, but part of its substance is drawn out into long threadlike processes called dendrites which branch intricately to make many connections with dendrites from other cells (Figure 7).

There are about a million million (10^{12}) neurons in the brain, and a cortical neuron has about 30,000 nerve processes from 3000 or so other neurons connecting with it (Tanner 1978, pp. 105–6). By the time a foetus is eighteen weeks old, its developing brain contains almost as many neurons as this, though not the full mesh of interconnecting dendrites: connections between neurons continue to develop for a long time after birth. In rats and kittens environmental stimulation after birth can increase dendritic growth and interconnections. Neuroglia begin to appear a little later than neurons, and new ones continue to develop until the second year of life, accounting for some of the postnatal increase in the brain's weight. Postnatal development also involves the formation of an insulating sheath of myelin along the neurons' processes.

Certain infections in the mother, or deficiences in her diet, may lead to the foetus developing fewer neurons, and hence also fewer dendritic branches and fewer connections with other neurons. Behaviour may be disturbed and

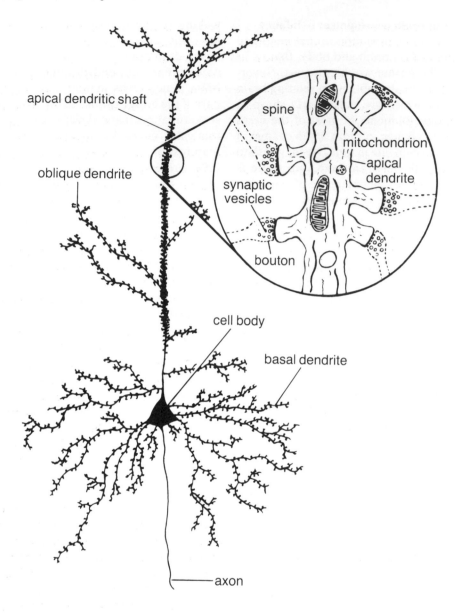

Figure 7 A typical Golgi-stained pyramidal neuron whose cell body is in Layer 5 of the cortex. The dendrites (apical, oblique, basal) receive synaptic input from other nerve cells. The axon conducts the neuron's output to other nerve cells. The enlargement presents a segment of the apical shaft as it might appear in the electron microscope. At high magnification (30,000 to 40,000 power) the dark projections from the dendrite appear as protoplasmic extensions called spines. These spines form synapses with the vesicle-filled axom terminals, or boutons, from other neurons. Synapses on the cell body do not utilize spines and hence cannot be visualized with Golgi-staining techniques.

Source: From Parmelee and Sigman (1983), p. 99.

intellectual retardation result. Other genetic or environmental difficulties may lead to malfunctioning of the brain. Among the best known of these is the genetic defect which causes phenylketonuria (PKU). This means that the sufferer's body cannot metabolize the amino acid phenylalanine. Normally phenylalanine from protein is converted into tyrosine by an enzyme called phenylalanine hydroxylase: this enzyme is defective in PKU so phenylalanine from the diet builds up in the body and cannot be got rid of. Developing nerve cells are vulnerable to it: it strips off the dendritic spines, breaking down the connections between neurons, and severe behavioural disturbance and mental retardation result. If the infant is fed on a diet which does not contain phenylalanine, no excess is built up, and the brain can develop more or less normally. The genetic defect is still there, but it has no effect in the special environment where there is little or no phenylalanine. Once brain development is complete, the individual with PKU is not harmed by a normal diet. However, if a woman with PKU, whose own retardation has been prevented by a restricted diet in infancy and childhood, takes an unrestricted diet during her pregnancy, the foetus may be born with severe mental retardation even though it has inherited the normal gene for phenylalanine hydoxylase from its father. The build-up of phenylalanine in the pregnant woman does not affect her because the mature nervous system is relatively resistant to it, but it swamps the neurological development of the foetus. The child is born with PKU mental retardation, although it does not itself have PKU (Konner 1982, Scarr and Kidd 1983).

Brain development and environmental pollution: the case of lead

High dosages of certain substances, for example mercury and lead, are known to poison the nervous system. Some of these substances are, at a low level, common environmental pollutants. It has been suggested that their pervasiveness may be such that they cause brain damage, particularly in the developing brains of children. Lead is perhaps the best known of these poisons/pollutants and so there has been some public concern about its effects.

Petrol has been thought to be an important contributor to environmental lead levels since lead use in cosmetics, in canning and in paint has declined in recent years. Airborne lead levels are high near roads with heavy traffic, and lead dust also contaminates the people, clothes and food it falls on. Children probably ingest a considerable amount of lead by licking dirty fingers, dropping and eating sweets and so forth, in addition to the lead inhaled in petrol fumes. Plants grown in contaminated soil may take in lead from it, and lead dust is not altogether easily washed off leaves. The evidence on what percentage of the lead found in children's blood samples comes from petrol is circumstantial, but it is certainly *a* major contributor and probably *the* major one (Rutter 1983).

High levels of lead in the blood or the teeth are associated with intellectual impairment, behaviour problems such as hyperactivity and, at the highest levels, gross neuropathology. The severity of these effects is greatest at highest lead levels, and decreases as they decrease. Until recently it was thought that lead levels below 40 micrograms (μg) per 100 ml in the blood had no adverse effects. Recent work reported in Rutter and Jones (1983), however, suggests that levels lower than this were associated with impaired psychological function, such as systematic inattention in the classroom and lower verbal IQ. Measurement difficulties, and differences between different studies, mean that this association at low levels is not certain, but Rutter (1983) summarizes the evidence so far as showing a consistent small effect of low levels of lead on psychological functioning. Harvey (1984) regards it as non-proven.

Interesting problems arise over the cause of the association. There is evidence on the neurophysiological damage caused by lead poisoning (it impairs nerve conduction velocities and EEG patterns also change), but not on what might be the psychological deficits linked with these neurophysiological ones. Damage from exposure to lead over a long period of time may be more like damage from chronic malnutrition than damage from a severe acute injury to the brain. There is usually considerable recovery from the latter, but persistent impairment may be more common after lead poisoning as after malnutrition. The effects of lead almost certainly interact with the effects of other socio-economic variables, being more severe for socially disadvantaged children than for middle-class ones, indeed being negligible for advantaged children (Shaffer 1985).

We do not yet know very specifically what cognitive or behavioural problems lead is associated with: most of the research is on its association with attention deficits, emotional reactivity and hyperactivity, where there is a consistent association. It is not, however, a strong association: lead level does not all by itself cause inattentiveness or educational retardation or delinquency, but it does contribute to some such problems. Preventing lead poisoning, provided the substitutes have fewer adverse effects, will lead to small but significant and not trivial benefits.

Brain organization and development

The brain is organized into different structures characterized by different clusters of neurons. Most of this general organization is recognizable by the seventh month *in utero*, by which time there has been a long and complex progress in development, from an initial pool of undifferentiated neurons to specialized neurons located in their proper places, a progress whose mechanisms are not yet understood. Different parts of the brain develop at different rates, and so are most sensitive to environmental influence at different times. The most advanced parts of the cortex are the primary motor and sensory areas: the areas where impulses are compared and integrated develop later. The brain areas which control movements of the hands, arms and upper body mature earlier than those which control the legs, a difference mirrored in the varying control infants and young children have over different movements. There are general positive correlations between maturity of brain structure and maturity of behaviour, but after the earliest stages both the causal sequences sketched at the beginning of this section are involved.

Recent studies have looked at the metabolism of the brain, including changes in the metabolic activity of the brain during specific activities. New techniques are allowing identification of which parts of the brain are most active during the processing of particular stimuli. There are some interesting results from adults (Parmelee and Sigman 1983, p. 106; Blakemore, personal communication) but not as yet any developmental studies. There are now known to be developmental changes in the speed and efficiency with which nerve impulses are transmitted and in the biochemistry of neurotransmitters. Further research is needed here, but changes in which neurotransmitters are present, and in their strength, would help to explain why certain drugs have one effect on adults and the reverse on infants.

Most of what I have said so far concerned neurons or even parts of neurons. However, they do, of course, work together in complex networks. Electroencephalogram recordings (EEGs) reflect the neurophysiological activity of networks of neurons in the cortex. The rhythm of activity in EEG recordings changes with what the person recorded is doing (for example sleeping, sitting quietly, thinking about a difficult problem), and developmentally. For example, adults have quite different EEG activity during sleeping and waking, while newborn infants have much less consistent patterns, and at a behavioural level go from sleeping to waking much more rapidly. EEG scans can show up pathological brain activity but do not help much in distinguishing within the normal range of behavioural development, temperament or intelligence (Parmelee and Sigman 1983, pp. 114–17).

EEG patterns can be analysed, perhaps by computer, to assess the time link between presentation of a stimulus and cortical response to it. Embedded in the spontaneous EEG activity is a peak which is due to the presented stimulus, the sensory evoked potential. In the immature nervous system, these responses tend to be rather slow, and less definite in their shape than in adults. They mirror the long transmission time taken over immature synaptic junctions and along immature axons which are not yet fully myelinated. The existence of sensory evoked potentials even in pre-term infants indicates that the sensory receptors can respond to the stimulus, that there are functioning connections between receptors and cortex, and that the neurons in the cortex can respond too, even if the whole process is on the slow side. They do not, however, indicate what processing is being done at any of these stages unless comparisons between stimuli are made. Recent studies (Parmelee and Sigman 1983, pp. 120–2) have begun to do this, in some cases as a measure of 'intelligence'.

The last aspect of brain development I want to refer to is the functional lateralization of the brain (Kinsbourne and Hiscock 1983). Much has been made of differences between the left and right halves of the brain: the popular literature on the subject abounds with suggestions that the left hemisphere is abstract, analytic and verbal while the right hemisphere is intuitive, artistic and concrete, or that educational failure is caused by being 'right-brained' in a 'left-brained' school system. We will see that such assertions are not well founded.

One very basic reason for this is that although some mental functions, such as perceiving the orientation of a bar of light, can be very precisely located in the brain, most higher mental functions are represented in several brain structures not localized in a single brain centre. Doing an arithmetic problem, for example, such as '2 + 3 = ?', will involve reading, memory, reasoning, computation and a variety of movements of eyes, head and the hand that writes down '5'. Each of these is certainly complex enough to involve many brain processes. (There is some discussion of their complexity in the next chapter.) It will be obvious that we cannot sensibly· talk about how 'arithmetic' is lateralized when many areas of the brain are involved and when indeed 'arithmetic' and ways of doing it vary in complexity so much.

Evidence from a large number of studies has now shown that most adults have their speech control in the left hemisphere, though the right hemisphere has a substantial capacity for language comprehension and some for control of expressive speech if the left hemisphere is not functioning. The right hemisphere's functions include control of tone perception and visual memory. A small proportion of right-handed people, and something under a third of left-handed people, have other patterns of lateralization of speech, some in the right hemisphere and some in both hemispheres. Recent EEG studies suggest that the left hemisphere is more active when tasks which are highly verbal are being done (Kinsbourne and Hiscock 1983, pp. 183–9). There are anatomical differences between left and right hemispheres, though how these are related to behavioural differences is generally not clear.

Although there are some changes between childhood and adulthood, both in anatomical differences between the hemispheres and in behaviour such as recovery from brain damage, Kinsbourne and Hiscock argue that the development of functional lateralization of the brain does not begin with two neutral hemispheres of equal potential and end with two definitely differentiated and specialized ones. They read the evidence as suggesting asymmetry from at least the first few postnatal weeks; as well as anatomical asymmetries rather similar to adults', infants seem to have a bias towards movement to the right, preferences for using their right hand or right foot, and better perception of speech sounds in the left hemisphere and of non-speech sounds in the right (Kinsbourne and Hiscock 1983, pp. 213–36). They attribute changes in apparent laterality not to changes in structural properties of the brain, but to different approaches to the task, shifts in the strategies employed.

Although developmental changes in asymmetry of visual perception have been attributed to an emerging hemispheric specialization for certain functions, it is curious that a brain that is lateralized from birth for the processing of speech sounds should become lateralized for other functions only after the passing of several years.

We suggested in the previous section of this chapter that developmental changes in degree of asymmetry probably reflect developmental changes in the behavioural organization of the skill rather than a shifting neural base for a constantly organized set of component skills. As a skill develops in the maturing brain, additional lateralized components may be recruited to the performance of the skill and asymmetries observed for the first time. When performance of the younger child is symmetric, this need not imply that the lateralized components have not yet become lateralized; instead the lateralized components may not yet be functional or integrated into the organization of the skill. In support of this explanation, we can point to evidence (previously described) that perceptual tasks are susceptible to influence from nonstructural variables, such as strategy, expectancy, and previous experience with the stimulus material.

Perceptual tasks are not merely measures of some structural property of the brain. It seems plausible that age-related changes in degree of asymmetry reflect different approaches to the task rather than different degrees of cerebral lateralization (Kinsbourne and Hiscock 1983, pp. 230–1).

I cannot assess the merits of their evidence and reasoning, but they are emphasizing yet again the problems of linking brain structure and behaviour in developmental theory. No facile conclusions can be drawn.

Cognition in infancy

I have outlined what is known about the physical status and the functioning of infants' perceptual apparatus in the preceding section. It would seem that they are able to get perceptual experience from birth, and in some modalities from before birth, indeed that perceptual experiences of various sorts are needed for the proper development of the sensory apparatus. However, there is a difference between the objective physical stimulus and what is made of it in the course of perception and cognition. Most stimuli are interpreted by the organism which perceives them, whether that organism be human or non-human, infant or adult. Sometimes the stimuli need little interpretation to be meaningful and effective,

sometimes a great deal is needed. Sometimes the interpretation made is objective, derived from the stimulus more than from the perceiver and likely to be identically derived by any other perceiver: sometimes the interpretation is subjective, a result of the perceiver's idiosyncracies not of the stimulus. Debates about the extent and the sources of interpretation of perception have been active in philosophy since well before any psychology or any systematic study of infants began: Hamlyn (1978) reviews the course of the arguments between the empiricists and the rationalists.

Piaget's theory

The central theory of infant cognition has been Piaget's. He emphasizes the importance of action for the development of thought. The infant acquires knowledge of the world by acting on it, actions which are initially crude reflexes but which develop into organized acts linked to their consequences. These are what Piaget calls 'circular reactions', that is, acts which tend to produce results which lead to the re-elicitation of the initial action. An example is sucking: this produces (among other sensations) mouth pressure which tends to elicit further sucking, so that the initial reflex meshes with feedback from its results. The circular reaction becomes differentiated and refined, so that the infant learns, for example, to suck in different ways suited to different objects. They also become integrated with other circular reactions, as in Bruner's experiments when infants co-ordinate the sucking which brings an attractive picture into focus with their looking at the picture (Bruner *et al.* 1966). The increasing differentiation, refinement, integration and deliberateness of circular reactions lead to progress in the infant's construction of a sensori-motor action-based representation of the world. The functional invariants of Assimilation and Accommodation are central to this progress, as new stimulation is interpreted in terms of old knowledge, and old knowledge extended by new information.

Thus Piaget's infant sets out into a world of varied stimulation equipped with a number of reflexes and assimilatory/accommodatory powers, and makes good cognitively by hammering out of the world a construction derived from his or her own actions upon it. The activity of the infant is what is emphasized, more than the possible structuring of information offered by either the physical or the social world. These possibilities are put nearer the centre stage by two other theories; Gibson (1979) emphasizes the orderliness of the physical world and the contributions that this makes to cognitive development: Bruner (1973) and others emphasize the contribution made by the infant's caretakers. I will spend more time on the former here, as the contributions of adults to infants' cognition are most obvious in the social and linguistic spheres and are therefore discussed in Chapters 4 and 6.

Gibson's theory

James J. Gibson is primarily concerned with non-developmental work on perception but the epistemological implications of his work are in some contrast to Piaget's, and are very relevant to understanding cognitive development in infancy. An important assertion is that the environment is rich in organized information. For example, changes in the apparent texture of objects indicate distance, as when we can see the separate blades of grass next to us but as we look further away the grass blades merge into a smooth uniform green. There is also a great deal of organization in features like the relative sizes of objects. If object A alone is getting bigger as we watch, while the rest of the visual field remains the same size, we see A moving towards us: if A and field both get bigger, remaining the same size relative to each other, we see A and the field getting nearer to us or ourselves moving nearer to the field. Treating perception by analysing it into separate bits of stimulation tends to obscure this organization.

Another important concept is that of 'affordances' (E. J. Gibson 1982). An affordance is a collection of properties of part of the environment relative to the organism being considered. For example, if a surface is more or less flat and horizontal, rather than sharp, slanted and verti-cal, and is large enough in extent relative to your size and rigid relative to your weight, then it *affords support*. 'It is stand-on-able, permitting an upright posture . . . it is therefore walk-on-able and run-over-able. It is not sink-into-able' (J. J. Gibson 1979, p.127). This affordance is an objective physical property of the world, but it is relative to you. A larger heavier animal might not be able to stand on the chair which affords support to you: you cannot be supported by the twig which affords support to the insect. A noise in the engine of a car affords information about how well the car is running: someone knowledgeable about the car will perceive this affordance, a non-driver will not.

Gibson's theory suggests that many of these relationships and affordances are perceived quite directly. The infant has, from birth, a perceptual system capable of detecting the rich organized information which the environment provides. Where Piaget suggests that information from different modalities or different moments of experience are separate to begin with, and have to be brought together by the infant's construction, Gibson suggests that environmental information comes in already organized and synthesized, in meaningful and useful packages, and little construction and reinterpretation is needed. Experience leads not to new insights but to clearer tuning and better discrimination of which features are most distinctive: the child becomes a more skilled and systematic observer, rather than Piaget's active little experimentalist.

Some cognitive developments in infancy

Harris (1983) reviews much of the literature on infant cognition in the light of these different theoretical emphases. I will discuss cross-modal integration, development of space perception and the development of the infant's understanding of the existence of objects, as these areas have received a great deal of attention and raise important theoretical points.

Cross-modal integration

Piaget, like the empiricist philosophers, argues that perception of space is gradually constructed from an integration of visual information into action. As a result of failure and success in reaching, and later locomotion, the infant comes to understand depth and distance. The integration of vision and touch, which began as separate modalities, leads to cross-modal perception, and an understanding that objects may continue to exist although no longer visible arises from multimodal knowledge and active experience of moving and finding objects. At first the world is haphazard, varying unstably from moment to moment and full of unintegrated stimulation: gradually the infant constructs a world of integrated schemes and permanent objects.

The Gibsonian infant has the benefit of linked sensory systems dealing coherently with linked information in the outside world. It is not necessary to construct correspondences between sound and sight, vision and touch: the physical world ensures that they often co-vary for the objects that surround the infant. What he or she has to do is learn which bits of co-varying information are most reliably associated with objects or events: this sort of discrimination does not have to be derived from the infant's own actions.

As far as the infant's ability to make links across sensory modalities is concerned, even infants in their first month of life can use information in one modality to guide another. For example, infants will probably look towards a sound, though it is not clear whether they also expect to see something at the place where the sound was heard. By the time they are about 4 months old they prefer to look at an object which is moving at the same tempo as the sound they hear (Harris 1983, pp.708–9, 740–1). Coordination between sight and touch also seems to originate very early, though there have been many replication failures here. Bower, Broughton and Moore (1970) reported that 2-week-old infants reached in the appropriate direction for the object they saw, shaping their hand appropriately to the object, and showing surprise and distress when, owing to some optical trickery, they reached to the place where the object appeared to be but really was not. Harris (1983, pp. 709, 742) cites only failures to replicate

this study. More recently, Meltzoff and Borton (1979) have produced data which suggest that neonates can recognize a visually presented object after a prior tactual experience; Bryant *et al.* (1972) showed that 8-month-olds can certainly do this. Thus the evidence is not easy to interpret.

Nevertheless, Harris concludes that sight probably does trigger reaching, and sound trigger looking. What is not clear is whether the infant really expects to see the source of the sound or touch the seen object, that is whether there is cross-modal integration at a deeper level. Infants have been shown to have more inter-modality coordination than Piaget allowed them, but they have to learn when to expect that information from different modalities should be correlated and when it need not be. For example, although voices often come from faces, non-speaking faces are quite common, and the infant will sometimes hear a voice without seeing a face. Lip movements, on the other hand, should always fit speech sounds.

Depth perception

Depth perception is thought by Piaget (and by the empiricist philosophers) to be gradually constructed from the infant's experience of reaching, grasping, and moving, which are constructively integrated with visual experience. Gibson suggests that depth is as directly perceived from environmental information as colour or shape is, and precedes the infant's experience of movement. As we saw when reviewing visual perception, the neonate has some capacity to achieve binocular vision which is one of the visual cues to depth, and can certainly achieve exact eye convergence well before accurate reaching is possible. From about 5 months old infants are unlikely to reach for objects which are beyond their reach, and at about this age also react by moving their arms between themselves and the object which is apparently on a collision course with them (Harris 1983, pp. 710–5). It appears, therefore, that infants show behaviour adjusted to spatial distance before they have had much opportunity to practise moving themselves, behaviour more consistent with Gibson's theory than with Piaget's. They certainly learn more about distance and depth perception with experience of locomotion, however.

Infant search and object permanence

Piaget claimed that infants for most of their first year believed that out of sight meant not just out of mind but out of existence. Objects, including people, existed while the infant looked at them and ceased to exist if not looked at. When the infant looked again, the object began to exist again, or a new but identical object began to exist. When the infant did not look, the object had no existence.

(While this belief seems bizarre and indeed infantile, it has been a real philosophical problem to determine whether something would exist while no one is aware of it. Two of the nineteenth-century Oxford limericks propose the problem and a solution to it which Piaget does not attribute to the infant.

> There once was a man who said 'God
> Must think it exceedingly odd
> If he finds that this tree
> Continues to be
> When there's no one about in the Quad.'

> 'Dear Sir, Your astonishment's odd:
> *I* am always about in the Quad.
> And that's why the tree
> Will continue to be,
> Since observed by Yours faithfully, God.'

We only 'know' that something continues to exist even though neither we nor anyone else are perceiving it because we have a theoretical model of the world which assumes objects have a stable existence, and we have learned a great deal about different sorts of disappearance and reappearance.)

There is a well-replicated sequence of infant search behaviours. To begin with, infants do not actively search at all, they simply stare in the direction of where the object was before it moved or disappeared. Next, they show some anticipation of the direction of movement of a moving object, follow it visually and manually if it is

taken from them, and will retrieve an object from a hiding place which only partly hides it. Later, they search for an object which has disappeared from view completely, but mainly in the place they are used to seeing it at, not in the new hiding place where they have just watched it being put. 'Faced with the disappearance of the object, the child immediately ceases to reflect and merely returns to the place where action was successful the first time' (Piaget 1954, p. 61). This is Piaget's stage 4, the most striking part of the infant search/object permanence data, and a popular research problem. In stage 5 the infant does not make this perseverative error but has difficulty with successive not fully visible displacements to new hiding places, and from about 18 months old the stage 6 infant can search for an object whatever displacements have been made.

There is some suggestion that infants at object search stages 1–3 may be a bit more sophisticated in their search than Piaget proposed, in that they do seem to treat objects which disappeared by being gradually covered up differently from objects which disappeared more suddenly or by fading or shrinking to nothing, and they may seem slightly surprised if the object when it reappears looks different. This suggests a Gibsonian position of the infant using rich information and gradually becoming more knowledgeable about the possibilities of objects may be tenable, but Piaget's observations of stages 1–3 are not in dispute. Replications of stage 4 do, however, suggest that infants do not invariably make the perseverative error which is central to his account of the stage. The Piagetian infant, having previously seen and found the object at A, then watches the object being hidden at B but searches for it only at A, apparently believing that the existence of the object is contingent on looking for it at A. Replication infants quite often search at B (about 50 per cent) (Butterworth 1975, 1977, 1978); they sometimes search at A even if the object is visible at B; they make very few errors if they are allowed to search immediately the object is hidden rather than being forced to wait (Gratch *et al.* 1974); they search more correctly in a conventional container such as an upright cup than in an unconventional one or under an inverted container (Freeman *et al.* 1980). That is, the infant's search is not so unreasonable or egocentric as Piaget implies, and the AB error may occur because the infant is confused about the object's whereabouts, not because he or she believes its *existence* is linked to A.

Harris (1983) places the emphasis on the infant coming to know *where to search* and what sort of thing he or she is searching for. A distinction has to be learned empirically between single objects and multiple identical objects. The former behave lawfully as to their position: an individual biscuit cannot be simultaneously in the tin and on the plate. The positions of multiple exemplars are not lawful: taking Biscuit One out of the tin does not preclude taking another biscuit out of the tin unless Biscuit One is the only biscuit there is. The infant has to learn how the successive positions of an object are related, which will involve considering these positions in relation to the infant, who can move and so change the relative position of the object, and in relation to a less mobile external framework. The biscuit is first seen in front of me, on the table; next in Daddy's hand, closer in front of me; next in my hand, moving to my mouth; next on the floor underneath my chair. It is suggested (e.g. Butterworth 1975, 1978; Bremner 1980) that infants initially code position relative to their own body, a strategy which works less well once they begin to crawl and hence to alter the relative position of the object and their body. A spatial framework specifying position relative to distinctive landmarks is developed. Some notions of the physical characteristics of landmarks and objects may be included; for example, Freeman *et al.* (1980) show that infants search more for an object hidden and moved about under an inverted container. Certainly there are differences later in understanding prepositions such as 'in', 'on', and 'under' (Clark 1983).

Recognizing the identity of objects
Detecting the invariant qualities of an object among the qualities which vary in appearance as the object moves, or is partially transformed, is an important cognitive activity in both Piaget's and Gibson's theories. For Piaget, the infant attains the object concept by deduction from his or her active experimentation on objects, gradually deducing that objects are permanent, external to the self and retain their identity whatever their changes in position (Piaget 1954). Later, this understanding of qualitative identity is developed into appreciation of what quantitative aspects of the object are conserved (see Chapter 3). For Gibson, on the other hand, much information about identity is given by the environment, and little deduction is needed. Invariance is detected not constructed (E. J. Gibson 1969; J. J. Gibson 1979). Harris (1983, pp. 731–9) reviews the evidence on how infants deal with invariance across changes of orientation and with objects which are different in some respects but invariant in being members of the same category.

Habituation techniques show that infants can distinguish different orientations of faces and geometric shapes, and, if they have seen several orientations of an object, they can react to a new object as if it were different from all that they have previously seen. That is, the old object, whatever its orientation, is more familiar than the new object. The age at which this distinction is made depends very much on the objects used. Infants shown several different exemplars of a category, for example male faces in a study by Fagan (Harris 1983, p. 732), show dishabituation to a member of a different category, for example a female face, but not to a new exemplar of the original category. The breadth of familiarization which they are given is related to the breadth of the concept they construct. There is some evidence that they use either the most frequent features or a form of averaging to build up a prototype example, just as adults do. This suggests that abstraction and deduction are involved in the detection of invariance, not just the detection of features which the Gibsons propose.

Recognizing the separation of self from objects
The dominant theory has been for a long time that infants do not distinguish between them-

selves and the outer world. They feel certain sensations but do not know where they come from, they cannot distinguish events which they are responsible for from events which are independent of them. They are utterly egocentric, subjective and solipsistic, with no way of distinguishing between internally-generated and externally-given information.

Recently, Gibson has argued that, on the contrary, infants do have a number of sources of information which would allow reliable distinctions to be made between them and the outside world. One source of information is the kinesthetic feedback supplied by any movement of the body. Another is the bits of body which provide boundaries to the visual field, the nose, the eyebrow ridge and the infant's fat cheeks. These are a fairly constant part of the visual field; they move whenever the head moves, faster than objects in the world beyond, and do not move when the head is still. Thus the infants can *feel* their own actions and *see* part of themselves, including of course the mobile bits of body such as hands.

While there is as yet little evidence to test Gibson's model, Harris (1983, pp. 744–7) proposes that it suggests that from the early months of life the infant is indeed sensitive to the ways in which the visual field specifies the existence, location and movements of the observing self. Full recognition of oneself as a person involves more than a separation of self from the external world, of course, and is discussed in the section on the self-concept (Chapter 5).

Play and cognitive development

It has often been suggested that play is the child's way of learning. This suggestion has been implemented in the classic early childhood curriculum of 'free play', which provides children in settings such as playgroups and nursery schools with materials and opportunities for play and encourages them in self-chosen means-dominated activities rather than involving them in achievement-directed training. Directive or didactic intervention by adults is seen as inappropriate for young children. The 'play way of learning' is backed up by the idealization of play

(see p. 24), by ideas derived from Piaget's views on learning (p. 34) and from Freudian ideas about play as therapy (p. 28) and more recently by suggestions from psychology experiments and observation that play with objects is an efficient way of learning how to solve problems (Sylva 1977; Sylva, Roy and Painter 1980). Smith and Simon (1984) review a number of such experiments which have compared the effects of a few free play sessions and a few directed training sessions on convergent or divergent problem-solving. Reviewing these studies they summarize them as suggesting that experience in 'play' and 'non-play' conditions contributes about equally to convergent problem-solving, where there is only one solution, and 'play' experience contributes more to success on divergent problems where many and novel solutions are required. The flexibility and lack of constraint that are assumed to characterize play would be expected to have this effect. However the experimental studies suffer from methodological problems. First, it may be doubted whether what the children do in the 'play' condition is 'play', in the sense of flexible, intrinsically-motivated activity rather than, for example, 'exploration' which typically precedes 'play' and is necessary if all the potential of the material is to be discovered (Hutt 1979). Second, the demonstration that 'play' is as good an inducer of learning as the training given does not mean that play is as good a way of learning as *any* training would be. In at least some of the studies reviewed the training is clearly not optimal for the subjects, and controls do not seem adequate. Smith and Simon also express concern about possible experimenter effects such as differential provision of hints to 'play' and 'training' groups or simply a more relaxed style of testing in the problem-solving phase for children from the more relaxed 'play' group. There is room for doubt also that one brief 'play' or 'training' session could be long enough to do any more than help the child feel at ease with the experimenter. After concluding that no conclusion on the question of the contribution of play experience to learning is possible from the experimental evidence available at present, Smith and Simon call for more ecologically valid work.

A considerable amount of observational data is available now from studies of British pre-schools done during the late 1970s (e.g. Sylva, Roy and Painter 1980; Hutt *et al.* 1979; Meadows and Cashdan 1983; Tizard, Philips and Plewis 1976). These studies have tried to assess the quality of children's play in part because of concern with its contribution to cognitive development. Sylva *et al.* (1980) used a binary categorization of quality, Tizard *et al.* (1976) two composite scales, Meadows *et al.* (1983) four 'cognitive' scales. These involved discrimination of symbolic, goal-directed and unfocused instances of play, four levels of how involved the child was in the play activity, how much use was made of play material, and how many operations were brought together in the activity. Rating play on these four dimensions showed positive but low correlations between dimensions, and differences between materials and children in which sort of 'complexity' characterized them. There are some problems in making detailed comparisons between studies, differences in how the 'quality' of play was assessed being one, but on the whole they agreed in two ways important for our present purposes. First, the general level of cognitive complexity of children's play in the wide range of pre-school groups observed was disappointing. Much of what children did when playing was pleasurable but simple, repetitive, unstructured, uninventive, uninvolving, brief and generally uninspiring. Second, on the rather rare occasions when teachers were more than casually involved, and in association with a limited range of materials which made it easy to define a goal and one's progress towards it (art activities are the clearest example), children showed play which was at higher levels.

It would be possible for those who are the greatest enthusiasts about the value of spontaneous play in cognitive development to dismiss this picture of how children play in pre-school groups as having managed to miss the learning that children were really doing, during what looked uninspired to someone not participating. However the research on different forms of early childhood education and the work on cognitive skills which I discuss in the next chapter both suggest, I think, that although children can and do learn through their play we need to recognize more explicitly what is learned through social interaction with adults and their deliberate teaching or model-giving.

Plate 6

Plate 7

3 The development of cognitive skills

In the previous chapter, I discussed the current theories of what 'cognitive development' consists of, and described perception and cognition in infancy. In this chapter, I am going to outline what we know about the development of cognitive skills. After the influence of Piaget's very abstract and general theory, interest has moved towards research which provides detailed accounts of children's behaviour in more limited areas of cognition. I will describe some of these areas, and draw some conclusions about the developmental processes involved.

It may be helpful to the reader to have in mind what I have emphasized already, that neither 'cognition' nor 'development' is simple, and that learner characteristics and task characteristics interact. Indeed, there should perhaps be implicit in our discussion something like the organizational framework proposed in a chapter by Brown, Bransford, Ferrara and Campione (1983)

which is the best current review of cognitive development that I know. I give here a slightly elaborated version of their tetrahedral framework (Figure 8).

Attention

Bearing this interaction in mind, then, we can look at some of the components of cognition and how they develop. 'Attention' seems a good aspect to start with since it could be taken as a necessary condition for further cognitive activity. It is however a somewhat vague concept, certainly polymorphous. Taylor (1978) gives examples: 'Attention can be directed, switched, captured, distributed, divided, narrowed, sustained or withheld. . . . "Distractibility" may imply that the child is not motivated to do the tasks he is given, or that they are too difficult for him to persist at; it may mean that he explores all

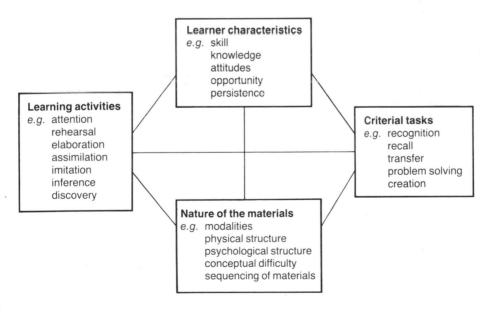

Figure 8

stimuli, or all prominent stimuli, or simply that the values he gives to stimuli are not that of the rater; it may mean that he becomes fatigued very rapidly and changes task frequently as a result' (Taylor 1978, p. 185).

Nor is 'attention' simple to measure: overt behaviour, task achievement, introspection and physiological indices of concentration such as changes in heart rate or EEG have all been used, and are all problematic. They do however give a moderately coherent picture of development. As development proceeds the direction of attention becomes more independent of what is conspicuous in the environment, more systematic and more flexible. In looking at a picture, for example, young subjects tend to focus on a point and work haphazardly away from it, while older subjects are more likely to scan the picture exhaustively or to attend more to information which is relevant to the task they have been set. One paradigm which shows this up very usefully is that of 'incidental memory' (e.g. Hagen and Hale 1973). Children are shown an array of cards and asked to recall where members of a specified subset (e.g. animals) are, while no instructions are given about the need to recall another subset (e.g. toys). They are then tested on their recall of both the subset they were told to learn ('central task') and the subset which they weren't ('incidental task'). Performance on the 'central task' improves very much with age: performance on the 'incidental task' does not change, and may decline in older, better educated or more effective learners. The older children have succeeded in directing their attention and their effort to learn where they are most needed: the younger children have not. As well as being less able to direct attention selectively they are less able to resist distraction (Taylor 1985).

Many school tasks require persistence and accuracy over a long period of time, and so 'he has a short attention span' is quite a serious complaint about a child. Sustaining attention, 'vigilance', is known to be affected by many different factors in adults: difficulties in remaining vigilant are commonly found in adults and children with psychiatric symptoms. However, observations of children doing school work (e.g. Meadows and Cashdan 1983; Galton *et al.* 1980) show that alternation of concentration with daydreaming, social chat and other activities less tightly related to the task is common. Hard work and rapid progress during concentration makes up, on most tasks, for periods of distracted or unfocused attention. (The accounts given of creative thinking and the role of subconscious activity are similarly comforting.) Sustained vigilance in the sense of attention which never omits to respond to target stimuli and never makes incorrect responses seems to be learned late, as a deliberate cold-blooded skill, and, at least in the forms which military tasks can require, needs special training. Given high motivation in daily life, however, children can be sufficiently vigilant: 'little pitchers have big ears'!

'Low attention span' and 'distractibility' have been related to neurological damage and immaturity and linked to 'hyperactivity', but there is little consensus about how strong the links are or to how physiological and psychological measures interact. Here as elsewhere (see, for example, discussion of aggression, Chapter 5) physiological (or biochemical) changes may cause or be caused by psychological ones, or both may be caused by some third sort of change. Psychosocial factors are also involved, both in choice of what is voluntarily attended to, and in the strategic aspects of attention. Family interaction and communication are probably involved, though a far more precise analysis of the ecology of homes is required than has been carried out so far (McGurk 1977).

'Attention' is a component of two of the best-known theories of 'cognitive style'. Witkin's 'Field dependence vs independence' model (Witkin *et al.* 1979; Witkin and Goodenough 1981) involves selective attention in the ability to process information analytically rather than holistically. The 'impulsivity vs reflectiveness' model of Kagan *et al.* (1964; Kagan 1984) also implies differences in what is attended to and how. Neither model seems to be making much progress at present (Kogan 1983), and doubts remain about the conceptual and methodological usefulness of rather simple models of cognitive style which are supposed to pervade all functioning. There is some danger that they become seen as important independent entities and so precise study of tasks and processes is precluded. Taylor (1978), concluding his review on the development of attention, and indicating how many gaps there are in our understanding, emphasizes that attention is not unitary and it is not something we simply get more of as we get older. He suggests that age (presumably he means the correlates of age, such as maturation and experience) 'brings an increase in the use of systematic, logical strategies of exploring the world; in the ability to be flexible and selective in one's approach to information; and in maintaining one's responsiveness for longer periods' (Taylor 1978, p. 195).

As the reader may already have anticipated, this sort of conclusion – lots of gaps in the evidence, but a picture of initial strategies and skills become more flexible and polished, in large part as a result of practice – will pervade my account of cognitive development.

Remembering

It is obvious that remembering of some sort is necessary for virtually any human cognitive activity. As we saw earlier it is hard to believe in the possibility of an intelligent organism which did not use accommodation and assimilation in its functioning, that did not make some comparison between the present stimulus and stimuli encountered earlier. This would be impossible without memory. Conversely, memory is rarely an isolated intellectual skill. Early researchers found it necessary to concentrate on memory for meaningless materials such as nonsense syllables in part because this was the only way to control for differences in subjects' knowledge, understanding and so forth (see, for example, Baddeley 1976). It is partly because of the interaction of remembering, understanding and acting that developmental changes in memory are important.

It is also obvious that 'remembering' is not one simple activity. There have been many suggestions about the structure of memory and the

processes which are involved at each stage. There is no clear consensus over the details of these models and they are in any case derived mainly from work done with adults, indeed mainly with undergraduates, rather than with children. However some distinctions and some processes drawn from these models appear in developmental studies, and point up both changes and lack of change with development.

Recognition memory

One distinction, due in part to differences in experimental method, is between 'recognition' and 'recall'. Recognition memory is investigated by presenting subjects with the material they are to remember, and then after an interval re-presenting it, either asking the subjects to judge whether it is familiar or novel, or requiring them to discriminate it from material which they have not seen before. In 'recall' tests, the material is not presented a second time, and subjects are required to retrieve and describe it from memory. All other things being equal, most people find recognition tasks easier than recall, and adults' recognition of meaningful material (such as pictures of familiar objects) is extremely good (Shepard 1967; Standing 1973; Bahrick *et al.* 1975). Recognition memory is virtually as good in children of 4 and older (e.g. Brown and Scott 1971; Brown and Campione 1972). In Brown and Campione's study, 4-year-olds were shown eighty pictures of familiar objects. After an interval they were shown 120 pairs of pictures; in sixty pairs one picture had been in the original set of eighty while the other picture had not but showed the same object (if, for example, the original picture showed a dog eating, it was paired in the recognition test with the same dog running). The other sixty pairs were entirely composed of new pictures. Recognition was highly accurate; after a two-hour interval, after a day and after a week. This is comparable with results in work with adults, though adults would often be shown more pictures.

Children as young as 4, then, have an impressive ability to say correctly whether or not they have seen a picture of an object before. Testing recognition memory in younger children by asking them to say whether pictures were novel or familiar would be problematic as it might be hard for a young child to produce the right words or to understand the instructions. A paradigm which allows the child to use well-mastered behaviour, particularly non-verbal responses, is more suitable for investigating recognition memory in babies and toddlers. Habituation techniques and measurement of the attention a baby pays to novel and familiar objects have produced some useful results.

In habituation experiments, subjects are repeatedly shown the same stimulus. On its first showing the stimulus evokes a lot of attention, as measured by how long it is looked at or by physiological measures such as deceleration of heart rate or changes in EEG. If on each successive showing it evokes less attention, the subject is said to have habituated: eventually the stimulus which was initially absorbing receives only a brief glance. This decline in interest or 'habituation' could only happen if the subject remembered the stimulus from one occasion to another. Since habituation to simple patterns can be demonstrated in babies from the age of 10 weeks, when babies start to prefer to look at novel patterns rather than ones they have seen before (Wetherford and Cohen 1973), there is clearly some recognition memory capacity in babies under 3 months old. The possibility of conditioning in neonates (e.g. Papousek 1967) suggests that there may be recognition memory earlier still. At these young ages, however, the time interval between stimuli must be very short if the baby is to show any remembering. As babies get older, they can recognize stimuli over a longer interval: in a study by Fagan (1973) 6-month-old infants looked more at a novel black and white photograph of a human face than at a familiar one after an interval as long as two weeks. They can probably also as they get older remember more information about the stimulus and therefore notice and attend to smaller differences between the familiar and the novel stimuli (Kagan, Kearsley and Zelazo 1978).

This dimension of complexity of stimuli, and the associated dimension of meaningfulness, may be among the most important aspects of the development of recognition memory. Although recognition memory for simple objects is almost as good in pre-school children as in adults, and there is not much more difference between them on harder stimuli such as abstract pictures or puzzle pieces (Nelson 1971; Nelson and Kosslyn 1976), older children and adults out-perform younger children on recognition memory of complex scenes (Newcombe, Rogoff and Kagan 1977). Young children seemed to make less use of the meaningful relationships between items in the scene: they may also have scanned the picture less exhaustively, even omitting to look at some parts of it. We will see that meaning and processing strategies play an important part in memory, a part which becomes more prominent as children develop. Discussion of these points will pervade the rest of our discussion of memory.

Recall Memory

We have seen that meaning and strategy become involved in recognition memory, but that even in cases where no particular effort is made to remember recognition memory may be very good indeed. Recall memory seems to be, on the whole, a much more difficult proposition. If adult subjects are shown a dozen or so unrelated stimuli once, and asked to recall them in any order immediately afterwards, they are likely to recall about seven items correctly; the last few items and perhaps the first few are most likely to be correct ('recency' and 'primacy' effects respectively). Only if the stimuli can be grouped, or if some deliberate mnemonic work is put in, or if the sequence has a meaningful structure, will the number of items recalled rise much above seven. There are developmental changes in this number, and indeed recall memory for a series of numbers – 'digit span' – is a standard intelligence test item. Children aged 3 years have a digit span of about two, 4-year-olds of three or four: the items they remember are likely to be from the end of the list not the beginning, that is they show a recency effect but not a primacy effect (Myers and Perlmutter 1978; Dempster 1981). The primacy effect in adults is thought to be due to subjects quietly naming items to themselves as they try to learn the list: that it is absent in young children implies that they do not do this naming. Naming or 'rehearsal' of items is one of the strategies which adults use to improve their memory. If children failed to use such mnemonic strategies, this might account for their poorer performances on recall tasks.

Children's use of mnemonic strategies

There is a great deal of evidence now that children under the age of 7 or so rarely use memorizing strategies in memory tasks. Kail (1979) reviews findings on children's use of rehearsal. There is little spontaneous rehearsal in under-7s; while 7-year-olds sometimes do some rehearsal, it is likely to be rudimentary and inefficient, for example limited to repetitions of only one name. Older children and adults are more likely to rehearse several items, to rehearse members of the same category together, and to adapt their rehearsal strategies to the particular demands of the task. Thus as subjects get older, their rehearsal techniques become more flexible and efficient. Rather similar results are found for other mnemonic strategies. Before school age children rarely use them at all. When the strategies are first used spontaneously, they are not used very well, but as children get older they use them more efficiently and more flexibly, and performance improves. Papers in Kail and Hagen (1977) review research on various mnemonic techniques: another improvement with age is the combination of mnemonics – a 'belt and braces' approach which also augments performance.

Why do young children rarely use mnemonics? One explanation would be that they are not capable of doing so. Work by Flavell and his colleagues demonstrates that this is not the case for rehearsal, since children of 6 or 7 can be trained to rehearse successfully. Similarly they can be taught to use categorization during learning, and during the recall phase to use cues, category labels and the strategy of exhaustive search of successive categories (Kail 1979, pp. 18–25). These young children showed themselves

perfectly able to use the mnemonic strategy they had been trained in while the experimenter required them to use it, so *inability* to rehearse, use cues, etc., was clearly not their main problem. However, a substantial proportion did not, even after training, use the strategy spontaneously. There is a gap between what they do off their own bat and what they can be trained to do. While this is probably true of us all (my memory for references, say, and I daresay the reader's, could certainly be improved by the practice of certain mnemonic strategies) one reason for the gap in small children is particularly important and interesting. It is that they do not appreciate how useful and necessary mnemonic strategies are.

Knowledge about memory

In order to know whether it is worth putting special effort into memorizing something one needs to know quite a lot about what the task demands and about one's own capacities. If the task is judged to be easier than it really is, or one's capacities are judged to be greater than they are, then one may conclude that no effort is necessary to succeed. Young children make mistakes on both these judgements. A graph from Kail (1979) illustrates this (Figure 9).

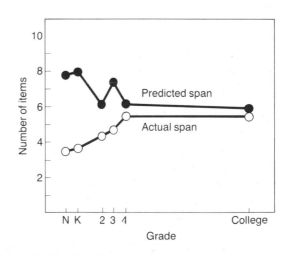

Figure 9 Predicted and actual memory spans as a function of grade level. N = nursery school children; K = kindergarten children.

Source : From Kail (1979), p. 42.

73

The young children from nursery and kindergarten believed that they would be able to remember many more items after a brief exposure than they actually managed. This inaccurate overconfidence about performance seemed to be due to ignorance about memory limitations, not to a general overestimation of abilities, since estimates of jumping distance were much more accurate than estimations of memory span, and the latter were slightly reduced by information about how well an 'average peer' would be likely to do (Kail 1977; Yussen and Levy 1975). It is fairly obvious that over-confidence is likely to lead to not making the extra effort which a more realistic assessment would show is needed for success, and hence to failure on the task. Failure on a memory task is peculiarly hard to judge, however; one may know that one has not remembered everything but not quite how many items one has failed to remember. Thus over-confident children may do badly on memory tasks but not notice their deficit: ecological studies of pre-school children might well show that they are rarely asked to do recall tasks and even more rarely have their failure brought home to them. Improvement in estimating memory span and in the use of mnemonic strategies comes after entry to school, where accurate memory performance increases in importance. A child who goes to school is also having to live in the two micro-systems of home and school, which will involve both relatively spontaneous reporting of school events at home and vice versa, and the deliberate carriage of information from one to the other. No longer can one caretaking adult take all the responsibility for the child's remembering; it is only the child who inhabits both micro-systems and knows all their details.

Improvement in memory estimation and in the use of mnemonics can be induced in the experimental situation by giving children feedback on their performance and showing that improvement is attributable to the use of mnemonics (Flavell and Wellman 1977; Whittaker 1983). Continued use of mnemonics is more likely if the demonstrated improvement is large, as if the mnemonics have to be seen to be cost-effective, and some generalization to other tasks may occur.

One of the important considerations here is the best way to remember in a particular memory task. Tasks vary in how easy the stimuli are to remember and in how easy different ways of demonstrating remembering are. These aspects too show developmental changes (Kail 1979). Pre-school children know that, all other things being equal, familiar items are more memorable than unfamiliar, and long lists are harder than short ones. They do not appreciate that a homogeneous set of items which show a consistent relationship may be very easy to learn irrespective of its length, thus they predict that a short paired associate list where there are arbitrary pairings will be easier to learn than a longer paired associate list where all the pairs are common antonyms. By the age of 9 or 10 children judge the antonym list to be easier (as it would be to adults), and if asked to generate a list which would be 'easy to remember' invent one with highly related items. Pre-school children know about the rapid decay of short-term memory, so they advise that having looked up a telephone number one should use it directly, not stop and do something irrelevant to telephoning; they tend to agree with adults that recognition is easier than recall. It is not until the age of about 10 that they say that to 'remember word for word' is harder than 'to tell you in my own words', i.e. that paraphrase is easier than verbatim memory. These results suggest that although children have achieved some understanding of the demands of memorizing by the time they enter school, considerable further experience of memorizing is necessary before they can gauge task demands with accuracy.

In addition to knowledge of oneself and the particular problems of the task set, performance is likely to benefit from self-monitoring of progress so that under-learned items are not neglected and no item is over-learned from too much attention. Young children do relatively poorly in their memory monitoring: they frequently stop their efforts to memorize prematurely, and on a second trial they relearn items already learned and neglect items which they have failed to learn first time. Here too feedback can improve performance (Kail 1979). Developing 'meta-memory' skills seems to be a necessary but not sufficient condition of good performance on memory tasks. 'Metacognition' is discussed later in this chapter.

Knowing and remembering

The first point I made when introducing discussion of the development of memory was that memory and knowledge are not independent (except in certain convenient laboratory techniques such as learning nonsense syllables where knowledge is deliberately made irrelevant to the situation). Chi's elegant experiments with chess players illustrate this point particularly neatly (Chi 1978). She compared children (average age 10) with adults on immediate recall of a string of digits and on immediate recall of stimuli placed within an eight by eight array. The adults performed better than the children on the digit list, as expected; but the children remembered more about the stimuli in the eight by eight array. This unusual finding of better performance by children is explained by the fact that the children were experienced chess players and the adults were not, and the 'stimuli placed within an eight by eight array' were chess pieces in a mid-game position on a chessboard. This array was meaningful and thus memorable to a chess player, meaningless and difficult to someone ignorant about chess. Experience highlights the salient points of an event which are most crucial for understanding and remembering it (Brown and De Loache 1978) and also makes complex events intelligible and easy to remember because reconstruction and inference can be used where otherwise it would be necessary to learn every detail. The novice/expert distinction (Brown and De Loache 1978; Flavell 1978) needs more specification (Robinson 1983) but may be useful in discussing cognitive development. Another example of the fact that knowing more makes remembering easier is the increased use of category-related mnemonics as children get older. Pre-school children may be relatively unlikely to use taxonomic categories either at the learning or at the retrieval stage (Kail 1979; Kobasigawa 1977), unless the instances of a category are prototypical members such as 'cat' and 'dog' rather than 'snail' and 'giraffe'. This may be associated with lack of knowledge, for example, that snails and giraffes are animals. The degree to which children's categories are the same as adults' is not yet clear (Rosch and Lloyd 1978; Clark 1983).

It must, however, be pointed out that prior knowledge may interfere with memory as well as help it. One classic example of this is Bartlett's 'constructive recall' evidence (Bartlett 1932) where subjects heard a strange little folk-tale of an encounter with ghosts by some North American Indians. When asked to re-tell the story they gradually anglicized it, losing or changing details which had significant meaning in the Indian mythology but had none to English minds. The distortion produced in this case is an informative but extreme example; usually in memorizing text the gist is retained even though the wording and some details may be lost. The error that increases with age is that information which was implied, but not explicitly stated, is inferred by the listener, so that implicit information is believed to have been made explicit. Acceptance of true inferences becomes more frequent as children get older, though false inferences continue to be rejected. Memory is normally holistic and inferential and in most cases this is advantageous, though it must contribute to the inaccuracy of eye witnesses which so concerns criminological psychologists (Loftus 1979).

Cultural demands for memory skills

It is speculative but possible that literal and verbatim memory require special skills rather different from what is done in ordinary daily remembering. (Tulving (1972) has made a possibly analogous distinction between episodic and semantic memory.) What is commonly called a 'photographic memory' or 'eidetic memory', is rare in adults but apparently commoner in young children who appear to be able to examine a stable mental image of the picture they were required to remember and 'read off' from it details, including details which have no meaning to them. Eidetic memory is, however, a somewhat

75

elusive phenomenon and a simplistic model of memory as stored images which are like photographs is untenable (see, for example, Bransford 1979, pp. 190–2). The possibility of verbatim memory for large amounts of material is one which interacts interestingly with the availability of external memory stores. It has been suggested that the possibility of recording information in writing and retrieving it by reading transforms cognition (e.g. Bruner 1966; Goody 1977; Cole and Griffin 1980; Olson and Torrance 1983). This is a controversial subject which receives more attention later. There are, however, certain groups of people in a variety of cultures, both literate and non-literate, who are required to recall long passages of words verbatim. One group studied – though by an ethnographic linguist (Lord 1960) rather than a psychologist – was the itinerant ballad singers of the remoter parts of Yugoslavia, who moved from village to village entertaining the men with traditional folk tales just as earlier reciters did Homer's poems, composed long before they could be recorded in writing. It had been believed that such storytellers must have achieved phenomenal powers of verbatim recall. A closer look at what they did showed that actually they remembered not every word but the order of events and a limited range of stock epithets, and with these and the help of strict rules of rhyme and rhythm they reconstructed a version of the story which differed slightly from previous versions, rather than remembering verbatim an unvarying text. Exact verbatim recall is required in the memorization of sacred texts, laws and property lists, which as Goody (1977) points out were among the earliest products when writing was invented, and also in the memorization of literary products such as poems and plays. There has not been much study of how this is done and whether it develops particular mnemonic powers. Wagner (1982) provides a rather brief account of a study of Moroccan boys, comparing various groups differing in educational experience and including boys from a traditional Islamic school where the curriculum centered on learning the Koran by heart, elementary literacy being virtually a by-product

of this. Their unusually extensive practice of verbatim memorizing, either by rote or by the organization of accumulated meaningful material, had no effect on their short-term recall or recognition of pictures of animals or of oriental rugs. It is to be regretted that they were given no opportunity to show how they remembered material more like the Koran; whether, for example, they showed better discrimination of explicitly presented information from information which is inferred not given. Groups of Moroccan boys who had had a more western type of schooling did rather better on the picture recognition and recall tasks. They also showed signs of the primacy effect in the recall task, which may indicate that they had used rehearsal as a mnemonic technique.

It would be very premature indeed to come to any conclusions about cultural effects on memorization or possible universals in memory structure or memory processing. All that can be said at present is that training with feedback can induce children to use mnemonic strategies and to persist in using them if they are efficient; and that a high degree of practice of a particular mnemonic technique can produce phenomenal remembering of material suited to that technique (see Luria 1969). Practice of one sort of technique on one sort of material may or may not lead to improved performance of other techniques or on other materials. If children are to be set to learn reams of poety, for example, this should be done for the sake of the advantages of remembering reams of poetry (which are various and by no means negligible) not because the memorizing is expected to 'train their memory' in any general way. That it may do so should be an incidental bonus.

Although experimental research has told us a great deal about the structure of memory and about remembering processes, we do not know as much as might be desired about memory in 'ecologically natural' settings. Early work by Istomina (1975) suggests that young children may do better on memory tasks which make sense to them than they do on artificial ones. In her study the comparison was between recalling items while playing 'shopping' and recalling the same items as a formally presented list. There are probably motivational differences in the two settings, and more knowledge of the demands of shopping meant more efficient strategies were recalled as appropriate. Work like this, a more sensitive approach to cross-cultural comparisons, and further investigations of 'the child as psychologist' (Harris 1983a) would be welcome.

Reading

Frith (1980a) calls reading and spelling 'complex and astonishing accomplishments', a description which is obviously correct. We do not yet have a full account of what people do when they read. Researchers agree that very many linguistic, perceptual, attentional, memory and cognitive skills are involved, but they vary considerably in which they emphasize. Research in experimental cognitive psychology often concentrates on 'bottom-up' analyses (see, for example, Crowder 1982) and emphasizes the reader's use of, for example, eye movements or pattern recognition processes. Other investigators may assert that the reader's knowledge of what is likely to be the meaning of a word or piece of text may be crucial in whether it can be read, and emphasize 'top-down' models (e.g. Smith 1978). In some cases there has been a regrettable tendency to make the 'top-down' or 'bottom-up' emphases too strong, so that some accounts of reading as a matter of comprehension have taken the perceptual components as uninteresting and mechanical, and some accounts of reading as a matter of decoding visual information into a verbal form have excluded anything more 'cognitive' than word recognition. 'Top-down' and 'bottom-up' have to be co-ordinated in theories as they are in ordinary reading, where most of the time processes at all levels are used. Recently theories which integrate different levels have appeared. Morton's 'logogen' system (Morton 1969, 1980) and Rumelhart's model (Rumelhart 1977; Ellis 1984) are important examples. It is clear that 'reading' includes many different activities at different perceptual, linguistic and cognitive levels, which no doubt interact in changing ways as the reader becomes more skilled, or when the reader is faced with different sorts of reading task or text. The 'reading' involved in recognizing 'cereals' in a supermarket is probably not quite the same as the 'reading' involved in understanding the same word in a newspaper article on the government's farming policy, and the 'reading' might well be different again when 'cereals' appears in a scientific article or a poem. Similarly, children learning to read may use different processes to make sense of the written message, varying according to, for example, familiarity, the availability of context, and the child's own preferences such as willingness to guess (Francis 1982).

Development in reading processes

Although we cannot yet specify the developmental course of interacting reading processes, it does seem likely that it is the basic perceptual processes which change least. Visual discriminations between symbols like b and d, for example, can be shown even in infants (see Chapter 2; and Banks and Salapatek 1983). There is, on the other hand, obvious and enormous development in the child's knowledge of language, of the world, and of reading and literature. Variations here are predictive of success or failure in learning to read. I shall have more to say about these 'top down' constituents of reading than about the perceptual basics, but I would not wish to imply either that the latter are unimportant or that they remain unchanged throughout the development of reading.

Children as they begin to learn to read probably have, then, most of the perceptual capacities – eye movements, pattern recognition and discrimination, attention – which they need. They are also very well used to dealing with the language that they hear. They have had much practice in extracting meaning from it: they have also probably analysed it into segments at the levels of phrases, words and morphemes (McShane, personal communication). In reading, they have to do rather similar things to language which they see rather than hear. There has been much debate over whether writing is decoded into imagined speech which is then processed as if it were really heard, or whether reading goes straight from symbol to meaning. The possible relationships between speech and reading are complex, and the evidence is so too (Crowder 1982; ch. 9; Ellis 1984). The debate may perhaps be resolving into an agreement that the skilled reader, at least, may use imagined sound or may go direct from written word to meaning. What is done depends on the reader's skills, the novelty or familiarity of words, the difficulty of the text and the purpose of reading, among other variables.

Sound–letter correspondences

Children learning to read often have problems over the relationship between sound and letter. In English there are many complexities in the correspondence between phoneme and grapheme – consider for example 'a' in 'cat', 'fate' and 'arm', and 'c' in 'cat', 'ceiling' and 'chuckle'. There may be more regularities in combinations of graphemes. As Stubbs (1980) points out, Bernard Shaw overstated his case for spelling reform when he suggested a pronunciation for 'ghoti' which followed precedents in other words ('gh' as in 'cough', 'o' as in 'women', 'ti' as in 'station', hence 'ghoti' is pronounced 'fish'), as 'gh' is always pronounced as a hard 'g' when it appears at the beginning of words ('ghost', 'ghastly', 'ghetto'). There are however many irregularities even in common words. The letter string 'ough' has a different pronunciation each time it appears in the words 'bough', 'cough', 'dough', 'lough', 'nought', 'rough' and 'through'. Further, Liberman *et al.* (1977) show that it is unlikely that speech sound is experienced as ready-segmented phonemes or that phonemes blend obviously into words. Young children and illiterate adults find it relatively easy to segment words into syllables and almost impossible to segment into phonemes. Symbol-sound correspondences are somewhat easier to learn in regularized alphabets such as the Initial Teaching Alphabet (i.t.a.) (Downing 1979) but such alphabets do not allow for regional pronunciation differences, nor do they preserve the lexical and syntactic information which irregular

spelling carries (for example the semantic relationship between 'bomb' and 'bombardment'). Stubbs (1980) argues that the English spelling system works extremely well for a native speaker who knows its phonological and morphological rules, that is it is better suited to adult fluent readers than to children (or foreigners) learning to read English. Awareness of language would thus appear to be a most important component of learning to read. Awareness of sounds is a predictor of speed of becoming a reader: teaching about sounds ('phonics') seems to be a useful part of teaching reading (Bryant and Bradley 1985). Phonemic analysis is quite hard to learn but becoming able to do it is an important breakthrough in the early stages of reading. 'Sounding out' words, if successful, reduces dependence on recognizing their visual pattern and supplements the child's knowledge of likely meaning and vocabulary. Experience of reading increases both the child's general knowledge and his or her knowledge of the underlying rules of written language so that gradually correspondences between letter and sound become less crucial to understanding what is being read. Adult fluent readers may only use sound deliberately in their reading when they are having problems with understanding or remembering what they read.

Language awareness in learning to read

Various studies have now picked up linguistic awareness and experience as an important predictor of learning to read, perhaps even a prerequisite for it. Wells (1981) found significant positive correlations between parents' and children's interest in literacy, particularly the frequency with which stories were read to the child, and the child's progress in learning to read, for his representative sample of 120 children. Francis (1982), in a sensitive case study of ten children, found that understanding the task of reading and writing was crucial both for doing it successfully and for appreciating why it was worth doing. Children who learn to read early and easily (Clark 1976) tend to have acquired such an understanding before beginning school. How much the child is read to, how much he or she sees other people reading, how much and how explicitly written material is used in daily activities like shopping, knowledge of concepts like 'sound', 'word' and 'sentence', are related to rate and efficiency of learning to read. These activities seem to contribute to achieving insight into the links between written symbol and word meaning: they also serve to establish that reading is or can be useful and entertaining.

Children who lack these experiences tend to be slower in learning to read. For some, lack of reading-related experiences may be due to a home background which also does not provide experience related to other school activities. Children from such homes may not know, when they first enter school, what is required of them. Classroom tasks may be relatively strange and incomprehensible. It is harder to learn to do something which makes no sense in itself and which you cannot link to your other experience than something part familiar whose purpose you appreciate, and when the 'something' is as complex and artificial as learning to read, it may be the best you can do to do it slowly, weakly and by rote, as some of the children described in Francis 1982 did. Only when the children achieved an insight into the general relation between reading and writing on the one hand and spoken language on the other, only when reading and writing became meaningful activities, did they make much progress.

Reading stages and strategies

The problem is certainly not a simple one of deficient home background, and it is not so much one of inadequacies of language or of concentration on the part of the child as of inexperience in reflecting on language and how it is used: in other words it is often essentially a metacognitive and metalinguistic problem, interacting with the social problem of adjustment to school life. Children solve the problem of learning to read in different ways. Ellis (1984) sketches a common developmental course. The 5-year-old beginning to learn to read recognizes and uses a spoken vocabulary of several hundred words, and speaks grammatically. The first step made in learning to read is often to 'glance-and-guess': a few words are recognized by shape, otherwise an unfamiliar word is guessed using the context as a guide, its graphemic or phonemic characteristics being rather unimportant in the guess. Unfamiliar words without context cannot be read at all. Errors tend to preserve meaning but look and sound different from the correct word. Later, in the second step of 'sophisticated guessing', the vocabulary recognized by sight is larger, and unfamiliar words met in or out of context are guessed in terms of their visual similarity with familiar words, with contextual cues used where possible. Visual cues from the beginnings of words are probably more easily used than those from the middle or end of words: words in context are easier than words isolated in word lists (an instance of the usefulness of top-down cues). Poor readers incidentally may tend to rely on pictures for cues, or even believe that the story is contained in the pictures rather than in the text (Francis 1982; Yule and Rutter 1985).

Francis (1982) also reports that even her quicker readers rarely used phonic cues until they had a fair grasp of visual and contextual cues. They then used sounding out unfamiliar words largely to supplement a not-quite-adequate visual and contextual analysis. Realizing, or being taught, that there is some consistency between words in how letters or groups of letters are pronounced, increases the child's chance of decoding written word into meaning. It may be particularly useful to do left-to-right sounding-out on words which are phonemically regular but visually nondescript, such as 'bun'; words which are phonemically irregular but visually distinctive, such as 'light', may be more easily recognized by their shape than by sounding-out. Bryant and Bradley (1980, 1985) report that some young children have separate reading and spelling strategies, and hence can read some words (such as 'light') which they cannot spell, and spell others (such as 'bun'), which they cannot read, a phenomenon found also among Francis' sample.

Insight into analysing words into phonemes,

Table 2 *Stages of reading development: an outline of the major qualitative characteristics and how they are acquired*

1 Stage designation	2 Grade range (age)	3 Major qualitative characteristics and masteries by end of age	4 How acquired	5 Relationship of reading to listening
Stage 0: Prereading, 'pseudo-reading'	Preschool ages 6 months–6 years	Child 'pretends' to read, retells story when looking at pages of book previously read to him/her; names letters of alphabet; recognizes some signs; prints own name; plays with books, pencils, and paper.	Being read to by an adult (or older child) who responds to and warmly appreciates the child's interest in books and reading; being provided with books, paper, pencils, blocks, and letters.	Most can understand the children's picture books and stories read to them. They understand thousands of words they hear by age 6 but can read few if any of them.
Stage 1: Initial reading and decoding	Grade 1 & beginning Grade 2 (ages 6 & 7)	Child learns relation between letters and sounds and between printed and spoken words; child is able to read simple text containing high frequency words and phonically regular words; uses skill and insight to 'sound out' new one-syllable words.	Direct instruction in letter-sound relations (phonics) and practice in their use. Reading of simple stories using words with phonic elements taught and words of high frequency. Being read to on a level above what child can read independently to develop more advanced language patterns, knowledge of new words, and ideas.	The level of difficulty of language read by the child is much below the language understood when heard. At the end of stage 1, most children can understand up to 4000 or more words when heard but can read only about 600.
Stage 2: Confirmation and fluency	Grades 2 & 3 (ages 7 & 8)	Child reads simple, familiar stories and selections with increasing fluency. This is done by consolidating the basic decoding elements, sight vocabulary, and meaning context in the reading of familiar stories and selections.	Direct instruction in advanced decoding skills; wide reading (with instruction and independently) of familiar, interesting materials which help promote fluent reading. Being read to at levels above their own independent reading level to develop language, vocabulary, and concepts.	At the end of stage 2, about 3000 words can be read and understood and about 9000 are known when heard. Listening is still more effective than reading.
Stage 3: Reading for learning the new Phase A Phase B	Grades 4–8 (ages 9–13) Intermediate, 4–6 Junior high school, 7–9	Reading is used to learn new ideas, to gain new knowledge, to experience new feelings, to learn new attitudes; generally from one viewpoint.	Reading and study of textbooks, reference works, trade books, newspapers, and magazines that contain new ideas and values, unfamiliar vocabulary and syntax; systematic study of words and reacting to the text through discussion, answering questions, writing, etc. Reading of increasingly more complex fiction, biography, nonfiction, and the like.	At beginning of stage 3, listening comprehension of the same material is still more effective than reading comprehension. By the end of stage 3, reading and listening are about equal; for those who read very well, reading may be more efficient.
Stage 4: Multiple viewpoints	High school, grades 10–12 (ages 15–17)	Reading widely from a broad range of complex materials, both expository and narrative, with a variety of viewpoints.	Wide reading and study of the physical, biological, and social sciences and the humanities; high quality and popular literature; newspapers and magazines; systematic study of words and word parts.	Reading comprehension is better than listening comprehension of material of difficult content and readability. For poorer readers, listening comprehension may be equal to reading comprehension.
Stage 5: Construction and reconstruction	College and beyond (age 18+)	Reading is used for one's own needs and purposes (professional and personal); reading serves to integrate one's knowledge with that of others, to synthesize it and to create new knowledge. It is rapid and efficient.	Wide reading of ever more difficult materials, reading beyond one's immediate needs; writing of papers, tests, essays, and other forms that call for integration of varied knowledge and points of view.	Reading is more efficient than listening.

phoneme–grapheme correspondences and the integration of phonic strategies, visual memory and use of context, with of course further vocabulary growth and increasing knowledge of the worlds which reading conjures up, combine to form the basic achievement of reading. Top-down and bottom-up strategies can now be used interdependently. They become, no doubt, more fluent with practice just as any other skills would, and the balance adopted between different reading strategies probably becomes more flexible and more efficient. There is considerable development, in other words, in the uses to which reading is put. Chall (1983) provides a table (Table 2) to illustrate this point: reading is an instrument for knowing, heavily influenced in its development by the demands of the ecosystem, and both an object and a result of practice in 'study skills' (Chall 1983, pp. 85–7).

Children and stories

There is a history several centuries old of producing special story books for children, and behind that a longer tradition of folk tales and rhymes and other narratives which also took children for their audience. Most children hear stories and tell them themselves: many read them or write them. In this country, at least (see Schieffelin and Cochran-Smith 1984 for notes on two other cultures), there is a positive correlation between being read stories during the pre-school years, on the one hand, and both metalinguistic competence (p. 137) and prospects of learning to read and write easily, on the other. Children learn a great deal about written language and about the structure of stories from being read to (e.g. Clay 1979; Clark 1976; Wells 1985). They also take part in a shared activity with the older person reading to them (and indirectly with the author). Where this is enjoyable for both parties, it doubtless provides motivation for further reading. Involving parents in hearing their older children read to them has proved a most effective way of improving children's reading skills (e.g. Tizard, Schofield and Hewison 1981).

Being read to can involve children in several different ways of 'taking from text' (Teale 1984).

Sometimes the child is required to be a passive audience. Sometimes adults encourage a great deal of active participation from the child, requesting identification of objects in pictures, comments on the action, and predictions about what will happen next. Sometimes analogies will be drawn between the events of the story and the child's own experience. If such elaborations of the reading and listening activity are sensitively used, children become adept at relating stories to a wider context and dealing with their implications more deeply, skills useful in the classroom (Hayward 1980; Heath 1982, 1983; Mills and Funnell 1983). Stories are a constant part of classroom social life, and a delight in many children's home lives.

Stories socialize children in other ways besides the interaction which is required of a reader or listener. They can convey the culture to the child and socialize him or her into culturally approved patterns of attitudes and values. They can do this both overtly and covertly, and can carry both admirable and deplorable messages. Hilaire Belloc's *Cautionary Tales for Children*, for example, has overt morals such as 'don't tell lies', 'don't slam doors' and 'don't play with loaded guns', which are, however, less memorable, and less enjoyed by children, than his gleeful callousness. Louisa May Alcott's *Little Women* proposes that girls should be quiet, ladylike, self-sacrificing and dominated by men, a mode of existence which was impossible and destructive for Alcott herself (Saxton 1978).

This sort of socialization is hard to quantify. Its existence has however been a source of anxiety to many adults who wish to censor the 'unsuitable' out of their children's reading (and indeed out of other adults' too), and often have wished to substitute more 'suitable' reading. There are a number of discussions of the socializing effects of traditional fairy-tales, for example (Tucker 1981; Steedman 1982; Zipes 1983). We do not know whether women were more self-effacing and long-suffering as a result of being told the story of Patient Griselda, the archetypal victimized wife whose patience wins her back the affections of her dreadful husband, or whether there was more

Plate 8

adultery between wives and servants after the publication of *Lady Chatterley's Lover*. Many of us may remember being (less strongly!) influenced by a story we have read. In so far as stories reflect the entire culture, and so are reinforced by other experiences, they may have a powerful effect. There is little clear evidence.

It is also argued that stories are important in children's emotional development. There are famous psychoanalytic interpretations of fairy stories in terms of children's need to resolve their Oedipus crisis or their penis envy, notably Bettelheim's *The Uses of Enchantment* (1978). Since these resolutions are normally of unconscious feelings and problems, it is again hard to demonstrate that stories have the 'uses' claimed. Stories may also model emotions more directly, as they illustrate their characters' behaviour. Hayward (1980) told a slightly simplified version of *Watership Down* to her class of 4-year-olds, and later observed a little boy with aspirations to toughness and bravado bump his head, and instead of crying say 'Miss Hayward, I've hurt myself bad, but don't worry, I'm Bigwig the strongest rabbit – I'm brave like Bigwig.'

Stories obviously commonly *evoke* emotions – like play, they provide a relatively risk-free and controllable form of being frightened, excited and exhilarated.

Children begin to understand the form of stories quite early in their experience of them. They are not as dependent on temporal order as Piaget (1969) suggested: given a logically structured story (his were ill-formed) they make inferences and build up a coherent shapely sequence of events even at the age of 4 (Wimmer 1980; Mandler and Johnson 1977). They develop 'story grammars' just as they develop 'scripts' of familiar events in their lives. Although their initial re-telling of stories contains mainly surface events, probing with 'why' questions elicits much inference about the characters' motives and intentions. Young children's limitations may be attributed to lack of world knowledge and memory problems rather than to lack of an ability to make inferences and other logical connections (Trabasso and Nicholas 1980). As children en-counter more stories they gain both more 'real world' knowledge and more knowledge of the conventions of stories. They begin to appreciate the distancing, reassuring opening 'Once upon a time'; they expect there to be good characters who triumph over their troubles and bad characters who get their due come-uppance; they know that foxes are 'sly' and witches are wicked. Traditional stories create a world simpler than the child's own but not entirely unlike it, so that they can try an alternative 'reality' just as they do in play.

Skills of learning from text

Being literate becomes increasingly important as one progresses through the educational system, both because of the possibilities of gathering, rearranging, comparing and passing on knowledge which it provides, and because it is one of the commonest social 'measures' of intellectual adequacy. As we have seen, reading involves many different levels of cognitive processing. Reading a text in order to *learn* from it requires the use of comprehension and study skills.

Comprehension
Collins and Smith (1982) describe some of the important comprehension skills necessary for dealing with written information. The first group are concerned with *monitoring* comprehension, that is checking whether the text is being understood, being aware of a breakdown in understanding and taking appropriate action to remedy it. The reader may fail to comprehend text at the level of a particular word, phrase or sentence, or at the level of fitting bits of text together. Children have limited vocabulary and general knowledge, compared with adults, and may make over-simple assumptions about grammar. When acting out the *spoken* sentence 'The cat was bitten by the dog', for example, they proceed as if the passive sentence had the subject–verb–object order characteristic of simple active declarative sentences. Similar problems may be found in many early readers: unusual grammar upsets the child's comprehension. Unusual vocabulary

items may puzzle the child too, but they are probably more easily clarified, and children often enjoy grand long words. However, children may have more marked comprehension problems than adults, even at the simplest levels. Ellen Markman suggests that they have major problems over comprehending the integration of separate bits of text into a consistent whole. They often do not notice, she says, what are to the adult glaring inconsistencies or omissions in verbal material, for example incomplete instructions about how to play a game (Markman 1979; Robinson and Robinson 1983).

Children's comprehension of text, then, runs into difficulties and the problem arises of how to solve them. Possible strategies include ignoring the uncomprehended words or passage; waiting to see if its meaning later becomes clear; guessing, the guess being confirmed or disconfirmed later; re-reading the immediate problem passage or the larger part of the text in which it occurs; seeking outside help, from peer, teacher, dictionary or another text. Which of these strategies the child uses will depend on the task requirements; casual reading uses the simpler strategies at the beginning of the list, while detailed mastery of difficult texts requires much more re-reading, analysis and comparison of different sources. Which strategy is used will also depend on the characteristics of the reader, and in the case of the very young reader on how he or she is being taught to read. However new reading is, the child has used skills very much like many of these for several years while trying to understand spoken language. The most obvious skill to be applicable to written language but not so readily to spoken language is re-reading, both because spoken words are much more ephemeral and because requests for repetition of an uncomprehended utterance often produce a rephrasing of what was said, not a verbatim repetition. Guessing, ignoring and seeking outside help (sometimes from the same sources) are however well-practised strategies. Children, like all who are relatively ignorant or novices, must rather often fail to 'comprehend'. It is, however, a question of some interest to identify what and when they

know *that* they don't know, and what and when they know *why* they don't know. This and other questions of 'metacognition' I will discuss later.

Collins and Smith (1982) point out that as well as guessing at the meaning of particular words or phrases, the reader will guess about the meaning of more global aspects of the text. Guesses will be made, or hypotheses constructed, about matters like what sort of story this is, what will happen in this situation, who are the 'goodies' and who the 'baddies', and so forth. (In many cases authors consciously use these hypotheses either to support the plausibility of their narrative (as in romantic novels) or to mislead the reader in a sequence of bluff and double-bluff (as in 'whodunnits'). Jane Austen's presentation of Mr Darcy and Mr Wickham in *Pride and Prejudice* is a particularly brilliant example of both uses.) Again, children beginning to read will have developed strategies of making sense of stories or events in terms of broad hypotheses which define what this sort of story is likely to be about, or what happens in this sort of event. Schank and Abelson (1977) called the latter 'scripts' (see section on social cognition, below). Careful observation of young children at home shows that they both use and seek to clarify 'scripts' (e.g. Tizard and Hughes 1982, 1984) and it has been argued that this use is a major opportunity for the development of reasoning (Mills and Funnell 1983). Children's experience of stories gives them something like 'scripts' for stories, as their filling-in of the frame 'Once upon a time . . . and then they all lived happily ever after' shows (e.g. Applebee 1978, and discussion of stories and of writing elsewhere in this chapter).

Study skills

Even when the reader understands the text bit by bit and as a whole, a considerable amount of work will have to be done on it if the learning task involves the memorization or the use of information from the text. Verbatim memorization requires rehearsal; remembering which is not verbatim requires other activities, which may also be appropriate to using the original text in creating one's own account of the area. These activities have been called 'study skills'. Ann Brown and her colleagues (Brown *et al.* 1983) have been investigating the types of knowledge and strategies which students bring to learning from texts. We are some way from the novice information-processors described in the earlier parts of this chapter, but Brown *et al.* conclude that there is a sequence of emergence of 'study skills' very like the sequence of emergence of remembering, attending and reading skills. There is an early period of sporadic use of appropriate activities; these activities become more and more stable, systematic and consolidated, and more easily applied flexibly to a range of tasks and situations, as development proceeds. 'Mature learning is in large part the result of strategic application of rules and principles, and the suppression of serviceable, but less mature, habits' (Brown *et al.* p. 90).

It is worth going into some detail on the 'study skills' reviewed because they illuminate developmental questions through their progress in schoolchildren, and because using them at a high and conscious level contributes to intellectual effort well beyond school level. Among the skills studied are: identifying the main points, the most important parts, of a text: identifying the organizing features of the text: paying more attention to and using more mnemonic activity on important and organizing features: accurately estimating one's current state of mastery and taking the appropriate action. Among other investigations, Brown *et al.* looked at how students worked on the task of summarizing a text. They compared schoolchildren of 12, 14, and 17, college students and teachers of rhetoric ('experts'). Two simple rules of summarizing which even the youngest children used quite accurately were 1 delete trivia and 2 delete redundancy. Further rules were 3 substitute a superordinate term or a superordinate event for lists of examples or episodes, a process which can easily be related to the use of category cues in recall; and 4 use (or invent) a topic sentence. There was more use, and more effective use, of these strategies as practice increased, but even college students did

not invent topic sentences on many occasions when it was appropriate to do so.

One important point to come out of these studies of summarization and note-taking was that the simple strategy 12-year-olds mostly used, that of copy-verbatim-with-deletions, is to some extent effective in that it does produce a recognizable summary or outline. However it is very passive and reduces the chance that understanding of the particular text will be linked to understanding of other texts. Experts are much more likely to depart from the text, to combine, rearrange, and interpolate information, to make synopses in their own words and to argue with what they read. This approach is more effective as a way of understanding text, but requires more cognitive resources (both process and knowledge). Students who are managing fairly well by using passive summaries (and who are not in their education required to do more) may never give up their partially adequate strategy in favour of one which is more efficient (and more fun, it risky). The general public level of information gathering and reading is not at all clear: sophisticated evaluation, comparison, criticism and re-creation of texts is probably a minority pleasure. However it is clear that both these highly elaborated ways of playing with text and the humbler study skills that underly them can be taught (Brown *et al.* 1983, 1984; Howe 1984; Biggs 1984/in press). They are implicit in much school activity, and many children gradually learn to use them through schooling, but they can also be deliberately developed. My own feeling is that they should be, more often than they are at present: this is an area where I regret my own state of bricolage!

Metacognition, motivation and study skills
I want to return for a moment to the Brown *et al.* tetrahedron model of interactions between the characteristics of learner, material, criterial tasks and learning activities, by which at present I mean study skills. Recent work by John Biggs (1984/in press) illustrates that these interactions are crucial to performance, and highly complex. He describes three basic motives for study:

to obtain a qualification with minimal effort (Surface motive), to actualize one's interests (Deep motive), and to manifest one's excellence publicly by obtaining the highest grades (Achieving motive). (He is mainly concerned with motives for study in secondary and tertiary education, but the same motives could no doubt apply in primary education; young children may read to get through the reading test, or to develop their own skills or interest, or to show off what good readers they are.) There are cases of mixed motives, particularly of Achieving motives mixed with the other two categories. Motives result from the interplay of student personality and the task situation.

The different motives are paired with different strategies. Thus the Deep motive tends to be associated with strategies which emphasize under-

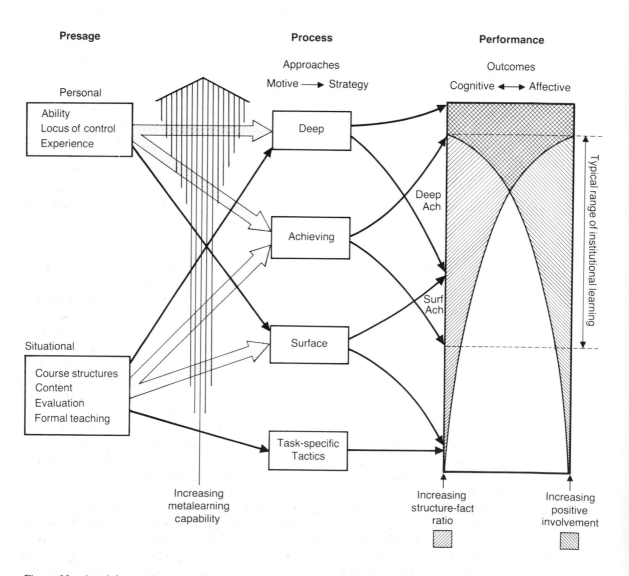

Figure 10 An elaborated model of student learning.

standing the meaning of the task and the material, the Surface motive with reproducing what is seen as the essential information or performance and ignoring all that is superfluous to getting by, the Achieving motive with organization which optimizes the use of time and effort. They have different outcomes. Surface learners' work is factual and superficial, and has little intrinsic interest to the student who may forget it the moment the qualification is obtained: Deep learners' is more complex, more structured and more affectively satisfying, hence more permanent; and so forth. The same study skill behaviours are differently effective for students with different motives; an Achieving motive student using an Achieving strategy generally does well, but a Deep motive student using the same strategy is likely to feel dissatisfied, aware of the discrepancy between desire and performance. Different educational institutions foster different motives and strategies, through their control of task materials and criterial tasks, and the different learning activities they propose or require.

Thus there is a complex interaction between student characteristics such as ability and self-concept, situational factors such as course structures and type of evaluation, the degree to which the student is aware of his or her learning strategies and activities, and the sort of knowledge and satisfaction that results, via the approach that the student takes to the learning task. Biggs (1984) provides a model (Figure 10).

This picture suggests that a Deep approach to study is more closely tied to the personality of the student, who feels 'I am doing this for me, and not because the school makes me'. A Surface approach tends to be seen as distant from the self, adopted in order to get a task done when it has been imposed from outside. The former is likely to involve more positive involvement on the part of the learner, a greater awareness of his or her learning activities, needs and achievements, and an outcome which shows more understanding and more links with other knowledge and less role learning of facts. Surface learning will be less involving, less enjoyable, often undertaken to cope with the demands of outside authorities,

and will have much less impact on the rest of the student's understanding: it may be useful for quiz games such as *Mastermind* but will never win you an FRS.

Writing

I have described some of the recent work on reading and using text. I want now to consider the 'second R', writing. Like reading, this is an activity which integrates many different processes – physical, linguistic, cognitive, even social – in different ways according to the writer's age, experience and purposes. Scardamalia (1981) lists the interdependent skills involved, among them questions of handwriting, spelling and punctuation, considerations of word choice, syntax and textual connections, and of overall purpose, organization, clarity and euphony. Each of these is itself of course highly complex and subject to developmental change. I shall focus here on the more cognitive issues, discussing the relation of writing to reading and speaking and the production problems, particularly the composition problems this involves.

Writing in relation to speaking
Written language and spoken language differ, though linguists disagree about how far the former is dependent on the latter. Stubbs (1980), reviewing the debate, points out that the relationship between written and spoken language differs for different writing systems, different authorial purposes, and different cultures. One consistent difference, however, is that the writer must construct the text without the assistance of signals from the recipient about whether the meaning is being understood, whether more information is needed, whether jokes are being appreciated or persuasive arguments are having the desired effect. The reader has to get meaning from the text in the absence of many of the signals that accompany spoken language: cues from the speaker's 'body language', pitch, speed of speaking, facial expression and so forth are not available in conventional written text, though devices of punctuation and typography may be used to

make up for some of this loss. Literary theorists debate how far 'the meaning' of a text is in the text itself, in text plus additional information about the writer and the context of writing, in the reader (with or without the context of reading), or in all of these in complementary or contradictory fashion. These debates are typically rather distant from psychology, though they do point to complexities which will be relevant to children's response to stories. My present point is that writers and readers interact much more distantly than speakers and listeners. Writers cannot, alas, monitor their readers' understanding. If they wish to be effective, they must therefore compose and review their writing more carefully than most speakers need to do, lest problems in any of the skills which Scardamalia (1981) lists should prevent satisfactory communication. They also need to appreciate some of the conventions which differ between spoken and written language. Normally, children learning to write have a good basic command of spoken language, which they have been using since early childhood and which they can use to serve a variety of social functions. Their communication in speech is, however, still commonly dependent on context and on paralinguistic cues to carry subtle or precise meaning. They may also have little experience of writing themselves or seeing others write, and particularly of the uses to which writing can be put.

Writing in relation to reading

Before I discuss children's achievements in learning to write, I wish to point out that with reading and writing or spelling the one is not simply the inverse of the other. There is evidence that at least at the early stages reading may be done by visual word recognition and spelling/writing by a phonological strategy (e.g. Bryant and Bradley 1980, 1983). Children and backward readers may read correctly, but spell *in*correctly, words which are visually distinctive but phonologically difficult, such as 'light', and read incorrectly but spell correctly words which are easy to construct phonologically (letter-by-letter) but are visually nondescript, such as 'bun'. Bryant and Bradley's subjects are producing some of their failures be-

cause they do not use their phonological and visual recognition strategies together: reading and spelling were unfortunately too independent. As reading progresses beyond the 8-year-old level, the different processes intertwine, and the experienced writer may find it commoner to know that a word is spelled incorrectly because it looks wrong rather than because it sounds wrong. Given the complexity of the relations between phoneme and grapheme in English, embodying as it does an immense amount of historical information, and overlooking as it does considerable regional and subcultural differences in pronunciation, sound may be a less reliable index of spelling correctness than sight in many cases. Readers certainly come to recognize, understand and spell correctly words they have never heard. The hero of *How Green Was My Valley* reads 'misled' as the past participle of a verb 'to misle', pronounces it to rhyme with 'drizzled', and is beaten by his schoolmaster despite his comprehension of the word.

Writing as a physical skill

Writing involves the use of fine muscle movements in varied but co-ordinated patterns, with visual monitoring, at a speed (in experienced writers) far faster than the brain can send messages to the hand and receive feedback, though more slowly than thinking or speaking. As Thomassen and Teuling (1983) remind us, the hand is an extraordinarily intricate and delicate mechanism, controlled by a large number of muscles, and during writing movements in fingers, wrists, arms and shoulders, plus movements of the eyes (and perhaps head) for monitoring writing, have to be co-ordinated. These muscle movements have to be small, quick and precise, and because the speed of transmission of neural control messages along the length of the arm is relatively slow, the brain cannot wait for one movement to be completed before the next is begun. Even at this level the brain must plan ahead to get the hand in the right position at the right place at the right time.

To do this, we write not in single letters but in larger units. As an example, compare the ease of writing 'written backwards' with the difficulty of writing 'sdrawkcab nettirw': and note where the pauses and breaks in writing came. 'Units' may occur over words; we pause more between clauses than within them, for example. 'Over-unitting' may produce errors; I planned the first sentence of this section from 'Writing' to 'patterns' as it is now printed, but wrote 'final' instead of 'fine', as a conflation of 'fine' with the sound at the end of 'muscle' rather than as a semantic error. Motor skills of the highly complex sort involved in writing fluently are acquired mainly through practice. Smith (1982) advocates writing practice free from demands for correctness in spelling, punctuation or composition which may distract from establishing automatic motor patterns. This may or may not be a sensible bit of pedagogy, but certainly children do take a fairly long time to develop fine motor co-ordination sufficiently good for writing neatly: some people never really do it!

Learning about the basic skills of writing

Given a piece of paper and a pencil, a 2-year-old will make marks on the paper. Initially these scribbles are probably not unsuccessful attempts to write, rather they are successful attempts to make marks on the paper where there were no marks before. 'Writing' usually follows attempts at drawing representations of objects. Vygotsky (1978a) points out that writing is a second-order

symbol system: the letters stand for the spoken word, which itself stands for the object. Drawings, and idiosyncratic pictographs, are in a first order symbolic relation to the object they represent. This account obviously implies that writing will develop after drawing has begun; writing is a special sort of drawing which represents language. As children experience written language by reading or being read to, they learn that conventionally writing (at least in English) comes in horizontal lines and consists of particular sorts of patterns. Young children may 'write' in a scribble or string of letters running horizontally across the page, or accompanying a picture as an adult might provide a caption. A fascinating observation of a child just under 5 illustrates this.

Unlike the case in other writing episodes, Coline is not oblivious to the activity around her. She sits with a group of boys, rather than alone, and watches intently as Raymond draws rockets and creates the accompanying sound-effects. The entire writing episode seems to be surrounded by more language. For the first time Coline begins the composing by verbalizing her intentions. She lays two blank pieces of paper on the desk before her and announces: 'I'm going to do a picture on that one and write on this one.' This, in fact, is what she does. The numbers beside the p.i.'s indicate the order in which they are written by Coline [Figure 11].

1 - ✝KOIC

4 - ✝✝KOIC

3 - OKKI

5 - KK✝OIs

2 - KIOe

6 - ✝KOK

✝KKO

Figure 11

This product indicates more progress in Coline's writing. Her handwriting is more controlled, the size of her letters more uniform, her boundaries more defined than before. Her composing process shows how demanding this new step forward is. Coline spends 20 minutes just writing the first three p.i.'s and throughout the composing actively seeks interruptions. She chats with the boys and comments on their pictures. She writes two letters, then noisily taps her pencil on the table. She completes a p.i., then rocks her chair back and forth on its squeaky back legs. There is much physical turmoil in these pauses from the writing.

The length of time spent composing and the effort expended in making well-formed letters possibly affects Coline's page arrangement. Instead of composing horizontally as in the June piece, she returns to a vertical page arrangement. While composing, however, she does not proceed in a neat progression from the top of the page to the bottom. Instead, she begins by writing the first p.i. at the top of the page, the second at the bottom, the third in the middle as follows. The transcription to the right of the p.i. indicates Coline's reading:

1. tkoic	cat
2. kioe	sat
3. okki	mat

Coline pauses, then rereads what she's written as follows:

1. tkoic	cat
3. okki	sat
2. kioe	mat

Although she does not compose top to bottom, she rereads her writing in this way. She begins at the top of the page and moves down pointing to each word in the order it appears on the page, an order quite different from her initial composing. Still the meaning stays the same. She writes 4. *tkkoic* says, 'I'm finished' and reads again:

1. tkoic	cat
4. ttkoic	sat
3. okki	on
2. kioe	the

'Got to write mat' she says to herself, forgetting that a few moments before she not only called both *okki* and *kioe* 'mat' but also said she was finished. Each word addition demands a rereading by Coline. Each rereading in turn changes the correspondence between p.i.'s and her meaning for them. She writes 5. *kktols*, presumably to be 'mat'. But the positioning of the word on the page ensures that she calls it 'the' instead, as happens:

1. tkoic	cat
4. ttkoic	sat
3. okki	on
5. kktols	the
2. kioe	mat

Things seem to be going well for Coline. Her demand that voice and print match is being satisfied. She rereads again and maintains the same match. Then, composing at the point of her pencil, she says 'eating'. Realizing, of course, that there is no corresponding p.i. for 'eating' she adds one more, 6. *tkok*. The story complete, there are now six clearly defined p.i.'s on the page before her and six clearly defined words in the message in her head. The reading should be straightforward. This, however, is not the case. Seven oral rereadings follow until Coline finally makes the match as charted [Table 3].

Table 3

Written text	Rereadings 1–3	Rereading 4	Rereadings 5–6	Rereading 7
1. tkoic	cat sat	cat sat	cat	cat sat
4. ttkoic	on	on	sat	on
3. okki	the	the	on	the
5. kktols	mat	mat	the	mat
2. kioe	eating	eating	mat	eating
6. tkok		oranges	eating	oranges

For some reason in the first three rereadings she pairs two spoken words, 'cat' and 'sat' with the one p.i. *tkoic*. Consequently she has one p.i. left over at the end, *tkok*, and no spoken word to go with it. On the fourth rereading she solves the problem by adding another spoken word, 'oranges'. All should go well now. On the fifth and sixth readings, however, she returns to her earlier behaviour of matching one spoken word to one p.i. As a result she now finds there is no written p.i. left to match the spoken 'oranges'. At last, on the seventh rereading she remanoeuvres and makes the match.

Such persistence! Coline will not stop until she reaches such closure. She adjusts and readjusts her division of the message until she succeeds. This self-imposed reading seems to be her way of gaining control of the writing.

Following her seventh rereading, she makes her illustration on the second piece of paper she put aside at the beginning of the composing. She seems pleased with herself as she draws a picture of a smiling cat and affixes a label *tkko* saying, 'See, I writed cat at the top'.

The message itself sounds like a rehash of a basal reader story line and is not interesting as a product. The process of getting there, however, is fascinating. Getting the message down in primary inventions is demanding. Coline pays most attention to the demands of making print and controlling the letters, less to her information. It is possible that while she writes she first makes her random clusters of letters and only later attributes meaning to them. Certainly children do this with their art. Perhaps there is a stage in the development of young writers where they write first, mean later (Kamler and Kilarr 1983, pp. 187–9).

Once children have achieved a significant insight into what writing is (Jarman 1979, Smith 1982; Kamler and Kilarr 1983), they have now to curb their inventiveness and adopt the conventional symbols – and construction techniques and spellings – required to communicate with adults. Children do not write letters badly or incorrectly because of inadequate visual processing, but because of production difficulties: letters have to be precisely formed in direction, size, joins, spaces and so forth, and the motor control needed for this is very considerable. Practice gives us a fluent production system, but children lacking one make the sort of errors and attempt the sort of solutions that they do in drawing (see Freeman and Cox 1985).

Some recent observational studies of young children writing are integrated by Clay (1983) into an account of how children develop a theory of writing. As in developing spoken language or reading, the child's own experience of writing seems to be an important determinant of rate of development: children from highly literate families are more positively motivated and more knowledgeable than children whose experience of writing is scant. Some children invent their own 'letters' (Hughes, 1984, reports children who invented their own numbers and arithmetical representations, see p. 103). Many invent their own spellings. One fairly common system is to represent consonants but not the vowel sounds which are less prominent in speech, writing 'LTL' for 'little', for example. It is worth pointing out, perhaps, that vowel deletion is common in strategies for writing fast, and that some Middle Eastern orthographies do not write in the vowels. As children become more familiar with the standard spellings they meet in their reading they move towards the conventional system: pressure from adults also contributes to this shift.

The functions of writing

A reader is essentially concerned with extracting the meaning of a pre-existing text, with or without increase in enjoyment or knowledge. A writer may have any of a wider range of purposes, for example to inform, to entertain, to persuade, to criticize, to record, to express something personally felt, and so forth. This list is obviously similar to one listing the functions of spoken language: recording is the major exception, as generally it is better done by writing than by speaking. Children's spoken language will have been used for most of these functions by the end of the pre-school years (Wells 1985; and see Chapter 4 this volume). They may not have experienced all these functions in writing. Although most adults write sometimes, the main uses of writing at home are in response to social pressure or practical requirements: domestic messages, shopping lists and family letters.

Griffiths and Wells (1983) investigated use of writing in a sample of Bristol adults and found the group differences shown in Figure 12.

The Bristol Language Development Study found adults' literacy was related to that of their children; parents who write more probably also read more, thus giving their children more experience of how writing can be used. It must be rare, however, for pre-school children to have experience of adults writing to express themselves, to tell stories or to record their own experience, since when adults do these things they do them privately. There is little evidence on children's use of writing outside school. Tizard and Hughes (1984) describe some mothers teaching their daughters to write, sometimes as a session of letter forming or copying words written by the mother, sometimes as part of an activity

Explorations in the development of writing

	Jottings	Notes	Casual prose	Formal prose
Universal	Not investigated			Class: H > L, $p < 0.001$ Education: A > M, $p < 0.001$
Strangers		Class: H > L, $p < 0.01$ Education: A > M, $p < 0.02$		Sex: M > F, $p < 0.02$ Class: H > L, $p < 0.001$ Education: A > M, $p < 0.001$
Colleagues	Class: H > L, $p < 0.001$ Education: A > M, $p < 0.05$	Class: H > L, $p < 0.001$ Education: A > M, $p < 0.01$		Sex: M > F, $p < 0.05$ Class: H > L, $p < 0.001$ Education: A > M, $p < 0.001$
Family and friends		Sex: F > M, $p < 0.001$ Education: A > M, $p < 0.01$	Sex: F > M, $p < 0.001$ Class: H > L, $p < 0.05$ Education: A > M, $p < 0.01$	
Self	Class: H > L, $p < 0.01$ Education: A > M, $p < 0.01$	Class: H > L, $p < 0.001$ Education: A > M, $p < 0.01$	Sex: F > M, $p < 0.05$ Class: H > L, $p < 0.01$ Education: A > M, $p < 0.01$	

Sex: F = female *Class:* H = higher *Education:* A = additional
M = male L = lower M = minimal

(Note: only significant differences are reported)

Figure 12 Relationships between amount of writing in different categories and sex, social class and education.

Source: From Griffiths and Wells (1983).

such as writing a letter to grandparents. The latter is probably a fairly common real-life experience for quite a lot of children; most available examples seem to be conventional rather than expressive. Parents may encourage (or require) children to write to grandparents or to people who have given presents or hospitality: thus there is a real social purpose to writing. There are clear rules for beginning and ending the text of letters and since there is often a specific interpersonal reason for writing the letter, at least some of what it must contain is also specified. A thank-you letter from Z to X acknowledging a gift, Y, must include at least the phrases 'Dear X, 'Thank you for the Y', 'from Z'. Collerson (1983) collected the letters his daughter Juliet wrote between the ages of 5 and $9\frac{1}{2}$; they show an increase in length via the inclusion of informative or expressive material beyond the minimum demanded by the formal letter scheme, and an increasing tendency to use written language as a means to a continuing dialogue with people who are known but too far away to speak to. The child 'learns that letters can be a means of reporting and interpreting experience, a device for exchanging information, and a method of maintaining social interaction among friends' (Collerson 1983, p. 92). Some children have difficulty seeing these purposes in school writing (Francis 1982; Tamburrini *et al.* 1984).

This list of functions that are served by Juliet's letters resembles the lists of language functions provided by Halliday (1975), which is discussed in Chapter 4, by Smith (1982, p. 14), and others. Writing and reading differ from speaking and listening not so much in the language functions involved as in the possible distance between the participants. As I said when discussing the relationship between writing and speaking, writing is a more abstract activity. Written text has to convey its meaning more independently of paralinguistic context as writer and reader do not have the shared immediate context which speaker and listener enjoy. The text must create its own context, so the writer must assess what knowledge can safely be assumed and what must be incorporated into the text. The writer must also assess what is the best order for pieces of text and present each piece unambiguously and explicitly. It may be easier for the reader to go back and read text again than it is for the listener to recall speech to re-examine it, but the writer cannot adjust content, order or emphasis as the speaker can in response to the reader's cues of understanding or failure to understand. On the cognitive and social levels, writing differs from speaking.

Writing as composition
Cognitive and social considerations are mingled in the composition of text. Text has to be planned, composed and revised in terms of, among other things, its probable success in communicating with the reader and its own explicitness and coherence. Martlew (1983) reviews some of the errors that poor or inexperienced writers make: they write as they speak, leaving their writing dependent on a context which the reader does not share; they plan poorly, if at all, and prepare themselves for writing too briefly to produce clearly organized text; they do not review or criticize what they have produced. Some of these errors no doubt arise because the whole task of considering the adequacy of the text *plus* spelling correctly *plus* writing neatly *plus* producing the right amount to satisfy the teacher overwhelms the writer. Some, however, probably stem from young writers' uncertainty about what to do in composition and how to do it. Frederiksen and Dominic (1981) suggest that important cognitive resources

include the writer's knowledge, the already established strategies and procedures for constructing a meaning and expressing it, and the general characteristics of their cognitive systems such as processing capacity and both the automaticity and efficiency of component processes (Frederiksen and Dominic 1981, p. 4).

A number of researchers have recently investigated children's composition techniques (see, for example, the collections of papers edited by Frederiksen and Dominic 1981; Martlew 1983; and Kroll and Wells 1983; and a review by Brown *et al*. 1983; as well as the paper specified as reference below). An early problem in composing is generating content. Young children frequently produce the equivalent of one utterance on the topic and then stop, claiming that that is all they can think of to say. Bereiter and Scardamalia (1982) demonstrate that devices of various sorts increase the amount produced. Instructions to produce a large amount, the opportunity to speak or dictate the text instead of having to write it, the provision of simple prompts such as 'go on' or more directive ones such as 'on the other hand' or 'also', all increased both number of words and number of ideas expressed. Children clearly had not reached the limits of what was available on the subject. They welcomed prompts and appreciated their effect. Learning to provide yourself with prompts is part of the development of writing skills.

Bereiter and Scardamalia's subjects did not, however, seem to fit their additional content neatly to the prompts or to the sentence openers which later experiments provided. (I am glad to say that a group of Bristol 9-year-olds, less formally studied, did.) Prompts and openers produced more material, but not all children provided material on the same side of the argument as an 'also' prompt suggests, or material on the opposite side after a prompt of 'on the other hand'. Their productions resembled what has been called a 'knowledge-telling' strategy, where everything that is known on a subject or part of a subject is allowed to flood out without much evidence of organization. Writers who use this strategy often pay little attention to the demands of their title and the limits it sets, and do not adjust what they say to the characteristics of their reader. 'Knowledge-telling' writing lacks goal-related planning and significant revision. The text is not interconnected but made up of unrelated sentences produced one after the other without reference forward or, more particularly, back. It may thus contain repetitions and contradictions. Children seem to have difficulties spotting inconsistencies and inadequacies in text (Brown *et al*. 1983; Markman 1979) and find it difficult also to estimate accurately whether they know a little or a lot about a topic (Bereiter and Scardamalia 1982). In other words, they have problems of access to their knowledge.

'Knowledge-telling' is a strategy which even experienced writers may resort to under conditions of stress (such as writing examination answers!); Brown *et al*. (1983) point out that it may be hard to give up because it does produce text, indeed text which is high in quantity even if low in relevance and organization. Knowledge-telling followed by rigorous revision and ruthless discarding of weak material is a perfectly respectable composition technique. Since, however, only relatively experienced writers produce the evaluating and revising parts of this procedure, it may be more effective for young children to be trained to plan their text before they write it.

Bereiter and Scardamalia (1982) report various attempts to induce and improve planning. Planning is one of the ways in which composing written language differs from spoken language. Spoken language is much more likely to be influenced by the recipient who may interrupt, argue, anticipate and so forth, thus changing the course of the speech. Planning in speaking has to be flexible and adapted in use to the behaviour of the listener: planning in writing is much less disruptible, and it may be more important to get it right. Before the teens, young writers seemed to plan, if at all, on a 'what next?' basis, even when prompts suggested different developments in a text. Planning was local, of the present sentence in relation to the previous one, not in terms of how it might fit into the text as a whole. One strategy the researchers used to try to induce larger-scale planning was to provide the children with a final sentence for their composition. They report their best discussion, between 12-year-olds given the task of composing a story ending with the sentence 'And so, after considering the reasons for it and the reasons against it, the duke decided to rent his castle to the vampire after all, in spite of the rumour he had heard.' Discussion concentrated, unfortunately, on world-knowledge problems such as why a duke might consider renting his castle to a vampire, and on separate literary considerations ('this whole story is getting kinda dumb'), without managing to resolve the tension between the two. Most children stuck with the world-knowledge problems, and did not get on to the more abstract problems of creating a good story at all.

Constructing a complex story in a backwards direction is a difficult task, as indeed is doing so in a forwards one. A great many highly esteemed novels and stories consist essentially of a string of incidents which might well have been generated by a 'what next' strategy. *The Pickwick Papers* and *Don Quixote* could be seen as examples. The writers have however had in mind at least a unifying theme and possibly an overall shape to the novel which have subsumed the individual elements into what reads as a coherent whole. A sequential composition strategy such as children use works well in the context of an overall high level plan.

Revision

Experienced writers plan their texts: they also review and revise them. Children mostly fail to do so. 'Egocentrism' or attachment to one's own text is not an adequate explanation of this (or of many other childish foibles, see Cox 1980; Ford 1979), since children also fail to revise other people's productions. Revision requires a highly developed ability to correct and improve as well as to generate text, involving treating the output of the nth attempt at writing as input to be revised into the (n + 1)th attempt. Bereiter and Scardamalia (1982) argue that children do not have an internal feedback system to use in evaluating their text. Just as young speakers seem to have problems in distinguishing between what was meant and what was said (see Chapter 4), young writers find it hard to assess how well what is written conveys what is meant. As I have said, the writer does not have the feedback of incomprehension which the listener gives the speaker. If he or she also has no way of getting self-generated feedback which represents accurately what the reader would provide, there is very little prospect of diagnosing a need for revision, or, further, of acting appropriately to improve the text.

Scardamalia and Bereiter (1983) trained children aged 10–14 to evaluate each sentence of the text they had produced asking 'what's the main problem with this?' They had a list of evaluative phrases such as 'People won't see why this is important', 'I think this could be said more clearly', and 'I'm getting away from the main point', and a set of directive phrases such as 'I'd better give an example' or 'I'd better change the wording'. Even the youngest children could choose evaluative phrases which seemed appropriate judgements to adult experts' rating the text, and the children also said that the phrases were helpful and enabled them to review their writing in ways they did not feel they were able to do in their normal writing. However, the directives that the children chose did not appear to be helpful either in the view of the adult judges or in terms of the changes made in the text. There were more changes for the better than changes for the worse, but the revised essays were not on the whole noticeably better than the original ones.

These children were able to recognize problems in their texts but not to make effective revisions. In part this may be because their revisions seemed to be mainly of minor details, rather than changes which coped with major problems at levels nearer the whole text. Scardamalia and Bereiter suggest that

one likely cause is incompletely developed mental representations of actual and intended texts. These representations may be developed to the point where the child can detect that something is amiss, but not far enough for the child to discover what it is. This is analogous to the experience one may have in travelling somewhere over an indistinctly remembered route. One senses that things do not look right and therefore begins to suspect that one has taken a wrong turn, but the mental representation of how things should look is not sufficiently clear to indicate where the wrong turn might have been made, or even to establish definitely that one is off course. A common response in the travel situation is just to keep going and hope things will become clearer. This is what children seem to do in writing (Scardamalia and Bereiter 1983, p. 93).

It seems possible however that young writers who have the rather difficult and not quite clear task of producing a better approximation to the ideal text suffer from attention problems as well as a feeling of not knowing exactly what to do. They may have a repertoire of alternative phrasings but be mesmerized by the original version: words on the page often seem to take on a horrid inevitability. The alternative phrasings have to be thought of – the access to knowledge problem discussed above – and each evaluated in comparison with the others, which will place very formidable demands on memory and on the child's powers of switching between composing and criticizing. Again, Bereiter and Scardamalia (1982) suggest there may be some improvement through exercises such as highlighting the main idea of a sentence, planning the development of a passage, précis-making, reading with an eye open for technique and the various other activities that have been traditional parts of learning rhetoric.

These analyses of the demands and difficulties of planning, composing and revising may seem dry and more likely to stifle children's interest in writing than to increase it. It is certainly the case that the intrinsic interest of particular tasks often leads children to write with enormous enthusiasm and care, and at great length (see, for example, Steedman 1982). Often the spur seems to be an emotional drive from inside the child, a need to express and so control feelings about an important experience. Bereiter and Scardamalia's subjects however seemed to enjoy applying their skills to tasks they had not chosen, to value the craft skills they had learned for their own sake. Their feeling of having learned useful new techniques which they could use to win increased success on tasks which are highly esteemed is very reminiscent of what Griffiths and Wells (1983) report of English adults, that they did not feel competent as writers but that writing was important and necessary and they wished they did it better.

Children who are fluent writers

A number of children write for their own pleasure, producing a large opus of stories, poems, and non-fiction. How many such children there are is unknown. The Newsons (1976) found that 23 per cent of their sample of 7-year-olds 'wrote a lot' at home for pleasure: girls did so more than boys, and middle-class children more than working-class children. This, however, included writing domestic notes and letters, and copying words without much regard to their meaning. So far as creative writing is concerned, one expert I asked said at least 10 per cent and junior school teachers estimated that there would probably be a couple in each class. Habitual writing seems to be a feature of the early lives of literary figures far more often than not: the Brontë family, writing long chronicles of their imaginary islands, Jane Austen, writing a dramatization of her favourite novel *Sir Charles Grandison* and a burlesque History of England, and Edith Sitwell, composing poems and fairy stories, are typical examples. Some write as children but give it up in adulthood – Daisy Ashford followed *The Young Visiters* with some other novels, also parasites on the sort of novels by adults she was reading at the time, but as an adult published only writing done in childhood.

Children's writing reaches the world beyond the writer largely through adult attention. Secretive children who have a fair degree of personal space may not be known to be writers. Much writing which comes to the attention of parents (or teachers) gets no further. In terms of its literary merit this is not unreasonable, since much of what children write lacks the craft which would make it satisfactory reading to anyone at all distant from its producer. As Steedman (1982) cogently argues, however, adults often have ulterior motives for preserving and publishing children's writing. Literary merit *is* considered in some cases, particularly I think in texts concerned with how to teach writing. Parental pride is another fairly innocent motive. Very commonly, however, adults use children's writing to interpret children's development, much as they would also interpret their play, dreams and talk. They also select writing because it exemplifies what they believe is typical of childhood – in the mid nineteenth century, for example, childhood's innocence, transience and spirituality (Coveney 1967). Some is published because it amuses adults, its artlessness affording them relaxation, some because it provides a moral object lesson and edification. Adults may supervise and correct children's writing, and children may tailor their productions to the susceptibilities of adults. Given such multiform selection and censorship, the range of content, of style and of genre that children produce in their writing can probably not be discovered.

There are, however, examples which indicate what the range might be and allow some speculation about children as writers. The research of Donald Graves and his colleagues (Graves 1983; Calkins 1983) provides some material. Bissex (1980) published detailed observations of her son's writing (and reading) from age 5 to age 11. Paul Bissex wrote frequently, and used a considerable variety of forms; captions, stories, directions, catalogues, newspapers, messages, school-type exercises, rhymes, planned schedules, diaries and ultimately codes. Initially his writing's functions involved achieving competence in the act of writing, then sharing it with his parents, and using it to name the objects of his world, for example a sign on a cupboard door read:

PAULZ RABR SAF RABRZ KANT GT EN

(Paul's robber safe. Robbers can't get in.)

(The Zs are examples of his good phonetic spelling.)

As he grew older, he used his writing to categorize and organize the world, for example drawing up lists like this one (at age 8:7):

Hard words (to spell)

antidisestablishmenterianism

satisfaction	complicated	
carbonated	scientific	
corrosive	character	
exploition	exploraition	
developed	interesting	extinct
antimated	fictional	puncuation
individual	annahilliated	
irrataitional	antimated	intellectual

He wrote newspapers, poems, stories with inventive plots, developed styles appropriate to the recipient of his letters, and showed rather the same preferences in his writing as in his reading. Throughout, being literate was important to him and a source of great enjoyment.

Steedman (1982) presents a rather different example. She discusses one main text, a story called *The Tidy House*, produced by three 8-year-old girls over a week in 1976. The characters of the story are two couples and their children: the plot 'is simple: it is concerned with the getting and regretting of children', with how to bring them up and with what life is like in 'the tidy house'. The story is interesting in the literary devices used but also for the picture it provides of these little girls' understanding of domestic life. In her extensive discussion, Steedman argues that producing the text was a way of confronting the social system they lived in, so far as this could be done by children who were captive both in the classroom and in the sort of lives they were describing. It is perhaps significant that the last page of *The Tidy House* ends in mid sentence, thus:

soon they went home and had tea and went to bed and

At 8, it may not be altogether easy to accept or to reject a future consisting of loving children who cry and whine. These working-class girls display in their writing and their commentary on it a consciousness of their families' lives which must dispel any belief that children's social understanding is egocentric or naïve, and also a sophistication in their planning and revision of text which corrects some theorists' emphasis on children's disorderly production of writing.

Arithmetical skills

Having sketched the development of reading and writing, I want now to look at children's arithmetical skills. This is a busy research area at present, with many fine-grained analyses of mathematical tasks. Mayer (1985) provides a brief introduction to this work: among the important collections of papers are books edited by

Brainerd (1982), Ginsberg (1983) and Lesh and Landau (1983). I will discuss some aspects of the development of number concepts and their role in children's handling of addition and subtraction. I will try throughout to bring together task analytic approaches, ecological work on children's spontaneous mathematics and considerations of mathematical language.

Learning number words

One rather basic aspect of using numbers is knowing number words, their names. Observations of pre-school children at home and at school show that they quite frequently encounter number words and number word sequences in nursery rhymes, songs, and adult conversation (see, for example, Tizard and Hughes 1984; Davie *et al.* 1984). Adults often make use of opportunities to use numbers; parents may deliberately teach their children to 'count' in the senses both of reciting number words and of applying those words in finding out how many objects there are. Fuson and Hall (1983) find that a majority of children can count to twenty or so by the time they are 5, and most can count to one hundred by the age of 6 given moderate practice in school.

In English, number words are regularly structured from the teens, with a units part, a 'decades' part and a hundreds or thousands part as appropriate. Thus 1986 is 'one thousand, nine hundred, eighty, six' (or 'nineteen hundred, eighty, six'); '35' is 'thirty, five'; and so on. The number names up to the teens have to be learned more or less by rote, as do the names of the decades; the rest can be generated by rule. Children's learning of number names seems to be initially by rote. It is usually after they have learned to recite the sequence beyond twenty that they realize there is a repetition of 'something-one, something-two' and so on, and after they have grasped the sequence to one hundred that they can really generate numbers iteratively *ad infinitum* (Siegler and Robinson 1982). Understanding zero and infinity (and negative numbers, fractions, etc.) comes of course later still.

Counting

Knowing the number words is not, as Piaget (1952) pointed out, the most important part of number concepts. Number words have to be matched to countable objects if the child is to 'count'. Accurate counting requires that each and every object must be tagged with one and only one number word. To do this, objects and words have to be kept in step, and objects have to be repeatedly and accurately divided into 'already counted' and 'not yet counted' groups. Children often use pointing or touching or moving objects to help themselves do this correctly: rhythms in the counting may also help. There is quite a lot of evidence (Fuson and Hall 1983) that children's counting does mostly allocate one number word to one object; it is less clear whether children regard this as a necessary principle of counting as Gelman and Gallistel (1978) suggested. They do not always use the conventional number sequence; young children's number lists are often idiosyncratic with an initial conventional and correct sequence such as 'one, two, three' followed by a stable but unconventional portion 'five, eight, nine, eleven' and a final non-stable portion which varies from occasion to occasion.

Having applied a stable list to the countable objects in a one to one fashion, the last number used indicates the numerosity of the set: its cardinal number. Adults can produce the cardinal number for small sets (up to four) and very well learned larger sets (such as the configurations on dominoes and playing cards) very quickly and without counting. This capacity is known as 'subitizing'. It is possible that young children can also subitize small sets of two or three items. It is however hard to distinguish between rapid covert counting and pattern recognition or 'subitizing' (see Gelman and Gallistel 1978, pp. 64–8, 219–25; and Fuson and Hall, pp. 59–61): until it is clearer exactly what subitizing consists of, it will be difficult to find out how counting and subitizing are related in development.

To find out how many objects there are in a set, one should count them and then report the last number used which is the cardinal word for that set. Young children often fail to report the last number, but when they have counted the set aloud they may be expecting the experimenter to realize that the last number said while counting is intended as the answer; it is indeed somewhat disingenuous of the experimenter to require further telling. It appears that most middle-class children do repeat their last counting word with added emphasis to indicate that it is their answer by the age of 4 (Fuson and Hall 1983). Appreciating that you would get the same cardinal number for *any* correct count of the objects in any order is a rather later achievement, as Piaget pointed out years ago, and as in the case of his mathematician friend (p. 33) it may be an exciting thing to realize. It is of course an achievement which depends on accurate counting: if your procedure in counting is a bit shaky, you may get a different numerosity each time and not realize the source of the variation.

Comparing numerical quantities

Although there are possible comparisons of numbers implicit in producing strings of number names and in counting a single set of objects, once there are two (or more) sets there are inevitably comparisons which involve judgements of more, less, fewer, same, equal, greater than, etc. Siegel (1978) reviews studies of children's problems with these terms. One source of confusion is that comparatives are correlated in the natural world: certainly when comparing sets of the same objects, the longer line does more often than not have more in, or the taller heap contain more objects. Sorting out the comparative dimensions, deciding that 'less' is *not* a synonym for 'more' (Donaldson and Balfour 1981) and sorting out exactly which entities are being compared (Siegel *et al.* 1978) seem to be among the harder preliminaries to making a comparison.

Up to a point, perceptual comparison strategies may give quite successful results. If numbers are small, or if there is a big difference between the sets to be compared, or if an approximate answer will do, relative judgements work quite well, and young children use them quite readily (Bryant 1974). They work less well

with exact comparisons between larger sets nearer in size, and do not work at all of course on number symbols: 71 is not obviously bigger than 48. New strategies therefore have to be developed, and the old ones given up, which, as we have seen, is difficult.

One possibility is matching each item in one set with an item from the other: if a set has one or more items left over after this procedure it has more items. The evidence reviewed by Fuson and Hall (1983) suggests that if children have perceptual cues like touching, moving and linking with drawn-in lines (techniques which also helped with counting, as we saw in the previous section), they can use matching to establish relative numerosity by the age of about 6. If matching is perceptually harder fewer children use it (Brainerd 1979).

Another possible strategy for establishing relative numerosities is of course counting. If the cardinal numbers of sets are the same, they are equal in quantity: if not, the *order* of the cardinal numbers in the sequence of number words shows which set has more and which fewer items in it – at least to someone who knows the number sequence and that if number a comes before number b then number a is smaller than number b. (Exactly how children make these order judgements is still controversial (Fuson and Hall 1983, pp. 93–8; Siegler and Robinson 1982, pp. 267–86). They are probably easier to make if the smaller number is very small and the gap between the numbers is large: Siegler and Robinson suggest that there is categorization of the number sequence into smallest, small, medium and big numbers. Pre-schoolers judge nine to be a big number in all contexts: adults judge it to be a big number in the context of one to ten but not in the context of one to a million.)

Counting may be of two separate sets existing simultaneously, or of one set before and after a transformation. In the classic number conservation test, both comparisons are involved. It is a well-replicated finding that children who have counted both sets before the transformation, and agreed that they are equivalent, will deny that same equivalence when one set of counters is spread out, even though they may count again and reach the same numbers. Nevertheless, counting does help in conservation of number tasks (Siegler 1981; Klahr and Wallace 1976). It is presumably *not* used as the best cue to numerosity in conservation when the child has a strong perceptual strategy and a low level of confidence in his or her own ability to count accurately.

Ordinal numbers

We have discussed using numbers to find the numerosity of a set or the relative sizes of several sets. Numbers can also be used to describe relative positions within a set: I am the fourth of my parents' children, the second tallest woman in my department, an inhabitant of the seventh largest city in England. Children do learn ordinal words

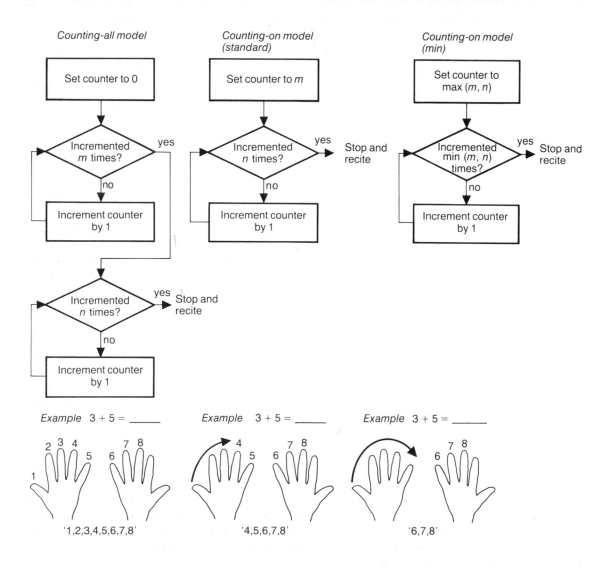

Figure 13 Three counting models for simple addition of $m + n$.

Source: From Mayer (1985), p. 141.

such as these, but some time after they have learned the conventional counting sequence, and probably the ordinal number sequence becomes systematic and iterative through school practice. Using the ordinal words to refer to the correct items of an ordered set – indicating the third, fifth or whatever item – is also difficult. Putting items in order of size or some other physical quality is something pre-school children enjoy doing, though as Piaget's seriation experiments show they may stick at comparisons of pairs of objects and not systematically complete an ordered set (Piaget 1952). They find it easier to identify the smallest and largest or first and last of a set than the 'middle-sized' or 'next to last' one (Siegel 1972, 1978). How ordinal number development is related to cardinal number development is not known: ordinal number development may lag behind because it is ecologically less common (though ordinal numbers are used daily in the calendar) or because its vocabulary is acquired later or both.

Doing addition and subtraction

There has been a great deal of work recently on children's strategies for adding and subtracting numbers. There are a number of useful reviews of the area, including Carpenter, Moser and Romberg 1982, Carpenter and Moser 1983, Resnick 1983 and Siegler and Robinson 1982. Children's most basic strategy is to construct sets of physical objects or fingers to represent the two numbers to be added, move the two sets together and then *count all* the joint set from one to the total. A more sophisticated (and quicker) strategy is to *count on* from the cardinal number of the first set through the members of the second set to the total number of the combined set. More efficiently still, the child may count on from the larger number through the smaller set to the total – the *counting on (min)* algorithm. These three algorithms are shown in Figure 13.

Reaction time evidence (Groen and Parkman 1972) suggests that in their first year of school children use the counting-on (min) algorithm, as it took longer to reach the correct answer if the minimum addend was two than if the minimum

addend was one and so on. The mean response times for 1 + 6 and 6 + 1 were identical and over a second shorter than the mean response times for 3 + 4 and 4 + 3, for example. 'Double' sums such as 1 + 1 and 2 + 2 were notably easy: this probably reflects a fourth strategy for coping with addition, the memorization of number facts. Resnick (1983) suggests that adults do most of their addition and subtraction by using mental shortcuts such as using memorized number facts and repartitioning numbers to fit well-learned facts (for example turning 18 + 23 into 18 + 2 + 21). Even in the early school years, as Groen and Parkman's data show, children use these strategies (Figure 14). These addition strategies form a hierarchy which most children pass through in one way or another before reaching automatic response.

Carpenter and Moser (1983) describe similar strategies for coping with subtraction problems. A concrete strategy is *separating from*; making a set of the larger numerosity, separating from it the smaller number and counting the remainder. This is an enactment of phrasings such as '5 take away 3', which Conroy (1984) found to be the preferred and easiest phrasing for Australian 6 to 13-year-olds. There is a parallel counting strategy called *Counting Down From*; the child counts backwards starting with the larger number for as many number words as the given smaller number. The last number in the counting sequence is the correct answer.

Other strategies include starting with the smaller number and *counting up* until the larger one is reached: the number of objects added is the answer. The most efficient of all strategies is to combine counting down and counting up to involve the minimum action: for example, counting down from eight is the quickest way to solve 8 – 2, while counting up from six is the quickest way to solve 8 – 6. As I said when discussing addition, using number facts supersedes these counting strategies to a considerable extent.

The early language of arithmetic

We have seen that children as young as 5 know that adding increases quantity and subtracting

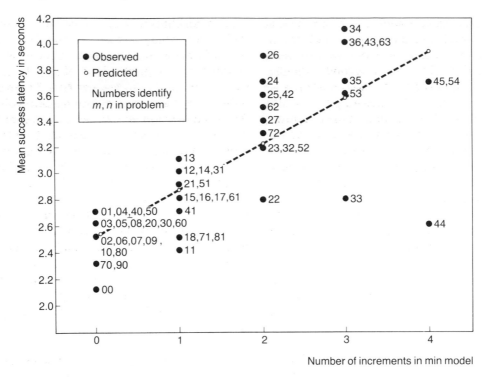

Figure 14 Response time depends on the number of increments required in the min model. Number pairs represent the two numbers to be added; e.g. 13 means 1 + 3.

Source: From Groen and Parkman (1972).

decreases it, are able to recite number names, and quickly learn ways of quantifying addition and subtraction. They have a good understanding of some of the language expressions of addition and subtraction, mainly the more concrete forms. For example, the 4-year-old boy recorded by Martin Hughes does very well with concrete questions but does not translate his knowledge into an abstract number system at all:

Adult   How many is two and one more?

Child   Four

Adult   Well, how many is two *lollypops* and one more?

Child   Three

Adult   How many is two *elephants* and one more?

Child   Three

Adult   How many is two *giraffes* and one more?

Child   Three

Adult   So how many is *two* and one more?

Child   (looks adult straight in the eye) Six.

(Hughes 1983, p. 211)

One of the things this child has to learn is the formal code of arithmetic, for example 'one' and 'two' used alone rather than with accompanying nouns as in 'one elephant' and 'two elephants'; 'and' as a synonym for 'plus'; 'is' (or 'makes') as synonymous for 'equals'. Corran and Walkerdine (1981) point out that children rarely learn this formal code from adults before school, and also that the different ways of saying a string of mathematical symbols such as 5 + 2 = 7 are not trivially different. 'Five and two *makes* seven' for example emphasizes the addition, the production of 7 from 5 and 2: 'Five plus two *equals* seven' emphasizes the equivalence of the two sides of the equation. To take a second example, Coleman 1982 lists various 'translations' of '8 − 5 = ?' – 'take 5 from 8', 'reduce 8 by 5', 'by how much greater is 8 than 5', 'what is the difference between 8 and 5' and so on. These seemed to reflect different ideas about what subtraction meant and how to do it. Conroy 1984 looked at children's success rate on different orally presented subtraction sums; 6-year-olds got 'what is 2 less than 8' right only 21 per cent of the time ('8 − 2 = ?' was right 67 per cent of the time) and 'what is 7 take away 5' right 70 per cent of the time ('7 − 5 = ?' was right 76 per cent of the time). How children translate from symbols to metaphoric language and vice versa can be seen to affect the solution procedures they use, as I shall describe. At some time the child has to reach a level of fluency and flexibility in using these terms that allows recognition that they are interchangeable verbal forms for the one symbolic statement.

Hughes (1983) gave 5 to 7-year-olds the task of showing on paper how many bricks there were on the table. They found this easy, drawing the objects or an equivalent number of tallies or writing the appropriate conventional number. They were also asked to show what happened when a few more bricks were added or subtracted. Most just drew the final number of bricks: there were a few attempts to represent initial number, final number and what had been added on or subtracted, for example by showing hands adding bricks or putting bricks away in the box, or the ingenious if slow strategy of drawing a line of British soldiers marching from left to right to represent added bricks, and a line of Japanese soldiers marching from right to left to represent subtracted ones. Not one of the seventy-two children tested used the conventional operator signs of + and −, although they were using them regularly in their arithmetic lessons, and, if they were comparable with Conroy's children, probably using them correctly most of the time.

Resnick (1982, 1983), examines subtracting algorithms and 'bugs', the errors which arise from

using algorithms in ways which violate some of their rules. Many of the bugs she describes resulted from failure to understand the meaning of subtraction, and particularly of how to manage subtraction problems such as 61 − 37 which require 'carrying' between tens and units columns. As such understandings became more secure and children's algorithms became more flexible, children could combine different operations to produce an answer and then check it, thus debugging themselves. How their informal self-generated strategies map on to the formal skills taught in mathematics lessons needs further research. So does the question of the extent, nature and causes of individual differences in arithmetic skills. It seems probable that a lack of matching between informal and formal mathematics is one important component of poor mathematical achievement. So are metacognitive skills.

Some further developments in mathematics
I have been describing what children do at the beginning of their work with numbers, and we have been dealing with small numerical quantities, mostly below ten. Dealing with larger numbers – 'hundreds, tens and units' – also has to be managed. This involves consideration of the base ten number system, computations using written versions of it, and crucially, a recognition that numbers can be interpreted as made up of other smaller numbers: 35 = 30 + 5 = 20 + 15 and so forth. There has been quite a lot of research on how children learn to manage more advanced forms of addition and subtraction (e.g. Resnick 1982, 1983) partly because difficulties are frequently found. Lesh and Landau (1983) also provide material on children's handling of proportions, fractions, geometrical concepts and algebraic problems. As was the case with simple addition and subtraction, children need to understand both the 'reality context' of the calculation, its mathematic structure and the appropriate algorithms, and to relate all these, if they are to work successfully. A great deal more research ideally involving collaboration between mathematicians, psychologists and educators, is needed.

Metacognition

'Metacognition refers to one's knowledge and control of the domain cognition' (Brown *et al.* 1983, p. 106). It thus involves a range of different psychological contents. Among them would be awareness of cognition, of understanding or not understanding, remembering or forgetting, at a particular moment; knowledge about one's own cognitive skills and about a task's difficulties ('I won't be able to do this because I can't remember how to do square roots'); and regulation of cognition, for example planning how to do a task, monitoring progress on it, checking the solution. Some of this metacognitive knowledge is stable and stateable, though it may not be objectively true. For example, I would know all the time that I remember epigrams rather badly and the general meaning of a play or novel quite well, and that in order to record the detail I should make a note of it. Some metacognition is much harder to describe and much harder to employ stably and systematically; as the introspectionist psychologists found long ago, people who reported on their thinking while they were working on a problem found their thinking disrupted (Valentine 1982, Russell 1984).

Recently, metacognition has taken a prominent place in discussion of cognition and cognitive development. This is partly because of the influence of the information-processing models of cognition which I briefly reviewed in the previous chapter (see also Klahr and Wallace 1976; Siegler 1981; Sternberg 1984; Case 1985). The concept of a central executive system which controls cognitive processes has been a powerful metaphor for developmentalists, who see cognition as becoming increasingly skilled and controlled as development and education proceed. Another reason for the rise of metacognition has been Piaget's emphasis that it is the child's awareness of a problem in his or her thinking which is crucial for cognitive development: a contradiction between two of my schemes of thought forces me to develop a resolution between them, or conflict between my thought and yours makes each of us review thinking we were previously complacent about.

A number of questions have been asked, then, about the development of metacognition. I will outline some of the relevant areas of research, and then briefly address the implications of this work for theories of cognition and for educational intervention. The sections of this chapter which discuss remembering and comprehension also contain relevant material.

Sources of metacognitive experiences

When do children know that they don't know? What effect does such an experience have? Piaget believed that experiences of knowing that you had contradictory ideas or that your ideas contradicted someone else's were common even in young children and served as one of the important pressures towards cognitive development. Autonomous regulation of thought, automatic small adjustments of actions, were inherent in cognitive activity: conscious reflection on thought was a late achievement. Awareness of the intended outcome and discrepancies from it comes much earlier than awareness of what exactly is wrong. Thus children might be expected to know that there was a contradiction without knowing what to do about it and without being able to take appropriate action (Piaget 1976, 1978). It can be very difficult to make this progress.

Experiments by Karmiloff-Smith and Inhelder (1974/5) illustrate one way in which the development is made. They gave 4 to 9-year-olds the task of balancing blocks of wood on a narrow bar. The simplest strategy was to use physical trial and error, nudging the blocks on to the balancing point: slow but successful. This strategy was, however, supplanted by simple theories which worked for some blocks but not for others, for example to balance the block by the geometric centre, which was successful for uniform blocks but not for ones with an uneven distribution of weight. These latter gave rise to an alternative theory, so the child operated two juxtaposed theories without co-ordinating them. Constructing a higher level procedure, which combined the simpler theories and left no exceptions, was slow and painful in that it gave rise to more errors as it was developed than its predecessors had done. Simple theories applied perfectly to a limited set of blocks: those blocks the theory couldn't cover were rejected as 'impossible to balance', until there were an intolerably large number of exceptions. Philosophers of science have observed a similar reluctance in professional scientists to take on board the accumulating instances which the present theory cannot incorporate (Kuhn 1962).

Social conflict as a source of metacognitive development

Another source of metacognitive conflict which Piaget emphasized is disagreement with peers. Experiments by Doise and his colleagues deal with this area (Doise and Mugny 1984). They have used various Piagetian paradigms. Pairs of children are required to reach agreement on a task organized so that they are likely to begin by giving contradictory answers. For example, in a conservation of length task, each child might judge the stick that came nearer to himself or herself to be longer than the one nearer the other child: thus their two judgements are contradictory, since it cannot be the case that both sticks are 'longer'. (In fact, of course, in the standard conservation test *both* children are wrong as the sticks are identical in length.)

Children who have experience of this sort of conflicting judgement often do better when working with the other child than they did on the pre-test, and the improvement may carry over to the post-test when they are alone again. The child is more likely to learn from conflict with peers if he or she already has some grasp of the principles involved in the task, and if there has been real involvement in the situation rather than a desultory partial attention. It is not necessary for one child to give the correct answer: evident conflict between two wrong answers also leads children to realize that they need to rethink their answer. Research by Emler and Valiant (1982) suggests that intra-individual conflict, confronting the child with a previous contradictory answer, can also induce metacognitive progress.

However, it has to be stressed that awareness of conflict is not quite the same as awareness of

contradiction, and knowing how to resolve the disagreement is something else again. There is some evidence that young children treat judgements of size as being much like judgements of preference: 'You think this one's more, I think that one's more' is regarded as the same sort of situation as 'You like this one, I like that one' (Russell 1981a, 1981b, 1982). Children who have some understanding of the physical principles of Piagetian tasks such as conservation are less likely to make this sort of mistake.

Beyond awareness to diagnosing the problem

One source of evidence on children's ability to diagnose the problem which is giving them a feeling of not having understood is the work on comprehension monitoring referred to on p. 83. Children may not be terribly good at reporting text comprehension problems but they do show some behavioural indices of comprehension monitoring, such as pausing and frowning (Brown *et al.* 1983, pp. 114–16). Another body of information comes from studies of verbal communication. Robinson (1983) reviews work in this area, much of it her own. Typically children are given an ambiguous message, for example one where the main referent is not specified sufficiently so that more than one object might be referred to, although only one particular one is meant. Thus the child might be told to pick 'the man with the red hat' when more than one red-hatted man was available, or told to use 'a big brick' next to construct a building when there are several 'big' bricks of different colours and shapes. Young children tend to act on such messages with great confidence that they have understood what was meant: when things go wrong they are likely to say it was the listener's fault for not listening properly. Older children, like adults, blame the speaker for giving an imprecise message, and say that more exact information should have been given.

It seems likely that this can be related to the ecology of the small child's life. Examination of the tapes from the Bristol Language Development Study suggested that when adults met an ambiguous utterance from a pre-school child they tended to guess what the child probably meant. Thus if the child said 'wanna drink' the adult's response was 'do you want some orange?' or 'orange or Ribena?'; thus the adult took responsibility for constructing a clear message. A few adults said things like 'I don't know what you mean. Tell me what you want to drink': *all* the children who were relatively precocious speaker-blamers had had this sort of treatment from their mothers (Robinson and Robinson 1981). Many children, however, must be told 'you haven't listened', 'now listen carefully', and so forth.

One of the important points that arises from considering how ambiguity and confusion arise in real life (by which I mean outside tests of cognitive development) is that they are frequent and that not all confusions are important enough to need noticing, let alone resolving. Often someone else will cope, as in the example where the adult listener takes responsibility for clarifying the child's ambiguous message. Or one may understand a concept very adequately for day-to-day purposes but not be familiar with all its more technical manifestations. Or ambiguity and contradiction may be deliberately employed as a literary or rhetorical device. At least in this last case, the point may be precisely in the pointing of levels of contradictory meaning. What 'conflicts' are diagnosed as, and how they are resolved, is an important question for research in the development of children's thinking (Rotman 1977).

Knowing what to do about a cognitive problem
There is an extensive literature now on children's knowledge about how to tackle cognitive problems: among useful reviews are Brown *et al.* 1983, Cavanaugh and Perlmutter 1982, Flavell and Wellman 1977, and Robinson 1983. There is also relevant discussion on memory, text construction and comprehension and awareness of language elsewhere in this chapter. One basic finding is that older children know more about their cognition than younger ones do. There is disagreement about the age at which children begin to make deliberate efforts to remember, notice text contradictions, plan their stories and so forth, partly because it is not always clear what are

reliable indices of such behaviour, and partly because the early stages of strategies or skills typically involve fragmentary and spasmodic use. Thus, as in the Piagetian literature, when evidence that children cannot do X until they are M + 2 years old is followed by evidence that on the contrary children can do x when they are only M years old, we need to examine very carefully the relationship between X and x. Babies may distinguish between two beats at a time and three, but is that the same as the adult's recognition of two and three? (Gelman 1982).

A more interesting question than the age one is how to describe the differences between the young child who does not use a metacognitive strategy and the older child who does. One possible description is the novice-expert dimension (Brown and de Loache 1978; Shatz 1978). Novices lack the necessary skills for a task and probably also an adequate 'feel' for the task as a whole. As managing the component parts of the task takes up all the available processing space in the early stages, there is little opportunity for metacognitive activity such as deliberate self-regulation. As the task parts become more familiar and take their places in the whole task, there will be more space for metacognition, and the learner can step back, consider the way the entire problem is going and make his or her performance more systematic and better organized. The children I described doing the balance task set them by Karmiloff-Smith and Inhelder (1974/5) seem to follow this pattern. Children will constantly be novices on tasks where adults have become experts with many more well-learned routines. Task familiarity will be a crucial variable (Shatz 1978).

It seems likely however that adults will not just have learned many routines well enough to find it easy to perform the routines and to think about them; they may also have developed more generalized metacognitive skills which they can transfer flexibly from task to task. Thus although the specifics of a task may be equally new to child and adult, the latter may both have a better sense of what sort of task this is, more knowledge of his or her own capabilities and more general routines for controlling his or her performance. (On the other hand, he or she may have acquired more emotional blocks to learning – 'you can't teach an old dog new tricks', 'I'm too old to handle micro-computers'.) Child 'novice' and adult 'novice' cannot be assumed to be the same.

Making metacognitive progress

One difficulty in giving an account of how and why children's metacognition develops is that much of the research is cross-sectional, establishing that children of, say, 5 do not have a particular metacognitive skill and children of, say, 9, do. This approach tells us nothing directly about the mechanisms of the change. Training studies, however, provide one way in to cognitive change, particularly if we compare successful training strategies with the events that occur in children's normal upbringing. Brown *et al.* (1983, pp. 129–46) review studies which have attempted to train 'learning skills'.

Inducing subjects to use a strategy *without* any explanation of why the strategy was important or an explicit noting that it was effective, generally led to improved performance on the task while the strategy was being used, but little transfer to other tasks, and the strategy might be given up even for the target task once the experimenter stopped reminding the subject to use it. Experiments by Whittaker (1983) illustrate this. He set up paradigms for memory tasks which forced the child to recognize the difference between performance using the strategy and performance without it: this greatly increased children's persistence in using the strategy.

Providing subjects with information about the importance and effectiveness of the activity that they're being trained to use greatly enhances the prospect of them continuing to use it and transferring it to other tasks. This sort of information seems to be particularly necessary for retarded children who rarely show spontaneous transfer of learning. Convincing information about why it is worth using a particular strategy presumably increases people's motivation to use that strategy. Metacognitive activity requires some effort on the part of the thinker, and if there are limitations on 'thinking space' (see Chapter 2) it may seem to be too much bother or not worth the effort. Demonstration that it does enhance performance and produce rewards greater than its initial cost may make it more likely to be used.

Children are, in practice, rarely given explicit metacognitive training of the sort used in the intervention studies reviewed by Brown *et al.* (1983). However they do have some opportunities to see older people making special efforts to remember, plan, review their learning and so forth. Such activities are probably more common at school than at home but do occur there too, particularly perhaps in conversations between the child and older people (Tizard and Hughes 1984). It seems likely that parents undertake some of the responsibility for their child's metacognition. One example is the joint activity of looking at books, where mothers often say to their 2-year-old things like 'I know you know that one', 'We'll find you something you know very well' (Ninio and Bruner 1978). Mothers are often used as a memory by their children (e.g. Kail 1979), as well as modelling external memory devices such as the use of shopping lists, which children understand well (Istomina 1975). Nursery rhymes and stories also provide obvious opportunities for metacognitive activities. The adult gradually hands over to the child more and more responsibility for the success of the activity. There is some reason to believe that children whose parents go in for quite a lot of *explicit* modelling of metacognitive and metalinguistic behaviour become advanced in their learning of these skills (e.g. Robinson and Robinson in press; Mills and Funnell 1983; Brown *et al.* 1983). We do not at present know exactly what effects parents' metacognitive behaviour has, or how those effects come about, and we certainly cannot conclude that the more metacognitive modelling there is the better. I do, however, propose that we should take very seriously the hypothesis that one important aspect of metacognitive development is a progress from cognition supported by, and regulated by, other people more skilled than oneself, to cognition which is relatively independent and self-regulated. To quote Brown *et al.* (1983, p. 124) mature thinkers are those who provide conflict trials for themselves, practice thought experiments, question their own basic assumptions, provide counter examples to their own rules, and so on. Although a great deal of thinking and learning may remain a social activity, mature reasoners become capable of providing the supportive-other role for themselves....

Social cognition

Most of the work on cognitive development deriving from the Piagetian or information-processing tradition centres on an individual thinker trying to understand the objective physical world. Lately, an interest has grown in an area which poses alternatives to each half of this individualist model, and centres on the thinking individual whose thinking comes from interaction with other individuals as much as from within himself or herself, or on individuals' thinking about the subjective social and interpersonal world. It is this newly important area which is called 'social cognition'. It is a diverse field, including, for example, the effects of social conflict on performance of conservation tasks, children's descriptions of 'friends', the role of emotion in understanding other people, children's ideas about techniques for achieving social goals such as joining groups, the use of social 'scripts', and children's theories of how social institutions work. There is much debate about conceptual and methodological issues, and not as yet a unifying theory (indeed only a high level theory could unify so wide an area): I will not attempt to do more than discuss selected work in the field. For reviews see Isbell and McKee 1980, Shantz 1983, Flavell and Ross 1981, Butterworth and Light 1982, and Forgas 1981.

Cognitive development as a social process
There is no room for doubt that children's cognitive development takes place within a social world and is influenced by other people. Children use other people's knowledge in their own development: the ways that other people treat the child shape his or her cognition not just about people but about many aspects of the non-human

world. Knowledge and influence come not just from the micro-system, as I shall describe, but from the wider social world. Religious teaching, for example, was a significant factor in the historical development of thinking about the relationship between Man and Nature (Thomas 1984). The questions that need to be answered are not about *whether* social interaction influences cognitive development but *when* and *how* it does.

Piaget placed his main emphasis on the dialectic between the child and the physical world, but included social interaction as a motivator of development, particularly through conflict of ideas between peers. Discussion and criticism involving peers forced the child to 'decentre', to resolve the contradictions between different viewpoints or opinions. Recently Doise and his colleagues in Geneva have carried out a series of studies on the effects of peer interaction on children's performance of Piagetian tasks (Doise and Mugny 1984). They paired children on conservation and perspective taking tasks set up in such a way that the children would disagree on the answer. This conflict led to more advanced judgements on subsequent tasks, provided that the children had the beginnings of a grasp of the principles underlying the correct answer. Children with no understanding at all of conservation or whatever were likely to treat the disagreement with the peer as a matter of disagreement over some subjective preference (Russell 1981, 1982; Light 1983): that is, there was an interaction between metacognition and ability to learn from social interaction.

There has been some debate about whether inter-individual conflict is a better motivator of cognitive development than either intra-individual conflict (children seeing that their present judgement is incompatible with their previous one) or inter-individual co-operation. Self-contradiction has seemed to be as effective in inducing cognitive development as other-contradiction (Emler and Valiant 1982), though Doise and Mackie 1981 argue that such situations are in fact socially produced (by the experimenter or another adult 'setting up' the child) or that the child may have 'decentred' enough to treat his or her previous and present views as objective and thus contrastable. In Chapter 2 I touched on the difficulties of knowing how to resolve a conflict and pointed out that recognizing its existence does not in fact solve the problem. Co-operation with another person, on the other hand, may both provide new information and confirmation of the participants' ideas where they agree (Bryant 1982). This sort of behaviour by adults does seem to advance cognitive development (Vygotsky 1978; Bruner 1968; Mills and Funnell 1983; Wood 1980; and see Chapters 2, 5 and 6). While children are developing cognitive skills and models within an area, commentary by other more expert people which helps to integrate the developing thinking into a coherent whole may serve to support the novice's understanding. Such behaviour seems to lead to the optimum cognitive development if it is contingent on the child's behaviour and interest (Mills and Funnell 1983), and if it is a reflection of the expert's expertise rather than his or her misunderstandings!

Children's understanding of the properties of persons and objects

'Social cognition' implies a distinction between social and non-social, between persons and other objects. Exactly what is the basis for such a distinction is a matter of some debate, particularly in contentious areas such as whether non-human animals or complex computers are 'persons' (Midgley 1979; Searle 1984). The central criteria seem to be:

– persons are *agents*, that is they are capable of initiating actions, while objects can only move if something or someone else initiates the action

– persons know, think, learn and have emotions, while objects do not

– persons are alive, that is they develop and reproduce themselves

– persons typically act and react in a wider variety of ways than objects do, thus they may be less predictable.

Some of Piaget's early work (Piaget 1929, 1930) showed children attributing animate characteristics, such as independent movement, to inanimate objects, such as bicycles or the moon. This he called 'animistic thinking', and it was supposed to be a pervasive feature of 'pre-operational' children's thought. More recently, a number of studies have failed to find much animistic thinking even in 3-year-olds. Shields and Duveen 1982, for example, asked nursery-school children which of a farmer, a cow, a tractor and a tree could eat, sleep, move by itself, talk, feel angry, and so forth. The children's answers drew a clear distinction between the tractor and the tree, which could not do any of these things, and the farmer and the cow which could. (There was some disagreement over whether cows could talk or have emotions, but children who claimed they could, maintained that cows talked with other cows or the farmer, 'talk' being extended slightly to mean 'communicate'.) Similarly, studies reviewed by Gelman and Spelke (1981, pp. 48–51) suggest that children as young as 2 may make some adult-type distinctions between animate and inanimate objects if the objects are familiar to them and if the questions asked are fairly straightforward. Some of Piaget's animistic answers may have stemmed, it is argued, from asking problematic questions like 'Does the sun know where it is moving?' *Explaining* difficult phenomena, however, may draw out animistic reasons: some of Shields and Duveen's subjects, like some of Piaget's, said that the wind was caused by the voluntary movement of the trees.

A distinction between animate and inanimate objects, and between people and other animate objects, seems to be discernible in quite young children. It is not entirely clear what the distinction is based on and we have only speculation at present as to how it is built up in the first three years of life. One probable source is no doubt differences in the ways persons act on the child and react to his or her actions compared with the actions and reactions of objects. Careful analysis of the lives of babies and toddlers would perhaps inform us about this.

Children's understanding of people

Research on the development of children's understanding of people is one of the largest bodies of work in the social cognition area. It has been heavily influenced by Piaget's theory that children are egocentric, that is that they are unable to appreciate that other people have knowledge, feelings or views different from their own. The notion of 'egocentricity' no longer seems as credible as it once did in the light of evidence that even very young children can and often do show a practical understanding of other people's feelings and knowledge (see p. 157). There is also a strong probability that children operate an intricate social world with, on the whole, about as much success as adults, which again suggests they have a fair understanding of their familiar peers and adults (see p. 192). Nevertheless, it is possible that the understanding which manifests itself in successful interpersonal action does develop. What evidence is there?

Shantz (1983) and Rogers (1978) review studies where children were asked to describe or judge people's behaviour. One of the best known of these is work by Livesley and Bromley (1973). They elicited free descriptions from each of their 7 to 15-year-old subjects of eight people personally known to the subject. They found that the younger children's descriptions were predominantly in 'peripheral' and 'external' terms, such as appearance, age, and surroundings. As children got older, their descriptions become more abstract and involved more inferences about stable psychological traits, initially rather global ones such as 'nice' or 'good', but gradually with more qualifications and balances. This sort of picture, initial descriptions which are mostly concrete and based on behaviour and later descriptions which are more abstract and in terms of psychological dispositions, emerges from most studies which have used this sort of approach (Shantz 1983; Rogers 1978).

They have been taken as indicating that young children have a poor understanding of other people and older children a better one. Abstract decriptions based on generalized dispositions may allow more general predictions than specific concrete descriptions do: if this is the case, and it is still a debatable issue in personality theory (see, for example, Cook 1984), the development of person perception may be from poor to better. However, it is not really very clear how well children's free descriptions represent their ideas about people. Describing people is a different activity from engaging in social interaction with them, and may not use the same information. There are also likely to be problems of interpreting what is meant, particularly with children whose vocabulary is limited and who may not mean by a particular term what an adult would mean by it. Research which uses more probing and more rating scales may be needed, even if such methods do restrict subjects. A study by Flapan, which Rogers (1978) describes, apparently found responses to questions were more sophisticated than free descriptions.

Children's attributional judgements

Young children do seem to be rather less likely than older ones to infer inner psychological dispositions from outward behaviour: there also seem to be some differences in what evidence they use when making attributional judgements about the causes of an event. Attribution theory (Heider 1958; Kelley 1979; Ross 1981; see also Chapters 5 and 6) distinguishes between personal causal factors, such as a person's timidity, and impersonal causal factors, such as the size and muscularity of the threatening opponent, which come into consideration when decisions have to be made about questions such as whether it should be fight or flight. It also uses the 'covariation principle'. If an act is done in that situation by most people most times, but not in other situations, then the situation, an impersonal causal factor, is more important than the person, whereas if that person acts that way in most situations most times then the cause lies in the person. Attributions like these are potentially useful in social interaction. They do need, however, to be based on representative evidence, preferably a great deal of it; to be available for use and revision; and to be unbiased (most adults under-estimate situational factors relative to personal ones when they are spectators (Ross 1981), though not so much when they are themselves actors).

It is probably premature to draw conclusions about what evidence children use and what judgements they come to in considering causal attributions. However, the work summarized by Rogers 1978, Ross 1981, Shantz 1983 and others, suggests that they do seem to make inferential use of both personal and impersonal information using the co-variation principle, though young children emphasize the situation at the expense of the person. They do integrate information, though young children may not manage to handle so many separate pieces of information and do much better when the person they are talking about is familiar to them or like themselves. They also live in social worlds which may be significantly unlike adults' social worlds, though what the likenesses and unlikenesses are has not been adequately conceptualized. This too might account for some of the apparent inconsistencies and inadequacies of children's judgements about people.

Understanding social events and institutions

The range of social events and institutions that children encounter is of course enormous, particularly if vicarious encounters through reading, television, etc., are included. I propose only to discuss one potential general model, the 'script', and one social area, aspects of the economic world, here. Research on children's knowledge of the world of school is discussed on pp. 198–200.

Scripts as representations of social knowledge

The notion of 'scripts' derives mainly from the work of Schank and Abelson 1977, which was concerned with describing a model for computers' understanding of inferences in a story setting. A script is basically an ordered sequence of actions, appropriate to their context and organized round a goal, a generalized set of expectations about who is likely to do what during this sort of event. There are obligatory actions and optional ones, points in the script where one particular thing has to be done and other points where there are alternative possible actions, essential rules and props whose omission would be very surprising indeed, and others which are less predictable. The best known prototype script is the restaurant script, which would look something like this:

Roles   Customer, waiter or waitress (chef off-stage, possible cashier)

Customer's goal   to obtain food to eat (maybe other goals such as being sociable)

1   go to restaurant, enter it, move to empty table, sit down (customer or waiter/waitress may choose table)

2   receive menu, study menu, decide what to eat, give order to waiter/waitress

3   receive food, eat it (possible repeat of 2 and 3 for later courses)

4   ask for bill, receive it, leave tip for waiter/waitress, pay bill (pay waiter/waitress or cashier: order of paying bill and leaving tip may be reversed), leave restaurant.

This sort of organization seems to be convenient for adults: elicitation of scripts from children suggests that they too use an organization based on a sequence of actions within a particular context (Nelson 1981). What is particularly interesting about these scripts is that they are *general*, not accounts of one particular episode. For example, a distinct language style is usually used, the impersonal pronoun and timeless present tense (such as 'you go to the restaurant, you go in and sit down', etc.). The events included (in temporal order) are more likely to be the routine components than the exceptional ones, though some components may be so routine and inevitable that they are not mentioned. Scripts look like generalized knowledge about a social routine, organized by experience and elaborated by further exposure: they seem likely to scaffold understanding of past and present events and prediction of future ones.

We do not know a great deal about how scripts are acquired. It seems likely that they are picked up from routines and contexts which adults structure for the child (see Chapter 6). Children take part in many activities which adults direct and organize. Children have to play their part more or less as determined by the adult partner, who may even supply the lines – 'Say thank you to Granny for the nice present', 'In this school we say "Good morning Miss Church"', "Please Miss Church may I . . ." not just "Miss, Miss"; it's politer.' Scripts provide a context of general expectations which reduce the uncertainty in particular problems. It seems quite a strong possibility that children show better understanding and more social sensitivity if they have shared script routines with familiar adults and if there have been explanations for particular events in generalized terms (Light 1978; Tizard *et al.* 1982; Mills and Funnell 1983). It is possible that the scripts themselves might be better articulated, though as yet there is no evidence for this.

Having a script for an event or context means that taking part in it can be automatic to a considerable extent. Attention and cognitive processing space is thus freed for other things: the idiosyncrasies of this particular instance of a general type of event, for example, or even remembering or planning events quite separate from the present very routine one. *Not* having a script means that the activity is far more problematic: we are less able to predict what will happen or to interpret what already has happened. Children, being inexperienced and ignorant compared with adults, are more frequently in this position. They may therefore be preoccupied with building scripts, and may focus on details which are incidental rather than typical; their scripts may not show a good match either to the situation or to other people's scripts for it. Nelson and Gruendel (1979 pp. 80–1) provide an example of two 4-year-olds comparing scripts and showing great interest in achieving agreement on their essential features.

G–1   And also, at night time, it's supper time.

G–2   Yeah, at night time it's supper time. It is.

G–1   It's morning.

G–2   At morning, it's lunch time!

G–1   At morning, we already had breakfast. Because at morning, it's lunch time!

G–2   RIGHT!

G–1   Yeah, at morning, it's lunch time.

G–2   At morning it's lunch time.

G–1   But, *first* comes snack, then comes lunch.

G–2   Right . . . Just in school, right?

G–1   Yeah, right, just in school.

G–2   Not at home.

G–1   Well, sometimes we have snacks at home.

G–2   Sometimes.

G–1   Sometimes I have a snack at home.

G–2   Sometimes I have a snack at my home, too.

G–1   Uh-hum. Because when special children come to visit us, we sometimes have snack. Like, like, hotdogs, or crackers, or cookies or, something like that.

G–2   Yeah, something. Maybe cake. (Laughs)

G–1   Cake.

G–2   Cake. Yeah, maybe cake.

G–1   Or maybe, uh, maybe, hotdog.

G–2   Maybe hotdog.

G–1   But, but, but, Jill and Michael don't like hotdog. Don't you know, but, do you know Michael or Jill?

G–2   I know another Michael.

G–1   I know, I know another Michael.

G–2   No, I know just one Michael. I just know one Michael.

G–1   Do you know Flora?

G–2   No! But you know what? It's a, it's it's one, it's somebody's bro . . . it's somebody's brother.

G–1   Are you eating your dinner? (Laughs) But not for real.

G–2   Not for real.

G–1   Because at morning, it's lunch time.

G–2   Right, at morning it is lunch time.

G–1   Right, at morning it is lunch time.

G–2   Yeah.

G–1   I think . . . I'll have . . . lunch. [Nelson and Gruendel, 1979, pp. 80–81]

'Scripts' could apply to a wide variety of events and understandings, and the notion may prove fruitful in analysing many phenomena in children's development. As well as the social settings discussed in this section, it seems to be applicable to children's construction and reading of stories (p. 83), to their language development (p. 118) and to their beliefs about their self-efficacy (p. 150). It might even be script violation that is the root of many pre-school emotional upsets: if the 'getting dressed' script specifies that the left foot should be shod before the right foot, or that teeth are brushed before hair, the adult who does otherwise risks protests and tears. Not having events go according to the script is a disorientating and unpleasant experience.

Children's understanding of socio-economic systems

Children's development, including their social cognition, has mainly been studied in terms of microsystems such as home or school, or mesosystems such as the relationships of agreement or discrepancy between home and school (Bronfenbrenner 1979; see Chapter 1 this volume). Children also live however within wider worlds: their part in these worlds is less prominent (people concerned with children's rights (e.g. Leach 1979) argue that it needs more recognition), but it is none the less of potential interest to developmental psychologists. There is some work on children's understanding of social institutions such as shops, banks, and governments, mainly conceived of as exosystems in which other people play roles that the child can observe, rather than as macrosystems or ideologies, which are more abstract and inferred rather than observed.

Studies of children's understanding of social institutions tend to involve questioning children, perhaps necessarily, since they do not normally vote, have bank accounts, or play many of the roles of economic or political persons directly rather than through or on behalf of adults. Their answers to questions such as 'What things, jobs, people, are important in a town?' (Furth 1980) are often full of charm but hard to analyse. Furth, like several other investigators, has used neo-

Piagetian stage analyses although data about uniformity of 'stage' across contexts or the separation of 'stages' are not usually impressive. More precise questions, script elicitations, and perhaps role play, may provide complementary information.

Understanding shopping

The central transaction in a shop might appear to be a simple exchange between customer and shopkeeper of goods and their value in cash. The shopkeeper has, and the customer wants, a bar of chocolate costing 15p: the customer gives the shopkeeper 15p and receives the chocolate in return. This is certainly the most visible part of shopping but it is far from the whole. The retail shopkeeper is a customer to the wholesalers who supply the shop with goods: the shop has assistants who exchange their labour for wages, and also various running costs such as rent, rates, lighting, etc. These components of the shop are less salient to the shopper, but they have significant effects on the cost of the items in the shop. Children seem to have some difficulty, as we shall see, in grasping the existence of these components and their effects, let alone their scale. A further source of confusion is that the passage of money between customer and shopkeeper may be two-way: the customer gives 20p and receives the chocolate bar and 5p change. To a small child with little grasp of the monetary values involved, this may look like a ritual, or a profit to the customer who ends up with goods *and* money, rather than the exchange it is.

Jahoda (1979, 1984) studied Scottish and Dutch children. The youngest, aged about 6, seemed to see the transactions as rituals; goods were given to the shop, not bought by it, and shop assistants were not doing a job and so were not paid. Even when these last two misconceptions were beginning to weaken, at around 7 to 8, the idea that the price the shop charges the customer is the same as the price the wholesaler charged the shop remains strong. The shopkeeper merely passed on goods at the same price as their original cost: the overheads of the shop, if recognized at all, were met from some external source such as

113

the Mint or the government. Children at about 11, with a better understanding of money, jobs, and costs, had begun to understand the concept of 'profit', though the size of profit made, the extent of the 'mark-up' between wholesale and retail prices, probably wasn't grasped – it is often enough a surprise to adults!

Understanding banks

Jahoda (1984) also summarizes the results of a study of children's understanding of the functioning of banks as economic institutions. He questioned Scottish children aged between 11 and 16. The youngest, who might have shown a little understanding of profit in the context of shops, showed no idea of it in banks. They viewed banks as being much like money boxes and borrowing from friends: you got out exactly what you put in, to get more or to pay for a loan would not be fair. Even if they knew about interest they had little idea where it came from, and still thought of the bank in interpersonal terms.

As children moved through early adolescence, they showed more appreciation of interest and the bank's use of the money deposited in it. Only a minority, however, mastered the reciprocity of interest in the bank's lending and borrowing, even after questioning designed to induce new insights. Again, appreciation of what scale banks' profits are on, and what is done with them, is probably unusual in adults.

Representing economic inequalities

Emler and Dickinson 1985 have studied children's representation of economic inequalities. They asked children aged between 7 and 12 to estimate the weekly incomes of doctors, teachers, bus drivers and road sweepers, to explain why the incomes differed and to say whether equality of income would 'be better'. The average estimates of middle-class children for each job were higher than those of working-class children: doctors were seen as having the highest incomes followed by teachers, bus drivers and finally road sweepers. As Figure 15 and Table 4 show, middle-class children gave much more differential in their estimates of income than working-class children

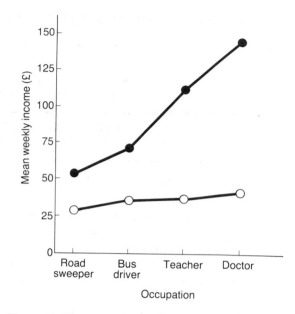

Figure 15 Income estimates for each occupation by middle-class and working-class children. ●———●, middle class; ○———○, working class.

Source: From Emler and Dickinson (1985), p. 194.

did, as well as judging incomes to be higher overall.

The children were asked about the 'fairness' of the different amounts they had estimated for each job and of a hypothetical equality of income. There were no significant differences in judgement of fairness by age or by social class, though it was less common for the oldest children or for middle-class ones to say that equality of income would be better. Most of the children justified inequality of income by reference to some form of equity consideration, such as differences in the work or the responsibility involved in the job or the amount of training required for it. Middle-class children were more sophisticated in their justification of inequality, producing more (and more varied) reasons.

Thus, although most children believed that income inequalities were justified, middle-class children estimated that the inequalities were larger (though even they probably underestimated their scale). The absence of age differ-

Table 4 *Ratios of income estimates for doctor and road sweeper by age and social class*

| | Age level | | | | | | | | | |
| | 7–8 | | 8–9 | | 9–10 | | 10–11 | | 11–12 | |
	$\bar{X}$	SD	$\bar{X}$	SD	$\bar{X}$	SD	$\bar{X}$	SD	$\bar{X}$	SD
WC	1.31	0.66	1.91	1.34	2.63	0.67	1.59	0.72	1.61	0.52
MC	3.32	3.25	2.94	2.66	4.79	5.35	2.88	1.22	2.64	1.42

Source: From Emler and Dickinson (1985), p. 194.

ences argues against this class difference being caused by a developmental increase in the complexity of understanding of social systems, faster in the middle-class children than in the lower-class. The different estimate levels seem more likely to be due to different information about incomes. Emler and Dickinson argue that social representations of economic inequalities are more detailed, extensive and salient in the middle class, and hence middle-class children have had more opportunity to assimilate their community's shared knowledge and belief about income inequality. Exactly where in the community economic knowledge comes from remains to be investigated.

Sources of socio-economic understanding

The three studies I have discussed in this section illustrate some of the recent work on the development of children's understanding of the socio-economic system. They use information derived from their participation in their community to construct representations and justifications of the workings of the economy. Limitations on this information which are caused by their own status as observers, not participants, or by the community's particular beliefs or values, restrict their models of economic life to simple versions. Although internal cognitive limitations may also restrict their conceptualization, sheer ignorance seems a likely cause of inadequate models. Children can learn to be sophisticated and critical observers of at least such parts of the economic system as advertising (Ward *et al.* 1977). Further work on the social origins of children's economics could produce findings which will be relevant also to the wider issue of social representation.

Plate 9 'Pa's Bank' from *The Book of Shops*, 1899, by E. V. Lucas, illustrated by Francis D. Bedford

Plate 10

4 Language development

Language

The development of language provides a good example of epigenesis, and its later stages also involve consideration of eco-systems. Human infants clearly start with a great many capacities and pieces of behaviour suited to language, but they are also born into communities which use language and expect the infant to use it too. All except the severely impaired develop language in very similar ways, though at varying rates: but the details of the language and how it is used are heavily influenced by the child's experience. Through development, language functions as a means of communication, as a means of reflecting on and re-organizing experience, and as a way to receive and transform the accumulated knowledge and values of the community. Using language is thus a central part of human existence.

Methodology

Studies of young children's language have relied heavily on 'naturalistic observation'; that is, on recordings of children's spontaneous language in their ordinary activities at home. One reason for this was an admirable concern for 'ecological validity', a belief that what children could be induced to do in experimental settings was not representative of what they did outside them. The tendency of children aged between 18 months and 3 years old to prove extremely difficult subjects for standardized experimental methods no doubt reinforced researchers' concern for ecological validity. Reliance on naturalistic observation, however, meant, here as in other areas of research, that very large amounts of data had to be collected in order to find sufficient instances of interesting phenomena which naturally occur only infrequently. This meant researchers had to have access to the child for long periods of time:

thus samples tended to be small in number and to have parents who were unusually interested in developmental psychology, many being psycholinguists themselves. The use of small samples biased towards the intellectual middle-classes raises problems of the representativeness of the findings of many studies.

There is need also to look very carefully at the ecological validity of naturalistic observations. In the first place, they involve the 'Observer Paradox' – as Labov has put it, 'to obtain the data most important for linguistic theory, we have to observe how people speak when they are not being observed' (Labov 1972, p. 113). Further, many studies do not specify exactly what settings are observed. Language produced at home playing with mother may differ from language produced at home when playing with a baby sibling (Dunn and Kendrick 1982), from language produced when out shopping with mother, from language produced at playschool with other children, from language produced at playschool with teacher. Systematic studies are needed of how situational variables (including the presence of an observer), affect children's language production and comprehension. Generalizing from the one situation observed to all others, particularly if allied to a belief that if children *don't* do something it is because they *can't*, has led to some false conclusions and misguided remediation programmes. One notable instance of this is the debate over social class differences in language which is discussed later in this chapter.

At the root of the problem of what 'ecological validity' really is, there may be the difficulty of defining what behaviour a particular situation requires as well as describing what it actually evokes. We do not have more than the very beginnings of anything relevant to such definitions. Grice (1975; see also Searle 1975) discusses the 'co-operative principle' which is necessary for effective communication. Speakers normally try to ensure that their contributions to discourse give information which is neither insufficient nor superfluous in quantity, which is known to be true rather than false or merely supposed, which is relevant to the aims of the conversation and which is not obscure, ambiguous, wordy or disorderly. Contributions which flout these requirements usually lead to breakdowns of communication or to indirect implications where what is actually said may be only part of what is meant. Participants in conversations tend to have an understanding of the implicit meaning of utterances and events which is affected by who is speaking, when, how, why and where. They may also have 'scripts' (e.g. Schank and Abelson 1977; Nelson 1981) which define what ought to happen in a particular setting or encounter. We will look at what is known about children's use of indirect speech acts and of scripts later. For the moment, my intention is merely to point out that the significance of what is observed in a natural setting cannot be fully understood unless the 'script' or the 'task demands' of the setting are known. The richness of naturalistic data forces selection and categorization on the observer, and unless this is done carefully, explicitly and consistently error and ambiguity may result. Corrigan (1982) suggests that naturalistic observation has to be supplemented by careful controlled experiment: 'a full picture of language acquisition requires information about what children choose to produce given less structured situations, as well as the limits of what they are capable of producing when required to do so' (Corrigan 1982, p. 182). Gordon Wells, director of the Bristol-based 'Language Development at Home and at School' project, the largest study to use naturalistic observation, discusses the methodological problems involved and discloses that with hindsight he would have collected more experimentally-elicited utterances (Well 1982). The Bristol study does nevertheless have more and in some ways better data than most others, and some of its findings are prominent in the discussion of language development that follows.

Language can be analysed at many different levels, including the sounds made, the words used, the sentences constructed, the meaning conveyed and the functions served. Each level is, of course, involved in the others most of the time, and children and adults alike do not learn or use them in isolation. Nevertheless the different levels have often been investigated separately, and there are differences as well as similarities in their developmental courses. We have now good descriptions of much of the sequence of children's language developments, as I shall outline, but there remains much to discover about precisely how and why this development happens.

Infants' perception of speech sounds

At the level of language sounds, newborn infants have been shown to have a preference for speech-like sounds over musical or non-speech noises (see Chapter 2; Eimas *et al.* 1971; Wolff 1966; for a review see Aslin *et al.* 1983), and an ability to discriminate between the voice of their mother and that of another woman (DeCasper and Fifer 1980). From a few days old, if they hear human speech their limb movements will become synchronized with the rhythm of the speech (Condon and Sander 1974). These are likely to be useful characteristics to child and parent alike: the baby's selective attention and close response to language will both increase its own opportunities for learning from language and help to make the parent believe that the baby is particularly interested in and responsive to the language-producing person. Interactional meshing, as we will see in discussing the development of relationships with other people, has to be got more or less right somehow, if relationships are to go well. The capabilities of newborn infants suggest that there may be some genetic preprogramming, perhaps of brain structures, which may possibly be very specific about speech sounds. There certainly has been shown to be, in infants of a few months, categorical perception of some consonant sounds (e.g. Eimas 1971; Trehub and Robinovitch 1972; Streeter 1976), at the same points as adults place the discrimination. Adults discriminate between /b/ and /p/, for example, in terms of whether they are pronounced with vocal-cord vibration (voicing); so do infants, including those growing up in a community using a language (such as the Kikuyu) where /b/ and /p/ are not regarded as different in meaning. This suggests that the auditory system is 'wired up' very early on in ways that mean there are points of particularly great sensitivity on the physical characteristics of speech sounds, and that languages place category limits between different phonemes at these sensitive points. However, if a language does not use a particular discrimination its speakers lose it, and have great difficulty in hearing (or producing) the appropriate sound. The programming of babies here too is not more specific than it needs to be. Ideas of a species-specific 'plan' for language perception in humans may have to be abandoned in the light of recent evidence that chinchillas (and possibly monkeys) categorize some speech contrasts as humans do. Aslin *et al.* (1983) review the evidence.

Infants' production of speech sounds

Just as it could be said that babies begin their language career by hearing more sounds than adults, it appears that when they start babbling they produce sounds which the adults around them do not produce. Babbling initially involves vowels; consonants start to appear in a fairly orderly way (see Clark and Clark 1977, ch. 10) in the second half of the first year. Babies have quite often been observed to do what looks like deliberate experimenting with sounds, contrasting the noises produced with different tongue and lip positions and at times moving mouth and tongue systematically but without making sounds. As the child gets older, strings of babble with varying intonation are produced; gradually the range of sounds made comes to resemble the range present in adults' language; and particular sounds are regularly produced in association with particular events. There may be good reason (Halliday 1975) to regard these sound-event pairs as the first 'words'. Adults are certainly likely to interpret them as meaningful, and babble noises which appear often may become important parts of adults' 'baby-talk'. The expected words for

young children to call their parents, for example, tend in many languages to resemble babble noises – 'mama', 'papa', 'baba', and so forth. A baby randomly producing such a noise may get a great deal of reward from parents who believe or pretend to believe that they are being addressed by name. Such reward has been shown to increase not specific noises in babble but on the one hand the amount of babble in general and on the other the probability that what was in its early stages something the baby did when alone will be done as part of a social activity. Parents clearly 'shape' their baby's early talk, requiring more and more precise articulation of words and later meanings, and also requiring the child to take part in conversation in an increasingly self-directed way, as we shall see.

The stable sequence of babbling and its appearance in virtually all children in much the same way at about the same time suggest that there is a high degree of genetic programming and maturation involved. Nevertheless experience is also necessary. Children who are congenitally deaf start babbling like normal children but give it up at about 8 or 9 months, almost certainly because they have not been able to hear themselves. If they are made able to hear at this point, babbling is restored and the child learns a spoken language (Fry 1966).

Maturation (in this case of articulation) is also clearly involved in the timing of children's first conventional words, which commonly appear between 10 and 15 months. Children have usually showed understanding of words, and may have produced their own idiosyncratic words, before then, and deaf babies learning sign language produce their first conventional signs for objects at about 8 months (de Villiers 1979) because the muscular control needed for manual signs is less fine than that needed for speech. Spoken words need more or less mature articulation, and the planning of the sequence of speech sounds, not just the ability to associate words with objects or events. The latter is also important, however; children who are growing up in a bilingual environment where the number of labels attached to objects is greater, where objects have more variable names, are commonly slower in their early vocabulary development.

Early words often involve phonemic simplification and the use of context to carry some of the meaning: /da/, for example, may serve as a simplified version of 'dog', 'duck' and 'daddy' and be acceptably unambiguous most of the time because only one of the possible referents is present or being played with or pointed to. Later in phonemic development, the child may begin to use systematic rules and strategies to produce intelligible words. Children commonly, for example, simplify consonant clusters which are hard to articulate, saying 'mack' instead of 'smack'. They replace two different consonants in a word by a repetition of the same one, as 'goggy' for 'doggy'. They may avoid the use of words which contain a difficult sound, something which gets easier to do as one's vocabulary of synonyms increases. Certain sounds are difficult for many children and may not be produced correctly for many years (or ever). Phonetic mistakes are not always due to incapacity, however, as in the case of one linguist's son (Smith 1973) who at 25 months said 'puggle' when he wanted to talk about puddles, but pronounced 'puzzle' as 'puddle'. A rule of some sort seemed to be involved here. The same child provided evidence of an ability to perceive and store discriminations which could not be produced: he said /maus/ for both 'mouse' and 'mouth', but would not accept adult usage of /maus/ to mean 'mouth'. In early language comprehension is quite commonly in advance of production. This may be analogous to song development in some birds who learn their song from other birds one season but do not sing it themselves until the next year (Nottebohm 1970).

Beginning to use words

Children tend to begin by talking about what they already know, familiar commonplace objects, people, or events, particularly objects or events that the child is concerned with as actor. Early words tend to be nouns or regulatory words such as 'more', 'no', 'up' and so forth. They are not necessarily the same as adult words in how they are used or in their exact range of reference.

Using words as names

It may seem obvious that when a child says a word he or she is referring to an object or event, that the word names or represents the referent. McShane (1980) argues otherwise. He sees early 'words' as inseparable from the functions that, in the context, they perform for the child. Thus, if the child says 'mummy' only when making requests to his or her mother and in no other context, 'mummy' is certainly functioning as part of the child's request. It is not certain that, as far as the child is concerned, it represents 'mummy' or is her name; adults are likely to believe it has these functions but it could just be for the child a noise one makes when trying to get something, as 'please' or 'help' or a certain sort of cry might be. If 'mummy' was used not just as a vocative, as in requests, but to perform a variety of functions, for example to answer questions, direct attention, make statements and so forth, in a variety of contexts, then it is safer to conclude that the child understands it is his or her name for mother, and that the word represents the person.

McShane's suggestion highlights the importance of considering the functions of language and the construction of meaning (see pp. 135–40). It avoids some of the difficulties which earlier theories of the meaning of early utterances have run into (McShane 1980, ch. 2) but rather more evidence is required to support it. The hypothesized sequence of events is as follows. The child's caretaker systematically responds to the child's utterances as if the child intended to convey a particular meaning (see below Chapter 6) and the child thus comes to learn that there are contingent relationships between his or her utterances and other people's behaviour. Adults' difficulties in interpreting the child presumably 'shape' utterances towards a form which is more intelligible and usually more conventional, for example if the contingent relationship between saying 'wow!' and getting what you want is less regular than the contingency between saying 'help' and getting what you want, 'help' will tend to be preferred. The child learns to communicate and to intend to communicate, but what is communicated is pragmatics – needs, requests, directions, and so forth. At about the same time, parents are introducing children to 'the naming game' (Ninio and Bruner 1978). In joint activities such as looking at picture books the adult helps the child participate in the ritual of 'what's that?' 'That's a doggie.' To begin with the adult plays both parts, but gradually pauses, prompts and other devices lead the child to make an increasingly large contribution to the routine. The child utters names at appropriate points of the ritual, but does not at first understand that this is 'naming', a particular sort of activity relating language and the world. It is worth pointing out that the concept of 'naming' is not a simple one: feeling that names are an inseparable and unalterable part of their referent (so that 'milk' could not be called 'ink', for example), or that one's name is private or even secret (Sinclair *et al.* 1978) seems to be rather common. McShane suggests as a result of taking part in the highly-structured ritual of naming the child comes to the insight that the words originally embedded in the ritual are names. That quite a lot of children show a rapid increase in vocabulary between 18 months and 2 years, and behaviour which looks like asking the name of every object they set eyes on, supports this notion, though as Wells (1985) points out, many parents deliberately teach names at about this time.

One documented instance of insight comes from Helen Keller, who after being blind and deaf from the age of 8 months had words finger-spelled to her by the governess, Anne Sullivan, who was put in charge of her education when she was 6. Anne Sullivan tried to spell out on Helen's fingers 'everything we do all day long, although she has no idea yet what the spelling means'. Helen quickly imitated the hand signs but made no connection between them and the objects they symbolized. The insight came in an incident which has become famous.

They had been wrestling with the words M–U–G and W–A–T–E–R, recorded Helen, and she persisted in confusing the two. Later they went for a walk by the well-house. Someone was pumping water. Annie placed Helen's hand under the spout and 'as the cool stream gushed over one hand, she (Annie) spelled into

the other the word water, first slowly then rapidly. I stood still, my whole attention fixed upon the motions of her fingers. Suddenly I felt a misty consciousness as of something forgotten – a thrill of returning thought; and somehow the mystery of language was revealed to me. I knew then that W–A–T–E–R meant the wonderful cool something that was flowing over my hand. . . . I left the well-house eager to learn. Everything had a name, and each name gave birth to a new thought. As we returned to the house every object which I touched seemed to quiver with life.'

Annie Sullivan wrote 'She has learned that everything has a name and that the manual alphabet is the key to everything she wants to know. . . . She has flitted from object to object, asking the name of everything' (Lash 1981, pp. 57–8).

Not every development of the concept of naming would be dramatic, and like other concepts further development is to be expected. One development that McShane suggests follows the initial insight that objects have names is that attributes, events and actions have names too. Linguistic accounts grow in length and develop grammatical structure to convey these different sorts of naming and reference. Here too adult 'scaffolding' and extension of children's utterances provides a model and a frame.

Early vocabulary

The limits of early vocabulary items have been seen as of interest as possibly revealing how young children associate label and referent. Quite commonly children use an early word to refer to many more objects than an adult would, for example 'doggy' is applied not just to dogs but to cats and pieces of fur, in what is called 'over-extension'. (The converse, 'under-extension', is also found, as when 'doggy' is only used to refer to the family dog.) Eve Clark (Clark and Clark 1977, pp. 492–7) suggested that in 'over-extension' children first associate the word with one or two particularly salient characteristics of the object, for example furriness, and so use it over-extensively to refer to anything characterized by furriness. Later they add in other salient features as requirements for 'dogginess', such as four-leggedness, size, ability to bark, narrowing their definition towards the adult level. Word, and concept, are seen as proceeding from particular instance to generalized abstraction by the increasing specification of features. (See Chapters 2 and 3 for discussion of cognitive models and semantic networks.)

It must be noted that children's early words are not necessarily simple neutral efforts to label. Some involve more complex activities such as commenting and comparing ('doggy' might be appropriately glossed in some instances not as 'that's a doggy' but as 'that's rather like a doggy' or 'my doggy has fur like that too'). As children get older, simile and metaphor become more likely. So do other indirect language uses. One child is recorded as having said 'heavy' in many situations which involved her in notable physical effort, including not only pushing open doors or lifting bricks but also climbing a long steep flight of stairs. If she had been of the right generation and subculture, she might have appropriately used her favourite word to refer to situations involving social and interpersonal difficulties: 'Man, being arrested is a real heavy scene'. Overgeneralizations do not unequivocally indicate inability to distinguish between objects or events: they may involve confusion, or they may involve comment, comparison, metaphor or joke. Social demands may also enter into the situation; if one feels socially obliged to say something but lacks the correct vocabulary item, one may produce a slightly inappropriate word or phrase as an approximation in verbal terms but an adequate response in social ones. This sort of experience comes fairly frequently to people who are not fully competent users of the language in question.

It should also be pointed out that the vocabulary children use and their degree of 'over-extension' or 'under-extension' may be related to adult usage of language to children. Here adults seem to have a sense of 'level of appropriateness' related to the distinctions they want the child to make. 'Plant' is thus seen as a bit too general, 'rose' as a bit too specific, 'flower' as about right; and contrasts are drawn through the means of vocabulary between a flower which can be admired, smelled, not walked on, etc., and other plants such as grass, tree, vegetables, which can variously be walked on, climbed, eaten and so forth. The adult's own interest, and the adult's encouragement of the child's interest, will make notable contributions to the child's later vocabulary. So will the distinctions the local culture makes and uses. A country child may quickly learn distinctions of which a town adult remains unaware. There is a salutary story, no doubt apocryphal, of a school inspector testing the general knowledge of children in a small country school. He showed them a picture of a sheep, but his 'What's this?' was received with puzzled faces. Eventually a child said 'I ain't never seen one of those – it's got a face like a Cheviot but its back's like a Jacob but neither of them's got horns like that 'un.' Labov's work makes a similar point (see p. 131).

Generally it would appear that children begin with only one or a few appropriate vocabulary items but develop differential ranges. Halliday (1975) provides examples of initial single words being used in a variety of situations but being replaced by a range of words used selectively according to the circumstances. As we shall see in examining the development of language as a functional communication system, this is an important part of later development and crucial to successful social life.

From single words to sentences

As we have seen, developing words which refer stably to objects and events is a tremendous achievement for the child, but in order to get very far with communication words have to be combined into sentences, sentences into longer passages and so forth. Grammatical rules specify how words may be combined to express increasingly precise meanings. Children have to learn to combine their words in ways which obey the rules. They can do this in rudimentary ways very early: managing some of the most subtle language structures requires considerable practice if not explicit training (e.g. whether the word 'none' takes a singular or plural verb).

As my comments above on the interpretation of one-word phrases imply, the beginnings of grammar are obscure. Only when two morpheme utterances begin can we look for evidence of word order, which is, of course, an important grammatical device in English. Children's earliest word orders tend to take the adult form and to express salient grammatical cases such as action, possession, location and so forth. Both the meanings and the structures which 2-year-olds express are of very similar sorts in most of the languages studied: they are usually uninflected words, mainly in the order which an adult would use to express the same meaning, though the 'functor' words like 'the', 'by', 'but' are omitted in favour of the words that carry most of the meaning. Some phrases are taken on wholesale from adult language and used as 'unanalysed chunks' or single words – 'wossat', 'gimme' are obvious examples. Peters (1983) argues with some cogency that this reflects some fundamental problems in our concepts of 'word' and 'syntax'. Even adults use some phrases as units which although potentially analysable are not normally broken into their components – polite formulae such as 'how do you do' are of this type. Peters suggests that language learners acquire units which consist of one or more words or morphemes, and which then become candidates for segmentation into smaller units. If a 'unit' can be segmented into smaller units these are added to the lexicon, and the original 'unit' may be retained. For example, the original unit 'how do you do' can be segmented into its separate words but may also be kept as a social formula, 'howdjado', which expects a different response from its components as well as being used as a unit. Segmentation also contributes to knowledge of the language's structures.

Children do of course produce utterances which are unlike adults ('all gone sticky') or which over-extend adults' rules (mouses, goed). Thus their development of grammar is not learned in any simple automatic way from adults. Noam Chomsky, impressed by the speed, regularity and specificity of children's language development, by apparently universal features of language and by evidence of specialized language centres in the brain, proposed a model of language develop-

ment in which an innate understanding of fundamental linguistic rules (centring on using syntax to express meaning) was activated by the language the baby heard and accounted for the speed and regularity of development (see, for example, Chomsky 1976; Clark and Clark 1977; Dale 1978). A great deal of research has been carried out aimed at constructing grammars of child language in terms of Chomsky's model of transformational generative grammar (e.g. Bloom 1970), or in terms of case grammars focusing on concepts like agent, action, locative (e.g. Bowerman 1973). (Dale 1976 and Maratsos 1983 provide useful accounts of both grammars and the associated research.) A Chomskian model of grammatical competence, which centres on a syntactic component represented without respect to meaning and involving transformations, is not now seen as a good psychological model of young children's language development. Beyond that, it is not as yet clear what grammatical models are most appropriate for the description of early language, or indeed for adults' language (Maratsos 1983); one particularly important aspect of the debate is how far it is sensible to treat syntax separately from semantics and pragmatics, that is to separate the formal grammar of what is said from what is meant and what effect the utterance has or was intended to have. We will look at these aspects of children's language development presently.

The question of whether all children develop language in the same way is of some interest. It has been impossible to answer accurately because research on language development in young children is very time-consuming at both the data-collecting and analysis stages. Most samples have been very small and many have been drawn from middle-class intellectual families, often the researcher's own. The nearest approximation to a large and socially representative sample that I know is that studied since 1972 by Gordon Wells and his colleagues in the Bristol Language Development Research Programme. After a description of the structure and methods of this programme I will outline the answers it gives to the question of whether all children develop language in the same way.

The children studied were 128 Bristol residents. Each was observed at three-monthly intervals for twenty-seven months; that is, ten observations. Each child wore a small radio microphone which recorded the child's speech and other people's speech to the child for a number of brief periods spread through the day so that neither child nor family knew with certainty that the microphone was on. The researcher was not present during this day but checked the tape with the child's mother in the evening to complement the sound tape with contextual information. Half the children were observed from 15 to 42 months, the other half from 39 to 66 months. Further studies of some of the sample in school were made (and indeed some of the sample are currently being studied as second-language learners). The families of the children were representative of the entire social class range, except that the proportions of very high and very low social class were increased to give an adequate number for analysis. Thus the programme has produced a very large quantity of data which may be analysed in terms of sex, age and social class variables, which are representative of the spontaneous speech of British children between 15 months and 5½ years, and which are probably relatively unspoiled by the participants' consciousness of being observed.

Wells (1985) presents the resultant picture of the sequence of language development, and although the use of spontaneous language gathered at quite long intervals may mean that language items which occur infrequently appear later in the data sequence than they would if attempts had been made to elicit such items, the picture is almost certainly pretty accurate. There seems to be 'a universal sequence of development, at least in general outline' (Wells 1985, p. 224).

The data do not tell us exactly why we find this order of emergence. Theorists have suggested that uses and structures appear early or late because they are frequent or infrequent respectively in the language which the child hears, and the Bristol data lend some support to this hypothesis (Wells 1985, ch. 9). Another suggestion has been that emergence is correlated with linguistic and cognitive 'complexity', and although it is not unproblematic to define such 'complexity', the emergence of auxiliary verbs, pronouns, meaning relations and functions did seem to be correlated with complexity. It is, of course, rather likely that frequency and complexity of language influence each other: if we need to say something often we may gradually simplify it (acronyms such as BBC, USA and BPS are examples of this). Mothers' adjustment of their language to what they believe will fit their children's current competence will increase the frequency of less complex items in the child's language, providing another sort of interaction between frequency and complexity.

Adults' talk to children

It has been one of the most consistent findings in studies of language development that mothers and other adults (and indeed older children, for example, Shatz and Gelman 1973) adjust their speech to the child developing language. Among the many adjustments are attention getters and holders, such as a frequent use of the child's name, a high pitch or exaggerated intonation, and many gestures and touches; restriction of semantic content, for example by talking more than usual about the 'here and now' and by careful selection of vocabulary by rules like the 'level of appropriateness' mentioned above; syntactic restriction to brief and simple sentences without, for example, passives or subordinate clauses, but with lots of repetitions; a specialized strategy of discourse, high on expansions and extensions of the child's own utterances, high on contemporaneous comment on ongoing activities, and high on questions, directions, prompts and modelling of discourse, and produced more slowly than language to adults. This sort of language has been called 'baby-talk' or 'motherese': it is a relatively consistent, organized, simplified and redundant set of utterances. It is thus very unlike the disorderly and degenerate language which was all the child in Chomsky's account had to learn from: 'motherese' has been seen as quite the reverse, as a particularly good source for the child to learn language from.

Maratsos (1983) raises certain queries about this. He first points out, correctly, that parents do not use motherese in order to teach their children language; they use it because they are trying to keep the child interested and understanding. Wells (1985, p. 380) makes the point neatly:

for most of the time the relatively finely tuned modelling of meanings and forms that the frequency data reveal occurs incidentally, as adults carry on conversations with their children for quite other purposes – to control the child's behaviour in the interests of his safety and their joint well-being, to share in and extend his interests, to maintain and enrich their interpersonal relationship and so on. Success in achieving these aims requires that the majority of the adults' contributions be pitched at a level of complexity that is not too far beyond the child's linguistic ability. However, this is achieved quite spontaneously by most adults under the control of feedback from the child's comprehension and production and does not require deliberate attention. The tuning that occurs is thus as much a response to, as a determinant of, the sequence in the child's learning.

The Bristol data show a great deal of this 'fine tuned' linguistic input, frequently with an increase in the complexity of the adult's language just before an increase in the complexity of the child's. Wells comments on this (p. 381):

It appears, therefore, that the influence of the input on the child's learning is enabling rather than determining. Once the child has the prerequisite cognitive understanding of the distinction which is encoded by a particular linguistic category, frequent appropriately contextualized occurrences of the category in the speech that is addressed to the child provide opportunities for him to make the connection between linguistic category and non-linguistic experience.

Fine-tuned input should not be seen as either necessary or sufficient for children to develop language, since there are several accounts of children who do not seem to have been talked to in this way but did seem to develop normal language (Lieven 1978; Ochs and Schieffelin 1983; Brice Heath 1983; Romaine 1984). It does seem possible that fast developers encounter particularly finely-tuned language (e.g. Cross 1977, 1978) but otherwise differences seem to be not in what is possible but in what is usually done, that is, in the distributions of *tokens*, not in the range of *types*. However the facilitating functions of adult speech are probably broader than the categories used in studies of motherese which concentrate on features like Mean Length of Utterance, sentence types or syntactic expansions. Wells lists five relevant types of intention (pp. 398–9): 1 to secure and maintain inter-subjectivity of attention, 2 to express one's own meaning intentions in a form that one's partner finds easy to understand, 3 to ensure that one has correctly understood the meaning intentions of one's partner, 4 to provide positive responses in order to sustain the partner's desire to continue the present interaction and to engage in further interactions in the future, and 5 to instruct one's partner so that he or she may become a more skilled performer. This last intention applies only to some sorts of interactions, teaching vocabulary in conversation about picture books being a well-documented example. These intentions underlie the behaviour which has been seen in 'accepting' or 'responsive' mothers (Nelson 1973; Lieven 1978). They have the short-term effect of sustaining the current conversation, and the long-term effect of maintaining the child's general motivation to interact and especially to converse with his or her adults. They also provide an opportunity for modelling to the child ways of doing things with language which he or she needs and cannot quite produce alone, utterances which are within the Vygotskian 'zone of proximal development'. (They also contribute to the opportunity to discuss cognitive issues: Wood (1980) and Tizard and Hughes (1984) stress the usefulness of conversations between adult and child based on the child's current interest as a painless way of learning about the world.)

Children who take part in a lot of child-contingent conversations of this sort seem to develop linguistically (and cognitively) rather well. However we cannot yet conclude that the conversations *accelerated* their language development.

Bates *et al.* (1982) outline some of the reasons why such a conclusion would be premature. They point out that emphasis on 'motherese' as a teaching device neglects the ability and the willingness of the child to learn. The child's knowledge of language and the social world must be considered: we will discuss its development later (p. 137). So must children's ecosystems (see p. 132). Second, even if a feature of parental language is correlated with a feature of the child's language development, we cannot assume that the former caused the latter. It might be the reverse, that parents are responding to the child's idiosyncracies, or a two-way relationship where child and parent each react to the other; or there may be a more indirect relation between the two measures. They give an example (p. 51) from a study (reported at a 1975 conference) where Tulkin and Covitz found a significant correlation between the 'prohibition ratio' in parents' speech to the child at 10 months and child's performance on a vocabulary test at 6 years. Bates *et al.* decline to conclude that saying 'no' to children decreases their vocabulary in any direct way, and I think even people who advocate extremely permissive childrearing would hesitate to draw this conclusion. It is more likely that relationships which include a lot of prohibition by parents have other qualities which adversely affect the child's development. Perhaps they are short on joint attention, child-contingent conversation, parental warmth, and opportunities for the child to explore the world at will but with an appreciative adult to put his or her discoveries into an accessible model. Only very detailed analyses of the pattern of children's experience, in conjunction with experimental evidence, can sort out the pathways of causation.

Wells (1985, ch. 8) points out that there are marked differences in the language used in different social contexts in the Bristol data. For example, 'representational speech' was high during sessions of reading or watching TV, 'controlling speech' was high during caretaking, eating and imaginary play without adults (which involves a lot of defining or allocating roles, e.g. 'you be the dog', 'you gotta crawl and bark'). Davie *et al.*

(1984), observing 3 to 5-year-olds at home, similarly found context differences in language use. Looking at books, for example, was associated with highly informational talk from adults – a high rate of naming and labelling objects in pictures, and a low rate of general conversation. I will return to this point about context and language in its social class aspects presently; at the moment it serves as a warning that we must have a *representative* quantity of data before we draw conclusions about what language input a child is experiencing and how it is associated with developmental outcomes.

A quotation from Wells (1985, p. 394) summarizes the complexity of the enterprise of understanding language development, making points which we will see apply just as strongly to our discussion of social development (Chapter 6).

In various ways, therefore, the differences observed in adult behaviour may owe as much to differences between the children with whom they converse as to inherent differences in the adults themselves. But the reverse is also true, and so, in seeking to explain the differences in adult or child behaviour we must recognize that, ultimately they are as likely to emerge from the interaction between a particular pair of participants, as they are to be attributable to either participant considered separately. If we are to untangle the relationship between features of the input and progress in language learning, therefore, it will be necessary to develop models of multiple and reciprocal causation operating within a matrix of interaction, which, on any particular occasion, is also affected by the particular context in which it occurs. Since we are very far from having such a model, it seems for the moment safer to conclude more modestly that although the evidence supports a belief in the potentialy facilitating effect of the adult input, this facilitating input itself is the product of interaction to which both child and adult contribute to varying degrees.

Language differences and social class

As it was once for Jane Austen's matchmaking matrons 'a truth universally acknowledged, that a single man in possession of a good fortune must be in want of a wife', it was for some time 'a truth universally acknowledged' that a child from a working-class background must be in want of a language different from that of his or her home if failure in school was to be avoided. Both 'truths' have been intensively attacked: we will consider the latter here.

Native English speakers perceive differences of sound, syntax and vocabulary in people's speech which they relate to social class. (The concept of social class is a problematic one (see Giddens and Held 1982) which I do not propose to analyse here. In this section what is referred to is social status as indicated by occupation: in the case of children, father's occupation.) Romaine (1984), summarizing the results of surveys of people's speech in various countries, says that, 'simplistically', the finding is that the middle-class adhere more closely to the norms of the high prestige standard language, while the working-class speak in less standard ways, closer to the local vernacular. Sometimes research picks up enormous class differences: Romaine (pp. 85–6) cites a study by Trudgill of the use of verb forms such as 'he go', verbs without /s/, in Norwich. Speakers from the middle classes virtually never used this 'non-standard suffixless present tense', while working-class speakers used it from 70 per cent (upper working class) to 97 per cent (lower working class) of the time. Often class differences are much smaller, however, and there is more variation within classes: indeed many speakers adjust their speech to their situation and their listener. Nevertheless, members of the community of native English speakers hear the differences in people's speech and may use them to judge the speaker's social class and other characteristics (Giles and Powesland 1975).

There are also differences in educational achievement between children from different social classes. Again 'simplistically', children from working-class families are more likely to leave school at the earliest opportunity and with minimal formal qualifications, having been more likely to be poor readers or non-readers from primary school on. These differences may be larger on verbal measures (including reading tests and intelligence tests) than on less verbal ones. It has been suggested, and often believed,

that these two phenomena, language differences and differences in educational achievement, are closely related; particularly that the former cause the latter. Working-class children are said to fail in school because they 1 do not, and 2 cannot, use language in middle-class ways.

This hypothesis reflects in a popularized form the ideas put forward by Basil Bernstein. Bernstein's ideas have changed considerably over the last twenty-five years: the three volumes *Class, Codes and Control* contain papers from the period 1958 to the early 1970s. The more recent formulations are much more complex and subtle than earlier ones, and their psychological and educational implications are different. Since the early formulations are still current in some accounts of language and education, however, I will present a brief account of the successive models.

The original influential version of the theory was that there were two distinct types of language, usually called 'restricted' and 'elaborated' codes. 'Elaborated code' was said to be grammatically complex, with frequent subordinate clauses, passives, impersonal pronouns ('One sees'), and a wide and unusual vocabulary of adjectives and adverbs: these features were used in the service of precision and explicitness. 'Restricted code' was said to use short, simple sentences, often incomplete or elliptical, and was far more repetitive, rigid, imprecise and implicit: it contained many more appeals to a shared context of understanding, for example in the use of phrases like 'you know', 'sort of', 'innit?'. Middle-class speakers were said to use both language codes, but some (and 'some' came to imply 'all' in the popular version) working-class speakers were supposed only to have access to restricted code. This deficit affected the way they could express themselves, and, it was postulated, the way they were able to think (verbally) to themselves. Further, since the language of school work is said to require an elaborated code, the inability to use anything except a restricted code explained a good part, if not all, of the working-class child's poor school achievement. He or she had a language deficiency which would directly prevent good performance in school unless it was remedied by teaching the use of elaborated code.

This model was quickly given up by researchers in the area, including Bernstein himself and his colleagues, although it continued to influence teachers and classroom remedial programmes (e.g. Tough 1973, 1977). Among the problems was, first, lack of evidence that the two codes had a real existence as distinct entities rather than as different modes on a continuum of variation. The literature virtually never contained transcribed examples, and linguists found the defining criteria unsatisfactory (Gordon 1981). It was generally the case that the evidence said to support the existence of separate codes was merely that one group of speakers *tended* to use *more* of a particular language form (e.g. passive verbs, 'implicit' pronouns) *in a particular situation* than another group of speakers. For example in a much-quoted experiment by Hawkins (1973, 1977), 5-year-olds were required to tell the story depicted in a series of pictures given by the tester. Middle-class children used more nouns to convey who was doing what in the pictures: lower working-class children used more pronouns, relying on the pictures to make their referent unambiguous. Hawkins argued that these 'implicit' 'restricted code' children were conveying less information about the pictures: their version

makes enormous demands on the listener. It means that the context (i.e. the pictures) must be present if the listener is to understand who and what is being referred to. It assumes the listener can *see* the pictures (Hawkins 1973, p. 87).

Since, however, both the child and the listener/tester *can* see the pictures in the test situation, the 'demands' and the 'ambiguity' are more in Hawkins' judgement than in the social ecology of the setting. Subsequent work (e.g. Hughes *et al.* 1979; Labov 1969; Heath 1983; Wells 1979) has amply demonstrated the fallacy of arguing that 'tend not to in situation X' implies 'cannot in any situation'. Subsequent formulations of links between language, class and education have taken into account the effect of different social contexts and the question of how *use* of language relates to language capabilities. It has also been realized that the relationship between linguistic form and cognitive complexity is not as uncomplicated as might have been supposed. Simple syntax *can* express logical sequence, hypothetical possibilities and interdependent propositions: complex syntax can often enough be used to disguise banal ideas.

Linguists have also found Bernstein's notion of 'implicitness' or 'explicitness' in language to be problematic. In 'implicit' use of language the meaning of a statement is not completely spelled out, as the speaker assumes that the listener has enough basic information to understand the unspoken part of the message. Strictly, however, *all* use of language involves assuming some shared understanding. We have to assume for example some shared vocabulary, syntactic knowledge and understanding of the social rules of discourse: if we could not make this assumption we could not communicate at all. Suppose we say 'the cat wants his dinner'. This simple sentence assumes the listener knows what a cat is; knows that we are talking about a particular cat, since we've said '*the*' cat, and indeed we're very probably talking about our own familiar domestic cat; similarly understands 'wants' 'his' and 'dinner'; and understands that in normal discourse the sentence would convey (at least to English speakers and listeners) an obligation to feed the cat. What looks like an explicit sentence of minimal complexity actually depends on a large amount of implicit information and works within rules of discourse that are also implicit, at least until they are broken (see Grice 1975; and p. 135 of this volume).

'Implicitness' is thus a normal part of language use, and indeed it would be impossible (or at least tedious) to be perfectly explicit on all occasions. Certainly there are likely to be problems in communication if the speaker's assumptions about shared aspects of meaning are incorrect and too much is left implicit; the listener may not understand what is said. It may even be a more serious breakdown in communication than over-explicitness, which would presumably leave the listener in a state of adequate understanding, though probably some social resentment against the speaker ('pedantic old bore'). What degree of implicitness is appropriate is a social property of the participants' whole discourse, and one of the aspects of language we learn from our experience of communicating with others about our world.

Bernstein's analysis is unsatisfactory in that it deals with implicitness as a property of the text. As we saw in the case of Hawkins' experiment, paralinguistic means to explicitness such as pointing are not included.

There are various grammatical features which are used to make reference unambiguous (see Romaine 1984, especially pp. 143–6); the indices Bernstein uses, types of pronouns and ratio of pronouns to full noun phrases, are inadequate as they ignore the situational context of the speech and, in practice, underestimate the effect of links between utterances (Gordon 1981).

Empirical investigations of whether there really are class differences in explicitness or implicitness of speech suggest that on the whole there are not. In Tizard and Hughes' study (1984), for example, mothers of all classes were sometimes implicit in talking to their daughters, but took good care to be perfectly explicit when it was felt to be important that the child should understand. Mothers varied in how much they demanded the child should be explicit: Robinson and Robinson (in press) suggest that parental demand that children should think about how to make themselves understood is a cause of a faster understanding of communication (see p. 137). Wells (1985) also found more variation within classes than between them.

Bernstein's later work (e.g. Bernstein 1973) moves 'codes' into a level of abstraction some distance from observable speech. Codes are now seen as a sort of underlying 'competence' which give rise to speech variants which are, roughly, the general range of syntactic forms, vocabulary items, and sort of meaning expressed. (See Chapters 2 and 3 for problems raised by competence/performance distinctions.) Syntax and vocabulary in speech variants are very like those proposed for the early version of 'codes': in

'restricted' speech variants, meaning is said to concentrate on 'particularistic' 'implicit' meaning shared between speaker and listener, while meaning in 'elaborated' speech variants is more concerned to be 'universalistic' and 'explicit', appealing to high level general principles. For example, a restricted code explanation for a parental command would be something like 'Because I say so'; an elaborated explanation would be 'Because people need to eat their spinach all up to grow into nice big strong people.'

Much about language is undoubtedly learned through socialization (see Chapter 6). Bernstein (1971) differentiates between two sorts of families which have different status structures and different communication systems. 'Positional' families are said to have clear-cut definitions of the role and status of different family members: 'children shall be seen and not heard'; daughters-in-law must defer to their mothers-in-law; the oldest son inherits the land, the second goes into the regiment, the third becomes a clergyman and takes up the family living: rigid status positions and roles are filled according to characteristics such as age, wealth and sex, not according to the particular strengths, weaknesses or desires of individual family members. In 'person-centred' families these status distinctions and ascriptions of roles are modified and varied in terms of the idiosyncrasies of individuals: people can achieve their positions on the basis of their merits, rather than having greatness (or exclusion from greatness) thrust upon them. Person-centred families are said to have 'open' communication systems; having a more fluid status system they need to communicate, negotiate and explain, and hence use elaborated code. Positional families have 'closed' communication systems and thus use restricted code, with strict social control based on commands and prohibitions explained only in terms of family members' status – 'Do as your father tells you'; 'Little girls can't do that'. Bernstein suggests that working-class families are predominantly 'positional', and middle-class families 'person-centred'.

Diagrammatically, his model is shown in Figure 16, where heavy arrows indicate a strong link and light ones a less certain link.

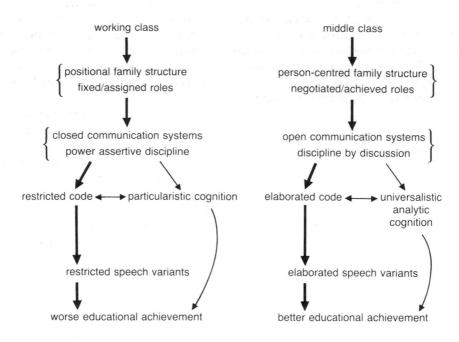

Figure 16

Both types of family structures may be found in each social class, and family types may vary in their communication system and codes: the version of the model drawn by Stubbs (1983) has, rather unkindly, all possible diagonal arrows drawn in between levels! However Bernstein (1973) is claiming tendencies to different class distributions, so there should be more emphasis on the vertical chains as drawn above, even if, exceptionally, diagonals may occur. It is expected that, on the whole, working-class families will be positional in structure; that, on the whole, positional families will generate closed communication systems; that, on the whole, closed communication fosters restricted code; that restricted code leads to restricted speech variants; and that restricted speech variants lead to educational underachievement.

This more elaborate formulation stands up to investigation little better than its predecessor. Just as there is no evidence for two distinct language 'codes' there is no evidence for two distinct family types, let alone two types clearly separable by class, and differences between families look like variations on a continuum, or, rather, on several continua which do not map on to the positional–person-centred distinction without loss of information (see Chapter 6). There is very little evidence that different family types talk in distinctly different ways. A few families are characterized by continual escalating conflict and non-communication (Patterson 1975; and see Chapter 6) but these aside, most families sometimes use explanations and sometimes not, sometimes ask or encourage questions and sometimes not, sometimes get involved in discussion of cognitively complex ideas, sometimes negotiate, sometimes command, and so forth. Wells (1985), reviewing the largest body of data available, emphasizes that by the time of their entry to school virtually all children had heard and used at home the same large range of syntax and language function. There are class differences in amounts of questioning, discussion, complex use of language, vocabulary and use of books and imaginative play between mother and pre-school child, but the differences are not large (Tizard and Hughes 1984; Wells 1979, 1985; Davie *et al.* 1984). There are more striking variations within classes than between them.

There is no good evidence at all on whether different sorts of language structure lead to different sorts of cognition. The difficulty of assessing cognitive structures is enormous (see Chapter 2 and 3): so is the difficulty of assessing the cognitive complexity of a language. Although there is a fairly plausible case that it is easier to talk about and think about things we have good vocabulary entries for (so that the Eskimo is more fluent in discussion of snow than the Spaniard, or the skier than the surfer), there is virtually no reason to believe that language structure severely restricts thought, and, especially, no good reason to believe that different languages vary in their possibilities of being explicit or logical (Labov 1969).

Differences in the *use* of language, however, including the social functions of language, may contribute to at least differences in knowledge about language and possibly also differences in cognitive processes. Children who have been encouraged or required to think about language itself, for example, seem to be faster in developing some aspects of knowledge about language. Elizabeth and Peter Robinson have carried out a careful and thorough series of experiments on developmental changes in children's understanding of communication failures due to the message having an ambiguous referent. These showed that children who had had their attention drawn (rather specifically) to the fact that the listener had not understood what the child meant, were better at playing a referential communication game and showed more understanding of why messages were not understood and of how to make them unambiguous (Robinson and Robinson 1982, 1983; and see p. 107 this volume). Children who have been taught about the sounds of letters

do more phonic processing in their reading and read better (Chall 1967; Bryant and Bradley 1985; and see p. 78 this volume). Children whose parents have talked to them in ways similar to those of their teachers probably understand rather better what their teachers require of them and how to provide it (Willes 1983; Wells 1981, 1982).

The emphasis shifts here to add an *indirect* link between the child's language and his or her performance in school, with the teachers' judgement of the child and its consequences (and perhaps the child's judgement of the teachers and school) being the crucial intervening variable. Teachers who think a child is stupid or inarticulate are likely to expect less and require less than they do of a pupil judged to be clever. A child who understands school as foreign, and teachers as people who impose meaningless tasks and ask bizarre questions, is presumably less likely to work hard and well than a pupil who finds school work and talk familiar, and understands why it is worth doing. This sort of fit or misfit is not likely to be simple, and the shifted emphasis is far from giving us an adequately detailed explanation of the educational failure which was the instigating problem. However the attention currently being given to the participants' view of education (see p. 198) to the sort of discourse that characterizes classrooms (see p. 132), to the patterns of stimulation, support, encouragement and motivation between parent and child, and teacher and child (see p. 184), and to self-concept development (see p. 150), seem likely to lead us to a better understanding of how to encourage everyone to be as clever as possible in as many ways as possible.

Language at home and at school

A popularized and radically cruder version of Bernstein's work argued, first, that children bring to school the language they used at home; second, that the middle class had access to what was called 'elaborated code' while the working class did not; third, that working-class children failed in school because they lacked the 'elaborated code' which school required; and fourth, that special language programmes should be run to remedy this deficit. Following a great deal of polemic, some careful collection and analysis of data has shown that there is a great deal to be said against each step of the argument just outlined.

It is necessarily true that children enter school having already developed many aspects of language. They have after all been using language for four or five years. If what I have said about the need for adult–child conversation and 'scaffolding' is at all true, this is just as well: no teacher could provide it for thirty children at once. Most children of 5 have shown themselves to be capable of constructing most of the sentence types and most of the semantic relationships of their language, including many complex ones (see, for example, Wells 1985, discussed earlier in this chapter). They still have things to learn about language, as we shall see, but they are basically linguistically competent. Do they bring this competence to school, as the first step of the argument asserts? The true answer is both yes and no, and the differences and discrepancies look important for the problems of social class and educational failure.

It *is* the case that some children are tongue-tied and monosyllabic when required to talk to teachers in school, and that such children often come from a background unlike the teacher's. This apparent inability to respond to the linguistic demands of the classroom is often interpreted as showing that the child *cannot* use language in the required ways, not merely that he or she *does not*. Closer observation of children shows, however, that in many cases they can and do use language perfectly competently when they are with their peers or members of their families (e.g. Wells 1982; Tizard and Hughes 1984; Wood 1981). This suggests that an explanation in terms of a deficiency in the ways the child *can* use language is untenable. An alternative explanation is that there is something unusual about the language usage required by schools, some factor in the demands that school makes on children which is unlike the demands of the home. Recent analyses (e.g. Sinclair and Coulthard 1975; Romaine 1984) of classroom language and behaviour suggest some focal differences. Most of

the discourse which children have taken part in at home has arisen from the participants' activity. It has a background of shared knowledge, so that each participant can assume the other knows roughly what is being talked about and what the aim of the conversation is. Much of the discourse is initiated by the child. School discourse is much more likely to be teacher-initiated, adult-structured and devoid of practical context. For example, a high proportion of teacher talk consists of 'display questions' such as 'what colour is the house?', where the teacher requires the child to give an answer which the teacher knows, and which the child knows the teacher knows. Questions at home are much more likely to occur because the questioner (child as frequently as adult) lacks information which he or she believes the respondent can supply, such as 'what would you like for dinner?'

Romaine (1984) points out that school conversations frequently have goals which are known to the teacher but not to the child, who is rarely told explicitly what the criteria for correctness are. She quotes (pp. 71–2) an example recorded by Dannequin of a French teacher who has strict but implicit criteria for what is an acceptable answer but expresses them so ambiguously that her pupils have to go through a long problem-solving process to get the 'right' answer.

T: *Avec quoi prend-on la température?*
What does one take a temperature with?

P: *Un thermomètre.*
A thermometer.

T: *Une petite phrase. Avec quoi prend-on la température? Véronique, une phrase.*
A short sentence. What does one take a temperature with? Veronica, a sentence.

V: *Un thermomètre.*
A thermometer.

T: *Tu me réponds par un mot. Je veux une phrase.*
You've given me a word. I want a sentence.

V: *Avec un thermomètre.*
With a thermometer.

T: *Ce n'est toujours pas une phrase. Tu me réponds par un autre mot. Je voudrais une phrase – Myriam.*
That's still not a sentence. You've just given me another word. I want a sentence – Myriam.

M: *Maman/prend/la température/avec un thermomètre* (utterance is syllable-timed with each chunk forming a separate tone group).
Mother takes a temperature with a thermometer.

T: *Voilà. Répète Véronique.*
There. Repeat, Veronica.

These pupils are being required to give up the normal discourse rule of not giving superfluous information (see the beginning of this chapter, p. 118) in favour of the showing-off of grammatical competence, and what is more, a grammatical competence somewhat arbitrarily defined by the teacher (*'une phrase'* can mean 'a phrase' in the English sense, so 'with a thermometer' or indeed 'a thermometer' would be technically adequate as answer). It is hardly far-fetched to feel that Véronique comes across as justifiably irritated and Myriam as getting rid of a pointless importunity. This is a particularly neat example because the teacher is requiring 'metalinguistic awareness', that is an ability to talk about language as having an objective existence, as being 'opaque' rather than 'transparent'. Dannequin's teacher is, however, representative here of a very high proportion of teacher–child discourse: Wells (1982) and Wood (1981) provide other examples. Heath (1983), in a brilliant study of children from different neighbourhoods in the south-east of the United States, reports awareness on the part of some children that different people used language differently, asking different sorts of questions, for example. One little boy, being given a lift in Heath's car a few weeks after he started nursery school, asked her a series of display questions about a fire-truck that passed, e.g. 'What colour dat truck? What colour dat coat? What colour dat car?' Such questions were rare at home, and Heath expressed her surprise at him asking questions to which they both knew the answer. The boy began laughing: he had been imitating the questions the teacher asked at school. If, as is probably the case, children playing at being teacher show even more stereotyped behaviour than children playing at being mothers, the reason may be somewhere in the oddness of much teacher–child dialogue.

Children become aware quite early that they are expected to talk in different ways with different people. Politeness rules, which are relatively systematically taught by many parents, are one example. Edinburgh schoolchildren reported to Romaine (1984) on the differences between 'polite' and 'rough' speech, the former being more like standard English and the latter more like Scots in features of pronunciation ('cannae' instead of 'can't', not 'down' but 'doon') and vocabulary ('ken' instead of 'know'). 'Dialect' differences such as these are associated by adults with differences in prestige, personality characteristics, education, occupation and so forth (see Giles and Powesland 1975), rural accented people being seen as nicer than urban accented people, and those using RP (Received Pronunciation or BBC/Oxford English) as being better educated and more powerful, though possibly not so trustworthy. Romaine's informants seemed to be making these sorts of distinctions by the later part of their primary school careers; by then, too, girls' language was usually nearer the prestige norm than boys' language, and they used fewer non-standard forms than boys. By this sort of age children used more non-standard language to their peers, too, sometimes seeing this as affirming (or required by) their social identity. Peer groups and other social groups often press their members into particular vocabularies, dialects or uses of language (see Romaine 1984, ch. 6.3; and p. 191 below).

School and home, then, show somewhat different ranges of language use. Some homes do include more school-type language than others, and homes which encourage relatively abstract and context-independent uses of language are quite likely to produce children whose language is advanced and who do cope well with school language (Wells 1982, 1985). A family which involves the child in literacy seems to be particularly advantageous (see also Osborn *et al.* 1984); no doubt this is partly because literacy is one of the major preoccupations of schools, but it is also probable that literacy encourages abstract and context-independent thought (see p. 140). There are class differences in literacy behaviour such as

Plate 11

reading, writing and discussing what is read or written, the middle classes indulging in them rather more, but otherwise there is as much variation in language use within social classes as there is between them. Talk of two homogeneous social classes, 'middle' and 'working' or 'lower-working', with two separate language codes, is seriously misleading (and to be fair, Bernstein would not have approved of such a model); so is an assumption that school language is exactly like any home language. The development of children's understanding of the demands of school is one of the growth areas for research at present (see Chapter 6). So is the search for explanations of children's school failure which examines the microsystem of the school for causes as well as the possible deficiencies of the child. So is the study of what language is used for, the subject which we now take up.

The functions of language

I mentioned the 'functions' of language in the first paragraph of this chapter, and they have been implicit in all that has been said since. The list of language functions which Michael Halliday (1975) observed in his young son provides an example of the range of uses which children's language can serve. A very early use is language in an *instrumental* function, a way in which the child satisfies his or her needs or wants; early language is also often *regulatory*, controlling others' behaviours, or *interactional*, used for establishing or maintaining interpersonal contact. Children also use language in a *personal* function, to talk about themselves, in the *heuristic* function, to find out about the world, and in the *imaginative* function of 'let's pretend'. Using language in the *informational* function is a relatively late development, but achieved well before pre-school. Initially language functions are simple, but they become more diverse and more are involved in any given utterance as people become more sophisticated speakers. Describing the function of the language being observed becomes problematic to a considerable degree.

The work of philosophers such as Austin, Searle and Grice on speech acts (see, for ex-

ample, Searle 1969) has provided important insights into 'how to do things with words'. One important distinction is between different levels of significance in an utterance such as the teacher's 'Somebody's making a lot of noise'. The first level is the *locution*, the linguistic form itself, in this case a possible neutral statement. The second is the *illocutionary* force, which is the type of speech act the speaker intends, here that the class should quieten down. The third is the *perlocutionary* force, the significance the hearer finds in the utterance, here perhaps that 'Miss wants everybody to be quiet' or 'Sir is making a fuss again'. Here we are mainly concerned with types of illocutionary forces, the functions which the speaker intends the utterance to serve.

Speech act theory provides definitions of speech acts such as requests, promises, threats and so on. For example, both promises and threats refer to future acts by the speaker, but promises refer to acts which will be of benefit to the hearer and threats to acts which will not. Children have to learn how to produce and comprehend speech acts in ways which are appropriate to their social and linguistic community, to the microsystems in which they take part. Problems may arise if the conventions for speech act usage differ between microsystems, such as the home/school differences I described above. A child who is used only to very direct speech acts, such as 'Shut up', may not see the illocutionary force of indirect ones, such as 'Someone's making a lot of noise'. Differences will apply at the level of single utterances and of whole long discourses: Heath (1983), for example, describes several different understandings of what 'stories' are and how to tell them.

Some examples of children's use of speech acts and of their awareness of the conditions that underpin them can be found in books and papers such as Garvey 1975, Ochs and Schieffelin 1979, Bates and MacWhinney 1979, Shatz 1983. Olson (1980a) provides a particularly nice example of the variety of social forms language can serve in the course of an interaction, in this case distributing dominoes equally between the two nursery-school children involved.

L: Let's make a domino house out of these.

J: Okay.

First by grabs.

J: Lookit how many I got . . . . You took a couple of mine!

L: Now *you* took a couple.

Then by commands.

L: Now you got to give me three back!

. . . .

L: Now give me just one more and then we got the same.

And then by requestful assertives.

J: Now, you got more than me–e.

And denials.

L: No! We got the same.

By fact collecting, assertions, and inferences.

L: [Begins to count her dominoes] One, two, three, four . . . twenty-eight, twenty-nine. [Then counts Jamie's dominoes] One, two, three, four . . . eighteen, nineteen . . . [short pause] twenty-nine.

J: I got nineteen and you got twenty-nine. . . . You got more than me.

L: No–o [shouting] I COUNTED. . . . You have the same as me . . . We got the same.

J: NO–O–O!

And when negotiations break down again, by grasping.
[There is a shuffle of dominoes across the floor and now Jamie has more than Lisa.]

And finally, by appeal to authority.

L: You got much more than me now.

J: Now we got the same
[Paul, a volunteer teacher, enters the room.]

L: Does he have much more than me?

P: Not too many more!

(Olson 1980a, pp. 95–6).

Some examples of these formal links are the replacement of nouns by pronouns on second and subsequent occurrences, or the use of items such as 'therefore', 'meanwhile' and 'in addition'. These devices refer back from the present word or phrase to earlier ones which it is not necessary to repeat verbatim because they can be understood from the whole linguistic context that has gone before. My use of 'these' and 'they' in the last three sentences are examples.

Very small children may merely string sentences together without using syntactical linking devices, but some instances of grammatical devices such as pronominal reference are produced and understood by pre-school children (Ervin-Tripp 1978; Karmiloff-Smith 1979). McTear (1985) describes the use of discourse connectors such as 'well', 'anyway' and so forth by his daughter Siobhan and her friend Heather. Over the period of recording the two little girls more such devices emerged and their discourse became both more flexible in structure and more continuous in theme. Devices for initiating, restarting and repairing conversation also became more varied and efficient. The children were able to monitor their own speech and the speech they heard and to take appropriate action to repair conversation and adjust its course so as to achieve the social interaction they desired. By the time they reached school-age Siobhan and Heather were effective as a conversational duo and in their talking with familiar adults. Differences of conversational style between these children and adults were mainly of degree – for example the adults, who had more world knowledge and more power, would use more indirect speech, innuendo and oblique references – though adults, of course, have more practice in specialized types of discourse such as counselling, chairing meetings or seduction routines. As they get older, children too learn more about how to use language to get the result they want (e.g. Clark and Delia 1976; Romaine 1984).

The picture of children's conversational competence which is emerging from research at present shows less of the incompetent egocentric language use which Piaget (1959) described and more of children using a variety of conversational devices in orderly ways similar to adults' usage. By school-age they have shown many complex skills: later conversational development is predominantly through increased world knowledge, better social cognition and mastery of rare linguistic forms. The integration of literacy and thinking and the world of school are perhaps the crucial problems and possibilities.

Children's metalinguistic behaviour

In Chapter 3 I discussed work on 'metacognition', children's awareness of and control of their thinking. There is a similar concept in the work on language development, children's awareness of and control of their language. As language has many different levels, metalinguistic competence has many components too and develops over a long period of time. Intuitive judgements about the sameness or difference of consonants such as 'p' or 'b' can be traced back to infants' discriminations (see Aslin *et al*. 1983, and Chapter 2 this volume), but picking the odd word out in a set containing contrasting items such as 'pat', 'bat', 'bee' and 'boy' is hard for children beginning to learn to read (eg Bryant and Bradley 1985).

Observations of pre-school children show use and awareness of different sorts of language, for example the child aged 2:10 who was recorded as saying 'When I was a little girl I could go "geek-geek" like that. But now I can go "this is a chair"', or the children who refuse to accept from other people the incorrect pronunciation or construction which they themselves use (Clark and Clark 1977; De Villiers 1979). Slobin 1978 provides an example of how 'flickering' children's awareness of grammar can be at this age:

Overgeneralizations planted in adult speech elicited protest from Heida only if the standard form happened to be momentarily present in her consciousness:

§25 (4;7). If she has just used the correct past tense of an irregular verb, she is annoyed with me if I respond to her with the overregularization; but if she has used the overregularization, she does not object to my following suit. If I follow her incorrect form with the correct form, she will often switch to the correct form.

The following dialogue is a good example of how the two forms flit in and out of consciousness in the course of natural conversation:

Dan: Hey, what happened last night after we left? Did Barbara [the baby sitter] read you that whole story? Remember you were reading *Babar*?

Heida: Yeah ... and, um, he ... she also ... you know ... `mama, mama, uh, this morning after breakfast, read the whole, um, book of the three little pigs and that, you know that book, that ... .

[digression of about one minute]

Heida: I don't know when she readed ...

Dan: You don't know when she what?

Heida: ... she readed the book. But you know that book – that green book – that has the gold goose, and the three little pigs, and the three little bears, and that story about the king?

Dan: M-hm.

Heida: That's the book she read. She read the whole, the whole book.

Dan: That's the book she *readed* huh?

Heida: Yeah ... *read*! [annoyed].

Dan: Oh.

Heida: Dum-dum!

[brief interlude about dressing]

Dan: Barbara readed you *Babar*?

Heida: *Babar*, yeah. You know, cause *you* readed some of it too.

Dan: Well I just started it.

Heida: Yeah. She readed all the rest.

Dan: She read the whole thing to you, huh?

Heida: Yeah ... nu–uh – *you* read some.

Dan: Oh, that's right; yeah, I readed the beginning of it.

Heida: *Readed*?! [annoyed surprise] *Read*! [insisting on the obvious].

Dan: Oh yeah – read.

Heida: Will you stop that, papa?

Dan: Sure.

(Slobin 1978, pp. 52–3).

Heida can monitor her language (and her father's) and correct it, but does not do so consistently. The pressure to communicate may have overcome the pressure to be grammatical; adults commonly accept ungrammatical utterances which are intelligible (see, for example, Wells 1982).

Segmentation is an important part of metalanguage. Segmenting words into sounds seems to be difficult for most children under about 7 and is a particular problem for poor readers (Bryant and Bradley 1985).

Training children to focus on sounds increased their metalinguistic awareness and their performance: in the case of the children Bradley trained it improved their reading. There are similar difficulties in segmenting sentences or utterances into words; again, children's ability to do this improves at around 6 or 7, and it seems likely that language awareness and reading practice influence each other. Ideas about words often confound the word itself and its referent: thus 'book' is a 'long word' because 'it has lots of letters in it', or 'primrose' a short one because primroses are small (Berthoud-Papandropoulou 1978). Words such as 'the' are not proper words: alternatively a 'word' given as response to the question 'tell me a word' might be a complete sentence. Again, reading is associated with understanding segmentation into words. Experience with written texts probably also helps children to deal with unusual grammatical constructions such as 'over and over rolled the ball'.

Awareness that what is said and what is meant are not necessarily the same is another fairly late achievement (e.g. Olson and Torrance 1983). For example, in one of Olson's experiments children were read a story about two children sharing some popcorn and then arguing about the distribution. One says to the other 'You have more than me!' 5-year-olds asked what was said are likely to reply that the child in the story said 'Give me more'. 7-year-olds report verbatim *and* can show they knew what was meant as well. In another study children of this age did not manage to deal with literal and expected meaning quite so well. Here a Sesame Street character said 'I'm going to divide this banana up so both of us can have some' and then ate the whole banana and gave his partner the skin. It was not until at least 8 that children realized that this division did fulfil the literal meaning of the sentence, though not the promise it implied. No doubt sad social experience contributes to understandings of this sort.

Children's handling of ambiguity is another source of evidence on their metalinguistic awareness. Again there are various sorts of ambiguity. It can be due to lexical double meanings (such as 'pipe') or syntactic ambiguities ('she hit the man with the glasses', 'he told her baby stories'). Children's jokes often exploit ambiguities of sound, vocabulary, syntax or expectation. Gleitman and Gleitman (1978, p. 118) provide some examples:

Sample jokes, classified in terms of the source of ambiguity

A: Phonological
1. If you put three ducks in a box what do you have? A box of quackers.
2. Bob coughed until his face turned blue. Was he choking? No, he was serious.

B: Lexical
1. How can hunters in the woods best find their lost dogs? By putting their ears to a tree and listening to the bark.
2. How do we know there was fruit on Noah's ark? Because the animals came in pairs.

C: Surface Structure
1. How would you run over a dinosaur? I'd start at his tail, run up his back, then over his neck and I'd jump off.
2. Where would you go to see a man-eating fish? A seafood restaurant.

D: Deep Structure
1. We're going to have my grandmother for Thanksgiving. You are? Well, we're going to have a turkey.
2. Will you join me in a bowl of soup? Do you think there's room for both of us?

E: Morpheme Boundary –No Phonological Distortion	1.	Why can one never starve in the desert? Because of the sand which is there.
	2.	How do trains hear? Through their engine ears.
F: Morpheme Boundary with Distortion	1.	Do you think that if I wash, my face will be clean? Let's soap for the best.
	2.	Did you read in the newspaper about the man who ate six dozen pancakes at one sitting? No – how waffle.

Understanding ambiguity, appreciating verbal jokes which use it, and developing the use of metaphor (Reynolds and Ortony 1980; Kogan 1983) are all aspects of language awareness which develop during the school years. All of them both require and make possible greater world knowledge and social understanding.

Word meanings and concepts

Words refer to concepts: concepts are labelled by words. There is an intimate interaction and mutual influence between cognition and language. I want here to look briefly at two aspects of this interaction: first the child's early use of concepts and of conceptual language, and then the question of how literacy affects language and thinking.

Early concepts

People's conceptual knowledge may be much more varied than their words for expressing it; for example, there are many more discriminably different colours than there are colour terms, and the culture's vocabulary of colour words is not a major determinant of accuracy of colour discrimination, though it does affect ease of labelling colours (Heider 1971, 1972; Rosch and Lloyd 1978). We do not have good descriptions of complete concept systems, though there are some interesting examples of attempts to map out some limited areas such as a 4-year-old's knowledge of dinosaurs (Chi and Koeske 1983), and patients' views on the significant people in their lives drawn up using Repertory Grids (e.g. Fransella 1976). Young children doubtless have

simpler concept systems, but it requires considerable ingenuity to elicit information from them.

Gelman and Baillargeon (1983) and Clark (1983) review some of the recent work on the beginnings of categorization and concept labelling. Both the habituation evidence from babies which I discussed in Chapter 2, and some evidence on very young children's manipulation of categorizable objects, suggest that the roots of categorization lie in the first year of life, before the child is producing language. Children's sorting behaviour can involve a significant amount of choosing objects consecutively from the same category before 18 months old, even an exhaustive search for a category, but at that age, and for a year or two to follow, sorting is in competition with pattern making, and the child may move freely from picking out items of a particular colour to arranging items in a pleasing pattern. This oscillation between interests leads to the apparently haphazard and conceptually confused 'collections' and 'chain concepts' which Vygotsky (1962) and others described. Markman, Cox and Machida (1981) report an experiment where children sorted items into plastic bags instead of on a table top: this procedure made 'arrangements' impossible and increased the frequency of logically based sortings. Thus there is some categorization of objects round about the time that children are producing their first words and sentences. Clark (1983) points out that early words, which typically first apply to a prototype object, are quickly used for all objects of that kind, not just the original prototype. Words such as 'dirty' are applied to objects which are 'dirty' in different physical ways but share the *conceptual* characteristic of being something you shouldn't touch, something taboo or literally likely to make you dirty. At this point in language use we find the 'over-extensions' I mentioned earlier, and also probably various other less conspicuous mismatches between word and referents. Children are already using sets of properties to define which objects are members of a category, and over-extended uses do tend to involve some similarities in appearance or other properties with the prototype instance. They try out different

139

assignments of objects to categories, picking up the community's conventional labels and judgements of 'same' or 'different'. Success in communication is an important criterion for the continued use of a concept–instance match. Children assume that there will be a word for a concept which is consistent from one instance of that concept to the next and which will also contrast with the words that belong to contrasting concepts. From very early on they ask for adult forms, try them and repair their own word choices (Clark 1983, p. 805). The goal is to fill lexical gaps by finding words for concepts the child wants to talk about. Gaps may be filled by finding the right word or by temporary measures such as overextensions or the use of general purpose words such as 'that', 'thing', 'do' or 'go', though these tend to be context-dependent. Children also coin new words, frequently using the standard devices of the language. In English, for example, nouns can be converted into verbs or vice versa, e.g. trumpet, attempt; affixes are used, e.g. garden–gardener–under-gardener; and there are compound words, e.g. darkroom, taxpayer. We need more data on children's word coinage, but they certainly use conversion ('Can you needle my shirt'; 'I'm gonna gun you'), and suffixes (where they prefer the more frequent '-er' to '-ist'), and make compound words (a smile-person, a knock-thing).

Appreciating the relationship between concepts and the overlapping of different words' referents requires a considerable amount of world-knowledge. In the absence of crucial knowledge, using a superordinate category may be impossible. Gelman and Baillargeon (1983) give as example some unpublished work by Susan Carey on children's concepts of animals. Characteristics such as breathe, think, have bones, were recognized as animal-like properties, and children recognized that mammals had most of these defining characteristics; then, in order, birds, insects, fish and worms, were seen as being the least 'animal' like. However, young children did not know accurately which animals had which characteristics and did not reliably judge one property to be more crucial than another. This

ignorance would lead inevitably to classifications which are biologically ill-founded. Ignorant adults make the same sort of mistakes; both adults and children may be deceived by words which are similar into believing that the objects they refer to are similar too. Adults' use of category hierarchies appears to influence children's learning of superordinate categories (Callanan 1985).

Literacy, language and thinking
I have emphasized throughout my discussion of children's cognition and language that they develop within a social context. Particularly once children attend school, literacy is an important part of this context. There are strong arguments in the literature that language and cognition skills are necessary for the development of literacy (notably awareness of language concepts, and awareness of language sounds, see p. 78) and also that literacy changes people's use of language and ways of thinking. It is this latter possibility that I want to concentrate on here.

There have been two main bodies of evidence for the assertion that becoming literate changes the ways in which people think and use language. One body of evidence centres on the marked change in children's thinking and talking which Piaget and many others have observed to happen during the early school years. An important part of this change is a growing ability to reassign descriptions or categorizations to the same object or event. This is seen as being related to the child's learning to read, an achievement which requires systematic thought about the alternatives and categorizations possible in language. Reading also opens up systematic access to the stored knowledge of the culture, and is thus what Bruner (1966) called a 'cultural amplifier'. Bruner sees the culture's supply of 'amplifiers' and the demands that life in the culture makes on an individual as being crucial determinants of the 'powers of mind' which will develop. For example, our society demands (among many other things) that people go through a formal educational process. Becoming literate is essential for coping with this demand; literacy is also one of the cultural amplifiers which the educational process offers, not just in school but in the use of books and other writing and reading outside school.

A similar suggestion comes from the second body of evidence which relates literacy, thinking and language. This consists of historical and ethnographic studies of the consequences of literacy or other social changes (e.g. Goody 1977; Luria 1976). In societies where literacy is newly introduced, those who become literate become able to do new thinking and language tasks rather as children becoming literate do in a culture where literacy is already established. Among the areas in which change has been claimed (for both children and literate members of developing societies) are deliberate remembering, logical and scientific reasoning, and various aspects of language use more characteristic of writing than of speech (see Goody and Watt 1968; Olson 1977; and Chapter 3 this volume).

There is debate about whether the consequences of literacy are *general* cognitive changes which extend far beyond reading and writing to other areas of language and thought, highly generalizable cognitive operations that are responsible for intelligent behaviour; or whether they are *specific* changes centering on literacy tasks and extending not terribly far from the business of reading and writing. Although the issue is very complex, the present emphasis seems to be on the *specific* possibilities which literacy allows rather than on literacy as a general 'cultural amplifier' which has strong effects even when literate skills are not being directly used. For example, Cole and Griffin (1980) describe experiments which show that most normal adults have the ability to correlate pieces of information and make correct inferences, whether they live in literate societies or not. What makes literate adults rather better at such tasks is that they use

writing and devices such as tables of instances to help them remember the information; if they are not allowed to do this, they forget information and so reason no better than illiterates. Similarly, provision of record-making materials lifted the performance of primary school children to the 'formal operations' level of systematic hypothesis testing on Piaget's science tasks (e.g. Brainerd 1978).

Further evidence that literacy's effects may be centred on the skills of literacy comes from Scribner and Cole (1981). They studied a society which has several different systems of literacy. The Vai people in Liberia use a syllable-based script, mainly for letter-writing and record-keeping: this script is learned at home. It is useful but not necessary for the Vai's traditional employments as rice farmers, small-scale entrepreneurs and craftsmen. About 20 per cent of Vai men use Vai script. Some people have attended American-type schools where they learn to read and write in and through English. There is also an Islamic influence; some Vai read Arabic, mostly just to decode the Koran and read it in religious services, but some also use it to write letters and records and to read commentaries on the Koran. Literates of these four different sorts were tested on a variety of skills based on analysis of literate practices, such as coding and decoding symbols, recalling information, playing a communication game and solving logical syllogisms. Test performance was very closely related to the specific functions of the particular literacy used by the subject. They argue that the apparent general effects of literacy are related to what it is used for and how it is taught. 'Cultural amplifiers' are embedded in the social context as language and cognition themselves are. Practice at meeting the demands of the microsystem makes perfect on the skills the microsystem requires: not necessarily on the skills it does not.

Plate 12 'The Castlemilk lads'

5 Personality

Just as there has been a tremendous variety of ways of understanding and investigating 'personality' itself, there have been many different approaches to its development. Developmental studies have encountered all the conceptual and methodological problems of general personality theories, plus difficulties associated with the interpretation of continuity of character or behaviour over time. Theories of personality development differ in their basic ideas about the origin of personality, about its consistency, and about the importance of life events and possible series of developmental stages. This chapter looks first at theories which place more emphasis on permanent 'dispositions', next at some 'stage' or 'life-event' approaches, and finally at the developmental evidence for certain aspects of 'personality'.

Physiology and personality

The belief that people differ in general character, that their approach to different situations is, say, consistently active or lethargic, melancholic or optimistic, is a very ancient one indeed. So is the attribution of such differences to an underlying physiological bias. Such ideas can be traced through millennia, surfacing strongly in the nineteenth century in phrenology and physiognomy (Gould 1984, in a vivid description of this work – and of early intelligence testing – provides a salutary warning to psychologists about the social implications of their research). They appeared again in this century in Kretschmer's and Sheldon's work on the link between body-build and character; and might be seen to be related also to Eysenck's accounting for introversion–extraversion and neuroticism in terms of the way the central nervous system works (e.g. Eysenck 1967). So far as the early theories were concerned, it was a case of 'anatomy is destiny';

for Sheldon, if you had a round, soft, plump sort of body you were destined to be a comfort-loving, relaxed, sociable sort of character, just as for Lombroso if you had ears which stuck out or unevenly set eyes you were almost bound to go in for one or the other sort of criminal activity. Personality was seen as genetically fixed, and as running in families. Jukes and Kallikaks bred true, and social reform depended heavily on eugenic breeding strategies.

These were seductive theories, corresponding plausibly with common-sense everyday experience, and they had a long run. However once careful and large-scale investigations were carried out, the correlations between body-build and character, let alone between skull shape and character, turned out to be too small to be much predictive use. The direction of causation of any such relationship is, in any case, likely to be unclear. The ectomorph, long, thin and weedy in build, with (less measurably) a highly sensitive nervous system and a low threshold for sensation, is unlikely to be easily competent or skilled at vigorous competitive athletic activities, or at settling disputes by physical means, and so may indeed concentrate on intellectual and symbolic activities. Conversely, however, avoiding strenuous exercise will affect how muscular the body becomes and indeed how efficiently heart, lungs and so forth work. Only if there is a self-induced 'experiment' in the form of a change of lifestyle can we know if body-type determines personality or vice versa. We know very little about how much changes in each are possible, or affect the other. People who change the amount of exercise they take quite often claim that they have experienced changes in psychological areas too: systematic study would be useful, here. So would studies of whether round, cuddly babies are treated very differently from hard muscular babies; given the apparent difference in both description and handling that boy and girl babies receive, it would seem quite possible that subtle differences in experience amplify initial small differences in physiology.

This sort of interaction, and these sorts of problems, no doubt also apply to Eysenck's model based on differences in the central nervous system. However there is little evidence about the continuity of extraversion–introversion over childhood (it seems to be fairly consistent in the adult years) and neuroticism, at least in terms of the prognosis from childhood depression or anxiety to similar states in adulthood, is not particularly consistent (Barker 1979). The theory is not entirely clear about the degree to which the 'balance' of the central nervous system is affected by – or determined by – experience. Again, answers to these questions would be very useful.

Thus there is not at present an adequately-grounded model of the relationship between physical and psychological characteristics in general personality. There is work on relationships between *variation* in physical characteristics such as hormone level and differences in aggressive, nurturant and other behaviour which we will look at later. One important and very interesting body of research has, however, continued to look at continuities in personality over childhood. Among the workers involved in studying 'temperament' have been Thomas and Chess and their colleagues (e.g. Thomas and Chess 1977; Buss and Plomin 1975; Halverson and Waldrop 1976; Kohn 1977). Dunn (1980) and Berger (1985) discuss the methodological issues involved, and a CIBA foundation symposium (CIBA 1982) reviews recent work.

Temperament

'Temperament' is seen as continuities of characteristic style of behaviour which can be observed and rated in infancy, and pervade all that a person does. Temperament interacts with experience to produce personality. Various 'temperament' dimensions have been suggested, among them activity level, general mood quality, how rhyth-

mic or predictable behaviour is, intensity of reaction, approach–withdrawal, distractability and fastidiousness. There is a tendency for clusters on these variables to be found which Thomas *et al.* label as 'easy', 'difficult' and 'slow to warm up' general types of temperament. 'Easy' babies are positive in mood, regular and predictable in behaviour, moderate in their activity and reaction, and highly adaptable to changes. 'Difficult' babies are intense, negative, irregular and slow to adapt. 'Slow to warm up' babies are inactive, withdrawn and slow to adapt. These characteristics are said to be highly stable over short periods of time, though continuities decrease as the time interval increases from babyhood to childhood. It is also claimed that early temperament differences are predictive of later psychopathology. Children whose early 'temperament' is irregular, unadaptable, negative, unfastidious and highly intense are particularly likely to be referred for psychiatric treatment in childhood or early adulthood. Children who are 'slow to warm up' may also have later problems, but these are likely to be of withdrawal and apathy, where the 'difficult' children are more likely to have more vigorous and disruptive behaviour problems (Rutter 1985a; Kohn 1977).

Temperament is generally assessed by means of detailed reports of the child's behaviour elicited from the mother or some other adult who knows the child well. Such reports are generally creditably accurate about present behaviour, though their accuracy in looking back over a period of months may be more doubtful. There are however more serious methodological problems. There may well be a quite marked relationship between baby differences, caretaker differences and continuity. Attentive mothers, for example, tend to have more alert babies; there are continuities in the mother's contribution to interactive style which may help to produce continuities in the child's (Ainsworth 1979; Dunn 1980). While temperament is often continuous in a stable environment, a change in caretaker, as in adoption, is likely to lead to discontinuities in the child's behaviour (see Chapter 6, and also Tizard (1977) on late adoption, which is discussed elsewhere). Similarly apparent 'temperament' varies in interaction with different members of the family: that is it has a substantial interactive or relational component. Finally, difficulties arise over the 'meaning' of behaviour and the assessment of continuity over time. To take an obvious example, crying on encountering a difficulty might be seen as adaptive for a baby, for whom it summons help, less so for a 5-year-old and actually maladaptive for a 10-year-old. Similarly, longitudinal studies show up subtleties in the patterning of continuities over time. Halverson and Waldrop (1976) found considerable stability in their general 'activity' dimension between $2\frac{1}{2}$ and $7\frac{1}{2}$ years. At $2\frac{1}{2}$, ratings of 'very high activity play' were associated with individual differences in 'social participation' and 'impulse high activity'. However these two latter variables were associated with quite different groups of behaviour measures at $7\frac{1}{2}$. High social participation at $2\frac{1}{2}$ was positively correlated with social participation at $7\frac{1}{2}$, with high verbal IQ and with high field independence. High impulsivity of action had *negative* implications for intellectual development. Possibly this difference might be related to the different demands made on children at the two ages: a child of $7\frac{1}{2}$ is expected to be able to control its impulses and fit them to outside constraints such as classroom requirements of sustained concentration and planful activity. A 'cognitive style' characterized by high impulsivity has often been seen as militating against academic achievement, and impulsivity might in excess (or in extreme lack) also have social implications.

These subtle relationships between characteristics over time are further complicated by the existence of differential socialization. Parents try to encourage ways of behaving in their child which will make the child better able to cope with the world. One interesting example – though ethnographic rather than the sort of work on which we are concentrating here – is found in Heath's (1983) account of language use in different Appalachian communities (see Chapter 4 this volume). Another, older, example in one of the pioneering studies of temperament and socialization, is

Kagan and Moss's (1962) findings on sex differences in dependence and aggression. In their longitudinal study of Midwestern children through the 1950s they found that the degree of dependence in infancy predicted to dependence in childhood and young adulthood in girls but not in boys: that is a highly dependent female baby was likely to be highly dependent as an adolescent girl, while a highly dependent male baby was not likely to be particularly dependent as a boy or youth. The reverse was true for aggression, which was fairly continuous in relative level in boys, but discontinuous for girls: aggressive little girls, and dependent little boys, were taught to change their behaviour towards the social stereotype of the passive nurturant female and the go-getting competitive male.

Stage models of personality

Whatever there may be in terms of personality differences 'innate' in the person – as temperament was first supposed to be – they are not easily measured or indeed conceptualized, and they will in any case interact with life stresses and the day-to-day experience of less extreme events in very complex ways. We do not know exactly how this happens, but general models of personality which emphasize development through a series of life-events have been put forward. Many have Freudian ancestry, many see life as a series of crises that have to be overcome but leave their scars on the developing personality. Erikson's eight stages (Erikson 1963) provide an example of this approach. Each stage is dominated by a conflict which has to be resolved. Thus, in the first stage the infant has to develop a sense of 'basic trust' that the world is basically benevolent and trustworthy: the mother's reliability and sensitivity (especially to the baby's oral needs) are crucial to this achievement, and if they fail the infant will have a sense of basic mistrust. The second stage's conflict is between autonomy and shame or doubt; developing control of anal reflexes and learning when to give and when to withhold faeces are the crucial events in this second year. Later conflicts include establishing a secure sense of identity rather than a sense of role diffusion (the fifth stage, adolescence), and resolving the contradictions between intimacy and isolation (the sixth stage, young adulthood).

As with other stage theories, Erikson's eight are presented as a series and appear to be discrete and relatively self-contained, though a poor outcome to a particular stage-conflict will lead to problems at later stages. What evidence there is on the existence of these stages comes from clinical material or from highly interpretive accounts of data which may not be much more reliable (Block 1971; Levinson 1978; Vaillant 1977). The conflicts themselves may have particularly acute periods at particular stages, but the difficulties they involve could equally well be thought to be constituents of human social life, at least in its modern western form. There is room for doubt over whether some of the stages appear at all in other social traditions, though Erikson regarded them as universal, and over whether they are common even in western experience. The 'identity crisis' of adolescence, for example, appears to be Eriksonian in only a small minority (Coleman 1980). Nevertheless, Erikson's emphasis on the different demands that are made on the developing child at different ages is a useful one. It raises two sets of questions: first, what are these demands and what stresses do they set up, and second, how far, and why, do the present stresses have links to past and future? There has been some interesting work done on the links between the demands parents make on their children, including how these are made, and the outcome in terms of children's personality and behaviour. This detailed work is discussed in the next chapter.

Self-concept development

Parental behaviour less explicitly specified has been seen for some considerable time as one of the most important sources of the self-concept. G. H. Mead in his classic book *Mind, Self and Society* (Mead 1934) says that via social interaction the young child begins to appreciate that other people (notably, parents) have views of him or her as 'good', 'bad', 'clever', 'a real boy', 'big for her age' and so forth. These views are inferred from others' behaviour towards him or her as well as from their talk, and are accepted as evaluative and categorical labels much like names. It is from these labels applied by others that the child builds up his or her self-concept – a 'looking-glass self'.

More recent theorists paint a slightly different picture. Lewis and Brooks-Gunn (1979) make Mead's account part of a wider development. They describe two rather different aspects of the 'self'. The subjective aspect, the 'existential self', is centrally the distinction of oneself from others, the awareness of the 'me' who is acting, experiencing, remembering and so forth. It probably involves the sensory self which may have a neurological base (Konner 1982) but it requires a sense of self-permanence which Lewis and Brooks-Gunn see as analogous to object permanence, and also an accumulation of learning about the patterning of actions and outcomes. As we have seen in discussing infancy, the rudiments of a distinction between self and not-self seem to become apparent increasingly clearly in the baby's first six months; by the last quarter of the first year distinctions between self and other are becoming independent of specific actions and contexts so that the child could be said to have a permanent 'existential self'.

From here on, the second aspect of the self develops too. This is the objective aspect, the 'categorical self'. This aspect refers to the characterization of oneself in terms of categories like gender, age, competence, attractiveness etc. The categories used may change between cultures or historical periods or may be universal, and may change over an individual's lifetime or remain constant. To give an example: my own 'categorical self' would include the following categories, all relative and not in any order of importance: 'tall', which appeared early, will remain constant and could be universal; 'female', also early, universal and constant, although the defining attributes and connotations of 'female' have undergone historical and cultural changes; 'distrustful of technology' which appeared late, is clearly not historically and culturally universal and possibly ought to be changed, in view of what I shall have to say about the effects of self-fulfilling prophecies! Such self-categorizations develop from babies' understanding of their own actions and from their use of others' categorizations of them, and language and other symbolic systems play an increasingly important part. During the second year, the self-concept develops rapidly: Kagan (1981) calls this the period of 'the emergence of self-awareness'. Verbal self-reference and use of pronouns 'you' and 'I' begin here. Research (e.g. Bertenthal and Fischer 1978) has identified landmarks in the process: from 10 months on the child who sees in a mirror a moving object whose movements are contingent on his or her own begins to be able to use the information in his or her reflection to locate the object; from about 18 months old, seeing in his or her reflection a trace of rouge which had earlier been surreptitiously put on his or her face, the child reaches out to touch not the reflection but the rouged spot on his or her own face. This achievement requires an image of what one's own face normally looks like and a recognition and location of the discrepancy. Gallup (1977, 1979) has demonstrated that given some hours of familiarization with mirrors, primates such as chimpanzees could similarly recognize themselves, but (so far) animals such as macaques, baboons and gibbons could not. Interestingly chimpanzees reared in social isolation did not show self-recognition. This is what Mead's account of self-concept developing through social interaction would predict, and it might be seen as analogous to the self-reports of humans who grew up with little social experience (Hartup 1978), but we really need a great deal more investigation of the competences and pathologies of social isolates before we can claim to understand the role of social interaction in the development of self-concept.

The mirror recognition experiments demonstrate young children's interest in observing their own actions and in discrepancies such as an unexpected rouge-coloured spot. Kagan (1981, 1984) points out that discrepancy becomes a preoccupation in the second year; things which are broken, or not as they should be, are enthralling and often distressing. Distress at something that is broken or 'dirty' might, of course, be seen as a conditioned result of the scolding, slaps or cold adult faces which accompany the child's breaking or soiling of objects (and toilet-training is likely to be part of the child's life at this age), but it could also be related to children's distress when their self-categorizations are teasingly denied. Once children have learned their gender, for example, the discrepancy of saying that a boy is a girl may evoke vigorous denial and upset: or may, in more favourable circumstances, be a big joke. Dunn and Kendrick (1982), presenting rich and fascinating data, provide a nice example which illustrates a child's play with categorization of herself, her teddy and her baby brother (it also shows her use of an adult label to describe herself, and a possible confusion of the referent of 'you' in her response to her father's first question).

Sally C:
Child (playing with her teddy) to father, F: Teddy's a man.

F: What are you?

C: You're a boy.

F: Yeah. What are you?

C: A menace.

F: Yeah, a menace. Apart from that are you a boy or a girl?

C: Boy (laughs).

F: Are you? What's Trevor?

C: A girl (laughs).

F: You're silly.

(Dunn and Kendrick 1982, pp. 110–11)

Several authors have pointed out that gender seems to be an early part of self-categorization, and as we shall see in the next chapter it becomes a salient aspect of children's social lives. Relative age seems to be another fairly early attribution, again salient in social relations (Lewis and Brooks-Gunn 1979) and, in Dunn and Kendrick's data on the first-born child's reaction to a new younger sibling, part of what appear to have been extensive discussions of people. In two examples, a child seems to have 'a triumphant sense of always being ahead':

Laura W:
1) C to Mother (after M comments to Baby about cutting teeth): I was cutting teeth. I was walking before he was. I walked before him..

2) C to Observer: He's a walloper. He'll smack me when he's bigger. I'm going to be huge when he's a bit bigger. Up to the ceiling. Like you.

   O to C: I'm not up to the ceiling.

   C to O: Well, I'll be up there. I'll grow so much. Up to the ceiling. So high.

(Dunn and Kendrick 1982, pp. 108–9)

Comparisons of self with peers and siblings seem to be increasingly recognized in the literature as important sources of the self-concept. Again, the contribution of interactions with other children will be discussed in the next chapter; but this new recognition has implications for the concept of 'identification' which I will discuss here.

Identification

Although it is a crucial concept in several accounts of the development of the self, the conscience and sex role, 'identification' has proved somewhat hard to define and very hard indeed to measure. On the whole, if A is to be said to be 'identified' with B, A must act, feel, think like B over a long period of time, in many different situations, and not by superficial or deliberate imitation but more unwittingly; and A must strongly want to be like B. Identification is both process and outcome; it is taking on a role in such a way that the role becomes oneself. It is differentiated from 'imitation', which is more likely to be temporary, fragmentary and deliberate, to have less emotional tone, although imitation can contribute to the process of identification. (Certain sorts of behaviour therapy and of actors' preparation for new roles illustrate this.) Simple overt similarity of behaviour is not a reliable index of identification, since similarity can result from

similar experiences (for example people who are slightly short-sighted are often said to be aloof and not to greet their acquaintances, whom they have not seen well enough to recognize) or from similar genes – as in the reports of similar postures and gestures among twins separated very young (Watson 1981).

Explanations of why identification happens have come from two main groups of theorists; Freud and his successors on the one hand and the social learning theorists on the other. Both centre their model on children identifying with their parents and particularly with the parent of the same sex. One motivation is to gain social approval and to avoid punishment; another is to lessen the risk or pain of losing the parent by becoming one's own parent-substitute. Maccoby (1980) gives an example supplied by Anna Freud:

A little girl, just two years old, had always been put to bed by her mother, and there was a familiar bed-time routine. For the first time, the mother was away overnight, and the child was being put to bed by a baby-sitter. The child had great difficulty going to sleep, and even though she was very tired, kept her eyes open after she was tucked in and the sitter had tiptoed out of the room. Through the open door, the sitter hears the child say, imitating her mother's voice: 'Goodnight my dearest' (Maccoby 1980, pp. 14–15).

Identification here provides comfort: it is also said to reduce anxiety about loss of love by making it less likely that the child will want to offend against parental prohibitions, to provide definition and models of the skills one ought to acquire, and to allow for vicarious experience and understanding. It is seen as especially important in the development of conscience (see moral development) and of gender identity and sex-roles. For both, identification with the parent of the same sex is said to be crucial: if this identification fails, the conscience will be weak and gender identity confused. This has been an influential theory to a wider audience than just professional psychologists: but this is how Eleanor Maccoby summarizes the research that has investigated it.

The research in child rearing that stemmed from this tradition was imposing both in conception and productivity . . . the importance of parental nurturance and of the way parents exercise authority have been amply demonstrated. Yet the yield of the work with respect to the theory of identification was disappointing . . . no consistent relationships were found among characteristics that ought to have been linked by their common origins in the process of identification (Maccoby 1980, pp. 17–18).

If, then, the definition, measurement and effects of identification are confused, it may be better to step back from it as an explanation and investigate at a more detailed behavioural level who 'identifies with' what in whom. Recent work on social relationships looks at some questions bearing on this, and results are discussed in the next chapter.

Beliefs about control of events

One aspect of personality which has received much attention from developmental psychologists is the extent to which people feel that they themselves are in control of their lives and responsible for their actions. It is suggested that feelings of being competent or helpless will affect what people choose to do, the emotions they have about what they are doing, and how they tackle problems. Such feelings have been conceptualized as 'locus of control' (e.g. Rotter *et al.* 1972; Nowicki and Walker 1974) attribution of causation (e.g. Weiner and Kukla 1970) and 'self-efficacy' (Bandura 1977, 1981). Beliefs about one's control of events are one likely source of achievement on difficult tasks, for example academic ones.

Locus of control

'Locus of control' is defined as a *generalized* expectation of internal or external control of reinforcement. People with an 'internal' locus of control believe that they are responsible for what happens: their own effort brought about success, their negligence led to failure. Someone with an 'external' locus of control would interpret success as being due to good luck or the favouritism of

powerful people, and failure as due to bad luck or persecution by the powerful. The 'external' would be less likely, it is argued, to work hard and effectively and therefore achieve success than the 'internal' would.

Most research studies on locus of control use questionnaire scores as a measure of how 'internal' or 'external' a subject is. There is some debate about questionnaires' adequacy as measures (Stipek and Weisz 1981, and see also the general literature on personality assessment). Nor is it simply the case that locus of control leads to achievement: experience of success or failure might also affect locus of control, for example. A related point to this is that it is not clearly a truer understanding of reality to have a more internal locus of control: whether you get good examination results or a university place, for example, depends not only on your own efforts but on public policy about what percentage of candidates are to be put in each marking grade or how many university places are to be available. However it does seem likely that children with a more internal locus of control do tend to show higher academic achievement (Osborn, personal communication on the findings of the Child Health and Education Study), possibly because they manage their own learning and their use of resources supplied by teachers better than 'externals' do.

Attributional models

An alternative model emphasizes situational specificity in identifying the causes of events. Attribution theory (e.g. Weiner 1979; Weiner and Kukla 1970) examines characteristics of the person and of the task or situation which may differ in how internal, how controllable (that is, contingent on your own actions) and how stable they are. For example, how much effort you make is seen as being internal, controllable and unstable; ability is internal, uncontrollable and stable; task difficulty is external, uncontrollable and stable. Attributing success to your own ability and effort is said to result in greater motivation to achieve, particularly if the task you have succeeded on is a difficult one, and thus to greater confidence in taking on further tasks. Attributing failure to stable characteristics of yourself, such as lack of ability, will be more demoralizing than attributing it to unstable characteristics such as lack of effort, or to external uncontrollable factors such as bad luck or an excessively difficult task. While most work on the attribution theory model has been done with adults, there is some evidence from children (e.g. Nicholls 1975, 1978). The model specifies more relevant variables than the 'locus of control' model and is therefore less ambiguous in its predictions about achievement behaviour and reactions to success or failure.

Self-efficacy

Bandura's work on 'self-efficacy' (Bandura 1977, 1981) links the cognitive and motivational components of attribution theory to the development of social understanding. He is concerned with how children come to think of themselves as efficacious, and how they act on such a judgement. He sees four principal sources of information on self-efficacy. The first is children's own accomplishment or performance, their history of success or failure on tasks and their attributions of causes for achievement. The second is vicarious experience, seeing other people's success or failure similarly attributed. The third is other people's judgement of the child's own efficacy: credible suggestions by others that he or she is bound to fail may persuade the child not to try and therefore not to achieve success. This is a form of the 'self-fulfilling prophecy' which may operate in schools (see, for example, Rogers 1982). Bandura's fourth source of evidence is emotional arousal; if it is very high, arousal probably debilitates performance, and judgements of lack of self-efficacy may increase arousal and thereby lead to the poor performance that was expected. What children know about how their emotional state affects their performance is also an important influence.

How people combine these different sorts of information, none of which is simple, is not as yet understood. Bandura (1981, p. 210) suggests that judgements of self-efficacy will tend to be more egocentric and emotionally toned than objective and dispassionate. Accurate appraisal is, however, much more advantageous for effective performance. Coming to such an appraisal is part of metacognitive development.

The development of self-efficacy

Even infants seem to take a particular interest in environmental events which are contingent on their own actions, and to be better able to learn about contingent events than non-contingent ones (see Finkelstein and Ramey 1977; and Chapter 2 this volume). Children seem to learn language best when they experience child-contingent conversations with adults (Wells 1985; and Chapter 4 this volume). Comparisons with siblings and peers also give information to the child about his or her competence, though much more research is needed about how this happens and what its effects are (Dunn 1984; Bandura 1981).

School is a very powerful source of information about academic achievements, including, it is currently thought, influences which leave girls in co-educational groups less confident about their own self-efficacy than boys are (Dweck and Elliott 1983, pp. 658–9). School practices may be associated with not only children's ideas about their own self-efficacy but also their sources of pleasure in their achievement and their reactions to their failure. It has been suggested (Harter 1981) that the intrinsic interest which infants show in being effective actors in their environments becomes overtaken by extrinsic motivation such as teacher approval, gold stars and the need to get good marks to get a job. Children who are made to seem ineffective at academic tasks may react by alienating themselves from school values and setting up a counter-culture (see, for example, Hargreaves 1967). Again, much work needs to be done on exactly how self-efficacy develops.

Aggression

In considering 'aggression' it is necessary, as in other areas, to point out the definitional problems. Olweus (1979) offers this definition:

any act or behaviour that involves, might involve, and/or to some extent can be considered as aiming at, the infliction of injury or discomfort; also manifestations of inner reactions such as feelings or thoughts that can be considered to have such aim.

Aggression thus defined would include some possibly doubtful cases, such as the professional activities of a dentist filling teeth and a judge pronouncing a sentence of imprisonment, and accidental injury, since 'can be considered as aiming at' follows an 'and/or' conjunction. It also includes feelings or thoughts which are not put into action, so that, for example, hoping that the Prime Minister will be ousted from office is aggressive in the ordinary voter as well as in the plotters in Opposition. What is more it does not specify who is to do the 'considering' that the behaviour 'aims at' injury and discomfort: all too often 'aggressor' and victim have had different ideas about this. Beating children, for example, has been seen in various groups at various times as necessary evil, moral duty, parental right and barbaric brutality: so has *not* beating children.

Narrower definitions run into similar problems. So typologies of 'aggression' have been suggested (Cook 1984), excluding predation and 'assertion' and distinguishing 'pro-social' and 'anti-social', 'intro-punitive' and 'extra-punitive', 'instrumental' and 'hostile' acts, and also the 'degree' of aggression. This would need to be considered, presumably, in terms of intent in the aggressor, extremity of behaviour, *and* degree of injury or discomfort inflicted. Bearing these distinctions in mind helpfully emphasizes the complexity of 'aggression', and they do reflect distinctions which we commonly use in judging the culpability of an aggressive action, but how accurately any particular action can be classified is very uncertain. As in the analysis of language, other events not only before but after will affect the classification, and different classifiers, with different knowledge and approaches, may judge differently. What was done to Steve Biko in the last few days of his life illustrates the naïvety of believing that different types of aggression can be simply and easily distinguished. The policemen,

prison officers and doctors involved hardly saw themselves as being aggressive (perhaps they saw Biko as not a member of the human species and so their behaviour as more like predation between species); in so far as they admitted aggression, it was mild, prosocial and instrumental, in that it contained and eventually removed someone hostile to the social system. To the liberals and opponents of apartheid both in and outside South Africa, the same behaviour was inexcusable and, in their terms, severe, anti-social, hostile and extreme. The failure of those who caused Biko's death to see anything extraordinary or culpable in what they had done seems to the liberals to be one further sign of their moral inadequacy.

Since children rarely if ever act like those South African prison officers (or like the similar examples which could easily be found in almost any day's newspaper) this example may seem to be an extravagant digression from the subject of child development. However the question of how far children's 'aggression' is like adults' is unanswerable until we know a great deal more about the causes, forms and functions of aggression than we do at present. Physiologists and ethologists have expended a great deal of effort on studies of aggression in man and other animals, with results which as yet just indicate the complexity of the picture and elucidate a few details (Konner 1982). Aggressive behaviour involves high activity in particular brain structures, notably the hypothalamus, the amygdala and the septal area, but also circuits in the midbrain, and at least in mice there are psychopharmacological changes in neurotransmitters. Slower-acting chemicals such as the 'stress' hormones and testosterone seem also to be involved in aggression; at least in males and in some species more testosterone can increase aggressiveness, but also successful aggression increases testosterone levels and unsuccessful aggression decreases them. Differences in hormone levels in the distant past as well as the present may also affect the level of aggression shown: cross-breeding experiments show genetically based differences in aggression in mice, dogs and bulls. However, even in non-human animals learning, experience and social structure have a great deal to do with aggressive behaviour. Imitation, place in the dominance hierarchy, and experience of social isolation all affect aggression. To quote Konner's summary:

early rearing in social isolation [the animals discussed are rhesus monkeys] . . . will produce a lifelong tendency to social hyperreactivity, unaffected by the usual sorts of later social experience. In males, such hyperreactivity frequently results in a high level of threat, attack, and fighting behaviour, often inappropriate and unsuccessful. To a lesser extent, the same behavioral abnormalities occur in rhesus monkeys that have been raised normally with their mothers in the first year of life, but without contact with peers. [In free-ranging rhesus monkeys] . . . high-ranking females have female infants – and possibly also males – that grow up to be high-ranking themselves and not just for genetic reasons. Infants of such mothers are frequently observed to imitate their mothers' threat-and-chase behavior, even in relation to adult animals. Obviously they are not capable of defeating the adults in individual combat, but the infants make their moves in the mother's shadow – even if she is not in the immediate vicinity – a phenomenon called by ethologists 'protected threat'. In this context, the infant has innumerable conventional learning experiences and opportunities for imitation and social facilitation that lead eventually to effective dominance behavior and high rank.
(Konner 1982, p. 199)

Thus aggression in animals involves genetic proclivities, subtle chemical and electrical influences in the central nervous system, and a history of learning, particularly learning in social contexts. The same could be said of human beings, with learning, as usual, of enormous importance, and with the existence of a genetically-based trait of 'aggression' less apparent than in animals which have been selectively bred to increase, for example, their tendency to attack a matador's red cape. In so far as there is evidence of 'heritability of aggressive offences' it can account for only a small percentage of the range of aggression found in the population, and alternative explanations such as heritability of alcoholism (which is asso-ciated with aggression, social disadvantage etc.) cannot be ruled out (Wells 1980; Rutter 1980a). It is necessary to remember, also, that 'aggression' can take many forms: precisely this point is made clear in observations of developmental changes in children's aggression.

If, as seems wise, *intention* to hurt, frighten or distress is seen as a necessary condition for defining an action as 'aggressive', children in their first year are rarely aggressive, though they may be angry (Lewis and Michalson 1983), and they may do things that in fact hurt, such as biting the nipple or pulling hair that comes within reach. Lacking the intention to hurt, and also knowledge of how their actions affect other people, they are not properly aggressive. Bronson (1975), describing behaviour changes in the second year, found that children showed increasingly intense frustration and anger at having a favourite toy taken from them or withheld. Tussles over property become commoner, but 2-year-olds who hit their opponent during such a disagreement often seem surprised that the other child is hurt. Realizing that one's actions can cause distress in others, and how 'best' to do this, requires considerable cognitive sophistication, Maccoby (1980) argues. Thus although there are many incidents of conflict in pre-school groups, not all of these incontrovertibly involve aggression. They do however serve as a 'training ground for learning effective strategies for initiating and terminating conflicting aggressive interactions' (Parke and Slaby 1983). Early strategies and conflicts tend to involve physical aggression (hitting, grabbing), and to be instrumental, that is they are relatively brief acts directed towards attaining a toy or other desired resource. These strategies decrease as verbally mediated interaction becomes more sophisticated, so that by around 7 aggression has become more verbal, more personal and more hostile – 'Don't play with A, he's a rotten smelly meanie.' Retaliatory aggression also becomes more common as children move from the pre-school through the primary school. Successful retaliation does inhibit the original aggressors, while a weak reaction encourages them to act aggressively again.

On the other hand, the experience of having retaliated successfully encourages aggressive behaviour in the original victim, including pre-emptive attack as well as simple retaliation after the event (Patterson *et al.* 1967). Children develop techniques for keeping aggression within bounds: these include non-verbal appeasement gestures (Camaras 1977, 1980), verbal rituals (Opie and Opie 1967; Heath 1983) and social rules about the conduct of fighters (Davies 1979; Sluckin 1981). Children who contravene these peer group regulations and act in highly aggressive ways tend to be unpopular with their peers and lacking in positive social skills (Parke and Slaby 1983). It is not, of course, a simple causal sequence: aggression may cause you to be rejected by your peers, or rejection by your peers may cause you to be aggressive, or both. The importance of social skills is worth noting, however. Training in social behaviour which is co-operative and aggression-avoiding has proved to be an effective way of treating aggressive patients.

There are developmental changes in what and who makes children angry (Feshbach *et al.* 1984). As Parke and Slaby (1983, pp. 570–1) describe, development also brings changes in children's understanding of stories about people's intentions and thus in their judgement of aggressive acts. There is an increasing tendency with age to distinguish between accidental and deliberate provocation, reacting less strongly to the former. Similarly, more discrimination is made between aggression committed with good intentions and aggression committed with selfish motives. These distinctions will probably be harder to make in real life, of course. Parke and Slaby argue that some children who consistently respond with aggression to behaviour which is non-intentionally negative may be having particular difficulty in making such distinctions. They misinterpret other people's behaviour and react to it as if it was more hostile than it was actually intended to be. Some work by Dodge (e.g. Dodge 1980; Parke and Slaby 1983, pp. 571–3) provides support for this argument. Dodge suggests that there may be an intricate self-sustaining process involved:

Given a negative outcome in the context of unclear intentions, an aggressive child may be likely to attribute a hostile intention to a peer who is responsible for this negative event. This attribution may confirm his general image of peers as hostile and may increase the likelihood of his interpreting future behavior by the peer as hostile. Consequently, he may retaliate against the peer with what he feels is justified aggression. Subsequently, the peer, who has become the recipient of a negative outcome, may attribute a hostile intention to the aggressive child. This attribution confirms the peer's view of the child as being inappropriately aggressive in general and increases the peer's likelihood of interpreting future behavior by the aggressive child as being hostile. Consequently, the peer may aggress against the aggressive child, which could start the cycle over again. Given a series of negative outcomes, which is inevitable, the cycle could turn into a self-perpetuating spiral of increased hostile attributions, aggressive behavior, and social rejection (Dodge 1980, p. 169).

Dodge is implying here a model of aggression as part of the network of social action, social cognition and social affect. Developing cognitive skills, especially understanding other people and moral issues, are seen as central to the ability to control aggression. It is also necessary to act and feel appropriately; thus social skills are important. While this sort of social–cognitive model is likely to lead to a more useful understanding of aggression than did regarding it as a biologically given instinct, there is not as yet much evidence that changes in cognitive skills lead to changes in children's aggression. Nor does it account for why people begin to behave aggressively. Personality differences, notably on temperament dimensions such as activity, impulsivity and low tolerance for frustration, seem likely to be involved.

It is probably a combination of continuity in temperament and stability of social skills which lies behind the rather considerable degree of continuity of aggressiveness found in a number of studies. Olweus (1979, 1984) reviews the evidence and finds that boys' aggression, as revealed in observations, adult ratings or peer nominations, is highly stable over periods of less than a year, and still pretty stable (correlations of around 0.4 or 0.5) over periods as long as ten years. It is thus comparable with intelligence in its consistency, and more stable than its opposite of inhibited, withdrawn behaviour. Evidence from other studies (Kelso and Stewart 1986; Kohn 1977) contributes further to this picture.

It is well known that boys act more aggressively than girls. They show more physical *and* more verbal aggression from pre-school onwards (Maccoby and Jacklin 1980; Meadows and Cashdan 1983; Smith and Green 1974). They almost monopolize violent crime, though the rate of female delinquency is increasing (Rutter and Giller 1983). They are somewhat more likely to initiate aggression and much more likely to retaliate aggressively. Girls are said to be more likely to be indirectly aggressive, for example to set up the situation so that they are not blamed and someone else gets into trouble (e.g. Pollard 1985). They are certainly more vigorously socialized into feeling guilt and shame about aggression. J. and E. Newson (1968, 1976) document this particularly well in their Nottingham sample. Mothers reported that fighting is much more likely to occur if the child is a boy or if the

antagonist is a sibling. Girls 'rarely' fight outside the family, and have a lower rate of fighting with siblings 'often', but they 'fight siblings sometimes' as frequently as boys. Girls are more often advised to withdraw from fights or conflict. The picture is one where girls are consistently discouraged from fighting, particularly in public. Biological differences lead to different social learning experiences.

Family socialization techniques and personality characteristics contribute to the level of aggression in children. In a study of boys in their early teens, Olweus (1980) showed the effect of four variables. The first was negativism in the basic emotional attitude of the principal caretaker (the mother). If she was hostile, cold, indifferent or rejecting this had a powerful effect on her discipline techniques and also a direct effect on the boy's aggression. A permissive attitude towards aggression was the second variable, and this also contributed directly to the boy's aggression: mothers were more likely to be permissive about aggression if they had a negative attitude to their sons. The third variable was both parents' use of discipline techniques which relied

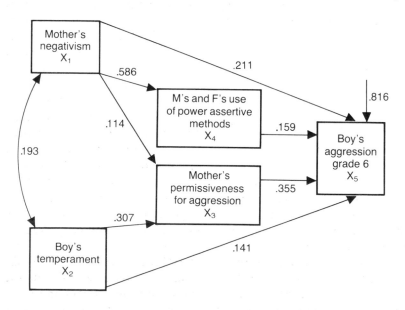

Figure 17 Path model relating child-rearing variables to boy's aggression.

Source: From Olweus (1980), p. 650.

on the assertion of their power rather than on negotiation or reasoning; this was more common in negativistic parents and made some contribution to the boys' aggression. Finally, the boy's temperamental level of activity and intensity interacted with the mother's negativism, contributed to how much she permitted aggression and had a direct influence on the boy's aggression. The variables fell into the pattern shown in Figure 17. Further discussion of child-rearing practices and social development may be found in Chapter 6.

Finally, the social ecology of aggression has to be considered if 'aggression' is to be identified correctly. For example, Manning *et al.* (1978) distinguished different types of hostility in preschool children. Some children tended to get rather rough during vigorous physical games or to bully their peers in imaginative games, but to be timid otherwise. Some children went in for unprovoked teasing and showed a high level of hostility and violence. Some children only showed hostility when specifically frustrated or provoked. These different types of behaviour had different prognoses for the child's state four years later, and were linked to different family backgrounds. Moderate aggression at the right moment can be socially desirable. Definitions of 'moderate' and 'right' are of course offered by the culture (e.g. Walzer 1984). The child's task is to learn and act on those definitions.

The development of pro-social behaviour

It would appear that psychoanalytic theories of id-dominated impulses towards selfish pleasure, Piaget's theory of cognitive egocentrism and sociobiological theories of 'the selfish gene' (Dawkins 1976) all imply that the 'natural' state of unsocialized man – and hence of young children – is one where altruistic acts and empathy with other people will be rare (and capable of explanation in terms of other, less selfless motives). It has recently been argued, however, that such a picture is substantially false: young children are not incapable of distinguishing other people's feelings from their own or of acting on

this distinction in ways which benefit the other. I have already discussed some of the areas of 'egocentricity' which were claimed to dominate language and cognition: here I shall discuss the evidence on emotional egocentricity and the conditions that facilitate empathy and altruism.

It is not disputed that very young children, indeed babies, may react to other people's distress with distress of their own. However it has often been claimed that young children, unable to differentiate between themselves and other people, are unclear about who is feeling the distress.

Consequently the child probably reacts to another's distress as though his dimly perceived self-and-other were somehow simultaneously, or alternatively, in distress. As an example consider a child I know whose typical response to his own distress, beginning late in the first year, was to suck his thumb with one hand and pull his ear with the other. At 12 months, on seeing a sad look on his father's face, he proceeded to look sad and suck his thumb, while pulling his father's ear (Hoffman 1975, p. 614).

It is quite commonly observed that a child seeing someone else in distress will try to comfort himself or herself, or, more sophisticatedly, will offer to the distressed other his or her own comfort object. Theorists who are conservative about acknowledging empathy in children interpret this as showing the child's failure to distinguish between self and other, attributing to the child the (incorrect) belief that what ends his or her own distress will end other people's. Theorists with slightly more liberal views about egocentricity and empathy consider the same behaviour differently. Yarrow and Waxler (1976), for example, suggest that the 'egocentric' comforting behaviour might represent an attempt to act out and thereby understand other people's feelings. Self-comforting in the face of a parent's sadness, as in Hoffman's example, might also be an appropriate reaction if the child felt distress at what he saw in his father: what is more, self-comforting is particularly appropriate if the usual source of comfort, the father, is unavailable because of his own distress. Merely offering an 'inappropriate'

Plate 13

comfort to someone in distress (and an 'inappropriate' comfort might through its provision of distraction or its demonstration of goodwill prove partially or even completely comforting) is not a sufficient sign of an inability to empathize or of a belief that one's own sources of comfort will serve for everyone else. It is after all a rare adult who can always provide appropriate comfort.

One of the things children do have to learn in order to empathize effectively is what other people's lives are like; if another person's life is very unlike our own we may have more difficulty in understanding their feelings than if we have a lot in common. Thus we might expect children to show empathy towards people familiar and like themselves earlier and more effectively than they do towards people less familiar and less similar. Dunn and Kendrick (1982) show unequivocally that children as young as 14 months demonstrate awareness of the emotional experience of parents and older siblings, and elder siblings still under 3 years old respond to the baby's state in appropriate non-projective ways. Awareness and response can be quite sophisticated, as in the two examples which follow:

Bruce S (Baby playing with a balloon): He going to pop it in a minute. And he'll cry. And he'll be frightened of me too. I *like* the pop (Dunn and Kendrick, p. 106).

Laura W Callum repeatedly reaches for and manipulates the magnetic letters Laura is playing with. Laura repeatedly says NO gently. Callum continues trying to reach the letters. Finally, Laura picks up the tray containing the letters and carries it to a high table that Callum cannot reach. Callum is furious and starts to cry. He turns and goes straight to the sofa where Laura's comfort objects, a rag doll and a pacifier, are lying. He takes the doll and holds tight, looking at Laura. Laura for the first time is very upset, starts crying and runs to take the doll (Dunn and Kendrick, p. 116).

As these examples show, awareness of other people's potential feelings does not of itself produce altruistic behaviour. Callum uses his understanding of Laura to get his own back on her; Iago uses his understanding of Othello to destroy him. Lack of understanding of other people will probably make it harder to please or succour them, that is some degree of understanding may be *necessary* for altruism but it certainly is not *sufficient*. This is one reason why attempts to find a causal link between altruistic behaviour and the cognitive capacities of 'perspective-taking', 'role-taking' and moral reasoning have had inconclusive and unconvincing results (Radke-Yarrow, Zahn-Waxler and Chapman 1983; Kurdek 1978). There are no strong consistent positive correlations between frequency of altruistic behaviour and perspective-taking ability, stage of moral reasoning, IQ or even score on a test which measures 'empathy' (Hoffman 1977). In particular we do not have good reason to believe that more advanced understanding causes more altruistic activity, a point which has to be made also in respect of Kohlberg's theory of moral development (see next section). Feeling, and wishing to act, are essential components of human altruistic behaviour. Acting, and the consequences of acting, may contribute to understanding as well as the reverse.

Another reason for the inconsistency of the results of studies which correlated 'sociomoral reasoning' and 'altruistic behaviour' is that these have been assumed to be two homogeneous entities. Few psychologists have investigated how different sorts of 'altruistic' or 'prosocial' behaviour are related. Radke-Yarrow *et al.* (1983) point out that although the terms 'altruistic' and 'pro-social' are understood to refer to the whole spectrum of kind, helpful and self-sacrificing behaviour, what has actually been investigated has been a much smaller range of actions. The dependent variable in experiments, for example, has often been rather trivial behaviour such as sharing out sweets or donating small sums to hypothetical 'poor children'. Observational studies include a wider range of behaviour, but do not usually have enough data to show how different sorts of 'altruism' co-occur, alternate or substitute for each other. We badly need a natural history of pro-social behaviour, since we really do not know much about what children do or about what they think in this area.

Anthropological evidence suggests that western children act helpfully and altruistically much less often than children in non-western societies (e.g. Whiting and Whiting 1975). Psychologists observing western children in school classrooms and playgrounds also report a low frequency of 'pro-social acts', though as Yarrow and Waxler (1976) show the 'frequency' found depends on how inclusive the definition of 'prosocial acts' is. Undoubtedly one reason why western children apparently lack altruism compared with children from other cultures is the ecology of their lives, or at least the part of their lives which is most accessible to researching psychologists. Most observational studies of western children's prosocial behaviour are done at school, that is they tend to be studies of children in groups whose members are all much the same age and much the same level of skill, and who are more often than not within the supervision of adults. Helping behaviour is much less common in any such homogeneous group than it is in heterogeneous ones, where helping, protecting, care-giving and patronizing behaviours are a much more frequent part of the social interaction (Radke-Yarrow *et al.* 1983; see also Chapter 6 this volume). It might be an overstatement to say that western school settings emphasize individual competition at the expense of altruism and co-operation, but they certainly give fewer opportunities for altruistic behaviour than settings where children are important care-givers for other children. In particular, they give few opportunities for 'serious' altruism, behaviour whose cost to the actor is serious or which is seriously needed by the recipient. The success of charitable appeals made by children's television programmes such as 'Blue Peter' suggests that we should not altogether believe in the apparent 'selfishness' of western children, though there is clearly no room for complacency about the altruism of the western world.

If, as I have implied, some settings, social systems and experience make prosocial behaviour more likely than others do, which are they? There are some fairly firm islands of evidence in a quagmire of ignorance, here. Social sensitivity is associated with parental discipline, in that children whose parents reasoned with them, negotiated issues and explained their commands and prohibitions show more advanced understanding of other people than do children brought up under rigidly authoritarian or very *laissez-faire* régimes (Light 1979; Maccoby and Martin 1983; Rollins and Thomas 1979; see also Chapter 6 this volume). Children who readily participate in other people's feelings seem to have parents who show empathy towards their children's distress (Zahn-Waxler *et al.* 1979). Seeing a model behave altruistically has increased children's altruism in some experiments but by no means all (Radke-Yarrow *et al.* 1983), while outstandingly altruistic children seem often to have modelled themselves on their own outstandingly altruistic parents. Attempts at conditioning children to behave altruistically by giving rewards for helping, sharing and so forth have had inconsistent results (Radke-Yarrow *et al.* 1983), sometimes leading the child to act altruistically only when he or she is rewarded – which obviously makes it plausible that the 'altruistic' act is really a selfish one! Attributional remarks like 'I know you're the sort of person who really cares for other people' may have some effect on the child's behaviour but the effect depends on whether the remarks appear sincere and believable, and probably on other aspects of the social situation. Prosocial behaviour cannot be divorced from social behaviour in general. Children who are confident and experienced in their relationships with other children may be helpful and protective as part of their normal social role. Children who are anxiously on the fringes of a social group may seek to share their toys or sweets, and may give up their own immediate interest in favour of a group member's, in the hope of buying their way into a group. Children who are happy about themselves may be able to be more generous towards other people than children who are chronically miserable, or their general complacency may prevent them from noticing another person's need. We have so little in the way of a natural history of altruism, and so little of a convincing philosophical analysis of altruism, that we can say very little about what conditions promote it. Since it is an important part of moral development and social interaction, we must hope that better data and better theory will be forthcoming.

Moral development

Moral development in children is a complex subject: many different emphases are relevant to its analysis, and because of the social implications of morality, and the apparent importance of education and child-rearing practices to its development, discussion has often been very value-laden. As we shall see, there are real differences as to what are and are not moral problems, what are good or universal moral principles, and how they develop. As in other areas of developmental psychology, models which emphasize 'biology', 'social conditioning' or 'cognition' are in competition: so are different views about the 'natural' 'goodness' or 'badness' of human beings and the functions of society.

Morality and sociobiology

The most heavily 'biological' account of morality is relatively new and far from being fully worked out. It is part of the ambitious claim made by Wilson (1975) that 'sociobiology', which asserts that human behaviour is determined by natural selection in ways similar to the influence of natural selection on human morphology, should take over psychology and the other social sciences. At the centre of the account is 'altruism', that is self-sacrificing behaviour which has good results for people other than the person actually doing it. This sort of behaviour is often regarded as morally admirable in humans ('Greater love hath no man than this, that he lay down his life for his friend'), and in other animals, particularly perhaps if the benefited person is an infant (or a human being, as may be seen in the popularity of lachrymose stories in which a dog saves his master's child from predators or other danger, or keeps vigil at his grave like Greyfriars Bobby). Wilson's work brought to more general attention the fact that 'altruistic' behaviour was to be found

in a great many species where it could not plausibly be explained by social learning or conditioning. Since altruism involves sacrificing oneself for others, it is likely to handicap the individuals who display it and reduce their chances of living and reproducing themselves. It is thus hard to account for in terms of an evolutionary theory which says that genes for characteristics or behaviour which militate against reproductive success will tend not to be reproduced, and to die out. The proposed explanation is that although altruism is by definition of immediate disadvantage to the altruistic person, there are indirect advantages which may add up to a better total. Thus although the mother lapwing who tempts the predator hawk away from her nest by pretending to be injured, or the human father who rushes into a blazing house to bring out his children, may lose their own lives, if they have saved the lives of enough of their offspring the net result may be that as many or more of their genes survive for later reproduction. The closer the genetic relation, the greater the possibility of sacrifice will be. Indirect advantages may also come about through reciprocity of altruism: if the 'altruistic' action of A towards B makes it more likely that B (or indeed anyone else) will act to the advantage of A (or A's kin) in future, then the present risk which A takes may be less than the future benefits which B may be obliged to shower on A. Seen in this way, what was apparently morally admirable self-sacrifice is reduced to a somewhat sordid calculation of self-interest. To quote the most enthusiastic proponent of sociobiology in the days before be began to show much caution about its claims:

The theory of group selection has taken most of the good will out of altruism. When altruism is conceived as the mechanism by which DNA multiplies itself through a network of relatives, spirituality becomes just one more Darwinian enabling device (Wilson 1975, p. 120).

This view is, however, an example of excessive reductionism; it deflates the smug myth of natural human goodness but at the cost of setting up an alternative myth of natural selfishness. The kin selection model has had some considerable pre-dictive successes though it works less well where animals cannot estimate their genetic relatedness to each other with any accuracy. The view runs however into crucial difficulties, two of which I want to pick up as they are central to the field of moral development. The first, as I stressed in Chapter 1, is that the link between genes and behaviour is not a simple direct one.

The nature of the relation between [the] genome and the physical realization of the actual animal, or its phenome, is an extremely complex, and as yet quite unsolved conceptual problem. That is to say, it is not yet possible to state in just what way any physical and behavioral feature of an animal can be said to be 'determined' by its genes. . . . The conceptual obstacle to providing such an account lies mainly in the role played by the enormously complex context in which the genes find themselves in the course of embryonic and post-embryonic development. (Stent 1978, p. 18).

Developmental studies of social behaviour in various primates (see, Trivers 1985, Gottlieb 1983, Hinde 1983) have demonstrated that the most genes can contribute is a *predisposition to learn* the complex behaviours that make up 'altruism' or 'parenting'. Social experience and the opportunity for imitation and learning are essential; if they are absent, as in Harlow's depri-vation experiments, or adverse, as seems to have been the case in the Ik (Turnbull 1972), there is no morality. Even when they are present, it may be doubted whether we are essentially the calculating, prudent, consistent persons that sociobiology at its most Hobbesian claims. Our altruistic actions may *in fact* benefit ourselves, but, and this is the second point, our motives, our ideas about our actions, will also be worth con-sidering. As Midgley (1979) points out with admirable clarity, it is necessary to look at the whole pattern of motives and behaviours.

They [people with crude notions of Darwinism] confuse the mere *fact of competing*, that is, of needing to share out a resource, with the motive of *competitiveness* or readiness to quarrel. Where creatures are competing (as a fact), their success will be decided by whatever tendencies they have that best help their predicament. These need not be quarrelsome tendencies at all. A species may prevail because it is better at finding food or turns to a food that is more plentiful, or because it grows protective colouration, or indeed because it becomes *less* quarrelsome and more co-operative (p. 132).

The necessary complexity of such capacities points up the wrongness of an atomizing approach to impulses. It seems unrealistic to talk as though the tendency to rescue people were something that could be carried by a single gene . . . in any fairly complex creature, the undertaking of dangerous actions *must* involve other traits in the character besides the impulse in question; the whole character has to be such as to permit them. Such behaviour cannot stand alone (pp. 134–5).

All the creatures that it makes sense to suppose could develop positive altruism are already caring for their young . . . the development of sociability proceeds in any case largely by this extension to other adults of behavior first developed between parents and young – grooming, mouth contact, embracing, protective and submissive gestures, giving food. In fact, wider sociality in its original essence simply *is* the power of adults to treat one another, mutually, as honorary parents and children. It is enriched later with other patterns largely drawn from the interactions *between* infants. . . . But quasi-parental interactions come first. They work well because they are adapted to soothe, to conciliate, to forge a bond . . . those who, from whatever cause, are especially protective and good at rearing young, are likely to leave a disproportionate number of descendants in relation to those actually born (p. 136).

That is, moral behaviour is part of the results of evolution, but simplistic accounts which treat it atomistically, which ignore motives and reason-ing, and which isolate it from other parts of behaviour, will be unsatisfactory. That Midgley places adult–child relationships/behaviour at the centre of the development of social being is in-teresting, with obvious self-justificatory attrac-tions for the developmental psychologist: it reflects back on my early assertions about the inseparable development of the biological and the social. We will return to the notion, when we have considered some other accounts of moral development which pay more attention to Midgley's points about motives, reasoning and the total complex pattern of behaviour.

Morality and Freudian theory

There is both biology and emphasis on the importance of parenting behaviour, though more pessimistically viewed, in another and better known theory of morality and moral development, the more elaborate and extraordinarily seductive account given by Freud. At the centre is a dichotomous view of the individual and the social system. There is conceptual (and indeed emotional) opposition between the self and others, the individual and the group, personal fulfilment and social obligation.

It is impossible to overlook the extent to which civilisation is built up upon renunciation of instinct, how much it presupposes precisely the non-satisfaction (by suppression, repression or some other means?) of powerful instincts (Freud 1930/61, p. 44).

The 'powerful instincts' dominate the unsocialized individual, including the unsocialized child: they are the instincts of sexuality (Eros), which Freud discovered, if that is the word, early in his work (Sulloway 1980), and aggression (Thanatos), which grew in importance in his thinking after the horrors of the First World War and the early death of his daughter Sophie (Clark 1980). The social system, 'culture' or 'civilization', exists to protect individuals and both to restrict the satisfaction of their instincts and to allow it some limited safe expression. The individual has powerful instincts which demand release and reduction of their tension; they are kept within bounds by external coercion which becomes internalized as development proceeds.

Civilisation, therefore, obtains mastery over the individual's desire for aggression by weakening and disarming it and by setting up an agency within him to watch over it, like a garrison in a conquered city (Freud 1930/61, pp. 70–1).

Moral development thus centres on the mastery of the instinctual drives that seethe in the id and demand instantaneous satisfaction. The baby quickly experiences frustration of instinctual demands – milk, warmth, mother, cannot come fast enough or reliably enough – and the second part or aspect of the personality, the ego, develops or differentiates itself from the id. The functioning of the ego involves coping with delay in the discharge of instinctual energy, adapting the desires of the id to the reality of the outside world.

The ego's relation to the id might be compared with that of a rider to his horse. The horse supplies the locomotive energy, while the rider has the privilege of deciding on the goal and of guiding the powerful animal's movement. But only too often there arises between the ego and the id the not precisely ideal situation of the rider being obliged to guide the horse along the path by which it itself wants to go (Freud 1933/64, p. 77).

The horse is a fierce and powerful one, and the external world's rules about how and where to ride are multiform and stringent. The ego tackles the problem of balancing the two in increasingly subtle ways but the problem-solving process involves anxiety which sometimes threatens to overcome the ego. Defence mechanisms control and alleviate anxiety but do so by distorting reality: in 'reaction formation' for example the ego may deny an unacceptable desire by focusing on its opposite, so that it may appear to be, for example, demonstratively loving rather than jealously hurtful, altruistic rather than selfish. The sceptical may often see defence mechanisms at work in the activity of moralists, particularly those who see themselves as the guardians of virtues unappreciated by the more lax.

While both id and ego contribute to moral behaviour, the most important moral aspect of the personality is the late developer, the superego. This has two important parts, the ego ideal, which is what one thinks one should be, and the conscience, which tells one how far short of ideal one is, and consequently how deplorable and worthy of punishment. The superego is as self-denying as the id is self-gratifying, and can be as extreme and violent. People with very strong superegos punish themselves very harshly, and tend to have impossibly high moral standards – which they may apply to other people as well as themselves – 'Social justice means that we deny ourselves many things so that others may have to do without them as well' (Freud 1955).

The superego, and hence moral self-scrutiny, is said to develop in early childhood, largely as a result of the tensions of the 'phallic' stage. Earlier, young infants get their sensual gratification first from oral activity and may have made rudimentary moral distinctions between 'good' objects, such as breasts, which satisfy their needs, and bad ones which do not, and subsequently from anal activity, which because it is the object of parental training and anxiety is a source of ideas about being 'good' or 'bad' oneself. Both these stages leave traces in personality and morality. It is however in the third stage, round about the age range of 3 to 6, when the child's sensuality is said to be centrally phallic, that Freud places the social and emotional dilemmas which result in the development of moral structures such as the superego, and which have become famous (or infamous) as 'the Oedipus complex'.

At this stage the developmental courses of boys and of girls diverge as to their detail and their consequences, although the central dilemma of being in love with the parent of the opposite sex is common to both sexes – and Freud believed very strongly that human nature is inherently bisexual, writing to a friend in 1899 that he was accustoming himself 'to the idea of regarding every sexual act as a process in which four persons are involved' (Wollheim 1971, p. 120). In outline, what happens is as follows. The little boy is in love with his mother and wants her sexually and exclusively for himself. This brings him into conflict with his father, whom he feels threatened by but also loves; indeed in later versions Freud proposed that this love for the father was erotic too. In this crisis of ambivalence and conflict, the child represses his sexuality, metaphorically castrating himself, and identifies with his father. In this identification he adopts or 'introjects' all the father's beliefs and values *as the child sees them*; that is he internalizes a threatening, punitive,

hypercritical, powerful person who is an insuperable obstacle to the little boy's sexual gratification. This internalized version of parental authority is the superego, 'the heir of the Oedipus complex'.

Freud says that the little girl also starts by being in love with her mother, as mothers have been for all infants the first love-object because of being the first important supplier of oral gratification. She also loves and desires her father and comes to realize that he has 'a prized object which she does not have' – a penis. She blames her mother for this lack, and feels that she herself has been castrated and is inadequate. While the boy fears the loss of his penis as a punishment for his incestuous desires, the girl having lost hers already has less to fear now. Her penis-envy leads to a depreciatory attitude towards other people who lack penises, a possessive attitude towards her menfolk's penises, and a wish for a child as a penis-substitute. Although she does identify with her mother and introject her values, her identification is slower and weaker and her superego is consequently inferior (Freud 1925, v. 19, 1931, v. 21).

This Freudian scenario of the interaction of psychosexual and moral development derives of course from the retrospective accounts of their early life by Freud's patients. There is little in the way of evidence which unequivocally supports or refutes it: indeed it has been said that there could be no refuting evidence since a demonstration that a person did not experience an Oedipus complex, feel penis-envy etc. might be interpreted as evidence for the perfect repression of the person's Oedipus complex, penis-envy, etc. The account has been modified, notably by feminists reaching to what they took to be its misogynistic character (Sayers 1982; Archer and Lloyd 1982). Since the theory is centrally clinical and therapeutic, whether it is 'true' or not may be less important than whether it is helpful to patients. For our purposes in considering moral development, I emphasize only the fact that Freud's account of the development of the superego is of an interaction of biology (the instincts), society (parental authority) and cognition (the child's evaluation of parents and self) which together make up moral processes and moral standards. That it suggests major changes in morality at the age of 6 or 7 as a result of the resolution of the Oedipus conflict, and differences in morality between males and females, are empirically testable questions which we will give more attention to later.

Morality and social learning theory

Social learning theory (see, for example, Bandura 1977) accounts for moral development in terms of the child's reinforcement history. Moral development is the acquisition of cultural values, the conditioning of moral anxiety is conscience, and 'moral character' is learned habits. 'That which is "good" is that which is reinforced.' Moral values are inculcated by parents and teachers, or by the secondary reinforcement of association with them, and by imitation of models whom the child can identify with. There are developmental changes because the child's accumulated experience is growing, because children become able to take more and more varied reinforcement contingencies into account as they get older, because they become more able to anticipate and to infer potential reinforcement, and because of changes in adults' expectations and discipline techniques of the child. Social learning theory, unlike classical learning theories, does concern itself with people's ideas as well as their overt behaviour, and would allow that moral behaviour is influenced by internalized moral reasoning, though this is itself influenced by reinforcement histories. Nevertheless, the theory predicts situation-specific behaviour as 'moral judgement involves a complex process of considering and weighing various criteria in a given social situation' (Miller 1983, p. 222).

One major strength of learning theories has been their amenability to experimental testing. Unsurprisingly, there has been a great deal of experimental research on social learning theory predictions about moral development, and the results have generally supported its account of the learning processes which could be involved. The results of observational and correlational studies of more complex situations such as family interactions, parental discipline techniques, and the degree of similarity between parents' and adolescents' moral beliefs (e.g. Rutter 1980), which will be discussed more thoroughly when we consider adult–child relations, are also in accord with social learning theory. The suggestion that moral judgement and moral behaviour may not necessarily be the same, and that the outcome will vary from situation to situation although the underlying processes are the same, seems a useful recognition of the complexity of morality, though it obviously reduces the degree to which the theory in its present state can predict behaviour with any exactness. The increasing learning theory emphasis on reasoning which mediates between stimulus and response also of course makes the theory less testable, but it also makes it more similar to the influential theories derived from Piaget which have sought to describe the structure as well as the process of moral development. I will discuss these, giving a rather longer account of them, next.

Concepts of morality

The work outlined so far has concentrated on the dynamics, the motives, of moral behaviour and development, rather than on its organization. Piaget's work, and the further 'cognitive–developmental' work that it has inspired, was more concerned with moral judgement and the principles that people use in evaluating some action as 'good' or 'bad', deserving praise or blame. Questions of how to define what is good have been a recurring preoccupation of moral philosophers. There is some agreement about a core meaning of 'morality', though less about its content. Moral rules may compete among themselves, but they all have the following characteristics (Gewirth 1978). First, they are *obligatory*, that is they do not depend on what anyone happens to feel like doing. Second, they are *generalizable*, that is what is right or wrong for any particular person is also right or wrong for any other individual (assuming that there are no relevant differences of characteristics or situation). Third, they are *important*, that is, the moral rule which is the best moral rule in a situation should take precedence over other non-moral considerations, such as conserving one's energy by not bothering, or justifying contravening the moral rule by appeals to etiquette or the desire for a quiet life or one's momentary frivolities. (Although some cultures have, of course, elevated principles of etiquette to a pre-eminent moral status, as a great many nineteenth-century novels would tell us, this is usually seen as morally inferior to attention to purely moral principles, except in so far as etiquette itself can be justified in terms of moral principles. The most admired characters in novels are often those who flout etiquette in the service of abstract moral principles, the most tragic ones those whose moral strivings are stifled by convention. Mary Garth, Rosamund Vincy and Dr Lydgate in *Middlemarch* provide good examples: George Eliot was of course a moral philosopher worthy of serious consideration as well as a great novelist.)

The content or justification of moral rules would seem to be more controversial. Various thinkers have said that something is 'good' if doing it tends on balance to increase people's happiness, or to contribute to their welfare, or to avoid their harm, or to be congruent with principles like 'justice' or 'truth' or 'beauty' or 'rationality', or to contribute to the bringing about of some desirable state of affairs which is the goal of existence or history or whatever (such as 'Evolutionary Adaptedness' or 'The Kingdom of God on Earth' or 'The Revolution' or even 'the conquest of inflation'). It is quite evident that no single one of these will do as a necessary and sufficient and unchallengeable condition for every instance of the 'good': hence G. E. Moore suggested that 'goodness' was the same sort of quality as 'yellowness', not to be defined in terms of anything but itself. Alternatively one might sidestep this debate by suggesting that many of the characteristics listed above will be involved in the evaluation of an action. Activities which satisfy all the requirements will be incontrovertibly 'good', while those which only satisfy some will be 'good but', will be 'qualified goods' until they satisfy so few requirements that they have 'died the death of a thousand qualifications'. This would make it clearly a psychologically relevant matter as to how the various principles were evoked and ranked, and how people decided between them when they were in conflict. It is this sort of matter that the 'cognitive-developmental' theorists of moral reasoning address. They are concerned with how children judge 'good' and 'bad', with what sort of principles they invoke and use in decision and justification. Piaget (1932) made the first of the attempts to describe the development of moral reasoning discussed here; Kohlberg (e.g. Kohlberg 1981a,b,c) is the second major figure, while some subsequent studies reacting to Kohlberg's work (e.g. Mussen and Eisenberg-Berg 1977, Turiel 1983), are also touched on.

Piaget's theory of moral development

Piaget was an influence on studies of moral reasoning both through his relatively early work on children's moral judgements (Piaget 1932) and through his later elaboration of the structure of cognitive development. *The Moral Judgment of the Child* pioneered the method which has been much used since, of telling children a story involving moral conflict and asking them what the protagonists should do and why, or how their actions should be judged. Here are two examples (Piaget 1932, pp. 117–18, Penguin edition).

A.   A little boy who is called John is in his room. He is called to dinner. He goes into the dining room. But behind the door there was a chair, and on the chair there was a tray with fifteen cups on it. John couldn't have known that there was all this behind the door. He goes in, the door knocks against the tray, bang go the fifteen cups and they all get broken!

B.   Once there was a little boy whose name was Henry. One day when his mother was out he tried to get some jam out of the cupboard. He climbed up on to a chair and stretched out his arm. But the jam was too high up and he couldn't reach it and have any. But while he was trying to get it he knocked over a cup. The cup fell down and broke.

[. . .] About each of these pairs of stories we ask two questions: (1) Are these children equally guilty? (2) Which of the two is the naughtiest, and why? It goes without saying that each of these questions is the occasion for a conversation more or less elaborate according to the child's reaction.

Similar pairs of stories were used to probe children's ideas about lying (incredible but without any evil intention versus quite probable but told with intent to deceive), about the appropriateness of different sorts of punishment (expiatory or reciprocal), fairness and so forth, and ideas of justice and equality, and the nature and origin of the rules of games such as marbles were also investigated. Piaget discusses all these in terms of two different moralities. The one which predominated in the answers of the younger children he called a 'morality of constraint' or 'heteronomous' morality. The child believes that there are strict rules imposed from outside, which must be obeyed and cannot be questioned, altered or avoided, and are applied to wrongdoing without taking into account intentions, mitigating circumstances or the possibility of avoiding doing wrong. Piaget attributes the source of this harsh and rigid morality to the child's response to parental authority, which inevitably means the issuing of injunctions which make no sense to the child. He gives examples drawn from observations of his own children (pp. 170–1).

Jacqueline has never been punished in the strict sense of the term. At the worst, when she makes a scene, we leave her alone for a little while and tell her we shall come back when she can talk quietly again. She has never been given duties as such, nor have we ever demanded from her that sort of passive obedience without discussion which in the eyes of so many parents constitutes the highest virtue. We have always tried to make her understand the 'why' of orders instead of laying down 'categorical' rules. Above all, we have always put things to her in the light of cooperation: 'to help mummy', to 'please' her parents, to 'show her sister', etc. – are for her reasons for carrying out orders that cannot be understood in themselves. As to rules that are unintelligible to very little children, such as the rule of truthfulness, she has never even heard mention of them.

But in ordinary life it is impossible to avoid certain injunctions of which the purport does not immediately seem to have any sense from the child's point of view.

Such are going to bed and having meals at given hours, not spoiling things, not touching the things on daddy's table, etc. Now, these commandments, received and applied before being really understood, naturally give rise to a whole ethic of heteronomy with a feeling of pure obligation, with remorse in case of violation of the law, etc.

For example, one evening I find Jacqueline, aged 2; 6(15),* in bed, spoiling a towel by pulling out the threads one by one. Her mother has already often told her that it is a pity to do that, that it makes holes, that you can't mend the holes, etc. So I say to J.: 'Oh, but mummy will be sad.' J. answers calmly and even with an ill-concealed smile: 'Yes. It makes holes. You can't mend'. . . etc. I continue my lecture, but she obviously is not going to take me seriously. Still hiding her amusement with difficulty, she suddenly says to me 'Laugh!' in so comic a tone that in order to keep a straight face I quickly change the subject. J., very conscious of her powers of seduction, then says to me 'My little darling Daddy', and the incident ends. The next morning, however, J. wakes up full of it. Her first words refer to what had happened the night before. She thinks about the towel and asks her mother whether she isn't sad. So in spite of the first reaction showing such charming disrespect, my words had told and the command had brought about the usual consequences.

The evening of the same day, J. begins to pull the threads out of the towel again. Her mother repeats that it is a pity. J. listens attentively but says nothing. A moment later she is calling out and cries till someone comes to her: she simply wanted to see her parents again and make sure that they bore her no grudge.

The other major source of this 'moral realism' is the child's egocentricity. Immediately after the passage quoted above, Piaget points out that one begins to differentiate one's own intentional actions from one's involuntary ones at quite an early age (3–4), and quickly to use this as an excuse ('I didn't mean to', 'I didn't do it on purpose'). But it is harder to apply this insight to other people, particularly when one is oneself the victim of the other's wrongdoing but even more when the problem is in a story rather than part of an immediate practical situation (Piaget 1932,

* 2; 6(15) = 2 years, 6 months and 15 days.

p. 177). This last is an important point which has repercussions for research methodology and theories of moral development that have not been sufficiently considered. Piaget here suggests a gap between moral reasoning in the abstract and moral behaviour in real life – a problem for all the cognitive–developmental theorists – but also that 'real' moral behaviour may be, at least at early ages, more advanced than discussion of moral stories can be. We will see that a difference in the opposite direction has been suspected at later ages.

Although 'heteronomous morality' is strong in the young child, and can be seen to flourish in society (Piaget 1932, p. 383), a second (and, as far as Piaget is concerned, better) morality gradually develops. By way of interaction with peers and consequently more egalitarian experience, the child comes to experience the benefits of co-operation and reciprocity and to develop a morality of equality and autonomy. Adult behaviour to the child plays a part in this (Piaget 1932, p. 307) but equal interaction and particularly co-operation and mutual respect among peers is the main reason for development. Blind obedience to authority is no longer esteemed; punishment is no longer to be expiation but should as far as possible be reciprocal or make reparation for the wrong done; rules are the products of social interaction and may be changed by democratic agreement; justice should take into account extenuating circumstances, the protagonist's motivation, and so forth.

While social interaction is seen here as a major source of developmental change, Piaget is concerned to link levels of moral reasoning with levels of cognitive functioning. The decline of intellectual egocentricity is necessary for moral development; consciousness of oneself as a particular individual with particular limitations and resources is necessary for co-operation with others (Piaget 1932, p. 381). This linking of cognition with moral, social and emotional development did not progress into detailed specifications of links in Piaget's own work but has been developed since, notably by the Kohlberg school (e.g. Kohlberg 1964, 1981; Lickona 1976) which also

modifies the Piagetian theory and extends its stage sequence at both ends. In these modifications and extensions more emphasis is placed on the developmental role of changes in cognition than on changes in social experience where research evidence is said only to give 'mixed' or 'weak' support (Lickona 1976). Some more recent evidence bearing on the question of links between social experience and moral behaviour will be considered after Kohlberg's work has been described.

Kohlberg's theory of moral development

Kohlberg suggests that there is a sequence of six stages of moral judgement. Like Piaget's stages of cognitive development, Kohlberg's moral stages involve structured reasoning, are invariant in sequence, hierarchical and universal throughout the human species. They are concerned with what *ought* to be, rather than with actual behaviour, and the essential characteristic of a stage is the sort of underlying reasoning which leads a subject to a particular judgement, rather than the content of the judgement itself. While the sequence of stages and the underlying structures of each stage are invariant, progress through the stages will vary in speed and some individuals will not reach the later stages. Progress is a result of an interaction between the maturation of individuals and their experience, particularly their experience of social role-taking, with a neo-Piagetian equilibration playing an important part in the interaction as well as within the cognitive–moral structures. As Turiel (1973, p. 737) says

Stages in a developmental sequence are, then, successive levels of equilibrium in two respects. First, each stage is a more equilibrated form than the previous one (e.g. there is more internal consistency). Second, each stage represents a more equilibrated means of interacting with the environment. That is, each new stage is a more adequate way of understanding moral problems and resolving conflicts encountered.

As in Piaget's work, subjects are told stories involving moral dilemmas and invited to comment on what the protagonist should do, and why. This is perhaps the best-known story.

In Europe, a woman was near death from a kind of cancer. There was one drug that the doctors thought might save her. It was a form of radium that a druggist in the same town had recently discovered. The drug was expensive to make, but the druggist was charging ten times what the drug cost him to make. He paid $200 for the radium and charged $2000 for a small dose of the drug. The sick woman's husband, Heinz, went to everyone he knew to borrow the money, but he could only get together about $1000 which is half of what it cost. He told the druggist that his wife was dying and asked him to sell it cheaper or let him pay later. But the druggist said, 'No, I discovered the drug and I'm going to make money from it.' So Heinz gets desperate and considers breaking into the man's store to steal the drug for his wife.

Responses to stories of this sort are analysed, using a detailed handbook, in terms of the quality of the judgements, the ways in which the situation is perceived and what moral principles are considered and in what way, rather than in terms of the surface content of the solution recommended to the story's conflict. The inherent dilemma of the stories is between an act which would comply with social or legal rules but would neglect the welfare or human rights of an individual (for example, Heinz deciding he must not steal, even though this deprives his wife of the drug) and an act which violates the rules but serves human needs (for example, stealing the drug and giving it to the sick woman). The important criterion of the stages is however not 'Steal' or 'Don't steal' but the reasons behind this decision. Discussion of ideas about laws, rules, authority, responsibility, equality and justice is at the centre of the stage sequence and of Kohlberg's conception of morality.

The six stages are paired into three levels; Pre-conventional, Conventional, and Post-conventional. At the earliest level, which Kohlberg says is characteristic of most children under 9, the person does not understand society's rules and expectations, and considerations of personal interest and advantage are paramount. The first stage in this level is of 'heteronomous morality' and the emphasis is on avoiding punishment by obedience to authority. Piaget's 'heteronomous morality' involved respect for adults: Kohlberg's does not, as he found not 'respect' but self-interest and fear. In the second stage, the child is more concerned than before with the positive aspects of relations with other people: reciprocity becomes extremely important but on the pragmatic ground that 'if you scratch my back, I'll scratch yours', what Kohlberg at an earlier point in his work called 'instrumental relativism' (Kohlberg 1971). The beginnings of Piaget's 'autonomous morality' or 'morality of co-operation' may be seen in this stage: it is also reminiscent of the sociobiologists' 'reciprocal altruism', discussed above.

The Conventional level is preoccupied with maintaining the expectations of the social group and obeying the law precisely because they are the law and the social consensus. Conformity has become a matter of active support and identification not just of fearful or self-interested compliance. Increasingly as Kohlberg's work progressed, it appeared that the majority of adolescents and adults were to be found at this level. In the earlier of its two stages, stage 3, the person is concerned to win approval, particularly from the immediate social group. 'Behaving well' is still seen as important, but so is 'meaning well'. Kohlberg called this the 'good boy–nice girl' stage (it is not clear whether the different moral implications of these two phrases are intended at this point: we will discuss the question of sex bias in the theory later). In the later stage, stage 4, there is an emphasis on laws and duties which are seen as necessary for the maintenance of society, which is now understood as being wider than one's own social group. Justice is based on the authority of government, punishment is to expiate one's 'debt to society'. Equality before the law is important, as is equality of opportunity, but efforts to eradicate more specific economic or social inequalities by 'positive discrimination' or more generous treatment of the disadvantaged are likely to be seen as wrong; conserving the social status quo is preferred to bringing about social change.

It is in the minority of people who move into the third or Post-conventional level that this dependence on consensus and normative sources of morality begins to be replaced by truly autonomous moral reasoning based on universal moral principles. The stage 4 thinker believes it is important to obey the law simply because it is the law: the stage 5 or 6 thinker is prepared to say like Mr Bumble in *Oliver Twist*, and with reasons in terms of impersonal principle, that 'If the law supposes that ... the law is a ass – a idiot' and should be changed. In stage 5 democratic agreement and recourse to agreed procedures for changing the rules are supported: laws are respected in terms of the purposes – such as the providing of equal rights to life, liberty and the pursuit of happiness – which the laws are intended to fulfil. At this stage there is an explicit awareness that there may be conflict between moral principles. In the story of Heinz's dilemma, Kohlberg says that a stage 5 thinker might believe that Heinz would be morally right to steal the drug to save his wife's life but that he would at the same time be legally wrong so that it would be a judge's duty to punish him. Moral reasoning at this stage also tends to take up a utilitarian position, to uphold principles of the maximization of human happiness, which Kohlberg regards as ethically inferior to the absolute principles of justice and individual conscience that characterize stage 6.

At stage 6 the process of making moral judgements has become autonomous. Neither the egoistic desires which dominated the Pre-conventional level nor the social pressures which dominated the Conventional level and were also considered to some extent in stage 5 are involved any more. The crucial principle is the application to all individuals of a belief in the dignity of human life; all individuals must be given 'fundamentally equal consideration'. This may involve very careful consideration of what other people's needs, wishes and judgements would be in a situation of moral conflict in terms of the universal moral principles that should guide actions. Heinz, for example, would consider whether the druggist would continue to place property rights over a human being's right to life if it were the druggist who was mortally ill and someone else who was withholding the cure; and also whether the wife

would continue to demand the drug if she were the property-owner and someone else the invalid. Kohlberg asserts that the inevitable outcome of this balancing of role-taking would be to demonstrate quite clearly that the right of a human being to life takes precedence over another human being's right to property; if the druggist does not concede this, he is wrong, and Heinz's theft is morally justified.

Whether or not the principles involved in this stage are unarguably 'better' than any other, the reasoning processes involved are clearly very sophisticated. It is perhaps not surprising that they are described as 'isomorphic with' formal operations: or that the age at which we can expect stage 6 to be attained has been raised in successive accounts from early adolescence to early middle age. There have also been suggestions for stages 5 and 6 as well as for formal operations that not all thinkers progress so far, let alone always manage to reason at their highest possible level. In a recent paper (Kohlberg 1984) Kohlberg has linked his difficulty in finding Post-conventional moral reasoning with post-Watergate disillusion with political principle and with the 'privatism' that has accompanied the economic recession of the last few years. He has therefore advocated moral education which tries to bring about stage 4 or social duty reasoning as this may be the best that can be achieved in the face of the characteristically stage 2 or stage 3 reasoning of the 'new conservatism'.

Kohlberg, then, is describing a series of stages of moral reasoning which make a first transition from self-interest to social interest, and in some cases may make a second transition from considering the immediate society as it is to considering wider universal principles. He puts the moral principle of justice at the centre of his model, and sees cognitive development and one of its consequences, improved role-taking ability, as the main motive force for development. In many ways it is an impressive theory, but there are a number of problems both in how it is conceived and in the quality of the evidence. In outline, these involve questions about 'stages', about moral reasoning based on universal principle, about 'justice' as that principle, about relations between 'reasoning', 'feeling' and 'acting', about individual differences in morality, and about research methodology.

Criticisms of Kohlberg's theory

I have already pointed out some of the dangers of 'stage' theories. In the case of Kohlberg's model, as with all the other 'stage sequences' that have proliferated so much since Piaget developed a stage model, there are dangers of creating artificial separations and artificial uniformities, overlooking variation within 'stages' and similarities between 'stages', simplifying complex behaviours into linear models, and reifying into a unity what might be more usefully thought of as multiform. It cannot be said too often that although we may have as an ideal a belief that if something exists, we can measure it, we need not believe that if we can measure 'something', 'it' exists. 'Moral reasoning' is a case in point. There is really very little evidence that 'moral reasoning' is consistent within 'stages', hierarchical between them, accurately diagnosed over a wide range of situations and so forth. There is also no really clear account of exactly what they are stages *of*, moral 'development', 'judgement', 'reasoning' surely involving a number of different components – understanding, using, feeling, for example – which are conglomerated in Kohlberg's stages. If, as Peters (1974) argues, the order of the stages is logical rather than psychological, we are also in danger of doing pseudo-empirical research uselessly (see Smedslund 1980).

Kohlberg's model places universal principle at the centre of moral judgement, and is thus an ethical rule theory (Munsey 1980; Rosen 1980). Ethical rule theorists assume that one must have a moral rule to make a justified moral judgement. The general consideration, the moral rule, is especially important, as it is necessary both for the moral judgement and for identifying the relevant particular facts of a case before the judgement is made. There is an alternative to ethical rule theory in ethical act theory, which suggests that possession of a general moral rule may not be necessary for making a moral judgement, since relevant facts in a particular case can be identified without moral rules and may override moral generalizations. Act theorists see moral rules as summaries which may admit of exceptions, and morality as therefore situation-specific; rule theorists see them as *a priori* universals. Rosen (1980) 'supposes' some developments of the Heinz story to make this point. One of these, and Rosen's subsequent comment, follow and illustrate some of the difficulties of Kohlberg's work.

Suppose the wife has contemplated suicide for years and wishes to die with dignity now. Heinz wants her to stay alive because he and she live off the interest of a trust fund set up in her name. The druggist is the brother of the wife, knows his sister's intentions, and while he legally would have to sell the drug to Heinz if the latter had the money, he uses the legal excuse not to sell the drug in order to allow his sister to carry out her own ends.

We would have to know much more about Heinz, the druggist, the wife, the society they live in and many more relevant items, in order to construct our conditionals. . . . Moral dilemmas are real problems, faced by real people in a real setting. It is no test of an ethical theory, or of the moral reasoning of people for that matter, to pose artificial problems. The problems, note, are not artificial primarily because they are fictional. They are artificial because they do not represent realistic situations with all their complexity. Perhaps we should let the poets and the novelists describe the moral problems for the tests and not the philosophers and psychologists. The problems would be more difficult to solve, but at least they would be relevant to the real problems that human beings have (Rosen 1980, p. 259).

In addition to the inadequacy (pp. 163–4) and superfluity (above) of universal moral principles, it has been argued (notably by Peters (1974) and Gilligan (1977)), that elevating 'justice' to the top of the list of universal moral principles or even making it the source of all the rest of the list, is unsatisfactory. The principle of caring for others is seen as equally important. This is a particularly interesting point for developmental psychology because there is a great deal of evidence that even very young children are aware of, and frequently sympathetic towards, other people's feelings. A model of moral development centering on sensitivity to others would be a great deal more positive about young children than Kohlberg's justice model, and would have obvious educational implications. Such a model is sketched by Mussen and Eisenberg-Berg (1977). It would also reverse what has been seen as a sexist bias. Gilligan (1977) refutes the tendency in work on moral development to view women as morally deficient (Freud provides a slightly earlier example than Kohlberg, but one could produce many ancient instances). Kohlberg, finding that women's moral reasoning was frequently at stage 3 (behaving well, meaning well, pleasing people – the 'good boy–nice girl' orientation), interpreted this as 'lower' than men's, and 'both functional and adequate for them'! With admirable control, Gilligan comments

And yet herein lies the paradox, for the very traits that have traditionally defined the 'goodness' of women, their care for and sensitivity to the needs of others, are those that mark them as deficient in moral development. The infusion of feeling into their judgements keeps them from developing (one might prefer 'expressing') a more independent and abstract ethical conception in which concern for others derives from principles of justice rather than from compassion and care (Gilligan 1977, p. 484).

Gilligan's account of the 'feminine voice' in morality is of compassion and love, with associated non-violence, at the centre of moral judgement. While I find this more appealing and more admirable than Kohlberg's enthroned justice, I want for the moment only to use it to tie in with a point made by Peters (1974) and others: it is not enough to know what is 'right' and 'wrong'; one also has to *care*. It is this neglect of feeling and of action that is one of the most serious reasons why Kohlberg's theory must not be taken as a complete account of moral development. The theory does not address itself adequately to the relationship between judgement and behaviour, and what little evidence there is suggests that level of judgement does not predict behaviour at all well (Kurtines and Grief 1974). Kohlberg (1981b) says that 'a stage of judgements of justice is a

necessary but not a sufficient condition for moral action': given the diagnostic problems I have touched on above, even this may be a somewhat generous statement.

Recent work on moral development

Recently, work on moral development has taken some interesting new directions. One of these is the suggestion by Turiel and his colleagues that issues of morality and of social convention are differentiated by children as young as 4 to 6. Moral rules (such as not hurting other people) are seen as obligatory, important and generalizable, and conventional rules (such as wearing clothes to school) as alterable, less important and more context-specific, except in so far as they were related to moral principles (such as not embarrassing people at school by going naked). A number of studies (e.g. Turiel 1978; Pool, Shweder and Much 1980; Nucci and Turiel 1978) show children giving different rationales to account for rules that have a moral, a conventional or a practical base (practical rules are such things as 'clean your teeth twice a day'). This research does not provide a really convincing demonstration that morality and convention are separable areas, first because moral rules were used as the ultimate reason for conventional ones and second because of the confounding effect of the severity of the transgression. However, this approach has provided some interesting data about children's social cognitions, and a corrective (if one was needed) to the idea that 'morality' is one simple thing.

Another promising initiative (Weinreich-Haste, in press) examines the role of feeling in the moral experiences of real life. Helen Weinreich-Haste regards the use of hypothetical moral dilemmas as concealing the role of feeling: subjects do not react to Hans' dilemma as they would to a dilemma of their own, and thus their reasoning about Hans is not representative of all their moral reasoning. Kohlberg and his colleagues see moral cognition as leading to action, not the reverse. A high level of moral reasoning means that the reasoner perceives his or her responsibility to act in accordance with the moral rules involved in the issue: seeing this responsibility leads to a closer integration of moral judgement and moral action (Kohlberg and Candee 1984). Responsibility is an obligation to act appropriately; it organizes and energizes action. Feelings about the situation are not considered, so there is no account in Kohlberg's work of how they arise, how they affect reasoning, or how they are involved in moral action.

Weinreich-Haste argues that this unidirectional relationship between cognition and action, which also gives little place to affect, is inadequate. In real-life moral problems much more is involved. The first key concept is *responsibility*, which involves perception that this problem involves moral issues, a belief that you can be effective in taking action on them, and a belief that it is right and necessary that you, personally, should be involved, that it is not enough to leave the responsibility to someone else. Thus responsibility involves vision, efficacy, and commitment: all of them blending affect and cognition. If young children seem to be inadequate as moral agents, I would suggest that this may be to some extent because many of the responsibilities which could come their way are taken for them by adults, and because they know they are not skilled or powerful enough to be as effective as adults. A judgement that somebody else will cope is a barrier against commitment. We know that children are less helpful to each other in an adult-led peer group than in more heterogeneous groups (Radke-Yarrow *et al.* 1983, and see p. 158) and that participating in discussions within the family seems to facilitate the development of social responsibility (Maccoby and Martin 1983; Radke-Yarrow and Zahn-Waxler 1983; and Chapter 6 this volume).

Real moral problems commonly last for more than the few minutes spent considering Heinz's dilemma, and dealing with them involves a complex sequence of judgements and feelings. Weinreich-Haste presents material on five people who have experienced moral crises which have led to a change in their lives. For example, Sandra decided to become a vegetarian. The *triggering event* was a stay in France where she witnessed butchers slaughtering animals for meat and was also revolted by meat cooked so that it was burnt on the outside and bloody inside. She felt disgusted, and reflecting on her feeling decided that eating meat was a *moral issue* she could do something about. Her feeling of disgust turned to a *moral feeling*, 'I just can't face eating something like that which has been killed in that way and hasn't had its own life', a *moral judgement*, 'I think that's wrong . . . because the animals themselves haven't really had a life. We're just breeding them to kill them', and a *moral action*, the decision not to eat meat.

The model of moral crises derived from this and other case-studies involves cycles of events, reactive affect, cognitive reflection, moral affect, feeling of responsibility and commitment to action. Level of moral reasoning is important in perceiving the issue to be morally important and in perceiving personal responsibility to do something about it, but the subject's sense of personal responsibility and self-efficacy, and social legitimation and support from other people, may be crucially important too. The interplay of affect, cognition and action lasts a long time, and is complex. There is little data as yet on pre-adolescents' moral crises, but no reason to believe that they are always simple.

Plate 14

6 Social relationships

I have stressed throughout this book that children's development takes place in large measure through social relationships. Other people's behaviour towards the child, and the child's behaviour towards other people, influence the development of cognition, language, personality, emotion and, of course, social behaviour. If it were possible for a child to grow up without any social relationships at all, and it probably is not, that child would not be recognizably 'human': would not have spoken language, would not have the intellectual skills we revere, would not, probably, have self-awareness or empathy. Social interaction is necessary for all this: 'feral' children, who may have completely lacked interaction with other human beings resemble 'beasts', 'savages' or 'idiots' (Zingg 1940; for a recent review see Skuse 1984). Because such cases are, fortunately, rare, and usually, unfortunately, badly documented, we do not know how complete and how permanent the distortion of their development is. There are two famous cases where initial state, training given and degree of recovery are well documented. Victor, captured in the forests of Aveyron in 1800 after he had lived there for at least three years, and probably since early childhood, was put into the hands of Jean-Marc Itard and his housekeeper Madame Guérin. He was about 13 years old. Itard used patient and careful training procedures which remarkably anticipate twentieth-century behaviour modification techniques (Lane 1976/7). Victor progressed from purely sensori-motor intelligence, little emotional display and no social skills whatever, to some conceptual thought and moral and empathic feelings, but his language development was disappointing and his emerging sexual feelings were disturbing to the adults responsible for him (and to the boy himself). A rather similar picture emerges from accounts of Genie (Curtiss 1977) who was imprisoned by her psychotic father from infancy to early adolescence in a state of almost total sensory and social deprivation. She too was 'barely human' when rescued, has developed considerably with sympathetic teaching but shows remaining deficits in language use and social skills. Children less totally deprived of social lives may show more recovery than these two (Koluchova 1976; Clarke and Clarke 1976; Skuse 1984) if given carefully set up social and educational experience. Since similarly severe deficits arise in other species, such as rhesus monkeys reared in isolation (Harlow 1969), we would have good grounds for regarding the social world as a biological necessity for individual development.

If something is 'a biological necessity' it is likely or at least possible that structures and processes which facilitate it will have evolved through natural selection and will be programmed by genes or 'memes' (Dawkins 1976; Trivers 1985). Are there such structures and processes contributing to the social development of children? If there are, how do they work?

Infant–adult interaction

It is fairly clear that babies are, and do, and can do, things which are likely to be useful in their social world. They have the big shiny eyes, plump cheeks, high foreheads, fine skin, smell of milk and unco-ordinated movements which evoke automatic reactions of tenderness and nurturance in adults in our own species as in many others (Tinbergen 1951). They selectively attend to human faces and voices, and astonishingly early appear to discriminate the familiar voice of their mother from other non-familiar voices (Mehler *et al.* 1978), a preference and a discrimination likely to convince mother that she is 'special' to her baby. Their vocalizations and their movements indicate what they feel, and receive social interpretations from their caretakers. Adults treat them as individuals who are trying to communicate, as social beings with needs and wishes and intentions not unlike their own. Recent research has shown that babies' behaviour is also subtly patterned in ways which resemble the patterns of social interactions between adults, such as conversations (e.g. Trevarthen 1978), and the impressiveness of fit between baby and caretaker in their interactions has led some theorists to suggest that the baby is a social being from birth. Kaye (1984) argues that such a view is mistaken, that the 'fit' is due entirely to the adult, who seizes on any bit of the baby's behaviour which could possibly be understood as having a social or communicative significance and treats it as if it really did, although the baby was not in fact capable of intending anything of the sort. There are indeed patterns 'innate' in the baby's behaviour – cycles of arousal and the characteristic rhythm of sucking in a burst– pause alternation are central ones – but their function is to entice the mother into turn-taking interaction with the baby. When the baby pauses in sucking, for example, the mother tends to interpret this as loss of interest or 'falling asleep on the job' and takes steps to recall the baby's attention to breast or bottle by talking, jiggling the nipple in the baby's mouth, or changing the baby's position. Thus while the baby is actively sucking, the mother is relatively quiet: when the baby stops sucking, the mother becomes active. This could be seen as turn-taking or proto-conversation. Kaye, however, points out that the baby's part in this is entirely automatic. The pattern of 'turns' is due entirely to the mother who learns quite quickly that jiggling makes it less likely that the baby will suck, that what provokes sucking is the cessation of a brief jiggle, and who therefore changes her own behaviour to affect the child's. Similar 'turn-taking' and change in 'turn-taking' can be seen in games and conversations throughout the years of infancy (and beyond) as we have seen in our discussion of language development (Chapter 4). Adults fit into children's behaviour to produce a shapely sequence, or to achieve a goal, or to prolong interaction. The baby is genetically programmed to produce regularities and hence predictabilities of behaviour. The adult is genetically programmed to pick up and use (or at least to be capable of picking up and using) these predictabilities in ways which apprentice the baby to the social (and intellectual) ways of the adult expert. By first using rhythms and regularities for shared activity, later imputing intention and a desire to communicate that intention (Dunn and Kendrick (1982) show us children as young as 4 doing this for their baby siblings), later still using an assumption of shared memory and shared language, adults

treat the child as more mature and more of a partner than he really is. Admittedly, there are real cues from the child that show he understands more than he did last week or last month. But the higher forms of interaction into which the adults slip are inevitably more advanced than what the child is actually capable of at the time. Thus parents are constantly drawing the child forward into a more challenging apprenticeship, eventually into a full partnership (Kaye 1984, p. 68).

Parenting

Kaye uses the idea of adults providing functional 'frames' for their children, organizing for them the world of objects, people and events in ways which reduce potential chaos to intelligible order. Adults *nurture* children, meeting their needs for nourishment and comfort (in both physical and emotional senses) and in so doing allow and enhance communication and mutual understanding (intersubjectivity). They *protect* children from harm, ideally while still allowing them to do things which are not yet quite within their competence. They act as helpers or *instruments*, either doing for children things they cannot do for themselves or modifying the wished-for activities or objects so the child can achieve them. They provide *feedback* on the child's actions so that consequences can be more consistent or more salient or less dangerous than in nature. They provide *models* and demonstrations of skills and attitudes. They support and encourage *discourse*, which is a means of sharing and enhancing understanding. They act as a *memory* for the child and this helps in the organization of knowledge and the fulfilment of plans (Kaye 1984, pp. 77–83). I would add that they *modulate* the child's arousal and *invite* participation in culture. To do all this requires a great deal of adult sensitivity to what the child is feeling and doing, and a great deal of patience, as many, many repetitions of various 'frames' will be needed for all the child has to learn. What good parents do is make possible 'the guided reinvention of language' (Lock 1978) and of cognition, social convention and so on.

Bonding and maternal instinct

The first three of these 'frames', and perhaps modelling and feedback, can be seen in parents of other species: the full repertoire is distinctively human. Most parents, many adults and many older children fit their behaviour to babies and young children in 'framing' or 'scaffolding' (Ninio and Bruner 1978) ways. However to produce this fit consistently and effectively throughout the years of childhood requires an enormous investment of goodwill and energy and hence a major emotional (or professional) commitment to the child. The concept of 'maternal instinct' has been suggested as an explanation of why this commitment is usually forthcoming from the mother. A cultural expectation has grown up that mothers 'naturally' know what's best for their babies. More specifically there is a belief that the hormonal changes of late pregnancy make the mother ready to fall in love with her new-born baby so creating a mother–infant 'bond'. Winnicott (1958) called this 'primary maternal preoccupation', describing it as a 'state of heightened sensitivity, almost an illness' in which the mother has to identify herself with the baby in order to be able to identify and serve its needs. This bonding is supposed to happen rapidly in the first few days (or hours or minutes) after the baby's birth: it is implied that if bonding goes well all will be well thereafter, and that if it fails there will be serious and perhaps insuperable problems. These two implications about the conse-

quences of bonding or not bonding, and the existence of maternal instinct and primary maternal preoccupation themselves, need to be looked at very carefully.

At least some mothers (Oakley 1980), and given an opportunity to express it, some fathers (Jackson 1984), report feelings about their new-born child which resemble 'primary maternal preoccupation'. Some do not; reporting no emotion, negative emotions, ambivalence or sheer exhausted confusion. Many newborn children elicit from their parents the same stereotyped patterns of looking, touching and talking, and the same feelings of tenderness. Obstetric practice during the 1950s and 1960s reduced the amount of time new mothers had their infants with them, and in the interests of hygiene and routine separated mother and baby except for feeding. This separation came to be seen as interfering with bonding, and a series of researchers (Klaus and Kennell 1976; Field 1977; Richards 1979; Trowell 1982) have shown that if mother and baby have very little contact in the period immediately after the baby's birth the outcome may be worse than normal, all other things being equal, and if they have more contact than usual outcomes tend to be better than normal, again all else being equal. This has had a beneficial humanizing effect on obstetric practice. The differences are not however large (or consistent) and they certainly do not mean either that good early bonding guarantees good development despite later problems, or that failed early bonding leads to inevitable disaster. The reason why mother and baby were separated also needs examination. If it is because the baby was ill, prematurely born, or the product of a difficult labour (Trowell 1982 looked at caesarian births) it may be the illness, rather than the separation, which causes problems through the anxiety and loss of self-confidence which it engenders in the mother. It is a consistent finding that babies who are ill at birth and need a few days' treatment in an intensive care unit because of low birthweight, failure to breathe or to establish a normal heartbeat and so forth, are likely to show some developmental deficits in the first year of their lives but to catch up with the normal healthy baby by the time they reach school, provided they do not add major social disadvantage in their family to their poor state at birth. Economic or educational disadvantage in the parents are much stronger predictors of developmental problems in the child than whether the child was *medically* 'high-risk' at birth or whether there were difficulties in bonding. Unfortunately in this area as elsewhere different sorts of disadvantage co-occur. A socially disadvantaged mother is likely to have a large number of problems (see, for example, Rutter and Madge 1976) such as: being less well-fed, less well-grown, and less well-cared-for before becoming pregnant, and becoming pregnant when younger and more immature; having less good food, health, living conditions, medical care and freedom from physically demanding work during pregnancy; having her baby in a worse-staffed hospital or unexpectedly without good medical care; and to live with the baby in an overcrowded, unfit, lead-polluted environment with continuing poor diet, poor health-care, economic stress and so forth. Every single one of the disadvantages listed above is among those thought to have an adverse effect on the development of children: accumulating, they can seriously disadvantage parent and child even if the mother's 'maternal instinct' is strong and mother and child bonded well at birth. There is controversy over whether 'maternal instinct' and 'bonding' exist (Sluckin *et al*. 1983); whether they do or not they are clearly neither necessary nor sufficient conditions of 'good parenting'. A society where most first-time mothers have little personal experience of babies, where many expect that babies will resemble dolls or the photogenic cherubs of advertisements, and where many such mothers have no training and little support in dealing with the realities of post-natal life must expect there to be stress and problems (Boulton 1983). We will examine the extent and the implications of these later.

Intersubjectivity

I have said that babies' behaviour shows preferences and regularities which make it possible to treat them as social beings, and also that babies who never experience social interaction seem not to develop the specifically human characteristics of self-awareness and representational language unless given a long period of special care and training. Two issues here need some further discussion: the first, to be touched on only very briefly, is how and when the baby functions as a truly 'social' person, and the second, to be examined more fully, is what sort of social interaction is necessary for the good or adequate development of the baby and young child.

Some theorists have suggested that the baby is born 'social', is capable of 'intersubjectivity' (the sharing of meaning with another person) very early in life (Bullowa 1979; Trevarthen 1980). What is meant by this hangs on what is meant by 'meaning' and by 'intention' which are not at all simple concepts (Trevarthen 1982; Kaye 1984). The very early ability of the baby to express emotion in ways which affect the adult is seen by Trevarthen 1978 as 'primary intersubjectivity'. Other observers prefer terms like 'proto-intersubjectivity' (Hinde 1979), wishing to be cautious about attributing communicative intention to a baby of 2 or 3 months old, and also preferring to explain behaviour in the simplest possible terms. The baby's emotion-laden signals may be intended to communicate with other people, or they may be an automatic expression of the baby's feelings which other people respond to as if communication was intended, though at the time there was no intention. It will be hard to tell which of these is the case, since as well as the perennial difficulties of knowing anyone's intentions we have to cope with the difficulties of working with very young organisms, 'the baffling mixture they exhibit of psychological immaturity and readiness for a mental life in the company of other persons' (Trevarthen 1982, p. 77).

There seems to be disagreement about the best way to conceive of the earliest stages of social understanding and interaction in babies; there is, however, substantial agreement that parents' acceptance of babies as social partners and their consequent 'framing' or 'scaffolding' of joint activities and conversation form an extremely effective context for infants to learn about themselves, other people, and the outside world. Current theory emphasizes the contribution which other people make to every aspect of a child's development, redressing the under-emphasis of this contribution which characterized Piagetian and other theories (see Butterworth and Light 1982; Lamb and Sherrod 1981, etc.).

Attachment

Clinical models and theories of the development of emotion and personality have consistently seen the early social relationships of the child as of major importance. Early good experience and in particular the establishment of strong emotional ties – 'bonding' – to a mother figure who provided good care were seen as crucial for healthy later life. The baby, who was at first not notably choosy about people, comes to show preferences for one person over another; by the age of 7 months or so these preferences amount to a strong positive feeling for one or a few familiar caretakers, comforters and playmates, and a negative feeling of fear or caution or lack of interest for unfamiliar others. This differential positive feeling has been called 'attachment'.

'Attachment' is, centrally, 'the affectional bond or tie that an infant forms between himself and his mother figure' (Ainsworth *et al.* 1978, p. 302). This bond is seen as providing the baby with affection and, most of all, security. It is inferred from the baby's 'attachment behaviour', that is, from items of behaviour 'that share the usual or predictable outcome of maintaining a desired degree of proximity to the mother figure – behaviour through which the attachment bond is first formed and then later mediated, maintained and further developed' (Ainsworth *et al.* 1978, p. 302). Among the relevant items of behaviour are enthusiasm in greeting the mother figure, distress on being left by her (or him), following him, seeking her attention, showing less anxiety and more confidence in his presence and fear in her absence. Babies usually become attached to the person who gives them attention, opportunities for joint play, and pleasantly intense social interaction, particularly if that person is responsive,

co-operative and sensitive. Provision for the baby's physical needs seems to be less important, and bottle-fed babies become just as 'attached' as breastfed ones. Bowlby (1977) believes that attachments are normally formed to people who are seen as stronger and wiser, and that babies' attachments function to protect them from danger (including being left unprotected from predators, since he has taken an evolutionary perspective on the development of attachment, though he was also influenced by psychoanalytic and systems theories). Being near to a mother figure, and becoming anxious if separated from her, would be adaptive, particularly if there were complementary feelings and actions in the mother figure. The biological basis of the model and especially its synthesis of ethology, systems theory and psychoanalysis contributed to its considerable impact on theory and on practical recommendations for the care of young children.

There can be no doubt, first, that people (including children) do form 'attachments' to other people (including their mother figures), and, second, that these attachments are important both for the present happiness of the individual and for his or her future prospects. As in the case of 'maternal instinct' the theory has brought about some welcome changes in how young children and their parents are treated by professionals. A great deal of interesting and important research has been done on attachment (see, for example, Murray Parkes and Stevenson-Hinde 1982). There are, however, a number of problems which need to be worked out in defining 'attachment' and 'adequate mothering'.

As can be seen from the short list of items of behaviour which was given in the last paragraph but one, 'attachment' is seen in a rather varied range of actions. An even wider range could have been presented: Main and Weston (1982) seem to be willing to include angry behaviour like tantrums because within an established attachment relationship they may serve the function of increasing proximity between partners – 'an infant's tantrum may persuade the mother either to approach him or to permit his approach; in turn, a mother's angry behaviour often brings her infant towards her' (Main and Weston 1982, p. 33). It is clear that 'attachment behaviour' is heterogeneous and thus 'attachment' is not a simple unitary concept. It might be possible to measure each type of 'attachment behaviour' (minutes of crying, number of frowns or smiles, how much physical effort is put into removing the barrier between oneself and one's attachment figure); and it might be possible to assess the strength of each (more indicates stronger); and these 'strengths' might correlate highly positively, so that one could amalgamate them into an overall measure of strength of attachment. However it has turned out in a large number of studies with a variety of species that the different behaviours may not be correlated and that they vary from time to time and situation to situation (Ainsworth 1982; Hinde 1982; Rutter 1981). This complexity and variation has been seen as undermining the usefulness of the concept of 'attachment': reacting to such criticisms, attachment theorists like Ainsworth (1982) and Sroufe and Waters (1977) emphasize the need to look not at specific attachment behaviours but at *patterns* of behaviour, which are much more stable. Ainsworth has developed a typology of patterns of attachment displayed by infants towards their mothers. They were assessed using the 'strange situation' paradigm, where the children successively experience playing in a strange room in their mother's presence, being left alone there, her return and repeated departure, the entry of a stranger and so forth. The 'largest and normative' group of babies explored actively when their mother was present, were upset at her departure and stopped exploring, and showed a strong interest in interacting with her, mostly seeking close bodily contact, when she returned. These babies, who were distressed by their mother's absence, confident in her presence and wholehearted in their greeting of her on her return, were said to be 'securely attached'. A small group of babies were anxious before separation, very upset during it, and ambivalent during the reunion when they both sought and resisted contact. A third group of babies showed little distress at the separation and avoided contact or close-

ness with the mother on reunion; some ignored and some avoided her. Observed at home, their behaviour was rather similar. The first group, 'securely attached', cried least, were least anxious and unco-operative, and had mothers who were positive, sensitive and encouraged close physical contact. The other two groups were 'anxiously attached', cried more, showed more general distress, and were negative about close physical contact. Their mothers were less sensitive to all the baby's signals; the mothers of the second group, the 'ambivalent' babies, were warm but highly insensitive so that their warmth came at inappropriate times, the mothers of the third, 'avoidant', group were (relatively) cold, angry and rejecting (Ainsworth 1982, pp. 16–17). Differences like these are said to persist, and to be associated with differences in the child's social, emotional and intellectual behaviour, over the first five years of life (Sroufe *et al.* 1977; Sroufe 1983).

Describing relationships

We will return to the question of long-term effects of parent–child relationships later: there are important and delicate questions to be asked about how any effects are caused and what cognitive or affective systems are involved. It must also be recognized that the mother's side of the relationship needs more consideration than it has received and that the 'ecological context' is important. Variation in the baby's behaviour in different settings and towards different people (Lamb 1978), and the approach of defining attachment behaviour in terms of whether they 'usually or predictably' bring about proximity between baby and mother figure, imply that we must consider not just the actions of the baby but also the actions of the person he or she is seeking proximity with: in other words that 'attachment' is a property of *relationships* not just of individuals, and particularly not just of the baby who is by far the more intensively studied partner (Hinde 1979, 1982). Most children develop multiple attachments (Rutter 1981) and these differ somewhat in intensity, function and content. We need to consider how we describe and evaluate relationships.

Robert Hinde (1978, 1979) has suggested a number of dimensions and principles which may prove useful in constructing a 'science of interpersonal relationships'. His model is complex, as the subject requires, exploratory, as our present state of knowledge requires, and presented with characteristic care and wisdom. My discussion of it is necessarily brief, and is centred on the development of relationships in childhood. A 'relationship' involves interactions which happen over an extended period of time, have some degree of continuity, and involve each participant taking account of the behaviour of the other. Thus I would probably not have a relationship with the shop assistant who sold me a dress as it would be (unless the dress had to be returned or it was a favourite shop) a one-off interaction with no personal past or future for either of us. I do have a relationship with my (admirable) secretary because our interactions have happened over a number of years and what we do during each is affected by our accumulated history of working together, so that we each take account of what the other does now, has done in the past and will probably do in the future: and of what we ourselves do, have done and will do.

A relationship has properties which apply *to the relationship*, not simply to either partner. it involves behaviour which (usually) has meaning to the participants. In describing this behaviour we must make reference to content (e.g. kissing), to quality (e.g. kissing tenderly or passionately) and to the patterning of behaviour. To use Hinde's example (1979, p. 20) 'Clearly the relationship between a couple who always kiss after they quarrel will be very different from that between a couple who always quarrel after they kiss, even though the total amounts of kissing and quarrelling are the same in both cases.'

Relationships always take place in a social context, and are affected by the participants' social past outside the relationship and by their other contemporaneous relationships; and thus by many different levels of social structure, as Bronfenbrenner also points out. It is important to distinguish between social behaviour (which is usually studied quantitatively) and social relationships (where quality may be more important); behaviour and relationships may be related but they are not identical. Finally, relationships involve not just overt behaviour but expectations, goals, values, feelings, assessments, interpretations, memories, categorizations and norms: the participants are active agents not just passive subjects, and their understanding of the relationship may be as important as what 'really' happened.

In describing a relationship, then, we must attend to the content and the diversity of the interactions within it; to aspects of quality such as intensity, the sorts of communication by linguistic and other means involved, and the meshing of the participants' behaviour; and to the relative frequency and patterning of interactions. It may be worth looking to see whether interactions involve reciprocity, so that the participants show similar behaviour either simultaneously or alternately as in children's games of rough-and-tumble, or whether the interactions are complementary, as in mealtime interactions between mother and baby. Relationships also vary in intimacy or the degree to which participants are willing to disclose their personal secrets to each other, in commitment to the relationship's duration or content, and in the relations between the views held by the participants about the relationship, themselves, each other and the outside world. These characteristics too need examination.

Parent–child relationships

It will be clear by now that a 'science of interpersonal relationships' will be a very complex thing; it will become clear that there are as yet no studies that describe, explain or predict relationships or their effects in the detail that Hinde is proposing on anything but a very small sample. (Outside conventional psychology, some biographers approximate this sort of description: see, for example, Bate (1975) on Samuel Johnson, Thwaite (1984) on Edmund Gosse, Rose (1985) on five Victorian literary marriages.) There is, however, interesting research which bears on some of the issues raised, and an account of some of this follows. I would like first, however, to point out some of the implications of Hinde's sketch of a taxonomy of relationships for the idea that the social experience of infants and very young children determines or is a model for their later social relationships. The parent–infant relationship has a number of characteristics which differentiate it from all other interpersonal relationships. In the first place, there are marked cognitive inequalities between parent and infant. Certainly even very young babies show some remarkable cognitive and social achievements (see Chapter 2 and the earlier part of this chapter) and they develop even more impressive ones very fast; nevertheless on the whole parents are much more experienced, knowledgeable, skilled, deliberate and generally capable than their children for at least the first few months or years! The parent–infant relationship is thus more unequal than most child–child or adult–adult relationships, especially since status and power differences are added to the cognitive ones. Consequently, most parent–infant relationships involve complementary rather than reciprocal interactions, as we have seen. The content and diversity of interactive behaviour will be greater for the parent than for the infant, as will the range of communication techniques that may be applied; the meshing of parents' and child's behaviour will be largely under the control of the parent. Intimacy, in the sense of deliberately disclosing one's inner self to another person, and deliberate commitment are irrelevant to the very young, and the baby's and parent's capacity for having views of each other as persons and of the relationship as a relationship are markedly different. These differences between participants are vastly greater than in other relationships, and although the baby learns fast, the differences remain considerable for some years. Moreover, the fact that the baby is changing as time goes by inevitably means that the relationship changes as to content, quality, patterning and all the dimensions I have outlined. Precisely the recognition of this change and the provision of appropriately changed behaviour is an important part of being a 'good parent'; indeed, I have suggested that if parents wish to produce precociously competent children, what they need to do is slightly overestimate children's maturity, providing them with opportunities for achievements a little beyond their present ones, and 'scaffolding' them as they extend their accomplishments. This is part of the teaching models of Vygotsky (1978) and Bruner (1967) and of the effective behaviour documented in various areas by, among others, Kaye (1984) and Wells (1985).

It may be seen that relationships are multifaceted complex things; that the parent–child relationship differs from most other relationships so profoundly that we might have reservations about taking too literally any suggestion that it determines later relationships; and that it is potentially (and in most cases actually) an important source of learning for the child (and, incidentally, for the parent), which implies that it may have important effects on how and what children learn and so on their lives beyond the parent–child milieu. I want next to look at what we know about the effects of different sorts of parent–child relationship, starting with the relationships of parents and infants.

Early experience and later effects

There has been a long tradition of theory which proposes that children's experiences with their parents determine much of what they are like for the rest of their lives. Early experience was seen as particularly important. Weaning and toilet-training in classic Freudian theory, the neonate's experience of the breast in Melanie Klein's model, the establishment of a strong and uninterrupted bond with the mother in Bowlby's 1951 monograph, more widely the view traditionally attributed to the Jesuits that the course of the first seven years of children's lives established them forever, are examples. All these accounts of development placed its most easily influenced time right at the beginning and implied that change was difficult (or impossible) thereafter. This is a strong hypothesis which has turned out to be false, or to be correct through more subtle sequences of causation than were assumed.

Methodological and conceptual problems

The importance of early experience in terms of later outcomes is hard to assess because of the problems of first defining and second explaining continuity (as I discussed in Chapter 1). It is not always obvious what outcome or range of outcomes a theory implies that a particular early event should be expected to bring about; the Freudian child's reaction to severe toilet-training, for example, might range, via differential success with various defence mechanisms, from the extremes of anal-expulsive messiness and selfishness to the extremes of anal-retentive tidiness and obsessive orderliness. Similarly the forms taken by anxiety at the age of 2 may differ from the forms taken by anxiety at the age of 32. Further, and perhaps more importantly, the long-term effect attributed to an early experience may be due not to that experience itself but to the continuing effects of its short-term consequences, or to a pervasive chronic problem which caused both the acute early event and the longer term effects which are attributed to the acute event itself. For example, it has long been known that children whose parents divorce are more likely to have problems such as delinquency, poor educational achievement and disturbed social relationships. Some explanations of this centred on the traumatic effect on the child of being separated from one parent (and parents who were contemplating divorce were urged to stay together 'for the sake of the children'). It now seems to be a much more viable alternative explanation to attribute the child's behaviour problems to the discord in the family which preceded and accompanied the divorce and separation, and to the loneliness, impaired finances and changes in disciplining and affection which the divorce forced on the single parent left in charge of the child (Rutter 1981; Hetherington 1979). Distinguishing between different models of causation is important because their implications for prevention and treatment are different, as the example of divorce's effects on children makes clear.

Maternal deprivation

Much of the debate of the last two decades on questions of the effects of early experience centred on Bowlby's account (1951, 1969, 1973, 1980) of what has come to be known as 'maternal deprivation'. Rutter (1981) provides an authoritative review of this debate. Evidence has accumulated to show that Bowlby was right to argue that deprivation and disadvantage have important influences on children's psychological development: we will examine some of the ways in which this happens later. Deprivation, however, takes many different forms and these have different effects via quite different psychological mechanisms; some of the bad effects are rare, some common; some are irreversible and some quite easily made up for; some remain severe, some gradually wear off. Individual differences in reaction to stresses and disadvantage are a new and illuminating area of study (Rutter 1978, 1981; Rutter and Garmezy 1983; Garmezy and Rutter 1985). Emphasis on the early months and years as a period of particular vulnerability is also being re-examined, and the extent to which continuity of effect persists despite discontinuity of experience is providing some very interesting findings (e.g. Tizard 1977 on late adoption; Clarke and Clarke 1976; Doyle *et al.* 1984).

Child-rearing techniques

A very considerable amount of research has been done on the effects of parents' child-rearing techniques on children's personality and achievement. This work has to be interpreted with great caution and consideration of its theoretical bases, methodological soundness and freedom from cultural, historical or ideological bias. Caution is all the more necessary because parents are often judged or advised about how to bring up their children. Some research base to this advice is probably better than none, but only if the research is fairly sound. (Hardyment (1983) reviews advice books 'from Locke to Spock': a salutary story.)

One common problem has been theoretical or, more forgiveably, methodological, focusing on parent effects on children as if one could expect a one-way influence. On the contrary, it is quite clear that differences in actual or imagined characteristics of the child call forth different behaviour in the parent. Sex differences represent one rather intensively studied example (see p. 196). A more specific example comes from a study of mother–child prelinguistic communication in normal children and children suffering from Down's syndrome (Jones 1979). Mother–child pairs were carefully observed while playing at home with a supplied set of toys. The Down's children were as much involved in interaction and vocalization as the normal children but they phased their activities in ways which made it difficult for their mothers to take turns. Their mothers were correspondingly more directive and restricted. The result of this was that the Down's children seemed to be providing themselves with an environment which was less stimulating in both social and cognitive terms – which might be expected to contribute to the retardation of language and cognition usually seen in Down's syndrome children. Jones makes the crucial point in her discussion. 'It is noteworthy that these subtle communication difficulties were only brought to light when the mother–child interactive context was taken into consideration' (Jones 1979, p. 194).

Not only do different children call forth different behaviour from their parents because they themselves behave differently or are classified differently, but each side may *interpret* the same behaviour differently according to who is doing it. Again sex differences provide a wealth of examples: one of the most telling is the Newsons' data on parents' treatment of aggression in boys and girls at 7 years old (Newson and Newson 1976, see also my discussion of the development of aggression (Chapter 5) and of sex differences (pp. 195–8)). This interaction of behaviour and interpretation may be very complex indeed: Schachter (1982), for example, speculates that in families with more than one child siblings may try to be unlike each other ('sibling deidentification') and one child will identify with each parent ('split-parent identification'). While this is a useful counterweight to the commoner hypothesis

that it is 'normal' and 'right' for children to identify primarily with the parent of the same sex, all else being risky if not pathological, there is so far very little evidence on the validity of such hypotheses and almost none which deals with behaviour rather than interview or questionnaire data. 'Identification' as a concept is examined in Chapter 5 and is seen to have its difficulties.

We know little about how far behaviour is consistent over time or different situations. There may be inconsistency in parents' behaviour and in children's, and in their interpretations: and this inconsistency may itself be consistent or inconsistent. For example, it may be that what parents expect children to do, and how they deal with transgressions, is dependent on the setting. The Newsons' Nottingham parents said that they permitted more aggressive behaviour in the privacy of the family than they did in public places, particularly for girls (Newson and Newson 1976). There may be inconsistency over short periods of time; 5-year-olds are often more tired and more whiney at the end of the school week; a mother who suffered from 'premenstrual tension' (Dalton 1983) might be more irritable and more restrictive in the few days before her period than she was at other times, and her children might adjust to 'Mummy being in one of her moods again'. 'Consistent inconsistencies' like these pose problems for researchers seeking to classify parents' child-rearing techniques (or indeed any other sort of behaviour) on the basis of limited amounts of data, but are very much part of what we need to learn to be adequate social beings. They seem, as we shall see, to pose much less of a problem for children than 'inconsistent inconsistencies' where what is done is so unpredictable that the child cannot learn from it.

Inconsistency on a longer time-scale is to be expected on various levels. It is obviously necessary that different discipline techniques should be used on children of, say, 12 months, 4 years and 14 years. Inconsistency in *effects* of parenting may also be found over a long time-scale, as children experience other influences or change themselves. There have been few studies with a time-scale longer than early childhood to pre-adolescence, so there is little data beyond biography. The exception is work on children who were parented particularly 'badly': we will look at this later.

Most of the data we have on parenting techniques and child behaviour comes from studies done on samples limited as to nationality, class, race and historical period. It is not at all clear how far what is found with one group may be true of other groups. It *is* clear that we risk being egocentric in our interpretation of what we see and in what we prescribe as 'good parenting'. John Raven's account of a Home Visiting project in Edinburgh (Raven 1980) illustrates this. Lower working-class mothers were encouraged to interact with their pre-school children in middle-class ways. This experience changed what the mothers believed it was possible to do with children to encourage their cognitive development, but not what they felt they could actually do themselves: their confidence in their mothering skills was diminished. We need to realize that some part of what is 'good parenting' depends on what society outside the family allows to and demands of the child and family.

Society's ideas about 'parenting' will introduce methodological problems in at least two ways. One is by the biasing of the researcher's judgement and observation: as well as misinterpreting behaviour we may simply not see what we think is unimportant. The other is by the biasing of parents' behaviour towards social acceptability. This must be recognized as a potential problem in both observational and interview/questionnaire studies. What we actually do, what we think we do, and what we say we do may be different things.

It must finally be said that although there are statistically significant correlations between various parental practices and various children's characteristics, the correlations are not, typically, large. As in the case of maternal deprivation, some children do well despite horrific parental behaviour, and vice versa. The more we know about other characteristics of child and parent and about the child's experiences outside the family, the nearer we may get to understanding this variation in outcome. As far as research goes, we will need to study the co-variation of many variables in large samples; as far as recommendations on parenting go, we must be cautious and not doctrinaire.

With all these caveats about models, variation, interpretation, interaction, inconsistency, limited time spans and limited samples in mind, we can proceed to look at what variations in parenting are associated with what child outcomes. The main dimensions investigated have been parental 'warmth' or 'responsivity' and parental discipline techniques.

Warmth and responsivity

'Warmth' is hard to define, and is certainly not a simple single trait. In most definitions it involves parents being deeply committed to the child's welfare; responsive to his or her needs and actions; willing to become involved in joint activity with the child, especially activity that stems from the child's interests; enthusiastic about the child's achievements and virtues, and sympathetic and helpful about his or her difficulties and failures; and sensitive to the child's emotional needs. No-one could possibly be all these things all the time, so 'warmth' is relative. There is a tendency for children whose parents are high on 'warmth' to be relatively affectionate and sensitive themselves, to be willing to comply with reasonable commands, to be securely attached, to be altruistic, and to have good opinions of themselves, in other words to show a high degree of positive social behaviour (Maccoby 1980; Rollins and Thomas 1979; Shaffer and Brody 1981). If 'warmth' is notably lacking in the parent–child relationship there is a tendency for children to show the opposite characteristics and an increased probability of a range of difficulties (Rutter 1981). We will consider the pathological extreme of lack of warmth later (p. 185).

A paper by Wadsworth and Wingfield (1986/ forthcoming) reports findings from the unique second generation part of the MRC National Survey of Health and Development of a cohort of 5362 people born in 1946. Studied at intervals through their lives so far (Atkins *et al.* 1980), they have been studied as parents as they have produced their first-born children. 1684 children who are the oldest child of a member of the 1946 cohort form the second generation. This work has allowed studies of continuity and change between generations and of very long-term effects of parenting.

Interview data from the mothers of the second generation children includes their description of their emotional relationship with their 4-year-old children.

The 30 per cent of mothers who said they had 'reserved' or one-sided relationships with their children were much more likely to say that they disciplined their child by threatening withdrawal of love, physical punishment or separation from mother. They took part in pretend play less, they read or told stories to the child less, they tolerated the child's tall stories less, they less often told the 4-year-old truthfully where babies come from. They less often sent the child to pre-school playgroup or nursery, and they more often described the child as 'highly strung' or 'backward'. When the children were tested at the age of 8, their scores on tests of reading, sentence completion and vocabulary were significantly lower than those of children who had had more demonstrative and more stimulating relationships with their mothers at the age of 4. Some of the difference could be accounted for in terms of the lower educational level of the less demonstrative mothers, but even after this had been statistically controlled through multiple regression analyses, affection and verbal stimulation were still of significance for the verbal test scores. Some information was gathered on the children's friendships at the age of 8: children from 'reserved' relationships were much more likely to be unpopular at school and not to have any friends. 'Reserved' mothers were more likely to be rather young (17–19 at the birth of their first child), to have had some hospital treatment for emotional disturbance and to say that their own childhood had been unhappy. Lack of warmth seems in this large sample to be associated with under-stimulation, lower achievement and difficulties for the child in getting on with other children.

The differences are not large and many children did not seem to be much affected, however.

Discipline and control

The other much-studied dimension of parenting is discipline or control. Baumrind (1971, 1980) distinguished three major patterns: 'authoritarian' behaviour which tended to be coercive, rigid, intrusive and punitive; 'permissive', which placed minimal constraint on the child, avoided controlling him or her preferring to allow freedom and self-actualization; and 'authoritative', which balanced conformity and independence, encouraging discussion and negotiation in the context of firm standards. The findings may be summarized as follows:

Daughters of Authoritative parents tended to be socially responsible, as well as independent, whereas sons, though socially responsible, were no more independent than average. Authoritarian styles, meanwhile, were associated with less achievement orientation and independence in girls and more hostility in boys. Somewhat curiously, similar patterns emerged among children of Permissive parents. Daughters of Nonconformist parents resembled daughters of Authoritarian and Permissive parents, whereas the sons of Nonconformists were significantly more independent and achievement-oriented. Baumrind has speculated that the similarity between the children of Permissive and Authoritarian parents is due to the fact that both types tend to shield their children from stress and thus inhibit the development of assertiveness and frustration tolerance. By contrast, Authoritative parents value self-assertion, willfulness, and independence and attempt to facilitate children's attainment of these goals by assuming active and rational parental roles. Their children, on the whole, are socially responsible because their parents impose demands that are intellectually stimulating (that is, their expectations are demanding and clearly communicated but not unrealistic), as well as moderately tension producing (inasmuch as firm discipline necessarily results in occasional clashes of will).

The findings discussed here dramatize the fact that it is not particularly valuable to consider isolated parental attributes like punitiveness, warmth, or control. The effects of these attributes are only evident when we consider complex *patterns* of attributes. In other words, the effects of firm control, for example, can be understood only when we know more about parents' warmth and punitiveness (Lamb and Baumrind 1978, pp. 57, 59).

Results like these may be looked at in terms of underlying characteristics of behaviour instead of in terms of types of parenting. Rollins and Thomas (1979) review a large number of studies. One important dimension is, they say, parents' supportiveness, because supportive parents provide a responsive and facilitating environment for the child's activity. 'Inductive' control, which gives information about causes and reasons and encourages children to understand the world and the consequences of their actions is also important. Coercive control and punishment has bad effects because it decreases responsivity, the child's effectiveness and communication. Sociologists studying families as 'systems' (e.g. Garbarino 1982) produce similar lists of characteristics of 'well-functioning' families: mutual affiliation and affection, open communication, flexible structure balancing individual and family needs, spending time and energy on family matters and joint activity.

It might be a carping criticism to say that this picture, drawn mainly from work with middle-class Americans, resembles the cosy ad-man's dream. More fairly, it must be seen as limited in both historical and cultural terms, a model probably not much seen outside twentieth-century western society. Nevertheless, it is probable that families which have the reverse characteristics may fairly be called 'badly-functioning'. Both adults and children living in families with poor communication, hostility, low commitment, and generally negative relations are likely to have social, emotional, educational and employment difficulties, at least in the context of a society which subscribes to the 'authoritative' family as ideal. The British evidence (Rutter 1980a; West 1982, 1985; Wadsworth 1979) suggests that boys from hostile, disrupted, disordered, disadvantaged families, which provide models of anti-social behaviour in other family members and where discipline and surveillance of the child is lax, are particularly likely to become not merely delinquent but recidivist or involved in serious violent crime, or to avoid delinquency only by having such severe difficulties in getting on with other people that they are almost completely withdrawn from any social activity.

Very poor parent–child relationships

A majority of parents who batter their children had an unhappy, rejecting and cruel upbringing themselves (Kempe and Kempe 1978; Rutter and Madge 1976), though only a minority of children from battering families grow up to be battering parents and the evidence is that family members vary in their parenting style almost as much as the general population (e.g. McGlaughlin *et al.* 1980, 1983). It is unlikely, too, that unhappy families have their ill effects simply because they provide maladaptive models, or because their stresses tend to induce psychiatric disorders in their members, or because they are unstable, or because they lack resources (material, economic and political as well as social) and connections outside the family; no single cause is sufficient. It is likely that there is a chain of causation whose details will differ from case to case (Madge 1983): indeed, to quote the first sentence of *Anna Karenina*

All happy families are alike but an unhappy family is unhappy after its own fashion (Tolstoy, translated R. Edmonds 1954).

We are only just beginning to tease out how it is that disadvantage, deprivation and dysfunction arise, recur and are avoided. It is a complex issue on both methodological and conceptual levels, but of immense social importance. Among the important British sources of information are Rutter and Madge (1976), Wilson and Herbert (1978), Coffield *et al.* (1980), Essen and Wedge (1982), Madge (1983), Brown and Madge (1982).

Very poor parent–child relationships seem to be likely to set in train a complex sequence of disadvantaging events which may, if not broken by good fortune, lead to serious disturbance when the child grows up, including difficulties in second-generation parenting. Removing the child from the disturbed family might be seen as one way of interrupting the sequence. With the possible exception of adoption, which seems to be relatively successful even in the case of quite old children (Tizard 1977; Hersov 1985), this cannot be seen as a panacea. Rutter, Quinton and Liddle (1983) found that poor mothering and generally poor psychosocial functioning in early adult life were strongly associated with being reared in an institution; a harmonious relationship with the father greatly ameliorated mothering behaviour, but girls brought up 'in care' were particularly likely to become pregnant early and to marry men who themselves had psychosocial problems. Their samples were small and all the girls came from one Inner London borough, but the research was very carefully done. It is not possible to say whether problems are caused by the disorder and difficulties which originally led to children being removed from their families, or to subsequent deficiencies in the institutions' or foster parents' ways of rearing the child, or to purely administrative factors such as the abrupt termination of support when the child reaches 'adulthood' (Jackson, personal communication). It is all too common for children to be brought up in a Home where they never took decisions about any aspect of their own lives – or even boiled the proverbial egg – and to be expected to function independently the moment they leave it. Part-time removal from the family, into a daycare group or the care of a child-minder, is likely to help but to leave the child still at a disadvantage (Clarke-Stewart 1982; Tizard 1974). In part this may be because the supply of daycare for children is much less than the demand (Bone 1977; Hughes *et al.* 1980), and many providers are very poorly paid; not surprisingly the quality of provision is in many cases worryingly low (Jackson 1979; Bryant *et al.* 1980), and even in the most privileged sector, nursery schools, not as good as might have been hoped (Sylva *et al.* 1980; Meadows and Cashdan 1983). Parents who are already having difficulties may find it impossible to get good daycare for their child or to make the best of what is found. The Child Health and

Education Study reports on the pre-school experience of a national sample (Osborn 1984). Their results show that it was precisely the most disadvantaged families who were most likely to get no pre-school provision at all for their child (16.6 per cent to 2 per cent of the most advantaged group); similarly children living with both natural parents or two adoptive parents, and children from small families, were much more likely to have pre-school experience than children from other sorts of families. Direct support to mothers may be a more effective method of intervention (Bronfenbrenner 1976).

Daycare

The effects of daycare on children have been investigated but there are limitations in the research which make drawing conclusions rather dangerous. The daycare institutions studied have often been of above average quality, and comparisons of home and pre-school are made difficult because little is known of home experience (but see Davie *et al.* 1984, and p. 191 below) and because children cannot normally be assigned randomly to home care and daycare: children are in a pre-school group because of the choices of their parents or other selective factors which make them different in unknown ways from children at home. Nor is it obvious what measures of 'effect' are appropriate: IQ? behaviour problems? present happiness? later school performance? Clarke-Stewart (1982) and Clarke-Stewart and Fein (1983) review the research done; children who have attended good nursery schools and similar groups show advanced cognitive skills on entry to school, though the effect may 'wash out', and they are more socially skilled with their peers than home-reared children. They are still 'attached' to their mothers, but somewhat more independent and boisterous. It is probably the case, then, that it is a good thing for everyone concerned if the nuclear family rearing which dominates 1980s' Britain is supplemented or partially replaced by group experiences (see also Weikart 1978). Experience with adults and children outside one's own immediate family has after all been the usual pattern at most historical times and in most places.

Child effects on parents

Developmental studies of the socialization of children in the family must be concerned with the sequence of normative age changes, with individual differences within each 'norm', and with how both general and idiosyncratic sequences come about. As I have pointed out, we must accept that while parents do socialize children, children also socialize parents. Also, there are changes in the child (and quite probably in parents too) as the child gets older which are contributors to the socialization process rather than results of it. As they grow up children get bigger, stronger and better co-ordinated, for example. As a result, they pose different control problems at different ages. Almost all 2-year-olds can be outrun and overpowered by their parents; most 8-year-olds can be overpowered but many cannot be outrun, so it is a matter of 'first catch your child'; most 16-year-olds cannot be easily overpowered or outrun. Parents have to change their discipline techniques appropriately, and adjusting to changes in the child by changing their own behaviour is one of the important general principles that successful parents follow. Physical growth is relatively free from parents' influence after birth, though I cannot resist a quotation from Dickens illustrating how parents have influenced it to their own advantage. The subject is Miss Ninetta Crummles, from the theatrical family which Nicholas Nickleby joins:

... the infant phenomenon, though of short stature, had a comparatively aged countenance, and had moreover been precisely the same age – not perhaps to the full extent of the memory of the oldest inhabitant, but certainly for five good years. But she had been kept up late every night, and put upon an unlimited allowance of gin-and-water from infancy, to prevent her growing tall, and perhaps this system of training had produced in the infant phenomenon these additional phenomena (*Nicholas Nickleby*, ch. 23).

She had also, of course, had her motor development influenced by her parents' training in ballet;

sex differences in physical skills before puberty, and to a lesser extent after it, can be related to amount of practice, and variation in strength between individuals also derives in some measure from variation in experience. Parents often react to signs of desirable talents in the child by providing increased opportunities for them.

Other developmental changes seem to be more or less universal, among them language development and improvements in communication (see Chapter 4), metacognitive processes and a decline in impulsivity (see Chapter 3), a decrease in dependence and an increased demand for autonomy. It is not clear how far these are products of socialization pressure (or of biology, Trivers 1985); Maccoby (1984, p. 325) suggests that 'within large limits these changes are surprisingly independent [*sic*] of the way parents treat their children'. Whether or not a change is a result of socialization it must influence and should change parents' treatment of their children. A decline in impulsivity and an improvement in communication skills, whether or not they result from earlier parental practices, will themselves make direct physical control of the child less necessary because they allow the use of verbal discipline techniques such as prohibition and reasoning. Parental socialization techniques co-exist, that is to say, with developmental changes which have maturational, self-stabilizing, components; and also, of course, with the socialization techniques of other people. Children's relationships with other children form a lively new area of study. I will discuss sibling relationships first, and then peer relationships outside the family.

Sibling relationships

Most children grow up in a family which contains other children, brothers and sisters. Often these siblings are an important part of the child's life, both because children may spend at least as much time with their siblings as with their mothers, and more time with siblings than with their fathers (Dunn 1983), and because relationships between child and parent are likely to be affected by the relationships that each has with other family members such as siblings. We have only a small amount of data on what siblings do together, even less on what developmental effects sibling interaction may bring about, and very little in the way of theory about sibling relationships. This unfortunate state of affairs may change as researchers get to grips with the complexity of mutual influences within the family. The necessity of doing so is highlighted by the findings of behaviour geneticists such as Sandra Scarr. Although siblings share an average of 50 per cent of their genetic material and many aspects of the family environment, they differ in personality, intelligence and most sorts of psychopathology almost as much as unrelated people do (Scarr 1983; Scarr and Grajek 1982). This suggests that we need to examine both how a 'family environment' differs for the different members of a family and how siblings affect each other. Various theorists (see Lamb and Sutton-Smith 1982) have suggested that siblings may often try to be as different as possible. Schachter (1982) for example calls this 'sibling de-identification'; she also proposes 'split-parent identification', an ugly term referring to the possibility that if the first child identifies (or is identified with) parent I the second child will identify with parent II. What we need here is both good data on what actually happens, and a more precise understanding of both 'identification' (see Chapter 5) and family dynamics. It would seem to be possible that within families, as within other social groups, a range of 'roles' are available, and individuals may have some choice in their 'ecological niche-picking'.

One useful distinction made in Hinde's taxonomy of relationships (Hinde 1979; see p. 179 above) was between 'complementary' and 'reciprocal' activities. Earlier I argued that adult–child relationships, being in so many ways unequal, will be weighted towards complementary interaction; the activities of the adult differ from those of the child and the two partners complement each other. Relationships between peers, more alike in competence and status, are likely to involve more reciprocal interaction where the partners do the same thing together or in some sort of turn-taking. Siblings' interaction can be examined in terms of this distinction (Dunn 1983), and to do so illuminates some distinctive qualities of sibling relationships and their developmental effects.

Complementary interaction

Particularly in non-western societies, and in sibling groups with a large age-gap between the members, older children may be the caretakers for their younger brothers or sisters (Whiting and Whiting 1975). Child caretakers are responsible for much of the nurturing and socialization that babies and young children receive. Even in our society, it is common for older brothers or sisters to be informally responsible for 'keeping an eye on' younger siblings, protecting them in the school playground, fostering their début in the adolescent social world, and so forth. Recent observational studies have shown that most young children are concerned and helpful about their younger siblings (Dunn and Kendrick 1982) and the younger siblings are 'attached' to the older ones much as they are to their parents (Schaffer and Emerson 1964). Children as young as 3 adjust their speech when talking to their baby sibling in ways which would be likely to bring about better communication (Dunn and Kendrick 1982; Shatz and Gelman 1973, 1977); they exaggerate their intonation, use simpler sentences and give more repetitions and explanations. These are some of the features of 'motherese' (see Chapter 4 on language); what siblings *rarely* used from the motherese register were the various language elicitation behaviours such as questions and 'scaffolded' dialogues. In part this was because at least Dunn's Cambridge children talked most to their baby siblings when engaged in play: they were concerned either to direct the baby's activity or to prohibit the baby from interfering with the older child's own activity. 'Teaching baby to talk' would not be a sensible part of such interaction. The first-born child's advantage in language development is to have had unshared language 'teaching' from parents; they themselves do not provide such bad models of language as has been suggested (e.g. by Zajonc and Marcus 1975) but they do 'dilute' the tutorial motherese environment for their younger siblings. Older children frequently teach their younger brothers and sisters about skills and games and their own areas of knowledge, and may do so more successfully than unrelated teachers (Cicirelli 1972, 1976). It has been suggested that teaching one's own competence to someone less skilled is a particularly good way of achieving more oneself (e.g. Light 1983), since being faced with the cognitive difficulties of another person may force one to reflect on the problem in new and productive ways. This happens even for parents informally teaching their children (Tizard and Hughes 1984); it presumably would have even more potential for an older child teaching a younger one.

The amount of complementary interaction between siblings varies. The most frequently examined sources of differences are sex and age. The evidence on sex-based patterns is inconsistent (Dunn 1983). It has more often been found that same sex sibling pairs are more positive in their relationship than different sex pairs; but sometimes there has been no difference and sometimes the pairs with one girl and one boy have been the more co-operative, comforting and friendly. Possibly older girls are more strongly expected to be helpful and nurturant, while older boys are seen as more challenging, but the differences in observed behaviour are, so far, small or non-existent. The behaviour which siblings show to each other is intimately related to the interaction between the children and their mother (and no doubt any other significant adult). The patterns are complex (Dunn 1983; Dunn and Kendrick 1982) and change over time, and we have no firm grasp of what *causes* what. Possibly maternal treatment of children which is responsive and consistent towards each one, avoiding differential treatment and drawing children into discussion of their responsibilities towards each other's wants, needs and feelings, is most likely to lead to relatively good relationships between siblings.

Reciprocal interactions

I have, so far, discussed *complementary* interaction between siblings. Their relationships do,

however, also have strong *reciprocal* characteristics: siblings are relatively similar in age, competence and status within the family. Observational studies of young siblings show them to be close and familiar, and this intimate knowledge of each other allows both warmth and highly effective aggression and exploitation. For better *and* worse, the interaction of brothers and sisters frequently has a strong emotional tone (e.g. Furman and Buhrmester 1985).

One aspect of young children's interest in their siblings which Dunn and Kendrick (1982) emphasize is their frequent imitation of each other. Initially it is the older sibling who imitates the baby but as they both grow older the younger sibling more frequently imitates the older, and throughout childhood mutual imitation may be an especially pleasing and exciting activity. Imitation is more frequent in pairs who are also friendly and helpful towards each other, and also in same sex pairs. Warmth and perceived similarity seem to be important for this sort of reciprocal behaviour. An affectionate sibling relationship is also associated with higher levels of social sensitivity and role-taking skills (Light 1979), and siblings' interest in joint role play enables more experience of negotiating and enacting roles than the less frequent and less successful participation of an adult in role play can do. There is some evidence that children with siblings get on better with peers (Vandell and Mueller 1980; Hartup 1978) presumably because getting on with their siblings has provided them with practice in getting on with peers. Brothers and sisters will have experienced the similarity of their own with each other's needs, wishes, skills and interests which makes it easier to understand another person and one's self, and hence people generally. They will also have learned about mutual help and joint activity, and about mutual antagonism, jealousy and aggression. These social understandings and social skills can be applied outside the family, and some later friendships may strongly resemble sibling relationships in their interaction of closeness, support and teasing. It is worth noting that having poor relationships with siblings is quite strongly associated

Plate 15

with later pathology and antisocial behaviour. Sibling behaviour both elicits and maintains aggression, and aggressive behaviour is often used to settle sibling disputes. The vast majority of children are at least sometimes physically aggressive to their siblings (Parke and Slaby 1983) though there is only rarely any serious injury. Parents often allow their children to express aggression within the family while discouraging the same behaviour in public (Newson and Newson 1976), especially for girls. It may be easier to 'make up' squabbles within the immediate family than in a wider social group which is less obliged to go on living together. In some families, however, coercion and counter-coercion escalate, or aggressive activity continues even if the victim reacts in a pleasant or conciliating way. Boys from these families are particularly likely to be hyperaggressive 'out of control' children (Patterson and Cobb 1971, 1982) with a very low level of sensitivity to other people's needs, wishes and actions. Habits learned with siblings, like habits learned with parents, may affect a child's approach to the social world beyond the family.

Peers

An enormous amount of work has been done recently on children's relationships with other children. It has varied so much in research method (ethnographies, questionnaires, sociometrics, formal experiments) in underlying theories (neo-Piagetian, behaviourist, sociological, etc.) and in degree of insight (ranging from stunning banality and pomposity to an eloquent communication of shared experience) that I shall not attempt to summarize and integrate it. There are major reviews or collections by Hartup (1983), Lewis and Rosenblum (1975), Foot, Chapman and Smith (1980), Asher and Gottman (1981), among others, and an accessible introduction by Rubin (1980). Here I will focus on peer relations as they shed light on a number of developmental issues and as part of the ecology of the child's life.

I have placed a great deal of emphasis so far on the importance of adults for children's development. I must now correct that emphasis by point- ·

ing out that children spend a great deal of time (and energy, in the widest sense) with other children. In densely populated and age-graded societies like ours, those other children will probably be of about the same age, which implies relative similarity of skills, experience, interests and status: that is, they can reasonably be called 'peers'. In so far as this is the case, child–child relationships are likely to involve reciprocal interactions rather more than adult–child relations' complementary interaction (Hinde 1979; see p. 179 above). We do not have much detailed evidence on what is actually typical of child–child interactions in enough contexts (or on enough cases) to know how far this is true, but it does appear that from the pre-school years onwards children expect to 'play' with peers not with adults and to get help from adults not from peers (Edwards and Lewis 1979; Barker and Wright 1955). Even babies under a year old seem to take a different attitude to other babies from that they take to adults, being more friendly and less wary (Lewis and Rosenblum 1975), though they cannot sustain social interaction except with a partner who can 'scaffold' them as an adult would (Vandell and Mueller 1980). If the participants in a child–child interaction are unequal in age or competence there is more complementary interaction, with older or more skilled children helping younger ones, and younger children showing dependence on the older (e.g. Whiting and Whiting 1975). Interactions between equals involve more 'give-and-take', both aggressive and conciliatory. Clearly people need to develop the social skills used between peers or towards the weaker as well as those used towards the more powerful; it may be easier for the child to do this with other children than with parents. A minority of children have serious and lasting difficulties in peer interactions because they are very withdrawn or impossibly bossy (e.g. Newson and Newson 1976); poor peer relationships do seem to imply a bad prognosis for later psychological health (Rutter 1985).

Social skills in peer interactions

What then are the social skills involved in peer interaction? How do they develop? They clearly begin with mutual interest shown in looking and vocalizing, and by the time children reach 2 years of age there are sequences of interaction as well as isolated contacts (Vandell and Mueller 1980); if the children are familiar with each other the interaction is likely to be physically closer and more mature than if they are strangers (Young and Lewis 1979; compare also Dunn and Kendrick 1982). Pre-school children take part in more positive and co-operative interaction as they get older, especially becoming better at taking part in joint activities such as rough and tumble play, co-operative building and construction and dramatic role-taking play (e.g. Meadows and Cashdan 1983). They do not, as Parten (1932) suggested, give up solitary activity or 'parallel' play (alongside other children but not noticeably interacting with them); these activities continue to take up a considerable amount of time for pre-school children but no longer happen so often because the child cannot manage to play with other children. They begin to develop techniques for gaining access to other children's games, and also techniques for excluding would-be participants in their own games (Putallaz and Gottman 1981; Rubin 1980). There begin to be marked sex differences in choice of play activity and, largely consequently, sex differences in social interaction and other experience. In most nursery studies, girls have chosen the quieter activities of painting, sewing etc. which are done near or with the teacher, and the domestic role-play of the 'Wendy house': boys choose play with construction toys such as meccano, vigorous physical activities and rough and tumble. Through this choice girls spend more of their time with adults or with small groups of other children, mostly girls: boys spend more time in larger groups of children, mostly boys, and in rough, boisterous and overtly aggressive play. There is some evidence that same-sex interactions are commoner and more amicable than cross-sex interaction, (e.g. Serbin *et al.* 1977; Maccoby and Jacklin 1978; compare also Dunn 1983), and this pattern of self-segregation and mild hostility between the two sexes has proved very difficult for adults to change (e.g. Best 1983; Huston 1983). Indeed as children get older the ideology of separation gets stronger. Boys with 'feminine' interests may be forced by the ridicule of their male peers to give them up and adopt an attitude of exaggerated machismo, while girls who wish to take part in 'masculine' activities can only do so if they are as talented in them as the best boys. There is little in the way of a rapprochement until well into adolescence, though the public sexist rhetoric does not preclude all private cross-sex friendships.

Clearly as children move through the primary school years their social skills develop, becoming more sophisticated in themselves and being used differentially according to the setting, the people involved, the task in hand and the recent history of all these. They have more contacts with other children and, as the course of sex-stereotyping in play illustrates, have to accommodate themselves to the social norms of the group. They become more aware of the relative skills and statuses of their peers, and explicit and stable hierarchies and roles develop. A number of studies influenced by ethnography have described examples of these child social groups; among these are Sluckin (1981) on life in Oxford playgrounds, Best (1983) on a Maryland class, Davies (1979) on a group of Australian children and Fine (1981) on boys playing in Little League baseball teams. These detailed participant observation studies provide reminders that children's peer interactions are not all sweetness and light, and although much of what they show about children's behaviour is deplorable, they are a vivid counterbalance to some of the over-sanitized secondhand reports of children's social worlds that can be found in the literature.

Children's understanding of other children

Theoretical accounts of why children's interaction with peers changes as they grow older often place a great deal of emphasis on cognitive changes (e.g. Hartup 1983). Young children, it is suggested, are too egocentric, too limited in language, and too crude in their understanding of intentionality to take part in complex social relationships in an effective way. This hypothesis is weakened by recent evidence that young children are less deficient in these cognitive skills than was supposed (see Chapters 2, 3, 4), by recent observations of highly sophisticated social behaviour by young children with familiar partners (see the earlier part of this chapter, especially p. 189) and by the omission of an account of how 'cognitive' and 'social' skills interact. The cognitive developmental model of social development suggests that immaturities of cognition retard social interaction and better cognition advances it, but the connections are not well documented and it could equally be the case that social interactions advance or retard cognition (see Light 1983; and Chapter 3 above). However a greater emphasis on the ideas and understanding of the participants in social interaction has enriched theory, and the relatively new field of 'social cognition' seems to be flourishing.

Although the evidence so far is limited, there do seem to be developmental shifts in children's understanding of events and other people (Shantz 1983). Young children are more likely than older ones to describe the more obvious aspects of what they see without explaining them or making inferences about internal state, intention, or causes, although when the situation is extremely familiar and they have no recall problems even pre-school children can go beyond description. Pre-school children appear to assume that most acts are intended, and so may not recognize (or, more specifically, label) accidental acts as being accidental, though again familiarity and recall seem to be important. Attributions of intention, and indeed the concept of 'intention' itself, are, of course, by no means simple things, and it is hardly to be wondered at that social experience plays an important part in their development. What children say when asked to describe another person changes as they get older from descriptions of observable concrete characteristics and global evaluations such as 'nice' or 'bad', through more abstract inferred psychological qualities, to explanatory descriptions with more qualifications and accounts of specific person by situation interactions (e.g. Livesley and Bromley 1973). Thus children under 7 might talk like behaviourists or demographers and say 'She's a

lady, she's got yellow hair and a loud voice and she wags her finger a lot'; a child of 10 or so might talk like a trait personality theorist and say 'She's bossy and she always likes to get her own way'; an adolescent might talk in interactionist terms and say 'well, she seems to want to appear to be tough and totally in control but maybe she had to act like that to get where she has, and remember she did show some feelings when her son got lost in the Sahara.'

Children's views on friendship

Rather similar changes appear to occur in children's free accounts of 'friendship'. There is a shift from rather concrete behavioural definitions centering on giving things to and playing with, possibly with an emphasis on the satisfaction of the child talking, to a more abstract dispositional description involving caring for, sharing feelings with, comforting and so forth, with more emphasis on mutual satisfaction (Shantz 1983). Reciprocity underlies friendship at all ages; friends like each other in part because they do things together. Friends tend incidentally to be rather similar to each other (Hartup 1983); they also tend to be more responsive and co-operative than non-friends (Foot, Chapman and Smith 1980). These changes in free descriptions have been taken as indicating identical changes in the underlying ways of thinking about people. There are problems in this, however, as in all tasks involving interpreting verbalization. It is conceivable, though not entirely likely, that the conceptual structure has changed very little and all that is being assessed is vocabulary growth. Further, what is said has to be interpreted: typically probing is needed, and it is also dangerous to assume that a particular term means the same to all subjects, let alone the same to a child as it does to the researcher. A more structured research technique, with appropriate statistical analyses, is really needed. Among the possibilities are developments in Personal Construct elicitation, such as Beveridge and Brierley (1982).

Children's attributions

Children's answers to questions like 'why did he do that?' have also been studied and linked to attribution theory (see Chapter 5). Behaviour which a person shows consistently in most situations most of the time is attributed to characteristics of the person; behaviour which most people show in that situation most of the time is attributed to the situation. Children by 5 or 6 seem to use these attributional principles as adults do, though the evidence so far is limited (Shantz 1983). One area in which there has been important work is children's attributions of the causes of achievement (Weiner 1974; Dweck and Elliott 1983). Success or failure on a task can be attributed to internal causes such as one's effort, which is occasion-specific i.e. unstable, or one's ability, which is (relatively) stable, or to external ones such as luck (very unstable), teacher favouritism (which could be stable or unstable) or the difficulty of the task (relatively stable) or to some interaction of such causes. Thus if I, for example, won a fortune by backing the horse that won the Derby, I could not attribute my success to my own effort, since I made no effort, nor to my ability, since I have never applied it to studying form, conditions, and so forth, nor to favouritism shown me by horse, jockey, bookmaker or race officials, nor to the difficulty of the task, but only to luck – an external and unstable factor; and hence I would have no grounds to expect further success in my betting. If however I were the trainer or the jockey (or the horse), the success might well be attributed to aspects of my effort or ability or both, unless an explanation in terms of cheating by officials on my behalf or the peculiarly poor quality of the other horses provided a sufficient explanation. If there was no such alternative explanation I could reasonably attribute my success to internal factors and might expect future successes.

It appears that people differ in their attributions of their own achievement, possibly because of their developmental histories (see Chapter 5), and also that there are overall developmental changes, which I will outline here. Before the beginning of schooling, although children try to achieve goals set by themselves or by others and are pleased by their successes and sad about their failures, it is not clear how far they discriminate between different causes of their achievement. They will often enough say 'I can't do it' and show fear of failure, but it is rarely clear whether they discriminate between task difficulty and ability or compare themselves with peers. Indeed, their judgement of ability is often heavily dependent on the achievement of a 'difficult' task, and it is fairly unusual for teachers in pre-schools to comment with much exactness on children's achievement, ability or effort (Meadows and Cashdan 1983; Wood *et al.* 1980). Once children start school, however, they are confronted with learning tasks where success and failure are more clear-cut, with teachers who demand effort and achievement and with peers to compare themselves with. During the early school years children develop ideas about their own ability relative to other children's and become well aware of the need to put some effort into the tasks they are faced with. They start to differentiate between the contributions of ability, effort and external factors to particular successes or failures, making attributions on the basis of other people's judgements as well as their own. Somewhere around the beginning of adolescence, sex differences in attributions of achievement start to appear. Girls are more likely to attribute their failures to 'lack of ability', boys to 'lack of effort'. This difference rather closely resembles the many reports of differences in teachers' comments to boys and girls. Comments to girls, particularly on 'difficult' 'masculine' tasks like mathematics, seem more likely to be of the 'well, that's rather hard for you, don't bother your pretty little head about it' type; while comments to boys are more likely to be on the lines of 'you haven't taken much trouble with this, have you: you go back and try properly this time' (e.g. Dweck *et al.* 1976, 1978). Attributing one's failure to lack of effort implies that success is still possible and does not reflect on one's ability; attributing one's failure to lack of ability implies that one is inadequate, inferior and unlikely to succeed. The implications of ideas about achievement for personality development are discussed in Chapter 5.

Having outlined some of the developmental changes there seem to be in children's ideas about other people, we can return to the question of whether more advanced social cognition brings about more advanced social interaction. The evidence is patchy and inconclusive, and the most that can be said is that while social cognitive ability may be necessary for understanding other people it is not sufficient for pro-social behaviour (as I discuss on p. 157). Boys who are aggressive are more likely to interpret someone else's ambiguous action as being intentionally hostile (Dodge 1980); children who don't attend to the psychological characteristics of those with whom they interact may have problems interpreting other people's behaviour. Those who believe that they are helpless may fail to achieve anything; those who believe that they can achieve anything they want, if they only try, may do so (Dweck and Elliott 1983). All we can say at the moment is 'may': 'it all depends', and we know very little about what it depends on.

Sex roles, sex differences, sex typing

For reasons which remain obscure, one of the most common ways the human race categorizes itself is into male and female. This division seems to have been made in most cultures (e.g. Rosaldo and Lamphere 1974) and in most historical periods (e.g. O'Faolain and Martines 1974); it is also one of the discriminations very young children seem to make. Along with it goes an assumption that males and females are significantly different: this assumption underlies common-sense or lay discussion of what males and females are like, and has significantly affected the research literature, which reports differences far more often than similarities (Maccoby 1980; but see also Archer and Lloyd 1980). Furthermore, the assumed differences of 'common-sense' *and* of much research almost all involve taking males as being more representative of the human species (*homo sapiens*), or even simply better (e.g. field independence vs field dependence), and females as inferior or deficient in so far as they are different from males (e.g. Kohlberg's moral judgement work, Chapter 5). This sort of value judgement has been under a heavy attack for at least the last hundred years and has to some extent gone underground, at least so far as most western psychological literature is concerned. Elsewhere it remains strong, and it continues to support discrimination against females which worsens every aspect of many lives from the earliest moment that sex can be diagnosed until death (which, since selective infanticide and abortion almost always select against females, may not be separated by a long time gap). I would recommend that anyone who does not regard this as deplorable read Janet Radcliffe Richards's *The Sceptical Feminist* (1982); it is quite clear that it is a significant injustice to treat males as the norm and females as defective males. Such a bias needs to be eradicated: so do interpretations of sex differences which attribute them to universals (such as being more muscular) which just happen to be convenient for the discriminatory status quo (such as males' domination of politics). Throughout it must be remembered that with the exception of a few physical characteristics, mostly directly related to reproduction, *all* 'sex differences' are differences between the *averages* for male and female populations, and population distributions overlap. To give a rather obvious example, although there *are* more highly aggressive males than there are highly aggressive females, and the average level of aggression *is* higher for males than for females, our present Prime Minister, though genetically female, is conspicuously more aggressive than many of her male colleagues and predecessors. She disproves the stereotyped belief that only men are forceful and assertive, if not the stereotyped belief that women are unsuited to politics.

In the chronology of the development of sex differences (see, for example, Huston 1983; Tanner 1978), the first 'cause' is genetic: males have an XY chromosome combination and females have an XX pair. The effect of having the XY pair is to produce differentiation of primitive gonadal tissue in the 6-week-old foetus into what will be testes; if this differentiation does not happen, the tissue develops into ovaries at about the twelfth week. The male foetus's testes produce more androgen than females' gonads do, and high levels of androgens lead to the development of penis and scrotum. Female foetuses exposed to high levels of androgen, and male foetuses which are insensitive to androgen, develop external genitalia more like those of the other sex. At birth, gender is normally assigned on the basis of what the external genitalia look like: and the pink or blue infant blanket is followed by the child-rearing patterns that I will describe presently.

It is still a possibility that the genetic difference directly influences sex-typed behaviour other than that involved in reproduction, that, for example, males are more aggressive or females more nurturant because of biologically based factors such as the current level of hormones circulating in their bloodstream, or prenatal hormone exposure which has led to different brain development. Huston (1983), reviewing the research, points out the many defects in studies which make conclusions impossible at present. An interdisciplinary collaboration between psychologists and biologists is needed. The existence of a biological basis to any sex difference would not, of course, mean that social influences were unimportant, or that nothing can or should be done to change either sex's behaviour. That something is 'natural' does not mean that it is right or unchangeable, as I argued in Chapter 1.

Whatever genetic influences there may be on sex differences, there are certainly very pervasive social ones. I would argue that it is these that turn the biological 'sex' into the social 'gender'. Children observe adults: predominantly they see women fulfilling 'female' roles – domestic responsibilities, service or nurturing jobs, aesthetic or social recreations – and men fulfilling 'male' roles – heavy physical work, technical and scientific jobs, athletic and aggressive recreations. People as observed in the mass media, and in children's literature, are even more stereotyped than in real life (Lobban 1978; Delamont 1980). The models that children are exposed to, then, tend towards two contrasted stereotypes. Children develop concepts of what are appropriate behaviours for each sex as part of their learning about the social world.

Boys and girls are also treated differently by adults. This begins at birth, when boy babies are

seen by their parents as stronger and more vigorous, and girls as softer, more fragile and less alert (Rubin *et al.* 1974; Campos *et al.* 1983). Fathers show more differentiation than mothers do: they also later play vigorous physical games much more with their sons than with their daughters. Boys are encouraged in their gross motor activity and in goal-directed tasks: girls are given more quiet interpersonal stimulation and more encouragement to play with dolls. There is consistent evidence from studies of American and European children that suggests this pattern of differences in parents' behaviour persists through childhood (Huston 1983; Block 1984). What's more, where parents' behaviour is less sex-stereotyped, children's tends to be less stereotyped too. Girls in particular are probably more likely to have androgynous interests, activities and aspirations if their mothers are employed or career-oriented (Etaugh 1974, Gold and Andres 1978, Block 1984) though the evidence is not strong.

Adults playing other social roles towards children may also treat boys and girls differently. What evidence there is suggests that, for example, boys get more vigorous disapproval and scolding from their teachers, maybe more attention altogether in the secondary school (Huston 1983). Girls are probably under less pressure to persist independently with a task if they run into difficulties (Serbin *et al.* 1973, 1978); Serbin and others argue that this reduces their sense of being in control of their own achievement.

A major source of pressure towards separate gender roles comes from other children. Even in the pre-school years, interaction with a child of the same sex seems to be more likely to be mutually responsive and positive (Lamb and Roopnarine 1979), though the picture is more complex if the other child is a sibling (Dunn 1984), when it is heavily influenced by each child's relationship with their mother. As children move through the primary school, peer pressure amounts to a 'curriculum' second only to the official curriculum of the 3 Rs –

it 'taught the children the traditional role behaviour for their sex. It taught little girls to be helpful and nurturant. It taught little boys to distance themselves from girls, to look down on them, and to accept as their due the help that girls offered. Through its insistence that boys learn to be boys and girls learn to be girls, this second curriculum resulted in separate worlds for the two sexes within the classroom and on the playground' (Best 1983, pp. 4–5).

This picture of 'feminine' girls and very 'masculine' boys forming separate and somewhat hostile groups comes out of most studies of what children think gender roles and the social world should be like. There is much peer pressure on individuals to conform to these stereotypes. A girl may achieve honorary status as a boy if she has exceptional talents at some masculine activity, such as football, and girls' social worlds can be somewhat androgynous in the primary school years. For a boy to be 'girlish', at least where his peers can see, seems to be social death. The children Best studied insisted that boys must be strong, be good fighters, be 'able to take it and dish it out', be the leader, be best at everything. They must not show any weakness or sentiment, must not cry, must not associate with girls or with 'sissies' (boys who associate with girls), must not do 'feminine' activities such as housework or helping teacher, must not care more for another person's welfare or success than for their own. Only after adolescence do these stereotypes become less rigid, and androgynous and non-sexist behaviour in public begin to be a viable possibility.

Children's sexism, leading them as it does into separate social groups and different activities, gives them different experiences during their school years. On the whole, girls gravitate towards adults more, do more domestic activities, show more affection and nurturance towards their friends and to younger children, and because of their vulnerability to sexual assault and unplanned pregnancy are more carefully chaperoned than boys (e.g. Newson and Newson 1976). On the whole, boys keep away from adults more, play more competitive and vigorous games, fight more, have gangs rather than intimate pairings, and are freer to range over longer distances than girls. Differences in exposure,

practice and subjective importance might well account for sex differences such as males' tendency to be more aggressive and better at certain visual–spatial skills, and females' tendency to be more nurturant and neater at fine motor activities.

The development of children's gender roles through childhood which we find in the literature is complex and contentious. I would summarize it as follows. It begins with the chromosomal difference which leads to differences in the external genitalia, and thus to social assignment of a particular gender, and possibly also to other physical differences relevant to psychological development, though these have been hard to identify. Thereafter there is a tendency for parents to treat their sons as more active and independent and interested in masculine toys, and their daughters as more fragile and dependent and interested in feminine toys. Children themselves come to discriminate between males and females by the age of 2 or 3 and tend to choose to play the games of their own sex. They learn through the pre-school years what are 'appropriate' activities for each sex, and increasingly through the primary school years adopt for themselves and prescribe for others sex typed behaviour which is stereotyped. There is explicit influence by adults on sex-typed play and occupational choice – 'boys don't play with dolls', 'girls can't be train drivers' – and more implicit influence on social behaviours such as independence and persistence with hard tasks. Peer groups set up and to a considerable extent enforce separate stereotypes. The mass media confront children with virtually polarized sex roles.

This is a depressing picture, all the more so since children are often so adamant about their sexism. There are grounds for hope, though, in that sex stereotypes are changing and becoming more multi-dimensional. It is more acceptable than it has been in the recent past for men to nurture their children, show their feelings, and negotiate rather than fearing loss of face, all 'feminine' behaviours: and for women to assert themselves, seek public achievement and responsibility, and be recognized as having equal rights to men's. There has not been enormous, or steady, or uniform progress, but there has been some: even, as Best (1983) documents, among school children!

Learning the social world of school

Schooling is compulsory in Britain from the age of 5, and most children are in some sort of schooling by their fifth birthday. 'Good behaviour' in school is also more or less compulsory, and success at school tasks, while not compulsory, is desirable if life in school is to be satisfying, as well as for the certification which comes in its later stages, and for the job prospects which follow schooling and are supposed to be served and enhanced by it. Children are therefore obliged to learn what to do in school. Since schools are very complex social institutions, what is learned is also complex and in particular operates on many different levels. I shall do no more here than mention some recent attempts to investigate children's social worlds in school and to indicate some of the issues that are involved.

Even nursery and kindergarten children quickly develop a social 'script' which answers questions about 'what do you do in school'. Fivush (1984) found narratives about school which used the general present tense, relatively abstract language and correct temporal order in 5-year-olds on their *second* day in school. A sample protocol went like this:

Play. Say hello to the teacher and you do reading or something. You can do anything you want to. Clean up, then you play some more and then clean up. And then you go to the gym or playground. And then you go home. You have your lunch and then you go home. And you go out the school, and you ride on the bus or the train and go home (Fivush 1984, p. 1708).

British 4-year-olds, interviewed about what they did in nursery school, produced rather similar narratives (Meadows *et al.* 1977; Weaver and Meadows, in preparation); when asked what their teachers did their answers echoed the protocol's emphasis on clearing up, and teachers were predominantly organizers and controllers. Willes (1983) induced her sample to play with a toy school and complete a story about a school

day, and they too represented the teacher as being in authority.

It is of course the case that teachers are (and need to be) in authority over their class, though some of the ideologies of education disguise this, particularly for young children (King 1978). Part of children's learning about school is concerned with learning how to behave towards teacher, how to negotiate teacher–child interaction. As I discuss in Chapter 4, the discourse strategies and the etiquette of classrooms differ in significant ways from those of home. There is less shared knowledge, less child-contingent dialogue, a requirement that the child puts up his or her hand and waits to be called on rather than shouting out an answer, a much higher rate of questions from the adult where the adult already knows the answer and the child knows the adult knows it, and so forth. Children have to abide by such rules if the class is to function at the 'busy hum' which the ideology of early childhood education advocates. Teachers teach some of these rules explicitly through personal directives, 'Put your hand up if you know, otherwise I can't hear you' or statements of general rules and principles, 'Kind hands don't grab and snatch, they share' (King 1978). Some emerge more implicitly from their discourse strategies and the children's experience of classroom interaction. Typically, the classroom rules which young children encounter are phrased as either inviolable general principles which everybody always follows, or suggestions which are designed to benefit the children, and which they will therefore go along with if they know their best interests, but which allow for some negotiation of what is done and when. Complying with such rules is seen as good and sensible, since they are supposed to work to the benefit of all involved. Non-compliance in the very young pupil is 'silliness' or 'immaturity': in the worst young offenders, and in older children, it smacks of wilful disobedience or rejection of school. All these categorizations of failure to comply with school rules lead to negative evaluation of the child. Children who are used to other sorts of rules for behaviour and ways of achieving compliance and do not adopt the school conventions quickly may therefore be at particular risk of being frowned on by the teacher (Rogers 1982).

I said, and meant, that teachers need to be in authority over the children in their classes. Pollard 1985 provides an interesting analysis of the 'interests-at-hand' of teachers and pupils in primary schools. Teachers are supposed to ensure that the maximum amount of learning goes on in their classroom in an orderly way; achieving a reasonable approximation of this is essential if they are to feel they are competent teachers, if they are to avoid the stress of coping with classroom conflicts and the external threat of criticism from the head teacher and other authorities, and if their work is to be felt to be enjoyable and fulfilling. Pollard sees this maintenance of self-image as a person who enjoys and controls their work, autonomously and without undue stress, as the primary interest-at-hand of the teacher.

Pupils are also concerned to maintain an advantageous self-image. They are in the difficult position of having two reference groups within the classroom. In so far as they relate to the teacher (or other adults), it will serve this interest-at-hand to be successful learners and dutiful pupils, thus avoiding the stress, indignity and unhappiness of failing or being reprimanded. The uneven power relationship between teacher and pupil may make it a sensible coping strategy to seek to please teacher. However, the child has his or her peers as another reference group. Classrooms are crowded with children (another difference between home and school), playgrounds are dominated by them, and relationships with other children are an important part of school life. They contribute to children's self-images, their enjoyment of school, the stress they feel, and their dignity or indignities. Children's informal social systems are complex and demanding (Davies 1979, Sluckin 1981), and not always compatible with the demands that teachers make. Analyses of children in schools have often found children who belonged to a sort of counterculture opposed to the teacher-centred ethos. Typically, they would be doing less well on the tasks of the school curriculum than their peers, would get little intrinsic satisfaction from lessons (which are

'boring') and find more enjoyment in 'messing about', 'having a laugh', and a culture of toughness of which staging confrontations with authority was an important part. They may well be right in believing that the school system does little for their present happiness and their future prospects: their rejection of it, however, make this even more likely.

It is likely that any classroom, and certainly any school, will contain children who are coping with the demands of the school's social structures in different ways: teacher-centred 'goodies' and 'swots', peer-centred 'gangs' and 'roughies', some children who are virtually isolates, and some who, clever or socially skilled, are popular with both teachers and peers. Current detailed work on interaction in the classroom and the playground, and on pupils' and adults' concepts of school and of the functions of education, is just beginning to sort out how and why children transact the social networks of schools, and what the effects of their coping strategies are. Among useful sources are Hargreaves 1967, Rogers 1982, Best 1983, Davies 1982, Delamont 1983, Galton, Simon and Croll 1980, Hammersley and Woods 1984, King 1978, Newson and Newson 1977, Pollard 1985, Sluckin 1981 and Willes 1983.

As well as coping with the social systems of school, children have to cope with the formal curriculum of educational activities. They begin to categorize school tasks as early as the nursery class (Beveridge and Brierley 1982; Weaver and Meadows, in preparation). Links between home's and school's definitions and methods of education facilitate learning and the child's satisfaction (Newson and Newson 1977; J. Tizard, Schofield and Hewison 1981; B. Tizard, Mortimore and Burchell 1981). Anxiety over hard work is the first source of unwillingness to go to school discussed by the Newsons in their study of 7-year-olds: some children complained of being distracted from their work by their peers or by non-academic activities such as PE or prayers. Reading has a crucial place in the curriculum because it is so often necessary for other subjects. Taking control of their own learning processes, that is developing and using their metacognitive abilities, is another component of being a successful school learner, the more so because pupils must share limited access to the teacher's help and limits on the funding of schools have led to sparse provision of books and other materials for reference. Some children classify certain areas of the curriculum as outside their interests or their competence, not always to their advantage (as, for example, girls deciding not to do science subjects). Coping with the curriculum, with peers and with teachers are intricately mingled throughout school life.

Children's independent social worlds

Studies of life inside the school and inside the family form major components of the research literature on children's social development. Despite their possible developmental importance, studies of children's unsupervised social worlds are comparatively rare. Such settings are by definition (and often by the children's deliberate choice) away from adults' attention, so that it is difficult for researchers to gain access to them save through the children themselves acting as informants. Studies by Best 1983, Davies 1979, Fine 1980, Patrick 1973 and Sluckin 1981 illustrate the possibilities of such a method and provide fascinating pictures of the groups studied, but it is hard to know how representative these groups are. The Opies' work on children's 'lore and language' (Opie and Opie 1967, 1969, 1985) makes a notable contribution to our understanding of the social order of their worlds, but again needs to be placed in a wider picture of their discourse, relationships and activities.

There is a limited amount of evidence from large samples on what children's out of school activities are. The Newsons asked their Nottingham mothers some open-ended questions about the spare time activities of their 7-year-olds (Newson and Newson 1976) and also have similar unpublished data on these same 400 children at later ages (E. Newson, personal communication). In a study whose central concern was how children were supervised out of school hours and what recreation they enjoyed, Petrie and Logan (1984) collected information on the pursuits of 423

London 7-year-olds and 11-year-olds. The Child Health and Education Study, in its survey of its national cohort sample (14,000 children) at the age of 10, asked the children's mothers to rate how often their child took part in each of a list of activities. Medrich *et al.* (1982) surveyed the out of school activities of 764 children of 11 to 12 years old in Oakland, California.

Of these studies, those by Petrie and Logan and by CHES are not yet fully analysed, and Medrich *et al.* tabulate their data without conveying as vivid a picture of the children's lives as the Newsons do. The Nottingham 7-year-olds were beginning to achieve some independence of their families, playing outside and making their own way home from school, though still expected to get back promptly, say exactly where they were going before leaving the vicinity of home, and stay within specified geographical limits. Their outdoor pursuits including bicycling, playing on swings, ball-games (football for boys and bouncing games for girls), skipping (mainly girls), roller-skating, and making dens. Playground games such as hopscotch and marbles seemed rarely to be played outside school. As in the Opies' studies, special verbal rituals and magical beliefs flourished within groups of age-mates.

The most commonly mentioned indoor pursuit for these 7-year-olds was drawing, painting and colouring: 'reading', that is reading plus looking at books, magazines and comics was another major interest, particularly for girls and middle-class children. 'Writing' was also common (see Chapter 3). Other indoor activities included model making (mostly boys) and sewing or knitting (girls), making scrapbooks and collecting things. The Newsons provide a list of some of the things collected.

The following are *some* of the things collected by children in our sample: silver paper, acorns, matchboxes, string, buttons, tins, nuts and bolts, stones, conkers, tickets, boxes, religious texts, cigarette cartons, toffee papers, make-up, matchsticks, free gifts, 'rubbish', bottle-tops, nails, cheese-boxes, handbags, handkerchiefs, pens and pencils, plastic gardens, jigsaws, gollywogs, caterpillars, car numbers, marbles, model planes, soft toy animals, leaves, coins, chemistry set equipment, records, Meccano, costume dolls, dolls' clothes, books, little cars, feathers, money, Action Man sets, comics, jewellery, magazine pictures, scraps, beermats, dolls'-house furniture, labels, postcards, ornaments, railway accessories, drawings, badges, fir-cones, tea cards, Lego parts, stamps, soldiers, marbles, bubble-gum cards, bricks, cactuses, footballers (*sic*), sweets, insects, Premium bonds, Scalextrix accessories, shells, 'anything that's weird or ghastly', and pictures of Cliff Richard (Newson and Newson 1976, p. 134, Penguin edition).

The more recent data provided by Petrie and Logan, by CHES and by Medrich *et al.* pick up watching television as a major indoor pursuit: 'activity' would probably be an inappropriate word, since the detailed comments made in the American study suggest that television viewing was passive, non-critical, non-selective and non-social, even when several family members watched together. Bicycling, sport, swimming and reading were common activities among these other samples too, however. In each study, some children went to museums and cinemas or to organizations such as Scouts and Brownies. Substantial numbers of the Oakland sample and of some of the ethnic groups in the London sample went frequently to church or to church based activities: the CHES survey did not ask about this. Music or dance lessons were common in the CHES and Oakland samples but are not spotlighted in the London study. In Oakland and in London there were substantial differences in what children did associated with cultural and economic differences: the CHES data have not yet been analysed in these terms. Some of the activities of children included in these studies are heavily dependent on sponsorship and practical support by adults: the collaboration or at least tolerance of parents is necessary even for collections of 'pictures of Cliff Richard'. The less child-centred influence of the commercial world also, of course, shapes children's activities.

Adolescence

I have very little to say about adolescence: my main point is that I see a discrepancy between theories about it and the apparent facts. The theories are, on the whole, highly dramatic and subjective – 'storm and stress', 'identity crisis', etc. – and the facts, such as they are, seem to be much drier and more mundane. In so far as theory and fact can be resolved, I think the resolution lies in the social psychology of adolescence, hence its appearance in a chapter on social development. I am particularly conscious that I am writing at a time when the economic structure of society makes certain aspects of adolescence peculiarly difficult in ways that are possibly historically new. Being adolescent may not in itself be a problem, but being adolescent *now* plausibly is harder than other statuses now or being adolescent at other periods.

Theories of adolescent crisis

Coleman (1980), reviewing theories of adolescence, divides them into two groups. The psychoanalytically oriented theories, Freud's own, Erikson's, the work of Blos, Laing and others, stress an adolescent vulnerability of personality and maladaptiveness of behaviour, due to the pressure of sexual instincts surging up after the latency period, and to the need to disengage from parents and establish an adult identity. Sociological theories stress that adolescence is a period of role change: emerging from childhood, where roles are largely ascribed to the child by other people, he or she has far more choice of what role to undertake and of how to play it. This discontinuity, pressures from other people (and the culture via the mass media) which may give contradictory messages about 'what you should be', and a sense that adult responsibilities loom while adult rewards may be further off, lead to a problematic transition period. Both schools of thought thus emphasize difficulties and crisis. At the same time, there are the physical changes of puberty – clumsiness, spots, the first possibility of reproduction, settling with a body different in shape and size from what you've been used to. Gloom, anxiety and *sturm und drang* seem all too likely. They may seem so inevitable as to be necessary parts of development, essential contributors to the entire process of growing up.

201

Indeed, Erikson (1965) suggests that those who do not suffer an 'identity crisis' as adolescents are less mature and healthy as adults than those who have a crisis and resolve it successfully.

Self-concept in adolescence

A theory of 'adolescence as a period of confused identity, role change and crisis' surely suggests that it will be a period when people's views of themselves change a great deal, and that this change will amount to a significant disturbance. It is by no means easy to assess people's self-concepts (see p. 146) and there is little really sound evidence on the point at issue. However, during the early part of adolescence young people probably are more self-conscious and more self-critical than they were before puberty, with a fluctuating and rather unfavourable self-image and a loss of belief that other people can be relied on for favour and indulgence. A highly negative self-image and behavioural maladjustment tend to go together, those who depreciate themselves most being likely to be depressed, anxious, failing in school and feeling incompetent in social relations. The adolescents studied by Coleman (1980) expressed particular fear and anxiety in their concept of themselves *in the future*; the worsening of job prospects for adolescents since 1980 suggests that these fears were justified and the present generation might be worse off (Donovan *et al.* 1986).

It is clear, however, that although adolescents do experience doubts about themselves and do have to make difficult decisions about their future lives, to call this a disturbance is appropriate only to a minority. Most people do not experience an acute or dramatic 'crisis', a 'crucial moment when development must move one way or another' (Erikson 1968, p. 16): rather they manage a gradual adaptation. The twig bends, rather than either snapping or remaining rigidly straight. Nor is 'identity' ever completely resolved, except perhaps for the very fortunate extravert: most of us have to question what we are at points of moral or practical difficulty well after adolescence. Some theorists, recognizing this, produce descriptions of the post-adolescence stages of crisis in the self-concept: Harter (1983) describes the model put forward by Levinson, which appears to have a new crisis for each five-year period. These models are fortunately outside our current concerns, though there could be work to be done on how the parents' (or teachers') 'mid-life transition' crisis affects the child's 'adolescent crisis'.

Social relationships in adolescence

Relations between parents and children are popularly supposed to be at their worst in adolescence, with the 'generation gap' at its widest. Before adolescence, children have been dependent on their parents to a considerable extent; after it, western societies expect them to be independent. Being independent and being dependent each have advantages and disadvantages: children are likely to be ambivalent about the change. So are parents, for the same reasons. Inconsistent behaviour will accompany the inconsistent attitudes. Nevertheless, most of the adolescents interviewed say that they like, respect and feel close to their parents, use them as models and disagree with them mainly about minor issues of dress, taste in music, and so forth (Coleman 1980; Maccoby and Martin 1983). The patterns of family interaction I discussed earlier (p. 181) are relevant here; some families do show pronounced alienation and conflict between parents and children in adolescence, but on the whole they were functioning in pathological ways before the children's adolescence was reached (Rutter 1983).

The next component of adolescent conflict I want to glance at is the influence of the peer group. Again, in the popular imagination this is an unhappy influence; the child, once happy and innocent in the bosom of his or her family, is seduced away into the dissident, dissonant, discordant peer group of adolescence and becomes there interested in wicked things like sex, drugs, pop music and 'having a good time'. This stereotype too does not stand up to what evidence there is (Coleman 1980; Douvan and Adelson 1966; Hartup 1983). Peer group and parents tend to agree about fundamental moral principles, and conflicts seem to centre on socially trivial issues (such as, for example, taste in music). Hartup

(1983) sees parent and peer influences as being synergistic in adolescence, just as they are before and after. Thus, if neither parents nor peer group approve of something, the adolescent probably won't either; if either one approves, the adolescent's approval will rise but not so far as it would reach if both parents and peers approved. In early adolescence, however, there is much pressure to conform with peers and this may include conformity with antisocial norms (Berndt 1979). Again, the ecology of the child's life needs to be considered (Bronfenbrenner 1979); adolescence is perhaps a time when the individual's various microsystems are more varied and less linked into a tightly structured mesosystem than before or after.

Adolescence as marginal social status

A very interesting book by Bernice Martin (1981) is relevant to this point. She uses the models of anthropologists and sociologists to argue that societies have an intrinsic tension between formal responsible rational behaviour and anarchic free behaviour. The latter is disruptive and so has a marginal status, being controlled by restriction to certain social groups or certain times. Thus the bohemian very rich and the extremely poor are not really expected to work, though the rest of us earn our bread and simultaneously deplore and ogle their freedom. Or the whole town works hard and is compulsively respectable for fifty weeks of the year, but has a few major festivities such as Christmas and Wakes Week which are marked by large-scale spending, drinking, new clothes and a greater appearance of sexuality, what Hoggart (1957) called 'excursions into the Baroque'. Or, in the few years of independent income between leaving school and starting a family, the young are allowed to be a bit outrageous; 'sowing wild oats', 'you're only young once', 'gather ye rosebuds while ye may'. 'The culture of youth is marked by spontaneity, hedonism, immediacy and a kind of self-centred emotional intensity which, from some angles, can resemble individualism, non-conformity or even rebellion' (Martin 1981, p. 139).

How far 'youth' participate in 'youth culture' is

an open question. The likely answer is that most adolescents live in the interacting cultures of family, school and peer group as well as 'youth culture', seeing the latter as subjectively important but recognizing its transitory nature. Autobiographical, ethnographic and interview accounts (e.g. Kitwood 1980; Jenkins 1983; McRobbie and Nava 1984; and Griffin 1985) show the complexity of the social picture. At present, many adolescents have difficulty in achieving employment and financial independence and there may be less individualism and less freedom than there was in Martin's focal period, the 1960s.

It is part of the *sturm und drang* model to say that adolescence is a period of high rates of psychological stress and malfunctioning. The rates of manifest psychiatric disturbance do not support this view (Rutter 1980, Rutter *et al.* 1976). Rutter's Isle of Wight population showed very little increase in disorder between 10 and 14 overall, though there was an increase for girls. Psychiatric disorder became less likely to be associated with severe family discord than it had been in childhood. Depression seemed to be the central problem, mild depression being very common indeed, as it is among some adults (Brown *et al* 1978).

Thus although theories of adolescence emphasize its stresses and problems, most adolescents seem to manage a fairly smooth transition from being a child to being an adult. Coleman (1980) suggests they are able to do this by coping with one problem at a time: now examinations, now getting permission to stay out late, now achieving the current peer group desirable. A number of issues have to be got through, but they come into focus at different ages and are not so interdependent that solution of one requires prior solutions of others. So far as there is evidence, this 'focal theory' seems to fit it better than the 'crisis' theories which have dominated the literature. It is when there are multiple problems which have to be dealt with simultaneously, or which have become chronic, that real stress, storm and breakdown occur. One all too conspicuous example of this is juvenile delinquency.

Delinquency

Young children very rarely commit offences which bring them before the courts: only a small minority of adults over 21 come into conflict with the law. A substantial proportion of male adolescents, however, are found guilty of, or cautioned for, indictable offences; the proportion of females is much lower, but girls too are at their most criminal between 14 and 17. There has been a considerable rise in adolescent indictments since the 1950s:Figures 18 and 19 show the Home Office figures on criminal statistics for England and Wales.

Some of this rise is due to changes in legislation,

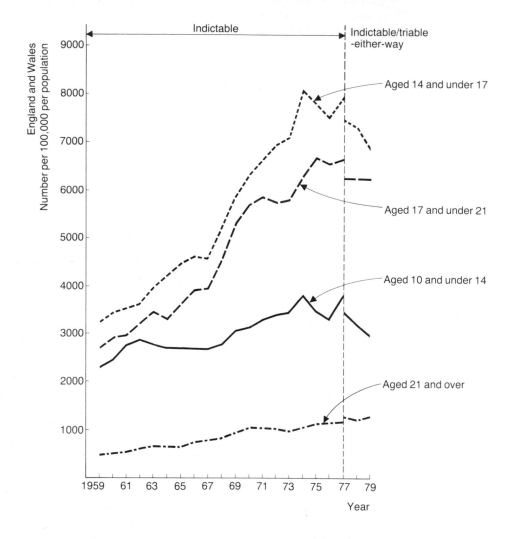

Figure 18   Males* found guilty of, or cautioned for, indictable/triable-either-way offences† per 100,000 population in the age group by age

Notes: *Other offender, i.e. companies, public bodies, etc., are included with males aged 21 and over because separate figures are not available before 1976; †Adjusted for changes in legislation.

Source: From Rutter and Giller (1983), pp. 69; using Home Office figures.

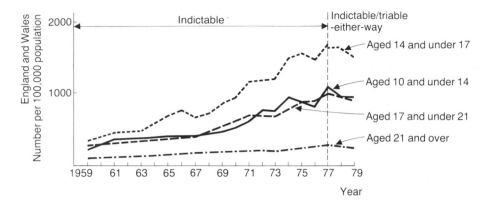

Figure 19 Females found guilty of, or cautioned for, indictable/triable-either-way offences* per 100,000 population in the age group by age.
Note: *Adjusted for changes in legislation.

Source: From Rutter and Giller (1983), p.70; using Home Office figures.

police recording practices and a trend towards dealing with antisocial behaviour formally rather than informally, but such factors cannot account for all the increase. Many offences do not get to court, and we know from self-report studies that many are committed but not detected; doing delinquent things must be seen as very common indeed among adolescents.

'Delinquent acts' cover, of course, an enormously wide range from the rather trivial to the very serious indeed. They include going to an X film when under age, which I and a majority of adolescents in West's sample (West 1982, p. 22) have done (I was taken by my father), to major offences against property or persons. Most delinquents' offences are from the less serious end of the range: the commonest concern theft and handling stolen goods (Maliphant 1979; West 1982) which account for more than 80 per cent of girls' crimes. About half of delinquents, mostly those who have committed relatively minor offences, are one-time offenders who never appear before the courts again. Most boys who are delinquent as adolescents, even those with several convictions, lead a normally law-abiding life as adults. Delinquents who only commit minor offences, once only or only a few times, and give it up in their late teens, are very similar

in personality and background to boys who have never been convicted. The picture is rather different for the persistent offenders and those who commit serious, particularly violent, crimes.

Rutter and Giller (1983) provide a very thorough review of the evidence on why people become delinquent. One of the most striking features of their survey is how thin and patchy the evidence is. One problem is the heterogeneity of 'delinquents', as I described in the last paragraph. Another is that measures are often weak, samples small and studies correlational. However they do tentatively identify a list of individual and psychosocial factors which characterize the prototypical persistent delinquent, the delinquent who repeatedly commits non-trivial antisocial acts. He probably comes from a large family, in worse economic straits than its neighbours and in worse housing, with poor relations between family members, ineffective supervision and discipline by parents and discord between them, and other members of the family also have criminal records. He is probably a school failure, has a lowish IQ and attention problems, has been unpopular with his peers and troublesome to his teachers since he was 8 or 10, and spends a lot of time alone watching TV, preferring violent programmes. He lives in an area where there is little constructive

205

amusement and lots of unsupervised public space. His social competence, and his attractiveness to potential employers, are both low. (We should not, of course, draw premature conclusions about which of these 'cause' delinquency either directly or indirectly.)

The same sort of picture comes from two important studies which followed their sample from a very early age through to adulthood. Wadsworth (1980) reports on delinquency in the 1946 cohort, West (1982) on a sample of Inner London working-class boys born in 1952–4 and studied from the age of 8 to the age of 21 (for some subgroups 24). These studies have the great advantage that they know something about the lives of their subjects before they were first found to be delinquent, and they have similar data on boys who do not become delinquent. West (1982, pp. 29–30) lists 'five major factors, each of which had a significant association with likelihood of delinquency, that could not be explained in terms of other, more basic items'. The factors were

1 coming from a low-income family (n = 93, percentage delinquent = 33.3 per cent)
2 having four or more siblings by your tenth birthday (n = 99, percentage delinquent = 32.3 per cent)
3 parents considered by social workers to be unsatisfactory as child-rearers (n = 96, percentage delinquent = 32.3 per cent)
4 IQ below 90 (Raven's Matrices Test) (n = 103, percentage delinquent = 31.1 per cent)
5 parent with criminal record (n = 103, percentage delinquent = 37.9 per cent)

These adverse factors overlapped considerably in the sample; of the sixty-three boys who had a combination of at least three of the five, thirty-one became juvenile delinquents.

These are unsatisfactorily high rates: each factor approximately doubled the rate of delinquency in boys who had it compared with the other boys in the sample who did not. Each factor was quite common, too, applying to about one in four of the sample. Boys who were in the worst 10 per cent on each factor, and among the most

'troublesome' according to teacher and peer ratings, were very likely to be among the 'persisting recidivists', the young men convicted at least twice before the age of 19 and at least once for further offences between their nineteenth and twenty-fourth birthdays. West calls their social histories 'little short of disastrous'. About half of these most disadvantaged boys were persisting delinquents, and of the remainder many more showed some degree of social disturbance. West and his colleagues did a special study of the eighteen men who, although they had a history of serious deprivation, had no criminal conviction by the time they were 22, in order to discover how they 'had managed to avoid becoming delinquents'. Depressingly, it turned out that some of them actually had committed offences, and 'the most prominent characteristic' of the group was their social failure. Many were chronically unemployed, or employed in ill-paid low-status jobs; their housing was often very poor; their social contacts were often limited and their emotional relationships unsatisfactory. West (1982, pp. 93–6) gives some case histories: this is the last one, which is said to be 'fairly representative'.

Case 011

This man's childhood was marred by impoverished conditions and extreme conflict between his parents. His father, who was chronically unemployed, was described as 'something of a hermit', hardly communicating even with his wife. He was 11 when his father died. His mother was an aggressive, quarrelsome woman with a long history of psychiatric disorder, diagnosed as 'paranoid psychosis with depressive features in a woman of low intelligence'. She made a number of suicide attempts.

At school he was no disciplinary problem, but was a poor attender and was taken before a juvenile court on that account. He was thought to be under his mother's domination. She would excuse his absences by complaining, falsely, that his classmates were picking on him. His mother and two of his siblings sustained criminal convictions.

He declined to be interviewed at 18, his mother writing on his behalf to order the interviewer to stay away, commenting that there were plenty of delinquents among the ignorant lot living in the same building who needed 'surveying'. She was at the time in great conflict with the housing authority who would not re-house her because she was such a troublesome tenant. When he was aged 20 the social services became involved with the household because his mother had attacked him with a knife. He was noted then to be an unemployed labourer who rarely went out in the evening.

At age 23 he did agree to an interview. He was still living with his now aged mother, but his siblings had all left and he no longer saw them. The home was in a very neglected state with the living-room floor partly eaten away by rats, the banisters and several doors fallen off and the sink almost permanently blocked. He had been continuously unemployed for eighteen months. He never went out in the evenings and his only two regular excursions each week were to collect social security money and to window gaze. He had no outside human contact apart from repair men and council officials. Asked about offences he replied pathetically: 'I can't get into trouble, I never go out' (West 1982, pp. 95–6).

Material on the 1946 cohort (Wadsworth 1979), while basically in agreement, provides further illustration of the range of problems associated with coming from a severely disadvantaged and disrupted family. Wadsworth shows that children from disrupted families, as well as being more likely to be delinquent, were more likely to be admitted to psychiatric hospitals or to be divorced or separated before the age of 26, and were more likely to have suffered from disorders like stomach ulcers or colitis. Wadsworth puts forward two possible ways in which there might be causal links between early disruption and later disorder. One is that the children have learned to handle stress differently; the other is that generally held social views of the effect of a disrupted family life have acted as a self-fulfilling prophecy. If teachers, social workers and other significant adults, and perhaps the children themselves too, believe that coming from a family which lacks unity and happiness *inevitably* leads to doom and gloom, they may behave in ways which make this progress more likely. The child who is continually told that he will come to a bad end, and who is given no opportunity to make good, may be trapped into a delinquent career which a positive intervention might have avoided.

It is very important to recognize that despite the tragedies shown in West's sample and corroborated in Wadsworth's, a substantial number of even the most disadvantaged boys do *not* become delinquent. Wadsworth (1979) shows that life history does not predict mild delinquency any better than chance would (p. 124), and although 87 per cent of the worst delinquents did have broken homes, large families and so forth in their backgrounds, 13 per cent did not and would not have been predicted to be delinquent from their biographies. Family problems should perhaps be eliminated for their own sake, not because they 'cause' delinquency.

We also need to investigate what factors have protected children against their poor life chances. Rutter, Wadsworth and West all emphasize how much more research is needed. However there are some indications as to what may be worth investigating.

We need to know much more about strategies for coping with stress and disadvantage. We need to know about the subtleties of adults' behaviour which may affect both the opportunities that children are given and their self-concepts. We need to know more about the peer group, about the ecology of the social world of the adolescent. Most juvenile delinquency involves acts undertaken with peers: West's delinquents particularly seem often to have begun by acting as lookout or fence to other boys and progressed, if that's the right word, to more personal involvement in the offence. Boys who persist in spending their time with a group of four or more other boys are more likely to remain delinquent than those who move to mixed-sex groups and give up 'the gang'. Parental supervision of friendships and moving away from the inner city's street corner society also decrease delinquency. Marriage, provided it was to a non-delinquent girl, also seems to reduce delinquent behaviour, in so far as it produces a change for the better in the social group and in personal relationships. Being employed possibly decreases aggression and delinquency, though decisive evidence is lacking. Living in a pleasant environment with neighbours feeling responsible for their surroundings is probably also important (Rutter and Giller 1983).

The core problem in persistent delinquency does seem, though, to be the quality of the relationships and the social training that the child has received in his family and other social interactions. We do not at present know enough to identify exactly which children are going through experiences which will leave them at risk for delinquency, nor do we know what to do about identified problem cases. Whipping a child away from an 'unsatisfactory' family into the care of the local authority, for example, is not the ideal solution. Potentially, a great deal could be done to reduce the disadvantages experienced by many families and to improve the stability and the harmony of child-rearing inside and outside the home. More work needs to be done to establish what prevention of individual predisposition to delinquency is possible. Changes in wider social spheres such as schools, the mass media, local ecology and the economy and political system we live in could also reduce delinquency. There are a multitude of influences which bring about antisocial behaviour; once their interactions are understood we will be better placed to prevent it. Prevention, here as elsewhere in the social system, is demonstrably cheaper than cure (e.g. Weikart 1978).

Overview

In this book I have tried to put together our current evidence on various aspects of child development to make a coherent picture of the patterns and sequences that occur. I have tried to indicate what general theories of child development might try to describe and explain, with some detail in certain well-studied areas. I have argued that we must try to achieve sound causal explanations of both continuities and discontinuities in development, not just 'getting age differences' but explaining in detail what has led to what within the ecosystems that the child inhabits, and where the sequence might have been different. Detailed studies of restricted areas of development are appropriate, but we must be cautious about isolating one aspect of children's development from others: cognition, emotion, social relationships and contexts, language, physical state, all co-occur and mutually influence each other. We cannot assume that what we see in one setting or one sample or at one time will be representative in detail of different settings, samples or times *unless* we understand very fully why things are the way they are.

Further reading

Chapter 1 Introducing the study of child development

Introductory reading

McGurk, H., *Growing and changing,* Methuen Essential Psychology (1975)

Wood, D., 'Models of childhood', in *Models of Man*, ed. A. J. Chapman and D. M. Jones, British Psychological Society (1980)

History

Ariès, P., *Centuries of Childhood* (Penguin 1973)

de Mause, L. (ed.), *The History of Childhood* (Souvenir Press 1974)

Hardyment, C., *Dream Babies* (Jonathan Cape 1983)

Pollock, L. A., *Forgotten Children* (Cambridge University Press 1983)

Scientific issues

Bronfenbrenner, U., *The Ecology of Human Development* (Cambridge, Mass.: Harvard University Press 1979)

Kessen, W. (ed.), *Handbook of Child Psychology*, vol. 1, series ed. P. H. Mussen (Wiley 1983)

Haith, M. M. and Campos, J. J. (eds.), vol 2 of the *Handbook of Child Psychology*

Rutter, M., 'Family and school influences on behavioural development', *Journal of Child Psychology and Psychiatry*, **26** (3) (1985a), pp. 349–68.

Rutter, M., 'Family and school influences on cognitive development', *Journal of Child Psychology and Psychiatry*, **26** (5) (1985b)

Play

Introductory reading

Garvey, C., *Play* (Fontana/Open Books 1977)

Further reading

Bruner, J. S., Sylva, K. and Jolly, A., *Play* (Penguin 1976)

Davie, C. *et al.*, *The young child at home* (NFER/Nelson 1984)

Rubin, K. H., Fein, G. G. and Vandenberg, B., 'Play', in E. M. Hetherington (ed.) vol 4 of the *Handbook of Child Psychology* (New York: Wiley 1983)

Schwartzman, H. B., *Transformations – the anthropology of play* (NY: Plenum Press 1978)

Smith, P. K. (ed.), *Play in animals and humans* (Blackwell 1984)

Sutton-Smith, B. (ed.), *Play and learning* (New York: Gardner Press 1979)

Chapter 2 Perceiving and understanding

Introductory reading

Donaldson, M., *Children's minds* (Fontana 1978)

Flavell, J. H., *Cognitive development* (Englewood Cliffs, NJ: Prentice Hall 1977)

Howe, M. J. A., *A teacher's guide to the psychology of learning* (Blackwell 1984)

Further reading

Brainerd, C. J., *Piaget's theory of intelligence* (Englewood Cliffs, NJ: Prentice Hall 1978)

Bruner, J. S., 'On cognitive growth', in J. S. Bruner, R. Olver and P. M. Greenfield (eds.), *Studies in cognitive growth* (New York: Wiley 1966)

Butterworth, G. and Light, P. (eds.), *Social cognition: studies of the development of understanding* (Harvester Press 1982)

Case, R., *Intellectual development* (New York: Academic Press 1985)

Flavell, J. H. and Markman, E. M. (eds.), vol. 3 of the *Handbook of Child Psychology* (New York: Wiley 1983)

Haith, M. and Campos, J. (eds.), vol. 2 of the *Handbook of Child Psychology* (New York: Wiley 1983)

Harris, P., 'Infant cognition', in M. Haith and J. Campos (eds.), vol. 2 of the *Handbook of Child Psychology* (New York: Wiley 1983)

Kail, R. V. and Bisanz, J., 'Information processing and cognitive development', in *Advances in child development and behaviour*, vol. 17 (New York: Academic Press 1982)

Meadows, S. (ed.), *Developing thinking* (Methuen 1983)

Perlmutter, M. (ed.), 'Intellectual development', *Minnesota symposium on child psychology*, vol. 19 (Hillsdale, NJ: Lawrence Erlbaum Associates 1985)

Chapter 3   The development of cognitive skills

Introductory reading

Howe, M. J. A., *A teachers' guide to the psychology of learning* (Blackwell 1984)

Kail, R. V., *The development of memory in children* (San Francisco: Freeman 1979, 1985)

Sternberg, R. J., *Human abilities* (New York: W. H. Freeman 1985)

Further reading

Brown, A. L. *et al.*, 'Learning, remembering and understanding', in J. H. Flavell and E. H. Markman (eds.), *Handbook of Child Psychology*, vol. 3 (New York: Wiley 1983)

Bryant, P. and Trabasso, T., *Nature* **232** (1971), pp. 456–8

Ellis, A., *Reading, writing and dyslexia* (Erlbaum 1984)

Kail, R. V. and Hagen, J. W., *Perspectives on the development of memory and cognition* (Hillsdale, NJ: Lawrence Erlbaum Associates)

Meadows, S. (ed.), *Developing thinking* (Methuen 1983)

Mills, M. and Funnell, E., in S. Meadows (ed.), *Developing thinking* (Methuen 1983)

Piaget, J. and Inhelder, B., *Memory and Intelligence* (Routledge & Kegan Paul 1973)

Robinson, E. J., 'Metacognitive development', in S. Meadows (ed.), *Developing thinking* (Methuen 1983)

Chapter 4   Language development

Introductory reading

de Villiers, P. A. and de Villiers, J. G., *Early language* (Fontana/Open Books 1979)

Wells, C. G., *Language, learning and education* (Centre for the Study of Language and Communication, University of Bristol 1982)

Further reading

Elliott, A. J. *Child language* (Cambridge University Press 1981)

Flavell, J. and Markman, E. (eds.), vol. 3 of the *Handbook of Child Psychology* (New York: Wiley 1983)

Heath, S. B., *Ways with words* (Cambridge University Press 1983)

Lock, A. (ed.), *Action, gesture and symbol* (Academic Press 1978)

Maratsos, M., 'Some current issues in the study of the acquisition of grammar', in J. H. Flavell and E. H. Markman (eds.), vol. 3 of the *Handbook of Child Psychology* (New York: Wiley 1983)

Romaine, S., *The language of children and adolescents: the acquisition of communicative competence* (Blackwell 1984)

Chapter 5   Personality

Introductory reading

Cook, M., *Levels of personality* (Holt, Rinehart & Winston 1984)

Maccoby, M., *Social development: psychological growth and the parent–child relationship* (New York: Harcourt Brace Jovanovich 1980)

Rutter, M., 'Psychopathology and development: links between childhood and adult life', in M. Rutter and L. Hersov (eds.), *Child and adolescent psychiatry: modern approaches* (Blackwell Scientific Publications 1985c)

Further reading

CIBA foundation symposium 1982, Ruth Porter and Geralyn M. Collins (eds.), *Temperamental differences in infants and young children* (Pitman 1982)

Bandura, A., 'Self-efficacy: toward a unifying theory of behavioural change', *Psychological Review*, **84** (1977a), pp. 191–215

Erikson, E., *Childhood and society* (Penguin 1963)

Parke, R. D., and Slaby, R. G., 'The development of aggression', in E. M. Hetherington (ed.), vol. 4 of the *Handbook of Child Psychology* (New York: Wiley 1983)

Radke-Yarrow, M., Zahn-Waxler, C. and Chapman, M., 'Children's prosocial dispositions and behaviour', in E. M. Hetherington (ed.), *Socialisation, personality and social development*, vol. 4 of the *Handbook of Child Psychology* (New York: Wiley 1983)

Chapter 6   Social relationships

Introductory reading

Coleman, J. C., *The nature of adolescence* (Methuen 1980)

Rogers, C., *A social psychology of schooling* (Routledge & Kegan Paul 1982)

Rubin, Z., *Children's friendships* (Fontana 1980)

Schaffer, H. R., *Mothering* (Fontana 1977)

Further reading

Coleman, J. C. (ed.), *The school years* (Methuen 1979)

Dunn, J. and Kendrick, C., *Siblings* (Grant McIntyre 1981)

Hetherington, E. M. (ed.), vol. 4 of the *Handbook of Child Psychology* (New York: Wiley 1983)

Hinde, R. A., *Towards understanding relationships* (Academic Press 1979)

Kaye, K., *The mental and social life of babies* (Methuen 1984)

Pollard, A. W., *The social world of the primary school* (Holt, Rinehart & Winston 1985)

Richards, M. P. M., *The integration of a child into a social world* (Cambridge University Press 1974)

Richards, M. P. M. and Light, P., *Children of social worlds: development in a social context* (Polity Press 1986)

Rutter, M., *Changing youth in a changing society* (Harvard: Harvard University Press 1980)

Rutter, M. and Giller, H., *Juvenile delinquency* (Penguin 1983)

Bibliography

Acker, S., Megarry, J., Nisbet S. and Hoyle, E. (eds.), *Women and Education: World Yearbook of Education 1984* (London: Kogan Page 1984)

Ainsworth, M. D. S., 'Attachment as related to mother–infant interaction', *Advances in the Study of Behaviour*, **9** (1979), pp. 2–52

Ainsworth, M. D. S., Blehar, M. C., Waters, E. and Wall, S., *Patterns of attachment: a psychological study of the strange situation* (Hillsdale, NJ: Erlbaum 1978)

Applebee, A., *The child's conception of story* (Chicago: University of Chicago Press 1978)

Archer, J. and Lloyd, B., *Sex and gender* (Harmondsworth: Penguin 1982)

Aries, P., *Centuries of childhood* (London: Jonathan Cape 1962)

Atkins, E. *et al.*, 'The 1946 British birth cohort survey: an account of the origins, progress and results of the National Survey of Health and Development', in S. A. Mednick and A. E. Baert (eds.), *An empirical basis for primary prevention: Prospective longitudinal research in Europe* (Oxford: OUP 1981)

Asher, S. R. and Gottman, J. M., *The development of children's friendships* (Cambridge: Cambridge UP 1981)

Baddeley, A., *The psychology of memory* (New York: Harper & Row 1976)

Bahrick, H. P., Bahrick, P. O. and Wittlinger, R. P., 'Fifty years of memory for names and faces: a cross sectional approach', *Journal of Experimental Psychology: General*, **104** (1975), pp. 54–75

Bandura, A., 'Self-efficacy: toward a unifying theory of behavioural change', *Psychological Review*, **84** (1977a), pp. 191–215

Bandura, A., *Social learning theory* (Englewood Cliffs, NJ: Prentice Hall 1977b)

Bandura, A., 'Self referent thought: a developmental analysis of self-efficacy', in J. H. Flavell and L. Ross (eds.), *Social cognitive development* (Cambridge: Cambridge UP 1981)

Banks, M. S. and Salaparek, P., 'Infant visual perception', in M. M. Haith and J. J. Campos (eds.), vol. 2 of the *Handbook of Child Psychology* (New York: Wiley 1983)

Barker, P., *Basic Child Psychiatry* (London: Granada 1979)

Barker, R. G. and Wright, H. F., *Midwest and its children* (New York: Harper & Row 1955)

Baring-Gould, W. S. and Baring-Gould, C., *The Annotated Mother Goose* (New York: Bramhall House 1962)

Barrett, J. H. W., 'Prenatal influences on adaptation in the newborn', in P. Stratton (ed.), *The Psychobiology of the human newborn* (London: Wiley 1982)

Bartlett, F. C., *Remembering* (Cambridge: Cambridge UP 1932)

Bate, W. J., *Samuel Johnson* (New York: Harcourt Brace Jovanovich 1975)

Bates, E., Bretherton, I., Beeghly-Smith, M. and McNew, S., 'Social bases of language development: a reassessment', in H. W. Reese and L. P. Lipsitt (eds.), *Advances in Child Development and Behaviour*, vol. 16 (New York: Academic Press 1982)

Bates, E. and MacWhinney, B., 'A functionalist approach to the acquisition of grammar', in E. Ochs and B. Schieffelin (eds.), *Developmental pragmatics* (New York: Academic Press 1979)

Baumrind, D., 'Current patterns of parental authority', *Developmental Monographs*, **41**, 1 (1971), pt 2

Baumrind, D., 'New directions in socialisation research', *American Psychologist*, **35** (1980), pp. 639–52

Beilin, H., 'Piaget's theory: refinement, revisionism or rejection?', in R. H. Kluwe and H. Spada (eds.), *Developmental models of thinking* (New York: Academic Press 1980)

Bell, R. W., 'A reinterpretation of the direction of effects in studies of socialisation', *Psychological Review*, **75** (1968), pp. 81–95

Belloc, H., *Cautionary tales for children* (London: Duckworth 1918)

Bereiter, C. and Scardamalia, M., 'From conversation to composition: the role of instruction in a developmental process', in R. Glaser (ed.), *Advances in Instructional Psychology*, vol. 2 (Hillsdale, NJ: Erlbaum 1982)

Berger, M., 'Temperament and individual differences', in M. Rutter and L. Hersov (eds.), *Child and adolescent psychiatry* (Oxford: Blackwell 1985)

Berlyne, D. E., 'Curiosity and exploration', *Science*, **153** (1966), pp. 25–33

Berndt, T. J., 'Developmental changes in conformity to peers and parents', *Developmental Psychology*, **15** (1979), pp. 608–16

Bernstein, B., *Class, codes and control*, vol. 1 (1971); vol. 2 (1973); vol. 3 (1975) (London: Routledge & Kegan Paul)

Bertenthal, B. I. and Fischer, K. W., 'Development of self-recognition in the infant', *Developmental Psychology*, **14** (1978), pp. 44–50

Berthoud-Papandropoulou, I., 'An experimental study of children's ideas about language', in A. Sinclair, R. J. Jarvella and W. J. M. Levett (eds.), *The child's conception of langauge* (Berlin: Springer-Verlag 1978)

Best, R., *We've all got scars* (Bloomington: Indiana UP 1983)

Bettelheim, B., *The uses of enchantment* (Harmondsworth: Penguin 1978)

Beveridge, M. (ed.), *Children thinking through language* (London: Edward Arnold 1982)

Beveridge, M. and Brierley, C., 'Classroom constructs: an interpretive approach to young children's language', in M. Beveridge (ed.), *Children thinking through language* (London: Edward Arnold 1982)

Biggs, J. B., 'The role of metalearning in study processes', paper given at BPS Education Section Conference Cambridge, September 1984 (1984/in press)

Bissex, G. L., *Gnys at wrk: a child learns to write and read* (Cambridge, Mass.: Harvard University Press)

Bjorklund, D. F. and Zeman, B. R., 'Children's organisation and metamemory awareness in their recall of familiar information', *Child Development*, **53** (1982), pp. 799–810

Blinkhorn, S. F. and Hendrickson, D. E., 'Averaged evoked responses and psychometric intelligence', *Nature*, **295** (1982), pp. 596–7

Block, J., *Sex-role identity and ego development* (San Francisco: Jossey-Bass 1984)

Block, J. H., *Lives through time* (Berkeley, California: Bancroft Books 1971)

Block, J. H. and Block, J., 'The role of ego-control and ego resiliency in the organisation of behavior', in W. A. Collins (ed.), *Minnesota Symposium on Child Psychology*, vol. 13 (Hillsdale, NJ: Lawrence Erlbaum 1980)

Bloom, K., 'Evaluation of infant vocal conditioning', *Journal of Experimental Child Psychology*, **27** (1979), pp. 60–70

Bloom, L., *Language development: form and function in emerging grammars* (Cambridge Mass.: MIT Press 1970)

Blurton Jones, N. (ed.), *Ethological studies in child behaviour* (Cambridge: Cambridge UP 1972)

Blurton-Jones, N., Woodson, R. H. and Chisholm, J. S., 'Cross-cultural perspectives on the significance of social relationships in infancy', in D. Shaffer and J. Dunn (eds.), *The first year of Life* (Chichester: Wiley 1979)

Boden, M. A., *Piaget* (London: Fontana 1979)

Bone, M. R., *Preschool children and the need for daycare: a survey carried out on behalf of the DHSS* (London: HMSO 1977)

Boulton, M. G., *On being a mother* (London: Tavistock 1983)

Bower, T. G. R., *Development in infancy* (San Francisco: Freeman 1974)

Bower, T. G. R., Broughton, J. M. and Moore, M. K., 'Demonstration of intention in the reaching behaviour of neonate humans', *Nature*, **228** (1970), pp. 679–81

Bowerman, M., *Early syntactic development: a cross-linguistic study with special reference to Finnish* (Cambridge, Mass.: Cambridge UP 1973)

Bowlby, J., *Maternal care and mental health* (London: HMSO 1951)

Bowlby, J., *Attachment and loss*, vol. 1, *Attachment* (1969); vol. 2, *Separation* (1973); vol. 3, *Loss* (1980) (London: Hogarth Press)

Bowlby, J., 'The making and breaking of affectional bonds', *British Journal of Psychiatry*, **130** (1977), pp. 201–10

Bradley L. and Bryant, P. E., 'Categorising sounds and learning to read: a causal connection', *Nature*, **301** (1983), pp. 419–21

Braine, M. D. S. and Rumain, B., 'Logical reasoning', in J. H. Flavell and E. M. Markman (eds.), *Handbook of Child Psychology*, vol. 3, series ed. P. H. Mussen (New York: Wiley 1983)

Brainerd, C. J., *Piaget's theory of intelligence* (Englewood Cliffs, NJ: Prentice Hall 1978)

Brainerd, C. J., *The origins of the number concept* (New York: Praeger 1979)

Brainerd, C. J. (ed.), *Children's logical and mathematical cognition* (New York: Springer-Verlag 1982)

Bransford, J. D., *Human Cognition* (Belmont, Cal.: Wadsworth 1979)

Bremner, J. G., 'The infant's understanding of space',

in M. V. Cox (ed.), *Are young children egocentric?* (London: Concord 1980)

Breslow, L., 'Reevaluation of the literature on the development of transitive inferences', *Psychological Bulletin*, **89** (2) (1981), pp. 325–51

Bretherton, I., 'Young children in stressful situations', in G. V. Coelho and P. I. Ahmed (eds.), *Uprooting and development* (New York: Plenum Press 1980)

Bretherton, I., McNew, S. and Beeghly-Smith, M., 'Early person knowledge as expressed in gestural and verbal communication: when do infants acquire a "theory of mind"?', in M. E. Lamb and L. R. Sherrod (eds.), *Infant Social Cognition* (Hillsdale, NJ: Erlbaum Associates 1981)

Bromley, D. B., 'Natural language and the development of the self', *Nebraska Symposium on Motivation 1977* (Lincoln, Nebraska: University of Nebraska Press 1978)

Bronfenbrenner, U., 'Is early intervention effective? Facts and principles of early intervention: a summary', in A. D. B. and A. M. Clarke (eds.), *Early experience* (London: Open Books 1976)

Bronfenbrenner, U., *The ecology of human development* (Cambridge, Mass.: Harvard Univ. Press 1979)

Bronson, W. C., 'Developments in behaviour with age mates during the second year of life', in M. Lewis and L. A. Rosenblum (eds.), *The origins of behaviour: Friendship and peer relations* (New York: John Wiley & Sons 1975)

Broughton, J., 'Development of concepts of self, mind, reality and knowledge', in W. Damon (ed.), *New directions for child development*, **1** (1978), pp. 75–100

Broughton, J. M., 'Genetic logic and the developmental psychology and philosophical concepts', in J. M. Broughton and D. J. Freeman-Moir (eds.), *The cognitive-developmental psychology of J. M. Baldwin* (Norwood, NJ: Ablex 1982)

Broughton, J. M. and Freeman-Moir, D. J. (eds.), *The cognitive developmental psychology of J. M. Baldwin* (Norwood, NJ: Ablex 1982)

Brown, A. L., 'The development of memory: knowing, knowing about knowing, and knowing how to know', in H. W. Reese (ed.), *Advances in child development and behaviour*, vol. 10 (New York: Academic Press 1975)

Brown, A. L., Bransford, J. D., Ferrara, R. A. and Campione, J. C., 'Learning, remembering and understanding', in J. H. Flavell and E. Markman (eds.), vol. 3 of the *Handbook of Child Psychology*, series ed. P. Mussen (New York: Wiley 1983)

Brown, A. L. and Campione, J. C., 'Recognition memory for perceptually similar pictures in pre-school children', *Journal of Experimental Psychology*, **95** (1972), pp. 55–62

Brown, A. L. and De Loache, J. S., 'Skills, plans and self-regulation' in R. S. Siegler (ed.), *Children's thinking. What develops?* (Hillsdale, NJ: LEA 1978)

Brown, A. L., Palincsar, A. S. and Armbruster, B. B., 'Instructing comprehension-fostering activities in interactive learning situations', in H. Mandle, N. Stein and T. Trabasso (eds.), *Learning and comprehension of texts* (Hillsdale, NJ: Erlsbaum 1984)

Brown, A. L. and Scott, M. S., 'Recognition memory for pictures in preschool children', *Journal of Experimental Child Psychology*, **11** (1971), pp. 401–12

Brown, G. and Desforges, C., *Piaget's theory: a psychological critique* (London: Routledge & Kegan Paul 1979)

Brown, G. W. and Harris, T., *Social origins of depression: a study of psychiatric disorder in women* (London: Tavistock 1978)

Brown, M. and Madge, N., *Despite the Welfare State* (London: Heinemann 1982)

Bruner, J. S., 'On cognitive growth', in J. S. Bruner, R. R. Olver and P. M. Greenfield (eds.), *Studies in cognitive growth* (New York: Wiley 1966)

Bruner, J. S., *Toward a theory of instruction* (New York: Norton 1968)

Bruner, J. S., 'Organisation of early skilled action', *Child Development*, **44** (1973), pp. 1–11

Bruner, J. S., 'From communication to language – a psychological perspective', *Cognition*, **3** (1976), pp. 255–87

Bruner, J. S., Goodnow, J. J. and Austin, G. A., *A study of thinking* (New York: Wiley 1956)

Bruner, J., Jolly, A., and Sylva, K. (eds.), *Play: its role in development and evolution* (Harmondsworth: Penguin 1976)

Bruner, J. S., Olver, R. and Greenfield, P. M. (eds.) *Studies in cognitive growth* (New York: Wiley 1966)

Bryant, B., Harris, M. and Newton, D., *Children and minders* (London: Grant McIntyre 1980)

Bryant, P. E., *Perception and understanding in young children* (London: Methuen 1974)

Bryant, P. E., 'The role of conflict and of agreement between intellectual strategies in children's ideas about measurement', *British Journal of Psychology*, **73** (1982), pp. 243–52

Bryant, P. E. and Bradley, L., 'Why children sometimes write words which they do not read', in U.

Frith (ed.), *Cognitive processes in spelling* (London: Academic Press 1980)

Bryant, P. E. and Bradley, L., 'Psychological strategies and the development of reading and writing', in M. Martlew (ed.), *The psychology of written language* (Chichester: Wiley 1983)

Bryant, P. E. and Bradley, L., *Children's reading problems* (Oxford: Blackwell 1985)

Bryant, P. E., Jones, P., Claxton, V. and Perkins, J., 'Recognition of shapes across modalities by infants', *Nature*, **240** (1972), pp. 303–4

Bryant, P. E. and Trabasso, T., 'Transitive inferences and memory in young children', *Nature*, **232** (1971), pp. 456–8

Bullowa, M., *Before speech: the beginnings of interpersonal communication* (Cambridge: Cambridge UP 1979)

Burghardt, G. M., 'On the origins of play', in P. K. Smith (ed.), *Play in animals and humans* (Oxford: Basil Blackwell 1984)

Burnett, J. (ed.), *Destiny obscure: autobiographies of childhood, education and family from the 1820s to the 1920s* (London: Allen Lane 1982)

Buss, A. H. and Plomin, R., *A temperament theory of personality development* (New York: Wiley 1975)

Butterworth, G., 'Object identity in infancy: the interaction of spatial location codes in determining search errors', *Child Development*, **46** (1975), pp. 866–70

Butterworth, G. 'Object disappearance and error in Piaget's Stage IV task', *Journal of Experimental Child Psychology*, **22** (1977), pp. 391–401

Butterworth, G., 'Thought and things: Piaget's theory', in A. Burton and J. Radford (eds.), *Perspectives on thinking* (London: Methuen 1978)

Butterworth, G. and Hicks, L., 'Visual proprioception and postural stability in infancy', *Perception*, **6** (1977), pp. 255–62

Butterworth, G. and Light, P. (eds.) *Social cognition: Studies of the development of understanding* (Brighton: Harvester Press 1982)

Byers, J. A., 'Play in ungulates', in P. K. Smith (ed.), *Play in animals & humans* (Oxford: Blackwell 1984)

Bynum, T. W., Thomas, J. A. and Weitz, L. J., 'Truth-functional logic in formal operational thinking', *Developmental Psychology*, **7** (1972), pp. 129–32

Calkins, L., *Lessons from a child: on the teaching and learning of writing* (Exeter, New Hampshire: Heinemann 1983)

Callanan, M. A., 'How parents label objects for young children: the role of input in the acquisition of category hierarchies', *Child Development*, **56** (1985), pp. 508–23

Camaras, L. A., 'Facial expressions used by children in a conflict situation', *Child Development*, **48** (1977), pp. 1431–5

Camaras, L. A., 'Children's understanding of facial expressions used during conflict encounters', *Child Development*, **51** (1980), pp. 879–85

Campos, J. J., Barrett, K. C., Lamb, M. E., Goldsmith, H. H. and Sternberg, C., 'Socio-emotional development', in M. M. Haith and J. J. Campos (eds.), vol. 2 of the *Handbook of Child Development* (New York: Wiley 1983)

Carpenter, T. P. and Moser, J. M., 'The acquisition of addition and subtraction concepts', in R. Lesh and M. Landau (eds.), *Acquisition of mathematics concepts and processes* (New York: Academic Press 1983)

Carpenter, T. P., Moser, J. M. and Romberg, T. A. (eds.), *Addition and Subtraction: a cognitive perspective* (Hillsdale, NJ: Erlbaum 1982)

Case, R., 'The process of stage-transition: a neo-Piagetian view', in R. J. Sternberg (ed.), *Mechanisms of cognitive development* (New York: Freeman 1984)

Case, R., *Intellectual development: birth to adulthood* (New York: Academic Press 1985)

Cavanaugh, J. C. and Perlmutter, M., 'Metamemory: a critical examination', *Child Development*, **53** (1982), pp. 11–28

Chall, J. S., *Learning to read: the great debate* (New York: McGraw Hill 1967)

Chall, J. S., *Stages of reading development* (New York: McGraw Hill 1983)

Chi, M. T. H., 'Knowledge structures and memory development', in R. S. Siegler (ed.), *Children's thinking: what develops?* (Hillsdale, NJ: LEA 1978)

Chi, M. T. H. and Koeske, R. D., 'Network representation of a child's dinosaur knowledge', *Developmental Psychology*, **19** (1) (1983), pp. 29–39

Chomsky, N., *Reflections on language* (London: Temple Smith/Fontana 1976)

CIBA foundation symposium: Ruth Porter and Geralyn M. Collins (eds.), *Temperamental differences in infants and young children* (London: Pitman 1982)

Cicirelli, V. G., 'Concept learning of young children as a function of sibling relationships to the teacher', *Child Development*, **43** (1972), pp. 282–7

Cicirelli, V. G. 'Sibling structure and intellectual

ability', *Developmental Psychology*, **12** (1976), pp. 369–70

Cicirelli, V. G., 'Sibling influence throughout the life span', in M. Lamb and B. Sutton-Smith (eds.), *Sibling relationships* (Hillsdale, NJ: Erlbaum 1982)

Clark, E. V., 'Meanings and concepts', in J. H. Flavell and E. M. Markman (eds.), vol. 3 of the *Handbook of Child Psychology*, series ed. P. H. Mussen (New York: Wiley 1983)

Clark, H. H. and Clark, E. V., *Psychology and language* (New York: Harcourt Brace Jovanovich 1977)

Clark, M. M., *Young fluent readers* (London: Heinemann 1976)

Clark, R. and Delia, J., 'The development of functional persuasive skills in childhood and early adolescence', *Child Development*, **47** (1976), pp. 1008–14

Clark, R. W., *Freud: the man and the cause* (London: Jonathan Cape 1980)

Clarke, A. M. and Clarke, A. D. B., *Early experience: myth and evidence* (London: Open Books 1976)

Clarke, R. V. G., 'Delinquency, environment and intervention', *Journal of Child Psychology & Psychiatry*, **26** (4) (1985), pp. 505–24

Clarke-Stewart, A., *Day Care* (London: Fontana 1982)

Clarke-Stewart, A. and Fein, G., 'Early childhood programs', in M. M. Haith and J. J. Campos, vol. 2 of the *Handbook of Child Psychology*, series ed. P. H. Mussen (New York: Wiley 1983)

Clay, M., *Reading: the patterning of complex behaviour* (Heinemann 1979)

Clay, M., 'Getting a theory of writing', in B. Kroll and G. Wells (eds.), *Explorations in the development of writing* (Chichester: Wiley 1983)

Coffield, F., Robinson, P. and Sarsby, J., *A cycle of deprivation? A case study of four families* (London: Heinemann 1980)

Cohen, G., *The psychology of cognition* (London: Academic Press 1983)

Cole, M. and Griffin, P., 'Cultural amplifiers reconsidered', in D. R. Olsen (ed.), *The social foundations of language and thought* (New York: W. W. Norton 1980)

Cole, M. and Means, B., *Comparative studies of how people think: an introduction* (Cambridge, Mass.: HVP 1981)

Coleman, J., *The nature of adolescence* (London: Methuen 1980)

Coleman, M., *Take one, leave one: young children's*

concepts of subtraction (Unpublished M.Ed. thesis, University of Bristol 1982)

Collerson, J., 'One child and one genre: developments in letter writing', in B. Kroll and G. Wells (eds.), *Explorations in the development of writing* (Chichester: Wiley 1983)

Collins, A. and Smith, E. E., 'Teaching the process of reading comprehension', in D. K. Detterman and R. J. Sternberg (eds.), *How and how much can intelligence be increased?* (Norwood, NJ: Ablex 1982)

Condon, W. S. and Sander, L. W., 'Neonate movement is synchronised with adult speech: interactional participation and language acquisition', *Science*, **183** (1974), pp. 99–101

Conroy, J. S., 'Towards a framework for language functioning in learning mathematics', Paper given at the Fifth International Congress on Mathematics Education Adelaide, Australia, August 1984

Cook, M., *Levels of personality* (London: Holt, Rinehart & Winston 1984)

Corran, G. and Walkerdine, V., *The practice of reason*, vol. 1 (London: Thomas Coran Research Unit, 1981)

Corrigan, R., 'Methodological issues in language acquisition research with very young children', *Developmental Review*, **2** (1982), pp. 162–88

Corsaro, W. A., 'Friendship in the nursery school: social organisation in a peer environment', in S. R. Asher and J. M. Gottman (eds.), *The development of children's friendships* (Cambridge: Cambridge UP 1981)

Coveney, P., *The image of childhood* (Harmondsworth: Penguin 1967)

Cowie, H. (ed.), *The development of children's imaginative writing* (London: Croom Helm 1984)

Cox, M. V. (ed.), *Are young children egocentric?* (London: Batsford 1980)

Crook, C. K., 'Taste perception in the newborn infant', *Infant behaviour and development*, **1**, pp. 52–69

Cross, T., 'Mother's speech adjustments: the contribution of selected child-listener variables', in C. Snow and C. Ferguson (eds.), *Talking to children: language input and acquisition* (Cambridge: Cambridge UP 1977)

Cross, T., 'Mother's speech and its association with rate of linguistic development in young children', in N. Waterson and C. Snow (eds.), *The development of communication* (Chichester: Wiley 1978)

Crowder, R. G., *The Psychology of reading: an introduction* (Oxford: OUP 1982)

Csiksentmihalyi, M., 'The concept of flow', in B. Sutton-Smith (ed.), *Play and Learning* (New York: Gardner Press 1979)

Curtiss, S., *Genie. A psycholinguistic study of a modern-day 'wild child'* (New York: Academic Press 1977)

Dale, P. S., *Language Development* (New York: Holt, Rinehart & Winston 1976)

Dalton, K., *Once a month: the menstrual syndrome* (London: Fontana 1983)

Damon, W. and Hart, D., 'The development of self-understanding from infancy through adolescence', *Child Development*, **53** (1982), pp. 841–64

Davie, C. E., Hutt, C. J., Vincent, E. and Mason, M., *The Young Child at Home* (Windsor: NFER–Nelson 1984)

Davies, B., *Life in the classroom & playground* (London: Routledge & Kegan Paul 1979)

Dawkins, R., *The selfish gene* (Oxford: OUP 1976)

Decarie, T. G., 'A study of the mental and emotional development of the thalidomide child', in B. M. Foss (ed.), *Determinants of infant behaviour*, vol. 4 (London: Methuen 1969)

Decasper, A. J. and Fifer, W. P., 'Of human bonding: newborns prefer their mothers' voices', *Science*, **208** (1980), pp. 1174–6

Delamont, S., *The sociology of women* (London: George Allen & Unwin 1980)

Delamont, S., *Interaction in the classroom* (London: Methuen 1983)

De Mause, L. (ed.), *The history of childhood* (London: Souvenir Press 1976)

Dempster, F. N., 'Memory span: sources of individual and developmental differences', *Psychological Bulletin*, **89** (1981), pp. 63–100

de Villiers, P. A. and de Villiers, J. G., *Early language* (London: Fontana 1979)

Dodge, K. A., Social cognition and children's aggressive behaviour, *Child Development*, **51** (1980), pp. 162–70

Doise, W. and Mackie, D., 'On the social nature of cognition', in J. P. Forgas (ed.), *Social cognition* (New York: Academic Press 1981)

Doise, W. and Mugny, G., *The social development of the intellect* (Oxford: Pergamon 1984)

Donaldson, M., *Children's minds* (London: Fontana 1978)

Donaldson, M., 'Conservation: what is the question?', *British Journal of Psychology*, **73** no.2 (1982), pp. 199–208

Donaldson, M. and Balfour, G., 'Less is more: a study of language comprehension', *British Journal of Psychology*, **59** (1981), pp. 461–71

Donovan, A., Oddy, M., Pardoe, R. and Ades, A., 'Employment status and psychological wellbeing: a longitudinal study of 16-year-old school leavers', *Journal of Child Psychology and Psychiatry*, **27**, (1) (1986), pp. 65–76

Dorval, B. and Eckerman, C. O., 'Developmental trends in the quality of conversation achieved by small groups of acquainted peers', *Monographs of the Society for Research in Child Development*, **49** (2) (1984), serial no. 206

Douvan, E. and Adelson, J., *The adolescent experience* (New York: Wiley 1966)

Dowdney, L., Skuse, D., Rutter, M., Quinton, D. and Mrazek, D., 'The nature and qualities of parenting provided by women raised in institutions', *Journal of Child Psychology & Psychiatry*, **26** (4) (1985) pp. 599–626

Downing, J., *Reading and reasoning* (Edinburgh: Chambers 1979)

Doyle, A. B., Gold, B. and Moskowitz, D. S. (eds.), *Children in families under stress* (San Francisco: Jossey-Bass 1984)

Dunn, J. F., 'The first year of life: continuities in individual differences', in D. Shaffer and J. F. Dunn (eds.) *The first year of life: psychological and medical implications of early experience* (New York: Wiley 1979)

Dunn, J. F., 'Individual differences in temperament', in M. Rutter (ed.), *The scientific foundations of developmental psychiatry* (London: Heinemann 1980)

Dunn, J., 'Sibling relationships in early childhood', *Child Development*, **54** (1983), pp. 787–811

Dunn, J., *Sisters and brothers* (London: Fontana 1984)

Dunn, J. and Kendrick, C., *Siblings: love, envy and understanding* (London: Grant McIntyre 1982)

Dweck, S. and Bush, E. S., 'Sex differences in learned helplessness I', *Developmental Psychology*, **12** (1976), pp. 147–56

Dweck, C. S., Davidson, W., Nelson, S. and Enna, B., 'Sex differences in learned helplessness II & III', *Developmental Psychology*, **14** (1978), pp. 268–76

Dweck, C. S. and Elliott, E. S., 'Achievement motivation', in E. M. Hetherington (ed.), 'Socialisation, personality and social development', vol. 4 of *The Handbook of Child Psychology*, P. H. Mussen (ed.) (New York: Wiley 1983)

Dweck, C. S. and Goetz, T. E., 'Attributions and learned helplessness', in J. H. Harvey, W. Ickles and R. F. Kidd (eds.), *New directions in attribution research*, vol. 2 (Hillsdale, NJ: Erlbaum 1978)

Edwards, C. P. and Lewis, M., 'Young children's concepts of social relations: social functions and social objects', in M. Lewis and L. A. Rosenblum (eds.), *The child and its family: genesis of behaviour*, vol. 2 (New York: Plenum Press 1979)

Ehrhardt, A. A., 'Gender differences: a biosocial perspective', *Nebraska Symposium on Motivation* 1984 (Lincoln, Nebraska: University of Nebraska Press 1985)

Ehrhardt, A. and Meyer-Bahlburg, H., 'Effects of prenatal sex hormones on gender-related behaviour', *Science*, **211** (1981), pp. 1312–18

Eimas, P. D., Siqueland, E. R., Jusczyk, P. and Vigorito, J., 'Speech Perception in Infants', *Science*, **171** (1971), pp. 302–26

Elder, G. H., *Children of the great Depression: Social change in life experience* (Chicago: University of Chicago Press 1974)

Elder, G. H., Nguyen, T. V. and Caspi, A., 'Linking family hardship to children's lives', *Child Development*, **56** (1985), pp. 361–75

Ellis, A. W., *Reading, writing and dyslexia: a cognitive analysis* (London: Erlbaum 1984)

Emler, N. and Valiant, G., 'Social interaction and cognitive conflict in the development of spatial co-ordination skills', *British Journal of Psychology*, **73** (1982), pp. 295–304

Emler, N. and Dickinson, J., 'Children's representation of economic inequalities: the effects of social class', *British Journal of Developmental Psychology*, **3** (2) (1985), pp. 191–8

Ennis, R. H., 'Conceptualization of children's logical competence: Piaget's propositional logic and an alternative proposal', in L. S. Siegel and C. J. Brainerd (eds.), *Alternatives to Piaget* (New York: Academic Press 1978)

Erikson, E., *Childhood and Society* (Harmondsworth: Penguin 1963)

Erikson, E., *Identity: youth and crisis* (London: Faber 1968)

Eron, L. D. 'Parent–child interaction, television violence and aggression of children', *American Psychologist*, **37** (1982), pp. 197–211

Ervin-Tripp, S., 'Some features of early child–adult dialogues', *Language in Society*, **7** (1978), pp. 357–73

Essen, J. and Wedge, P., *Continuities in childhood disadvantage* (London: Heinemann 1982)

Etaugh, C., 'Effects of maternal employment on children: a review of recent research', *Merrill-Palmer Quarterly*, **20** (1974), pp. 71–98

Eysenck, H. J., *The biological basis of personality* (Springfield, Illinois: Charles C. Thomas 1967)

Fagan, J. F., 'Infants' delayed recognition memory and forgetting', *Journal of Experimental Child Psychology*, **16** (1973), pp. 424–50

Fagan, J. F., 'Infants' recognition of invariant features of faces', *Child Development*, **45** (1976), pp. 351–6

Fagen, R., *Animal Play Behaviour* (New York: OUP 1981)

Falbo, T., 'Only children in America', in M. Lamb and B. Sutton-Smith (eds.), *Sibling relationships* (Hillsdale, NJ: Erlbaum 1982)

Fehr, L. A., 'Methodological inconsistencies in the measurement of spatial perspective taking ability: a cause for concern', *Human Development*, **21** (1978), pp. 302–15

Fein, G. G., 'Pretend play: an integrative review', *Child Development*, **52** (1981), pp. 1095–118

Feldman, C. F. and Toulmin, S., 'Logic and the theory of mind', in *Nebraska Symposium on Motivation* (Lincoln: Univ. of Nebraska Press 1976)

Feshbach, S., Feshbach, N. D., Cohen, R. S. and Hoffman, M., 'The antecedents of anger: a developmental approach', in R. M. Kaplan, V. J. Konecni and R. W. Novaco (eds.), *Aggression in children and youth* (The Hague: Martinus Nijhoff 1984)

Field, T. M., 'Effects of early separation, interactive deficits, and experimental manipulations on infant–mother face-to-face interaction', *Child Development*, **48** (1977), pp. 763–71

Field, T. M., Sostek, A. M., Vietze, P. and Leiderman, P. H., *Culture and early interactions* (Hillsdale, NJ: Erlbaum 1981)

Fine, G. A., 'The natural history of preadolescent male friendship groups', in H. C. Foot, A. J. Chapman and J. R. Smith (eds.), *Friendship and social relations in children* (London: Wiley 1980)

Fine, G. A., 'Friends, impression management, and preadolescent behaviour', in S. R. Asher and J. M. Gottman (eds.), *The development of childrens' friendships* (Cambridge: Cambrige UP 1981)

Finkelstein, N. W. and Ramey, C. T., 'Learning to control the environment in infancy', *Child Development*, **48** (1977), pp. 806–19

Fivush, R., 'Negotiating classroom interaction', *The Quarterly Newsletter of the Laboratory of Comparative Human Cognition*, **5** (4) (1983), pp. 83–7

Fivush, R., 'Learning about school: the development of kindergartner's school scripts', *Child Development*, **55** (1984), pp. 1697–709

Flavell, J. H., *The developmental psychology of Jean Piaget* (Princeton, NJ: Van Nostrand 1963)

Flavell, J. H., *Cognitive development* (Englewood Cliffs, NJ: Prentice Hall 1977)

Flavell, J. H., 'The development of knowledge about visual perception', *Nebraska Symposium on Motivation 1977* (Lincoln, Nebraska: University of Nebraska Press 1978a)

Flavell, J. H., 'Comments on Brown & DeLoach's paper in R. S. Siegler (ed.), *Children's thinking: what develops?* (Hillsdale, NJ: Erlbaum 1978b)

Flavell, J. H., 'On cognitive development', *Child Development*, **53** (1982), pp. 1–10

Flavell, J. H., Botkin, P. T., Fry, C. L., Wright, J. W. and Jarvis, P. E., *The development of role-taking and communication skills in children* (New York: Wiley 1968)

Flavell, J. H. and Ross, L. (eds.), *Social cognitive development* (Cambridge: Cambridge UP 1981)

Flavell, J. H. and Markman, E. M. (eds.), *Cognitive development*, vol. 3 of the *Handbook of Child Psychology*, series ed. P. H. Mussen (New York: Wiley 1983)

Flavell, J. H. and Wellman, H. M., 'Metamemory', in R. V. Kail and J. W. Hagen (eds.), *Perspectives on the development of memory and cognition* (Hillsdale, NJ: Erlbaum 1977)

Foot, H. C., Chapman, A. J. and Smith, J. R., *Friendship and social relations in children* (Chichester: Wiley 1980)

Ford, M. E., 'The construct validity of egocentrism', *Psychological Bulletin*, **86** (1979), pp. 1169–88

Forgas, J. (ed.), *Social cognition* (New York: Academic Press 1981)

Francis, H., *Learning to read: literate behaviour and orthographic knowledge* (London: George Allen & Unwin 1982)

Fransella, F., 'The theory and measurement of personal constructs', in K. Franville-Grossman (ed.), *Recent advances in clinical psychiatry* (London: Churchill Livingstone 1976)

Frederiksen, C. H. and Dominic, J. F., *Writing: the nature, development and teaching of written communication*, vol. 2, *Writing: process, development and communication* (Hillsdale, NJ: Erlbaum 1981)

Freeman, N. H. and Cox, M. V. (eds.), *Visual order: the nature and development of pictorial representation* (Cambridge: Cambridge UP 1985)

Freeman, N., Lloyd, S. and Sinha, C. G., 'Infant search tasks reveal early concepts of containment and canonical usage of objects', *Cognition*, **8** (1980), pp. 243–62

Freud, S., 'Three essays on the theory of sexuality', vol. 7 in J. Strachey (ed.), *The standard edition of the complete Psychological works of Sigmund Freud* (London: Hogarth Press 1905/53)

Freud, S., 'The ego and the id', vol. 19 (1923/61)

Freud, S., 'The dissolution of the Oedipus complex', vol. 19 (1924)

Freud, S., 'Some psychical consequences of the anatomical distinction between the sexes', vol. 19 (1924)

Freud, S., 'Civilisation and its discontents', vol. 21 (1930/61)

Freud, S., 'New introductory lectures on psychoanalysis', vol. 22 (1933/64)

Freud, S., 'Analysis of a phobia in a five year old boy', vol. 10 (1955)

Frith, U., 'Reading and spelling skills', in M. Rutter (ed.), *Scientific foundations of developmental psychiatry* (London: Heinemann 1980a)

Frith, U. (ed.), *Cognitive processes in spelling* (London: Academic Press 1980b)

Fry, D. B., 'The development of the phonological system in the normal and the deaf child', in F. Smith and G. A. Miller (eds.), *The genesis of language: a psycholinguistic approach* (Camb., Mass.: MIT Press 1966)

Furman, W. and Buhrmester, D., 'Children's perceptions of the qualities of sibling relationships', *Child Development*, **56** (1985), pp. 448–61

Furth, H., *The world of grown ups* (New York: Elsevier North Holland 1980)

Fuson, K. C. and Hall, J. W., 'The acquisition of early number word meanings: a conceptual analysis and review', in H. P. Ginsburg (ed.), *The development of mathematical thinking* (New York: Academic Press 1983)

Gallup, G. G., 'Self-recognition in primates: a comparative approach to the bidirectional properties of consciousness', *American Psychologist*, **32** (1977), pp. 329–38

Gallup, G., 'Self-recognition in chimpanzees and man', in M. Lewis and L. Rosenblum (eds.), *The child and its family: the genesis of behaviour*, vol. 2 (New York: Plenum 1979)

Galton, M., Simon, B. and Croll, P., *Inside the primary classroom* (London: Routledge & Kegan Paul 1980)

Garbarino, J., *Children and families in the social environment* (New York: Aldine 1982)

Garmezy, N. and Rutter, M., 'Acute reactions to stress', in M. Rutter and L. Hersov (eds.), *Child & adolescent psychiatry: modern approaches* (Oxford: Blackwell 1985)

Garvey, C., 'Requests and responses in children's speech', *Journal of Child Language*, **2** (1975), pp. 41–63

Garvey, C., *Play* (London: Fontana/Open Books 1977)

Garvey, C., *Children's talk* (London: Fontana 1984)

Gelman, R., 'Basic numerical abilities', in Sternberg, R. J. (ed.), *Advances in the psychology of human intelligence*, vol. 1 (Hillsdale, NJ: Erlbaum 1982)

Gelman, R. and Baillargeon, R., 'A review of some Piagetian concepts', in J. H. Flavell and E. M. Markman (eds.), *Handbook of Child Psychology*, vol. 3, series ed. P. Mussen (New York: Wiley 1983)

Gelman, R. and Gallistel, C. R., *The child's understanding of number* (Cambridge, Mass.: Harvard UP 1978)

Gelman, R. and Spelke, E., 'The development of thoughts about animate and inanimate objects: implications for research on social cognition', in J. H. Flavell and L. Ross (eds.), *Social cognitive development* (Cambridge: Cambridge UP 1981)

Gesell, A., *Wolf child and human child* (London: The Scientific Book Club 1942)

Gewirth, A., *Reason and morality* (Chicago and London: Univ. of Chicago Press 1978)

Gholson, B. and Beilin, H., 'A developmental model of human learning', in H. W. Reese and L. P. Lipsitt (eds.), *Advances in Child Development and Beha-*

viour, vol. 13 (1979)

Gibson, E. J., *Principles of perceptual learning and development* (New York: Appleton-Century-Crofts 1969)

Gibson, J. J., *The ecological approach to visual perception* (Boston: Houghton-Mifflin 1979)

Giddens, A. and Held, D., *Classes, power and conflict* (Basingstoke: Macmillan 1982)

Giles, H. and Powesland, P. F., *Speech style and social evaluation* (London: Academic Press 1975)

Gilligan, C., 'In a different voice: women's conceptions of self and morality', *Harvard Educational Review*, **47** (1977), pp. 481–517

Gilligan, C., *In a different voice: Psychological theory and women's development* (Camb., Mass.: Harvard UP 1982)

Ginsburg, H. P. (ed.), *The development of mathematical thinking* (New York: Academic Press 1983)

Gold, D. and Andres, D. 'Comparisons of adolescent children with employed and unemployed mothers', *Merrill-Palmer Quarterly*, **24** (1978), pp. 243–54

Goldman, R. and Goldman, J., *Children's sexual thinking* (London: Routledge & Kegan Paul 1982)

Goldsmith, H. H., 'Genetic influences on personality from infancy to adulthood', *Child Development*, **54** (1983), pp. 331–55

Goodnow, J. J., Compensation arguments on conservation tasks, *Developmental Psychology*, **8** (1) (1973), p. 140

Goodnow, J., and co-authors, 'Adult social cognition', in M. Perlmutter (ed.), 'Cognitive perspectives on children's social and behavioural development', *Minnesota Symposium on Child Psychology (vol. 18)* (Hillsdale, NJ: Lawrence Erlbaum Associates, in press)

Goody, J., *The domestication of the savage mind* (Cambridge: Cambridge UP 1977)

Goody, J. and Watt, I., 'The consequences of literacy', in J. Goody (ed.), *Literacy in traditional societies* (Cambridge: Cambridge UP 1968)

Gordon, J. C. B., *Verbal deficit: a critique* (London: Croom Helm 1981)

Gottlieb, G., 'The psychobiological approach to developmental issues', in M. M. Haith and J. J. Campos (eds.) vol. 2 of the *Handbook of Child Psychology* (New York: Wiley 1983)

Gould, S. J., *Ontogeny and phylogeny* (Cambridge, Mass.: Harvard UP 1977)

Gould, S. J., *The mismeasure of man* (Harmondsworth: Penguin 1984)

Gould, S. J. and Lewontin, R. C., 'The spandrels of San Marco and the Panglossian paradigm: a critique of the adaptationist programme', *Proceedings of the Royal Society of London*, **B205** (1979), pp. 581–98

Gratch, G., Appel, K. J., Evans, W. F., LeCompte, G. K. and Wright, N. A., 'Piaget's Stage IV object concept error: evidence of forgetting of object conception?', *Child Development*, **45** (1974), pp. 71–7

Graves, D., *Writing: teachers and children at work* (Heinemann 1983)

Grice, H. P., 'Logic and conversation', in P. Cole and J. L. Morgan (eds.), *Syntax and semantics*, vol. 3, *Speech acts* (New York: Academic Press 1975)

Griffin, C., *Typical girls? Young women from school to the job market* (London: Routledge & Kegan Paul 1985)

Griffiths, M. and Wells, G., 'Who writes what and why?', in B. Kroll and G. Wells (eds.), *Explorations in the development of writing* (Chichester: Wiley 1983)

Groen, G. J. and Parkman, J. M., 'A chronometric analysis of simple addition', *Psychological Review*, **97** (1972), pp. 329–43

Grotevant, H. D. and Cooper, C. R., 'Patterns of interaction in family relationships and the development of identity exploration in adolescence', *Child Development*, **56** (1985), pp. 415–28

Guttentag, M. and Longfellow, C., 'Children's social attributions development and change', in C. B. Keasey (ed.), *Nebraska Symposium on Motivation* vol. 25 (Lincoln, Nebraska: Univ. of Nebraska Press 1977)

Hagen, J. W. and Hale, G. H., 'The development of attention in children', in *Minnesota Symposium on Child Psychology*, vol. 7 (1973), pp. 117–39

Haith, M. M. and Campos, J. J. (eds.) *Infancy and developmental Psychobiology*, vol. II, *Handbook of Child Psychology*, ed. P. H. Mussen (New York: Wiley 1983)

Halliday, M. A. K. *Learning how to mean* (London: Edward Arnold 1975)

Halverson, C. F. and Waldrop, M. F., 'Relations between preschool activity and aspects of intellectual and social behaviour at age $7\frac{1}{2}$', *Developmental Psychology*, **12** (1976), pp. 107–12

Hamlyn, D. W., *Experience and the growth of understanding* (London: Routledge & Kegan Paul 1978)

Hammersley, M. and Woods, P., *Life in school: the sociology of pupil culture* (Milton Keynes: Open University Press 1984)

Hampson, S. E., *The construction of personality* (London: Routledge & Kegan Paul 1982)

Hardyment, C., *Dream babies: from Locke to Spock* (London: Jonathan Cape 1983)

Hargreaves, D., *Social relations in a secondary school* (London: Routledge & Kegan Paul 1967)

Harlow, H. F. and Harlow, M. K., 'Effects of various mother–infant relationships on rhesus monkey behaviours', in B. M. Foss (ed.), *Determinants of Infant Behaviour*, vol. 4 (London: Methuen 1969)

Harris, P. 'Perception and cognition in infancy', in K. Connely (ed.), *Psychology Survey No. 2* (London: George Allen & Unwin 1979)

Harris, P. L., 'The child as psychologist', in M. Donaldson, R. Grieve and C. Pratt (eds.), *Early childhood development and education* (Oxford: Blackwell 1983a)

Harris, P. L., 'Infant cognition', in M. M. Haith and J. J. Campos (eds.), vol. 2 of the *Handbook of Child Psychology*, series ed. P. H. Mussen (New York: Wiley 1983b)

Harter, S., 'A model of intrinsic mastery motivation in children: individual differences and developmental change', *Minnesota Symposium on Child Psychology*, vol. 14 (Hillsdale, NJ: Erlbaum 1981)

Hartup, W. W., 'Children and their friends', in H. McGurk (ed.), *Issues in childhood social development* (London: Methuen 1978)

Hartup, W. W., *Peer relations*, in E. M. Hetherington (ed.), vol. 4 of the *Handbook of Child Psychology*, series ed. P. H. Mussen (New York: Wiley 1983)

Harvey, P. G. 'Lead and children's health – recent research and future questions', *Journal of Child Psychology and Psychiatry*, **25** (1984), pp. 517–22

Hawkins, P. R., 'Social class, the nominal group and reference', in B. Bernstein (ed.), *Class, codes and control*, vol. 2 (London: Routledge & Kegan Paul 1973)

Hawkins, P. R., *Social class, the nominal group and verbal strategies* (London: Routledge & Kegan Paul 1977)

Hayward, C., *Literary theme development in the nursery classroom* (Unpublished M.Ed. thesis, University of Bristol 1982)

Heath, S. B., 'What no bedtime story means: narrative skills at home and at school', *Language in Society*, **11** (1982), pp. 49–76

Heath, S. B., *Ways with words* (Cambridge: Cambridge UP 1983)

Heider, E. R., 'Focal color areas and the development of color names', *Developmental Psychology*, **4** (1971), pp. 447–55

Heider, E. R., 'Universals in color naming', *Journal of Experimental Psychology*, **93** (1972), pp. 10–20

Heider, F., *The psychology of interpersonal relations*

(New York: Wiley 1958)

Hersov, L., 'Adoption and fostering', in M. Rutter and L. Hersov (eds.), *Child and adolescent psychiatry: modern approaches* (Oxford: Blackwell 1985)

Hetherington, E. M., 'Divorce: a child's perspective', *American Psychologist*, **34** (1979), pp. 851–8

Hinde, R. A., 'Interpersonal relationships: in quest of a science', *Psychological Medicine*, **8** (1978), pp. 373–86

Hinde, R. A. *Towards understanding relationships* (London: Academic Press 1979)

Hinde, R. A., 'Attachment: some conceptual and biological issues', in C. M. Parkes and J. Stevenson-Hinde (eds.), *The place of attachment in human behaviour* (London: Tavistock 1982a)

Hinde, R. A., *Ethology* (London: Fontana 1982b)

Hinde, R. A., 'Ethology and child development', in M. M. Haith and J. J. Campos (eds.), vol. 2 of the *Handbook of Child Psychology* (New York: Wiley 1983)

Hinde, R. A., Easton, D. F., Meller, R. E. and Tamplin A., 'Nature and determinants of pre-schoolers' differential behaviour to adults and peers', *British Journal of Developmental Psychology*, **1** (1983), pp. 3–19

Hinde, R. A. and Tamplin, A., 'Relations between mother–child interaction and behaviour in pre-school', *British Journal of Developmental Psychology*, **1** (1983), pp. 231–57

Hines, M., 'Prenatal gonadal hormones and sex differences in human behaviour', *Psychological Bulletin*, **92** (1982), pp. 56–80

Hirsh-Pasek, K., Gleitman, L. R. and Gleitman, H., 'What did the brain say to the mind? A study of the detection and report of ambiguity by young children', in A. Sinclair, R. J. Jarvella and W. J. M. Levelt (eds.), *The child's conception of language* (Berlin: Springer-Verlag 1978)

Hofer, M. A., *The roots of human behavior: an introduction to the psychology of early development* (San Francisco: W. H. Freeman 1981)

Hoffman, M. L., 'Developmental synthesis of affect and cognition and its implications for altruistic motivation', *Developmental Psychology*, **11** (1975), pp. 607–22

Hoffman, M. L., 'Empathy, its development and pro-social implications', in C. B. Keasey (ed.), *Nebraska Symposium on Motivation*, vol. 25 (Lincoln: Univ. of Nebraska Press 1977)

Hoffman, M. L., 'Is altruism part of human nature?', *Journal of Personality and Social Psychology*, **40** (1981), pp. 121–37

Hoffman, M. L. and Levine, L. E., 'Early sex differ-ences in empathy', *Developmental Psychology*, **12** (1976), pp. 557–8

Hoggart, R., *The uses of literacy* (Harmondsworth: Penguin 1957)

Horn, J. M., 'The Texas Adoption Project: adopted children and their intellectual resemblance to bio-logical and adoptive parents', *Child Development*, **54** (1983), pp. 268–77

Hotopf, W. H. N., 'An examination of Piaget's theory of perception', in B. A. Geber (ed.), *Piaget and knowing: studies in genetic epistemology* (London: Routledge & Kegan Paul 1977)

Houlbrooke, R., *The English family 1450–1700* (London: Longmans 1984)

Howe, M. J. A., *A teacher's guide to the psychology of learning* (Oxford: Blackwell 1984)

Hughes, M., 'What is difficult about learning arith-metic?', in M. Donaldson, R. Grieve and C. Pratt (eds.), *Early childhood development and education* (Oxford: Blackwell 1983)

Hughes, M., Carmichael, H., Pinkerton, G. and Tizard, B., 'Recording children's conversations at home and at nursery school', *Journal of Child Psychology and Psychiatry*, **20** (1979), pp. 225–32

Hughes, M. and Donaldson, M., 'The use of hiding games for studying the coordination of viewpoints', *Educational Review*, **31** (1979), pp. 133–40

Hughes, M., Mayall, B., Moss, P., Perry, J., Petrie, P. and Pinkerton, G., *Nurseries Now* (Harmonds-worth: Penguin 1980)

Humphreys, A. P. and Smith, P. K., 'Rough-and-tumble in preschool and playground', in P. K. Smith (ed.), *Play in animals and humans* (Oxford: Black-well 1984)

Huston, A., 'Sex-typing' in E. M. Hetherington (ed.), vol. 3 of the *Handbook of Child Psychology* (New York: Wiley 1983)

Hutt, C., 'Exploration and play', in B. Sutton-Smith (ed.), *Play and learning* (New York: Gardner Press 1979)

Isbell, B. J. and McKee, L., 'Society's Cradle: an anthropological perspective on the socialisation of cognition', in J. Sants (ed.), *Developmental Psychology and Society* (London: Macmillan 1980)

Istomina, Z. M., 'The development of voluntary memory in preschool-age children', *Soviet Psychology*, **13** (1975), pp. 5–64

Jackson, B., *Fatherhood* (London: George Allen & Unwin 1984)

Jackson, B. and Jackson, S., *Childminder* (London: Routledge & Kegan Paul 1979)

Jahoda, G., 'The construction of economic reality by

some Glaswegian children', *European Journal of Social Psychology*, **9** (1979), pp. 115–27

Jahoda, G., 'The development of thinking about socioeconomic systems', in H. Tajfel (ed.), *The social dimension*, vol. 1 (Cambridge: Cambridge UP 1984)

Jarman, C., *The development of handwriting skills* (London: Basil Blackwell 1979)

Jencks, C., *Inequality: a reassessment of the effect of family and schooling in America* (Harmondsworth: Penguin 1975)

Jenkins, R., *Lads, citizens and ordinary kids: working-class youth life-styles in Belfast* (London: Routledge & Kegan Paul 1983)

Jennings, K. D., Harmon, R. J., Morgan, G. A., Gaiter, J. L. and Yarrow, L. J. 'Exploratory play as an index of mastery motivation: relationships to persistence, cognitive functioning and environmental measures', *Developmental Psychology*, **15** (1979), pp. 386–94

Johns, M. A., 'The role of the vomeronasal system in mammalian reproductive physiology', in D. Muller-Schwarze and R. M. Silverstein (eds.), *Chemical Signals* (New York: Plenum 1980)

Johnson, C. N. and Wellman, H. M., 'Children's developing conceptions of the mind and brain', *Child Development*, **53** (1982), pp. 222–34

Jones, O. H. M., 'A comparative study of mother–child communication with Down's syndrome and normal infants', in D. Shaffer and J. Dunn (eds.), *The first year of life* (Chichester: Wiley 1979)

Jorm, A. F., Share, D. L., Maclean, R. and Matthews, R., 'Cognitive factory at school entry predictive of specific reading retardation and general reading backwardness', *Journal of Child Psychology and Psychiatry*, **27** (1986), pp. 45–54

Kagan, J., 'Information processing in the child: the significance of analytic and reflective attitudes', *Psychological Monographs*, **78** (1964), p. 578

Kagan, J., *The nature of the Child* (New York: Basic Books Inc. 1984)

Kagan, J., Kearsley, R. B. and Zelazo, P. R., *Infancy and its place in human development* (Cambridge, Mass.: Harvard UP 1978)

Kagan, J. and Moss, H. A., *Birth to maturity* (New York: Wiley 1962)

Kail, R., *The development of memory in children* (San Francisco: W. H. Freeman 1979)

Kail, R. and Bisanz, J., 'Information processing and cognitive development', in *Advances in Child Development and Behaviour*, vol. 17 (New York: Academic Press 1982)

Kail, R. and Hagen, J. W. (eds.) *Perspectives on the development on memory and cognition* (Hillsdale, NJ: LEA 1977)

Kamler, B. and Kilarr, G., 'Looking at what children can do', in B. Kroll and G. Wells (eds.), *Explorations in the development of writing* (Chichester: Wiley 1983)

Karmiloff-Smith, A., *A functional approach to child language: a study of determiners and reference* (Cambridge: Cambridge UP 1979)

Karmiloff-Smith, A., 'Getting developmental differences or studying child development?', *Cognition*, **10** (1981), pp. 151–8

Karmiloff-Smith, A., and Inhelder B., 'If you want to get ahead, get a theory', *Cognition*, **3** (1974/5), pp. 195–212

Kaye, K., *The mental and social life of babies* (London: Methuen 1984)

Kaye, K. and Furstenburg, F. F. (eds.), 'Family development and the child', special section of *Child Development*, **56** (2) (1985), pp. 279–501

Keasey, C. B. (ed.), *Social cognitive development Nebraska Symposium on Motivation*, vol. 25 (Lincoln, Nebraska: Univ. of Nebraska Press 1977)

Keil, F., 'Children's thinking: what never develops?', *Cognition*, **10** (1981), pp. 159–66

Keil, F. C., 'Mechanisms in cognitive development and the structure of knowledge', in R. J. Sternberg (ed.), *Mechanisms of cognitive development* (New York: Freeman 1984)

Kelley, H. H., *Personal relationships: their structures and processes* (Hillsdale, NJ: LEA 1979)

Kelso, J. and Stewart, M. A., 'Factors which predict the persistence of aggressive conduct disorder', *Journal of Child Psychology and Psychiatry*, **27** (1986), pp. 77–86

Kempe, R. S. and Kempe C. H., *Child Abuse* (London: Fontana 1978)

King, R., *All things bright and beautiful? A sociological study of infants' classrooms* (London: Wiley 1978)

Kinsbourne, M., 'Brain-based limitations on mind', in R. W. Rieber (ed.), *Mind and body* (New York: Academic Press 1980)

Kinsbourne, M. and Hiscock, M., 'The normal and deviant development of functional lateralisation of the brain', in M. M. Haith and J. J. Campos (eds.), *Infancy and Developmental Psychobiology* vol. 2 of *Handbook of Child Psychology*, series ed. P. H. Mussen (New York: Wiley 1983)

Kitwood, T., *Disclosures to a stranger: adolescent*

values in advanced industrial society (London: Routledge & Kegan Paul 1980)

Klahr, D. and Wallace, J. G., *Cognitive development: an information-processing view* (New York: Erlbaum 1976)

Klaus, M. and Kennell, J., *Maternal–infant bonding* (St Louis: C. V. Mosby 1976)

Klausmeier, H. J. and Sipple, T. S., 'Factor structure of the Piagetian stage of concrete operations', *Contemporary Educational Psychology*, **7** (1982), pp. 161–80

Kobasigawa, A., 'Retrieval factors in the development of memory', in R. V. Kail and J. W. Hagen (eds.), *Perspectives on the development of memory and cognition* (Hillsdale, NJ: Erlbaum 1977)

Kogan, N., 'Stylistic variation in childhood and adolescence: creativity, metaphor and cognitive styles', in J. H. Flavell and E. M. Markman (eds.), vol. 3 of *Handbook of Child Psychology*, series ed. P. H. Mussen (New York: Wiley 1983)

Kohlberg, L., 'Development of moral character and moral ideology', in L. W. Hoffman (ed.), *Review of Child Development Research*, **1** (New York: Russell Sage Foundation 1964), pp. 383–431

Kohlberg, L., 'Stages of moral development as a basis for moral education', in B. Munsey (ed.), *Moral development, moral education and Kohlberg* (Birmingham, Alabama: Religious Education Press 1971)

Kohlberg, L., '"From is to ought": how to commit the naturalistic fallacy and get away with it in the study of moral development', in T. Mischel (ed.), *Cognitive development and epistemology* (New York: Academic Press 1971)

Kohlberg, L., *Essays on moral development*, vol. 2, *The Psychology of moral development. The nature and validity of moral stages* (San Francisco: Harper & Row 1984)

Kohlberg, L., and Candee, D., 'The relationship of moral judgement to moral action', in L. Kohlberg (ed.), *Essays on moral development*, vol. 2, *The Psychology of moral development. The nature and validity of moral stages* (San Francisco: Harper & Row 1984)

Kohlberg, L., Levine, C., Hewer, A., *Moral stages: a current formulation and a response to critics* (Basel: Karger 1983)

Kohn, M., *Social competence, symptoms and underachievement in childhood: a longitudinal perspective* (New York: Wiley 1977)

Koluchova, J., 'Severe deprivation in twins: a case study', in Clarke, A. M. and Clarke, A. D. B. (eds.), *Early experience: myth and evidence* (London: Open Books 1976)

Konner, M., *The tangled wing: biological constraints on the human spirit* (London: Heinemann 1982; Harmondsworth: Penguin 1984)

Kopp, C. B., 'Risk factors in development', in M. M. Haith and J. J. Campos (eds.), vol. 2 of *Handbook of Child Psychology*, series ed. P. H. Mussen (New York: Wiley 1983)

Kroll, B. and Wells, G., *Explorations in the development of writing* (Chichester: Wiley 1983)

Kuhn, T. S., *The structure of scientific revolutions* (Chicago: Chicago University Press 1962)

Kurdek, L. A., 'Perspective taking as the cognitive basis of children's moral development: a review of the literature', *Merrill-Palmer Quarterly*, **24** (1978), pp. 3–28

Kurtines, W. and Grief, E. B., 'The development of moral thought: review and evaluation of Kohlberg's work', *Psychological Bulletin*, **81** (1974), pp. 453–70

Laboratory of Comparative Human Cognition, 'Culture and Intelligence', in R. J. Sternberg (ed.), *Handbook of Human Intelligence* (Cambridge: Cambridge UP 1982)

Labov, W., 1969, 'The logic of non-standard English', in Keddie, N. (ed.), *Tinker, Tailor ... the myth of cultural deprivation* (Harmondsworth: Penguin 1973)

Labov, W., *Sociolinguistic Patterns* (Philadelphia: Univ. of Pennsylvania Press 1972)

Lamb, M. E. and Baumrind, D., 'Socialisation and personality development in the preschool years', in M. E. Lamb (ed.), *Social and personality development* (New York: Holt, Rinehart & Winston 1978)

Lamb, M. E. and Roopnarine, J. L., 'Peer influences on sex-role development in preschoolers', *Child Development*, **50** (1979), pp. 1219–22

Lamb, M. E. and Sherrod, L. R. (eds.), *Infant social cognition: empirical and theoretical considerations* (Hillsdale, NJ: Erlbaum 1981)

Lamb, M. E. and Sutton-Smith, B., *Sibling relationships: their nature and significance across the lifespan* (Hillsdale, NJ: Erlbaum 1982)

Lane, H., *The wild boy of Aveyron* (London: George Allen & Unwin 1976)

Lash, J. P., *Helen and Teacher* (London: Allen Lane 1980)

Laslett, P., *The world we have lost* (London: Souvenir Press 1971)

Laszlo, J. I. and Bairstow, P. J., *Perceptual-motor behaviour: developmental assessment and therapy* (London: Holt, Rinehart & Winston 1985)

Lawton, J. T. and Coleman, M., 'Parents' perceptions of parenting', *Infant Mental Health Journal*, **4** (1983), pp. 352–61

Leach, P., *Who cares? A new deal for mothers and their small children* (Harmondsworth: Penguin 1979)

Lesh, R. and Landau, M. (eds.), *Acquisition of mathematics concepts and processes* (New York: Academic Press 1983)

Levinson, D. J., *The seasons of a man's life* (New York: Knopf 1978)

Lewis, M. and Brooks-Gunn, J., *Social cognition and the acquisition of self* (New York: Plenum 1979)

Lewis, M. and Michalson, L., *Children's emotions and moods: developmental theory and measurement* (New York: Plenum 1983)

Lewis, M. and Rosenblum, L. A. (eds.), *The child and its family* (New York: Plenum 1979)

Liberman, I. Y., Shankweiler, D., Liberman, A. and Fowler, C., 'Phonetic segmentation and reading in the beginning reader', in A. S. Reber and D. L. Scarborough (eds.), *Toward a psychology of reading* (New York: Wiley 1977)

Lickona, T., 'Research on Piaget's theory of moral development', in T. Lickona (ed.), *Moral development and behaviour: theory research and social issues* (New York: Holt, Rinehart & Winston 1976)

Lieven, E. V. M., 'Conversations between mothers and young children: individual differences and their possible implication for the study of language learning', in N. Waterson and C. Snow (eds.), *The development of communications* (Chichester: Wiley 1978)

Lieven, E. V. M., 'Context, process and progress in young children's speech', in M. Beveridge (ed.), *Children thinking through language* (London: Edward Arnold 1982)

Light, P. H., *The development of social sensitivity* (Cambridge: Cambridge UP 1979)

Light, P. H., 'Social interaction and cognitive development: a review of post-Piagetian research', in S. Meadows (ed.), *Developing Thinking* (London: Methuen 1983)

Liss, M. B. (ed.), *Social and cognitive skills: sex roles and children's play* (New York: Academic Press 1983)

Livesley, W. J. and Bromley, D. B., *Person perception in childhood and adolescence* (London: Wiley 1973)

Lobban, G., 'The influence of the school on sex-role stereotyping', in J. Chetwynd and O. Hartnett (eds.), *The sex role system: psychological & sociological perspectives* (London: Routledge & Kegan Paul 1978)

Lock, A. (ed.), *Action, gesture and symbol: the emergence of language* (London: Academic Press 1978)

Loftus, E. F., *Eyewitness testimony* (Cambridge, Mass.: Harvard UP 1979)

London, P., 'The rescuers: motivational hypotheses about Christians who saved Jews from the Nazis', in J. Macauley and L. Berkowitz (eds.), *Altruism and helping behaviour* (New York: Academic Press 1970)

Lord, A. B., *The singer of tales* (Cambridge, Mass.: Harvard UP 1960)

Luria, A. R., *The mind of a mnemonist* (London: Cape 1969)

Luria, A. R., *Cognitive development: its cultural and social foundations* (Cambridge, Mass.: Harvard UP 1976)

Lurie, A., *Only children* (Harmondsworth: Penguin 1980)

Maccoby, E. E., *Social development: psychological growth and the parent–child relationship* (New York: Harcourt Brace Jovanovich 1980)

Maccoby, E. E., 'Socialisation and developmental change', *Child Development*, **55** (1983), pp. 317–28

Maccoby, E. E. and Jacklin, C., *The psychology of sex differences* (Stanford, California: Stanford UP 1978)

Maccoby, E. E. and Jacklin, C., 'Sex differences in aggression: a rejoinder and reprise', *Child Development*, **41** (1980), pp. 964–80

Maccoby, E. E. and Martin, J. A., 'Socialisation in the context of the family: parent–child interaction', in E. M. Hetherington (ed.), vol. 4 of the *Handbook of Child Psychology*, series ed. P. H. Mussen (New York: Wiley 1983)

Macfarlane, J. A., 'Olfaction in the development of social preferences in the human neonate', *CIBA Foundation Symposium on Parent–infant interaction*, **33** (1976), pp. 103–13 (Amsterdam: Elsevier)

McGlaughlin, A., Empson, J., Morrissey, M. and Sever, J., 'Early child development and the home environment: consistencies at and between four pre-school stages', *International Journal of Behavioural Development*, **3** (1980), pp. 299–309

McGlaughlin, A. and Empson, J. M., 'Sisters and their children: implications for a cycle of deprivation', in N. Madge (ed.), *Families at risk* (London: Heinemann 1983)

McGurk, H. (ed.), *Ecological factors in human development* (Amsterdam: North-Holland Publishing Co. 1977)

McGurk, H., *Issues in childhood social development* (London: Methuen 1978)

McLaughlin, B., 'Early bilingualism: methodological and theoretical issues', in M. Paradis and Y. Lebrun (eds.), *Early bilingualism and child development* (Lisse: Swets & Zeitlinger BV 1984)

McRobbie, A. and Nava, M., *Gender and generation* (London: Macmillan 1984)

McShane, J., 'The development of naming', *Linguistics*, **17** (1979), pp. 879–905

McShane, J., *Learning to talk* (Cambridge: Cambridge UP 1980)

McTear, M. *Children's conversation* (Oxford: Blackwell 1985)

Madge, N. (ed.), *Families at risk* (London: Heinemann 1983)

Main, M. and Weston, D. R., 'Avoidance of the attachment figure in infancy: descriptions and interpretations', in C. M. Parkes and J. Stevenson-Hinde (eds.), *The place of attachment in human behaviour* (London: Tavistock 1982)

Maliphant, R., 'Juvenile delinquency', in J. C. Coleman (ed.), *The School Years* (London: Methuen 1979)

Mandler, J. M. and Johnson, N. S., 'Remembrance of things parsed: story structure and recall, *Cognitive Psychology*, **9** (1977), pp. 111–51

Manning, M., Heron, J. and Marshall, T., 'Styles of hostility and social interactions at nursery, at school and at home. An extended study of children', in L. A. Hersov, M. Berger, and D. Schaffer (eds.), *Aggression and anti-social behaviour in childhood and adolescence* (Oxford: Pergamon 1978)

Maratsos, M., 'Some current issues in the study of the acquisition of grammar', in J. H. Flavell and E. M. Markman (eds.), vol. 3 of the *Handbook of Child Psychology* series ed. P. H. Mussen (New York: Wiley 1983)

Markman, E., 'The facilitation of part-whole comparisons by use of the collective noun "family"', *Child development*, **44** (1973), pp. 837–40

Markman, E. M., 'Realising that you don't understand: elementary school children's awareness of inconsistencies', *Child Development*, **50** (1979) pp. 643–55

Markman, E. M., 'Comprehension monitoring', in W. P. Dickson (ed.), *Children's oral communication skills* (New York: Academic Press 1981)

Markman, E., Cox, B. and Machida, S., 'The standard sorting task as a measure of conceptual organisation', *Developmental Psychology* **17**, (1981), pp. 115–17

Martin, B., *A sociology of contemporary cultural change* (Oxford: Blackwell 1981)

Martlew, M., *The psychology of written language: developmental and educational perspectives* (Chichester: Wiley 1983)

Mayer, R., 'Mathematical ability', in R. J. Sternberg (ed.), *Human abilities: an information-processing approach* (New York: W. H. Freeman 1985)

Mead, G. H., *Mind, self and society* (Chicago: Univ. of Chicago Press 1934)

Meadows, S. A. C., 'The development of concrete operations: a short-term longitudinal study', (PhD thesis, University of London 1975)

Meadows, S., 'An experimental investigation of Piaget's analysis of class inclusion', *British Journal of Psychology*, **68** (2) (1977), pp. 229–37

Meadows, S. (ed.), *Developing thinking: approaches to children's cognitive development* (London: Methuen 1983)

Meadows, S. and Cashdan, A., *Teaching styles in nursery education: final report to SSRC* (1983)

Meadows, S., Philps, J., Weaver, J. and Mably, S., 'Adults' and children's views on education, and their behaviour at home and in nursery school: a report on two pilot studies', Paper given at the British Psychological Society Conference, London (December 1977)

Medrich, E. A., Roizen, J. A., Rubin, V. and Buckley, S., *The serious business of growing up: a study of children's lives outside school*

(Berkeley, California: Univ. of California Press 1982)

Mehler, J., Bertoncini, J., Barrier, J. and Jassik-Gerschenfeld, D., 'Infant recognition of mother's voice', *Perception*, **7** (1978) pp. 491–7

Meltzoff, A. and Boston, R. W., 'Intermodal matching by human neonates', *Nature*, **282** (1979), pp. 403–4

Meltzoff, A. and Moore, M. K., 'Imitation of facial and manual gestures by human neonates', *Science*, **198** (1977), pp. 75–8

Midgley, M. *Beast and man: the roots of human nature* (Brighton: Harvester Press 1979)

Millar, S., *The psychology of play* (Harmondsworth: Penguin 1968)

Miller, P., *Theories of developmental psychology* (San Francisco: Freeman 1983)

Miller, S. A., 'On the generalizability of conservation: A comparison of different kinds of transformation', *British Journal of Psychology*, **73** (2) (1982), pp. 221–30

Mills, M. and Funnell, E. 'Experience and cognitive processing', in S. Meadows (ed.), *Developing Thinking* (London: Methuen 1983)

Mischel, T. (ed.), *Cognitive development and epistemology* (New York & London: Academic Press 1971)

Money, J. and Ehrhardt, A., *Man and woman, boy and girl* (Baltimore, Maryland: Johns Hopkins UP 1972)

Morton, J., 'Interaction of information in word recognition', *Psychological Review*, **76** (1969), pp. 165–78

Morton, J., 'The logogen model and orthographic structure', in U. Frith (ed.), *Cognitive processes in spelling* (London: Academic Press 1980)

Munsey, B. (ed.), *Moral development, moral education and Kohlberg* (Birmingham, Alabama: Religious Education Press 1980)

Mussen, P. and Eisenberg-Berg, N., *Roots of caring, sharing and helping: the development of prosocial behaviour in children* (San Francisco: W. H. Freeman 1977)

Myers, N. A. and Perlmutter, M., 'Memory in the years from two to five', in P. A. Ornstein (ed.), *Memory development in Children* (Hillsdale, NJ: LEA 1978)

Nelson, K., 'Structure and strategy in learning to talk', *Monographs of the Society for Research in Child Development*, **38** (1973), serial 149

Nelson, K., 'Social cognition in a script frame-work', in J. H. Flavell and L. Ross (eds.), *Social cognitive development: frontiers and possible futures* (Cambridge: Cambridge UP 1981)

Nelson, K. and Gruendel, J., 'At morning it's lunchtime: a scriptal view of children's dialogues', *Discourse processes*, **2** (1979) pp. 73–94

Nelson, K. E., 'Memory development in children: evidence from non-verbal tasks', *Psychonomic Science*, **25** (1971), pp. 346–8

Nelson, K. E. and Kosslyn, S. M., 'Recognition of previously labelled or unlabelled pictures by 5 year olds and adults', *Journal of Experimental Child Psychology* **21** (1976), pp. 40–5

Nesselroade, J. R. and Baltes, P. B., *Longitudinal research in the study of behaviour and development* (London: Academic Press 1979)

Newcombe, N. E., Rogoff, B. and Kagan, J., 'Developmental changes in recognition memory for pictures of objects and scenes', *Developmental Psychology*, **13** (1977), pp. 337–41

Newson, J., 'Intentional behaviour in the young infant', in D. Schaffer and J. Dunn (eds.), *The first year of life* (Chichester: Wiley 1979)

Newson, J. and Newson, E., *Four years old in an urban community* (London: George Allen & Unwin 1968)

Newson, J. and Newson, E., *Seven years old in the home environment* (London: George Allen & Unwin 1976)

Newson, J. and Newson, E., with Barnes, P. *Perspectives on school at seven years old* (London: George Allen & Unwin 1977)

Nicholls, J. G., 'Causal attributes and other achievement-related cognition', *Journal of Personality & Social Psychology*, **31** (1975), pp. 379–89

Nicholls, J. G., 'The development of the concepts of effort and ability, perception of academic attainment, and the understanding that difficult tasks require more ability', *Child Development* **49** (1978), pp. 800–14

Ninio, A. and Bruner, J. S., 'The achievement and antecedents of labelling', *Journal of Child language*, **5** (1978), pp. 1–15

Nottebohm, F., 'Ontogeny of bird song', *Science* **167** (1970), pp. 950–6

Nowicki, S. and Walker, C., 'The role of generalised and specific expectancies in determining academic achievement', *Journal of Social Psychology*, **94** (1974), pp. 275–80

Nucci, L. P. and Turiel, E., 'Social interactions

and the development of social concepts in pre-school children', *Child Development*, **49** (1978), pp. 400–7

Oakley, A., *Women confined: towards a sociology of childbirth* (Oxford: Martin Robertson 1980)

Ochs, E. and Schieffelin, B. (eds.), *Developmental Pragmatics* (New York: Academic Press 1979)

Ochs, E. and Schieffelin, B., *Acquiring conversational competence* (London: Routledge & Kegan Paul 1983)

O'Faolain, J. and Martines, L., *Not in God's Image* (London: Fontana 1974)

Olson, D. R., 'From utterance to text: the bias of language in speech and writing', *Harvard Educational Review*, **47** (1977), pp. 257–81

Olson, D. R. (ed.), *The social foundations of language and thought: essays in honor of Jerome S. Bruner* (New York & London: W. W. Norton & Co. 1980)

Olson, D. R., 'Some social aspects of meaning in oral and written language', in D. R. Olson (ed.), *The social foundations of language and thought: essays in honor of Jerome S. Bruner* (New York: W. W. Norton & Co. 1980a)

Olson, D. R. and Torrance, N. G., 'Literacy and cognitive development', in S. Meadows (ed.), *Developing Thinking* (London: Methuen 1983)

Olweus, D., 'Stability and aggressive reaction patterns in males: a review', *Psychological Bulletin*, **86** (1979), pp. 852–75

Olweus, D., 'Stability in aggression and withdrawn, inhibited behaviour patterns', in R. M. Kaplan, V. J. Konecri and R. W. Novaco (eds.), *Aggression in children and youth* (The Hague: Martinus Nijhoff 1984)

Opie, I. and Opie, P., *The lore and language of schoolchildren* (London: Oxford UP 1967)

Opie, I. and Opie, P., *Children's games in street and playground* (Oxford: Clarendon 1969)

Opie, I. and Opie, P., *The Singing Game* (Oxford: Oxford UP 1985)

Osborn, A. F., Butler, N. R. and Morris, A. C., *The social life of Britain's five year olds. A report of the Child Health and Education Study* (London: Routledge & Kegan Paul 1984)

Paley, G., *Boys and girls: superheroes in the doll corner* (Chicago: Univ. of Chicago Press 1984)

Papousek, H., 'Experimental studies of appetitional behaviour in human newborns and infants', in H. W. Stevenson, E. H. Hess and H. L. Rheingold (eds.), *Early behaviour* (New York: Wiley 1967)

Paradis, M. and Lebrun, Y. (eds.), *Early bilingualism and child development* (Lisse: Swets & Zeitlinger BV 1984)

Parke, R. D. and Slaby, R. G., 'The development of aggression', in E. M. Hetherington (ed.), vol. 4 of the *Handbook of Child Psychology*, series ed. P. H. Mussen (New York: Wiley 1983)

Parkes, C. M. and Stevenson-Hinde, J. (eds.), *The place of attachment in human behaviour* (London: Tavistock 1982)

Parmelee, A. H. and Sigman, M. D., 'Perinatal brain development and behaviour', in M. M. Haith and J. J. Campos (eds.), vol. 2 of the *Handbook of Child Development*, series ed. P. H. Mussen (New York: Wiley 1983)

Parten, M. B., 'Social participation among preschool children', *Journal of Abnormal Psychology*, **27** (1932), pp. 243–69

Pascual-Leone J., 'A mathematical model for the transition role in Piaget's developmental stages', *Acta Psychologica*, **32** (1970), pp. 301–45

Patrick, J., *A Glasgow gang observed* (London: Methuen 1973)

Patterson, C. J., Cosgrove, J. M. and O'Brien, R. G., 'Non verbal indicants of comprehension and non-comprehension', *Developmental Psychology*, **16** (1) (1980), pp. 38–48

Patterson, G. R., *Families: applications of social learning to family life* (Champaign: Research Press 1975)

Patterson, G. R. and Cobb, J. A., 'A dyadic analysis of "aggressive" behaviours', in J. P. Hill (ed.), *Minnesota symposium on child psychology*, vol. 5 (Minneapolis: Univ. of Minnesota Press 1971)

Patterson, G. R., Littman, R. A. and Bricker, W., 'Assertive behaviour in children: a step toward a theory of aggression', *Monographs of the Society for Research in Child Development*, **32** (serial no. 113) (1967)

Perera, K., *Children's writing and reading: analysing classroom language* (Oxford: Blackwell 1984)

Perlmutter, M. (ed.), 'Parent–child interaction and parent–child relations in child development', *Minnesota Symposium on Child Psychology*, vol. 17 (Hillsdale, NJ: Erlbaum 1984)

Perlmutter, M. (ed.), 'Cognitive perspectives on children's social and behavioural development', *Minnesota Symposium on Child Psychology*, 1984, vol. 18 (Hillsdale, NJ: Lawrence Erlbaum Associates

1984)

Perlmutter, M. (ed.), 'Intellectual development', *Minnesota Symposium on Child Psychology*, 1985, vol. 19 (Hillsdale, NJ: Lawrence Erlbaum Associates 1985)

Peters, A. M., *The units of language acquisition* (Cambridge: Cambridge UP 1983)

Peters, R. S., 'Moral development: a plea for pluralism', in R. S. Peters, *Psychology and ethical development* (London: Allen & Unwin 1974)

Piaget, J., *The child's conception of the world* (London: Routledge & Kegan Paul 1929)

Piaget, J., *The child's conception of physical causality* (London: Routledge & Kegan Paul 1930)

Piaget, J., *The child's conception of number* (New York: Basic Books 1952)

Piaget, J., *The construction of reality in the child* (New York: Basic Books 1954)

Piaget, J., *The language and thought of the child* (London: Routledge & Kegan Paul 1959)

Piaget, J., *Play, dreams and imitation in childhood* (New York: Norton 1962)

Piaget, J., *Six Psychological Studies* (London: Univ. of London Press 1968)

Piaget, J., *The child's conception of time* (London: Routledge & Kegan Paul 1969)

Piaget, J., *Genetic Epistemology* (New York, Columbia U. Press 1970)

Piaget, J., 'The theory of stages on cognitive development', in D. R. Green, M. P. Ford and G. B. Flanner (eds.), *Measurement and Piaget* (New York: McGraw-Hill 1971a)

Piaget, J., *Biology and Knowledge* (Edinburgh: Edinburgh Univ. Press 1971b)

Piaget, J., *Structuralism* (London: Routledge & Kegan Paul 1971c)

Piaget, J., *The development of thought: equilibration of cognitive structures* (Oxford: Blackwell 1978)

Piaget, J. and Inhelder, B., *The Psychology of the Child* (London: Routledge & Kegan Paul 1969)

Pollard, A., *The social world of the primary school* (London: Holt, Rinehart & Winston 1985)

Pollock, L. A., *Forgotten children* (Cambridge: Cambridge UP 1983)

Pool, D. L., Shweder, R. A. and Much, N. C., 'Culture as a cognitive system: differential rule understandings in children and other savages', in E. T. Higgins, D. N. Ruble and W. W. Hartup (eds.), *Social cognition and social development: a socio-cultural perspective* (Cambridge: Cambridge UP 1983)

Putallaz, M. and Gottman, J. M., 'Social skills and group acceptance', in S. R. Asher and J. M. Gottman (eds.), *The development of children's friendships* (Cambridge: Cambridge UP 1981)

Pylyshyn, Z. W., 'When is attribution of beliefs justified?', *Behavioural & Brain Sciences*, **1** (1978), pp. 592–3

Rachlin, H., *Behaviour and learning* (San Francisco: W. H. Freeman 1976)

Radcliffe Richards J., *The sceptical feminist* (Harmondsworth: Penguin 1982)

Radke-Yarrow, M., Zahn-Waxler, C. and Chapman, M., 'Children's prosocial dispositions and behaviour', in E. M. Hetherington (ed.), *Socialisation, personality and social development*, vol. 4 of *Handbook of Child Psychology*, series ed. P. H. Mussen (New York: Wiley 1983)

Raven, J., *Parents, teachers and children: a study of an educational home visiting scheme* (London: Hodder & Stoughton for the Scottish Council for Research in Education 1980)

Ravenette, A. T., 'Grid techniques for children', *Journal of Child Psychology & Psychiatry*, **16** (1975), pp. 79–83

Resnick, L., 'A developmental theory of number understanding', in H. P. Ginsburg (ed.), *The Development of mathematical thinking* (New York: Academic Press 1983)

Rest, J. R., 'Morality', in J. H. Flavell and E. M. Markman (eds.), vol. 3 of *Handbook of Child Psychology*, series ed. P. H. Mussen (New York: Wiley 1983)

Reynolds, P., 'Play, language and human evolution', in J. Bruner, A. Jolly and K. Sylva (eds.), *Play: its role in development and evolution* (Harmondsworth: Penguin 1976)

Reynolds, R. E. and Ortony, A., 'Some issues in the measurement of children's comprehension of metaphorical language', *Child Development*, **51** (1980), pp. 1110–19

Richards, M. P. M., 'Effects on development of medical interventions and the separation of newborns from their parents', in D. Schaffer and J. Dunn (eds.), *The first year of Life* (New York: Wiley 1979)

Richards, M. P. M. and Light, P. H. (eds.), *Children of social worlds: development in a social context* (Cambridge: Polity Press, in press)

Richman, N., Stevenson, J. and Graham, P., *Pre-school to school: a behavioural study* (London: Academic Press 1982)

Robinson, E. J., 'Metacognitive development', in S. Meadows (ed.), *Developing Thinking* (London: Methuen 1983)

Robinson, E. J. and Robinson, W. P., 'Development in the understanding of the causes of success and failure in verbal communication', *Cognition*, **5** (1977), pp. 363–78

Robinson, E. J. and Robinson, W. P., 'Development of understanding about communication: message inadequacy and its role in causing communication failure', *Genetic Psychology Monographs*, **98** (1978), pp. 233–79

Robinson, E. J. and Robinson, W. P., 'Egocentrism in verbal referential communication', in M. V. Cox (ed.), *Are Young Children Egocentric?* (London: Batsford 1980)

Robinson, E. J. and Robinson, W. P., 'Ways of reacting to communication failure in relation to the development of children's understanding about verbal communication', *European Journal of Social Psychology*, **11** (1981), pp. 189–208

Robinson, E. J. and Robinson, W. P., 'The advancement of children's verbal referential communication skills: the role of metacognitive guidance', *International Journal of Behavioural Development*, **5** (1982), pp. 329–55

Robinson, E. J. and Robinson, W. P., 'Communication and metacommunication: quality of children's instructions in relation to judgements about the adequacy of instructions and the locus of responsibility for communication failure', *Journal of Experimental Child Psychology*, **36** (1983), pp. 305–20

Robinson, E. J. and Robinson, W. P., 'Teaching children about verbal referential communication', *International Journal of Behavioural Development* (in press)

Robinson, W. P., 'Social psychology in classrooms', in G. M. Stephenson and J. H. Davis (eds.), *Progress in Applied Social Psychology*, vol. 2 (Chichester: Wiley 1984)

Rogers, C., 'The child's perception of other people', in H. McGurk (ed.), *Issues in Childhood Social Development* (London: Methuen 1978)

Rogers, C., *A social psychology of schooling* (London: Routledge & Kegan Paul 1982)

Rollins, B. C. and Thomas, D. L., 'Parental support, power and control techniques in the socialisation of children', in W. R. Burr, R. Hill, F. I. Nye and I. L. Reiss (eds.), *Contemporary theories about the family*, vol. 1 (New York: Free Press 1979)

Romaine, S., *The language of children and adolescents: the acquisition of communicative competence* (Oxford: Basil Blackwell 1984)

Rosa, A., Ochaita, E., Moreno, E., Fernandez, E. Carretero, M. and Pozo, J. I., 'Cognitive development in blind children: a challenge to Piagetian theory', *Quarterly newsletter of the Laboratory of Comparative Human Cognition*, **6** (1984), pp. 75–81

Rosaldo, M. Z. and Lamphere, L. (eds.), *Woman, Culture and Society* (Stanford: Stanford Univ. Press 1974)

Rosch, E. and Lloyd, B. B. (eds.), *Cognition and Categorisation* (Hillsdale NJ: LEA 1978)

Rose, P., *Parallel lives: five Victorian marriages* (Harmondsworth: Penguin 1985)

Rose, S. A. and Blank, M., 'The potency of context in children's cognition: an illustration through conservation', *Child Development*, **45** (1974), pp. 499–502

Rosen, B., 'Moral dilemmas and their treatment', in B. Munsey (ed.), *Moral development, moral education and Kohlberg* (Birmingham, Alabama: Religious Education Press 1980)

Rosenblatt, D., 'Developmental trends in infant play', in B. Tizard and D. Harvey (eds.), *The biology of play* (London: Heinemann Medical Books 1977)

Ross, L., 'The "intuitive scientist" formulation and its developmental implications', in J. H. Flavell and L. Ross (eds.), *Social cognitive development* (Cambridge: Cambridge UP 1981)

Rotman, B., *Jean Piaget: Psychologist of the Real* (Hassocks, Sussex: Harvester Press 1977)

Rotter, J., Chance, J. and Phares, E., *Applications of a social learning theory of personality* (New York: Holt, Rinehart & Winston 1972)

Rubin, J. Z., Provenzano, F. J. and Luria, Z., 'The eye of the beholder: parents' views on sex of newborns', *American Journal of Orthopsychiatry*, **44** (1974), pp. 512–19

Rubin, K. H., Fein, G. G. and Vandenberg, B., 'Play', in E. M. Hetherington (ed.), vol. 4 of the *Handbook of Child Psychology*, series ed. P. H. Mussen (New York: Wiley 1983)

Rubin, K. H., Watson, K. S. and Jambor, T. W., 'Freeplay behaviours in preschool and kindergarten children', *Child Development*, **49** (1978), pp. 534–6

Rubin, Z., *Children's friendships* (London: Fontana 1980)

Rumelhart, D., 'Toward an interactive model of reading', in S. Dornic (ed.), *Attention and performance*, VI (Hillsdale, NJ: Erlbaum 1977)

Russell, J., *The acquisition of knowledge* (London: Macmillan 1978)

Russell, J., 'Dyadic interaction in a logical reasoning problem requiring inclusion ability', *Child Development*, **52** (1981a), pp. 1322–5

Russell, J., 'Why "socio-cognitive conflict" may

be impossible: the status of egocentric errors in the dyadic performance of a spatial task', *Educational Psychology*, **1** (1981b), pp. 159–69

Russell, J., 'Propositional attitudes', in M. Beveridge (ed.), *Children thinking through language* (London: Edward Arnold 1982)

Russell, J., *Explaining mental life: some philosophical issues in psychology* (London: Macmillan 1984)

Rutter, M., 'Early sources of security and competence', in J. S. Bruner and A. Garton (eds.), *Human Growth and Development* (Oxford: Oxford UP 1978)

Rutter, M., *Changing youth in a changing society* (Cambridge, Mass.: Harvard UP 1980a)

Rutter, M. (ed.), *Scientific foundations of developmental psychiatry* (London: Heinemann Medical 1980b)

Rutter, M., *Maternal deprivation reassessed* (2nd ed.) (Harmondsworth: Penguin 1981)

Rutter, M., 'School effects on pupil progress: research findings and policy implications', *Child Development*, **54** (1983a), pp. 1–29

Rutter, M., 'Low level lead exposure: sources, effects and implications', in M. Rutter and R. R. Jones (eds.), *Lead versus health* (Chichester: Wiley 1983b)

Rutter, M., 'Statistical and personal interactions: facets and perspectives', in D. Magnusson and V. L. Allen (eds.), *Human Development: an interactional perspective* (London: Academic Press 1983c)

Rutter, M., 'Family and school influences on behavioural development', *Journal of Child Psychology and Psychiatry*, **26** (3) (1985a), pp. 349–68

Rutter, M., 'Family and school influences on cognitive development', *Journal of Child Psychology and Psychiatry*, **26** (5) (1985b), pp. 683–704

Rutter, M., 'Psychopathology and development: links between childhood and adult life', in M. Rutter and L. Hersov (eds.), *Child and adolescent psychiatry: modern approaches* (Oxford: Blackwell Scientific Publications 1985c)

Rutter, M. and Garmezy, N., 'Developmental psychopathology', in E. M. Hetherington (ed.), vol. 4 of the *Handbook of Child Psychology*, series ed. P. H. Mussen (New York: Wiley 1983)

Rutter, M. and Giller, H., *Juvenile delinquency* (Harmondsworth: Penguin 1983)

Rutter, M. and Hersov, L. (eds.), *Child and adolescent psychiatry: modern approaches* (Oxford: Blackwell Scientific Publications 1985)

Rutter, M. and Jones, R. R. (eds.), *Lead versus health: sources and effects of low level lead exposure* (Chichester: Wiley 1983)

Rutter, M. and Madge, N., *Cycles of disadvantage* (London: Heinemann 1976)

Rutter, M., Quinton, D. and Liddle, C., 'Parenting in two generations: looking backwards and looking forwards', in N. Madge (ed.), *Families at risk* (London: Heinemann 1983)

Rutter, M., Tizard, J., Yule, W., Graham, P. and Whitmore, K., 'Research Report. Isle of Wight studies 1964–1974', *Psychological Medicine*, **6** (1976), pp. 313–32

Rutter, M. and Yule, W., 'Reading difficulties', in M. Rutter and L. Hersov (eds.), *Child psychiatry: modern approaches* (Oxford: Blackwell 1976)

Saxton, M., *Louisa May: a modern biography of Louisa May Alcott* (London: Andre Deutsch 1978)

Sayers, J., *Biological politics: feminist and anti-feminist perspectives* (London: Tavistock 1982)

Scardamalia, M., 'Information processing capacity and the problem of horizontal décalage: a demonstration using combinatorial reasoning tasks', *Child Development*, **48** (1977), pp. 28–37

Scardamalia, M., 'How children cope with the cognitive demands of writing', in C. H. Frederiksen, M. F. Whitemand and J. F. Dominic (eds.), *Writing: the nature, development and teaching of written communication* (Hillsdale, NJ: Erlbaum 1981)

Scardamalia, M. and Bereiter, C., 'The development of evaluative, diagnostic and remedial capabilities in children's composing', in M. Martlew (ed.), *The psychology of written language* (Chichester: John Wiley & Sons 1983)

Scarr, S. and Grajek, S., 'Similarities and differences among siblings', in M. Lamb and B. Sutton-Smith (eds.), *Sibling relationships* (Hillsdale, NJ: Erlbaum 1982)

Scarr, S. and Kidd, K. K., 'Developmental behaviour genetics', in M. M. Haith and J. J. Campos (eds.), vol. 2 of the *Handbook of Child Psychology*, series ed. P. H. Mussen (New York: Wiley 1983)

Scarr, S. and McCartney, K., 'How people make

their own environments: a theory of genotype → environment effects', *Child Development,* **54** (1983), pp. 424–35

Scarr, S. and Weinberg, R. A., 'The Minnesota Adoption studies: genetic differences and malleability', *Child Development,* **54** (1983), pp. 260–7

Schachter, F. F., 'Sibling deidentification and split-parent identification: a family trend', in M. Lamb and B. Sutton-Smith (eds.), *Sibling relationships* (Hillsdale, NJ: Erlbaum 1982)

Schaffer, H. R., *The child's entry into a social world* (London: Academic Press 1984)

Schaffer, H. R. and Emerson, P. E., 'The development of social attachments in infancy', *Monographs of the Society for Research in Child Development,* **29** (3) serial no. 94 (1964)

Schank, R. C. and Abelson, R., *Scripts, plans, goals and understanding* (Hillsdale, NJ: LEA 1977)

Schieffelin, B. B. and Cochran-Smith, M., 'Learning to read culturally: literacy before schooling', in H. Goetman, A. Oberg and F. Smith (eds.), *Awakening to literacy* (London: Heinemann 1984)

Schwartzman, H., *Transformations: the anthropology of children's play* (New York: Plenum 1978)

Scribner, S. and Cole, M., *The psychology of literacy* (Cambridge, Mass.: Harvard UP 1981)

Searle, J., *Speech acts* (Cambridge: Cambridge UP 1969)

Searle, J., 'A classification of illocutionary acts', *Language & Society,* **5** (1975), pp. 1–23

Searle, J., *Minds, brains and science: the 1984 Reith Lectures* (London: BBC Publications 1984)

Seitz, V., Rosenbaum, L. K. and Apfel, N. H., 'Effects of family support intervention: a ten year follow-up', *Child Development,* **56** (1985), pp. 376–91

Selman, R. L., 'The child as a friendship philosopher', in S. R. Asher and J. M. Gottman (eds.), *The development of children's friendships* (Cambridge: Cambridge UP 1981)

Selman, R. L. and Jaquette, D., 'Stability and oscillation in inter-personal awareness: a clinical-developmental analysis', in C. B. Keasey (ed.), *Nebraska Symposium on Motivation,* vol. 25 (Lincoln, Nebraska: Univ. of Nebraska Press 1977)

Serbin, L. A., Connor, J. M. and Citron, C. C.,

'Environmental control of independent and dependent behaviours in preschool girls and boys: a model for early independence training', *Sex Roles,* **4** (1978), pp. 867–75

Serbin, L. A., O'Leary, K. D., Kent, R. N. and Tonick, I. J., 'A comparison of teacher response to the preacademic and problem behaviour of boys and girls', *Child Development,* **44** (1973), pp. 796–804

Serbin, L. A., Tonick, I. J. and Sternglanz, S. H., 'Shaping co-operative cross-sex play', *Child Development,* **48** (1977), pp. 924–9

Shaffer, D., 'Brain Damage', in M. Rutter and L. Hersov (eds.), *Child & adolescent psychiatry: modern approaches* (Oxford: Blackwell 1985)

Shaffer, D. R. and Brody G. H., 'Parental and peer influences on moral development', in R. W. Henderson (ed.), *Parent–child interaction* (New York: Academic Press 1981)

Shantz, C. U., 'Social cognition', in J. Flavell and E. Markman (eds.), vol. 3 of the *Handbook of Child Psychology,* series ed. P. H. Mussen (New York: Wiley 1983)

Shatz, M., 'The relationship between cognitive processes and the development of communication skills', *Nebraska Symposium on Motivation,* 1977 (Lincoln, Nebraska: Univ. of Nebraska Press 1978)

Shatz, M. and Gelman, R., 'The development of communication skills', *Monographs of the Society for Research in Child Development,* **38** (5), serial no. 152 (1973)

Shatz, M. and Gelman, R., 'Beyond syntax: the influence of conversational constraints on speech modifications', in C. E. Snow and C. A. Ferguson (eds.), *Talking to children* (Cambridge: Cambridge UP 1977)

Shepar, R. N., 'Recognition memory for words, sentences and pictures', *Journal of Verbal Learning & Verbal Behaviour,* **6** (1967), pp. 156–63

Shields, M. M. and Duveen, G., *The young child's image of the personal and social world: some aspects of the child's representation of persons,* Paper presented at the International Sociological Association Conference Mexico City (August 1982)

Shultz, T. R., 'Play as arousal modulation', in B. Sutton-Smith (ed.), *Play and learning* (New York: Gardner Press 1979)

Shweder, R. A., Turiel, E. and Much, N. C.,

'The moral intuitions of the child', in J. H. Favell and L. Ross (eds.), *Social cognitive development* (Cambridge: Cambridge UP 1981)

Siegel, L. S., 'Development of the concept of seriation', *Developmental Psychology,* **5** (1972), pp. 135–7

Siegel, L. S., 'The relationship of language & thought in the preoperational child: a reconsideration of nonverbal alternatives to Piagetian tasks', in L. S. Siegel and C. J. Brainerd (eds.), *Alternatives to Piaget* (New York: Academic Press 1978)

Siegel, L. S., McCabe, A. E., Brand, J. and Matthews, J., 'Evidence for the understanding of class inclusion in preschool children: linguistic factors and training effects', *Child Development,* **49** (1978), pp. 688–93

Siegler, R. S., 'Developmental sequences within and between concepts', *Monographs of the Society for Research in Child Development,* **46** (1981), pp. 1–74

Siegler, R. S., 'Information processing approaches to development', in W. Kessen (ed.), vol. 1 of the *Handbook of Child Psychology,* series ed. P. H. Mussen (New York: Wiley 1983)

Siegler, R. S., 'Mechanisms of cognitive growth: variation and selection', in R. J. Sternberg (ed.), *Mechanisms of cognitive development* (New York: W. H. Freeman 1984)

Siegler, R. S. and Robinson, M., 'The development of numerical understandings', in H. W. Reese and L. P. Lipsitt (eds.), *Advances in Child Development and Behaviour,* vol. 16 (New York: Academic Press 1982)

Sinclair, A., Jarvella, R. J. and Levelt, W. J. M., *The child's conception of language* (Berlin: Springer-Verlag 1978)

Sinclair, J. M. and Coulthard, R. M., *Towards an analysis of discourse: the English used by teachers and pupils* (Oxford: Oxford UP 1975)

Skinner, B. F., *Walden Two* (New York: Macmillan 1948)

Skuse, D., 'Extreme deprivation in early childhood I Diverse outcomes for three siblings from an extraordinary family II. Theoretical issues and a comparative review', *Journal of Child Psychology & Psychiatry,* **25** (1984), pp. 523–42, 543–72

Slobin, D. I., 'A case study of early language awareness', in A. Sinclair, R. J. Jarvella and W. J. M. Levelt (eds.), *The child's conception of language* (Berlin: Springer-Verlag 1978)

Sluckin, A., *Growing up in the playground* (London: Routledge & Kegan Paul 1981)

Sluckin, W., Herbert, M. and Sluckin, A., *Maternal bonding* (Oxford: Blackwell 1983)

Smedslund, J., 'Analyzing the Primary Code: from Empiricism to Apriorism', in D. R. Olson (ed.), *The social foundations of language and thought* (New York: W. W. Norton 1980)

Smith, F., *Reading* (Cambridge: Cambridge UP 1978)

Smith, F., *Writing and the writer* (London: Heinemann 1982)

Smith, N. V., *The acquisition of phonology. a case study* (Cambridge: Cambridge UP 1973)

Smith, P. K. (ed.), *Play in animals and humans* (Oxford: Blackwell 1984)

Smith, P. K. and Connolly, K. J., *The behavioural ecology of the preschool* (Cambridge: Cambridge UP 1981)

Smith, P. K. and Green, M., 'Aggressive behaviour in English nurseries and playgroups. Sex differences and response of adults', *Child Development,* **46** (1975), pp. 211–14

Smith, P. K. and Simon, T., 'Object play, problem-solving and creativity in children', in P. K. Smith (ed.), *Play in animals and humans* (Oxford: Blackwell 1984)

Smith, P. K., Simon, T. and Emberton, R., 'Play, problem solving and experimenter effects', *British Journal of Developmental Psychology,* **3** (1985), pp. 105–7

Sroufe, L. A., 'Individual patterns of adaptation from infancy to preschool', in M. Perlmutter (ed.), *Minnesota Symposium on Child Psychology,* vol. 16 (Hillsdale NJ: Erlbaum 1983)

Sroufe, L. A. and Waters, E., 'Attachment as an organisational construct', *Child Development,* **48** (1977), pp. 1184–99

Standing, L., 'Learning 10,000 Pictures', *Quarterly Journal of Experimental Psychology,* **25** (1973), pp. 207–22

Steedman, C., *The tidy house* (London: Virago 1982)

Stent, G. S. (ed.), *Morality as a biological phenomenon* (Berlin: Dahlem Conferenzen 1978)

Sternberg, R. J. (ed.), *Handbook of human intelligence* (Cambridge: Cambridge UP 1982)

Sternberg, R. J. (ed.), *Mechanisms of cognitive development* (New York: W. H. Freeman 1984)

Sternberg, R. J., 'Mechanisms of cognitive development: a componential approach', in R. J. Sternberg (ed.), *Mechanisms of cognitive development* (New York: Freeman 1984)

Stillwell, R. and Dunn, J., 'Continuities in sibling relationships: patterns of aggression and friendliness', *Journal of Child Psychology & Psychiatry,* **26** (4) (1985), pp. 627–38

Stipek, D. J. and Weisz, J. R., 'Perceived personal control and academic achievement', *Review of Educational Research,* **51** (1981), pp. 101–37

Stockard, J. and Johnson, M. H., *Sex roles: sex inequality and sex role development* (Englewood Cliffs: Prentice Hall 1980)

Streeter, L., 'Language perception of 2 month-old infants shows effects of both innate mechanisms and experience', *Nature,* **259** (1976), pp. 39–41

Stubbs, M., *Language and literacy: the sociolinguistics of reading and writing* (London: Routledge & Kegan Paul 1980)

Stubbs, M., *Language, schools and classrooms* (London: Methuen 1983)

Sulloway, F. J., *Freud, biologist of the mind* (London: Fontana 1980)

Super, C. M., Clement, J., Vuori, L., Christiansen, N., Mora, J. O. and Herrera, M. G., 'Infant & caretaker behaviour as mediators of nutritional and social intervention in the barrios of Bogota', in T. M. Field, A. M. Sostek, P. Vietze and P. H. Leiderman (eds.), *Culture and early interactions* (Hillsdale, NJ: Erlbaum 1981)

Sutton, A., 'An introduction to Soviet developmental psychology', in S. Meadows (ed.), *Developing Thinking* (London: Methuen 1983)

Sutton-Smith, B. (ed.), *Play and learning* (New York: Gardner Press 1979)

Sutton-Smith, B. and Kelly-Byrne, D., 'The idealisation of play', in P. K. Smith (ed.), *Play in animals and humans* (Oxford: Blackwell 1984)

Sylva, K., 'Play and learning', in B. Tizard and D. Harvey (eds.), *The biology of play* (London: Heinemann 1977)

Sylva, K., Roy, C. and Painter, M., *Childwatching in playgroup and nursery school* (London: Grant McIntyre 1980)

Tamburrini, J., Willig, J. and Butler, C., 'Children's conceptions of writing', in H. Cowie (ed.), *The development of children's imaginative writing* (London: Croom Helm 1984)

Tanner, J. M., *Foetus into Man: physical growth from conception to maturity* (London: Open Books 1978)

Taylor, E., 'The development of attention', in M. Rutter (ed.), *Scientific foundations of Developmental Psychiatry* (London: Heinemann 1980)

Taylor, E., 'Syndromes of overactivity and attention deficit', in M. Rutter and L. Hersov (eds.), *Child & adolescent psychiatry: modern approaches* (Oxford: Blackwell 1985)

Taylor, M. C. and Hall, J., 'Psychological androgyny: theories, methods & conclusions', *Psychological Bulletin,* **92** (1982), pp. 347–66

Teale, W. H., 'Reading to young children: its significance for literacy development', in H. Goelman, A. Oberg and F. Smith (eds.), *Awakening to literacy* (London: Heinemann 1984)

Thomas, A. and Chess, S., *Temperament and development* (New York: Brunner/Mazel 1977)

Thomas, K., *Man and the natural world* (Harmondsworth: Penguin 1984)

Thomassen, A. J. W. M. and Teulings, H-L. H. M., 'The development of handwriting', in M. Martlew (ed.), *The psychology of written language* (Chichester: Wiley 1983)

Thwaite, A., *Edmund Gosse* (London: Secker & Warburg 1984)

Tinbergen, N., *Study of instinct* (Oxford: Clarendon Press 1951)

Tizard, B., *Adoption: a second chance* (London: Open Books 1977)

Tizard, B. and Hughes, M., *Young children learning* (London: Fontana 1984)

Tizard, B., Hughes, M., Pinkerton, G. and Carmichael, H., 'Adults' cognitive demands at home and at nursery school', *Journal of Child Psychology and Psychiatry,* **23** (2) (1982), pp. 108–17

Tizard, B., Mortimore, J. and Burchell, B., *Involving parents in nursery and infant schools* (London: Grant McIntyre 1981)

Tizard, B., Philps, J. and Plewis, I., 'Play in preschool centres, I and II', *Journal of Child Psychology and Psychiatry,* **17** (1976), pp. 251–74

Tizard, J., Schofield, W., Hewison, J., 'Collaboration between teachers and parents in assisting children's reading', *British Journal of Educational Psychology,* **52** (1981), pp. 1–5

Tolstoy, L. (translated R. Edmonds), *Anna Karenina* (Harmondsworth: Penguin Classics 1954)

Tough, J., *Focus on meaning: a study of children's use of language* (London: George Allen & Unwin 1973)

Tough, J., *The development of meaning* (London: George Allen & Unwin 1977)

Trabasso, T., 'Representation, memory and reasons: how do we make transitive inferences?', in A. D. Pick (ed.), *Minnesota symposium on child psychology*, vol. 9 (Minneapolis: University of Minnesota 1975)

Trabasso, T. and Nicholas, D. W., 'Memory and inferences in the comprehension of narratives', in F. Wilkening, J. Becker and T. Trabasso (eds.), *Information integration by children* (Hillsdale, NJ: Erlbaum 1980)

Trehub, S. E. and Rabinovitch, M. S., 'Auditory-linguistic sensitivity in early infancy', *Developmental Psychology*, **6** (1972), pp. 74–7

Trevarthen, C., 'Communication and cooperation in early infancy', in M. Bullowa (ed.), *Before speech* (Cambridge: Cambridge UP 1978)

Trevarthen, C., 'The foundations of intersubjectivity: development of interpersonal and co-operative understanding in infants', in D. R. Olson (ed.), *The social foundations of language and thought* (New York: W. W. Norton & Co. 1980)

Trevarthen, C., 'The primary motives for co-operative understanding', in G. Butterworth and P. Light (eds.), *Social cognition: studies of the development of understanding* (Brighton: Harvester Press 1982)

Trivers, R., *Social evolution* (Menlo Park, California: The Benjamin/Cummings Publishing Company 1985)

Trowell, J., 'Effects of obstetric management on the mother–child relationship', in C. M. Parkes and J. Stevenson-Hinde (eds.), *The place of attachment in human behaviour* (London: Tavistock 1982)

Tucker, N., *The child and the book* (Cambridge: Cambridge UP 1981)

Tulving, E., 'Episodic and semantic memory', in E. Tulving and W. Donaldson (eds.), *Organisation of memory* (New York: Academic Press 1972)

Turiel, E., 'Stage transition in moral development', in R. Travers (ed.), *Second handbook of research in teaching* (Chicago: Rand McNally 1973), pp. 732–58

Turiel, E., 'Distinct conceptual and developmental domains: social convention and morality', in C. B. Keasey (ed.), *Nebraska Symposium on Motivation 1977* (1978)

Turnbull, C., *The mountain people* (London: Pan Books 1974)

Vaillant, G. E., *Adaptation to life* (Waltham, Mass.: Little, Brown 1977)

Valentine, E. R., *Conceptual issues in psychology* (London: George Allen & Unwin 1982)

Vandell, D. L. and Mueller, E. C., 'Peer play and friendships during the first two years', in H. C. Foot, A. J. Chapman and J. R. Smith (eds.), *Friendship and social relations in children* (Chichester: Wiley 1980)

Vuyk, R., *Overview and critique of Piaget's genetic Epistemology 1965–1980*, vols. 1 and 2 (London: Academic Press 1981)

Vygotsky, L. S., *Thought and language* (Harvard: MIT Press 1962)

Vygotsky, L. S., *Mind in Society*, M. Cole, V. John-Steiner, S. Scribner and E. Souberman (eds.) (Cambridge, Mass.: Harvard UP 1978)

Vygotsky, L. S., 'The prehistory of written language', in M. Cole, V. John-Steiner, S. Scribner and E. Souberman (eds.), *Mind in Society: the development of higher psychological processes* (Cambridge, Mass.: Harvard UP 1978a)

Wadsworth, M., *Roots of delinquency* (Oxford: Martin Robertson 1979)

Wadsworth, M. and Wingfield, J., 'Preschool experience, parenting styles and later verbal attainment scores in a national longitudinal study', *Journal of Early Childhood Research* (in press)

Wagner, D. A., 'Ontogeny in the study of culture and cognition', in D. A. Wagner and H. W. Stevenson (eds.), *Cultural perspectives on child development* (San Francisco: W. H. Freeman 1982)

Walzer, M., *Just and unjust wars* (Harmondsworth: Penguin 1984)

Ward, S., Wackman, D. B. and Wartella, E., *How children learn to buy: the development of consumer information-processing skills* (Beverley Hills: Sage Publications 1977)

Wason, P. C. and Johnson-Laird, P. N., *The Psychology of Reasoning* (London: Batsford 1972)

Watson, P., *Twins: an investigation into the strange coincidences in the lives of separated twins* (London: Hutchinson 1981)

Weikart, D., *An economic analysis of the Ypsilanti Perry Preschool Project* (Ypsilanti: High/Scope Educational Research Foundation 1978)

Weiner, B. (ed.), *Achievement and attribution theory* (Morristown, NJ: General Learning Press 1974)

Weiner, B., 'A theory of motivation for some classroom experiences', *Journal of Educational Psychology,* **71** (1979), pp. 3–25

Weiner, B. and Kukla, A., 'An attributional analysis of achievement behaviour', *Journal of Personality and Social Psychology,* **15** (1970), pp. 1–20

Weinreich-Haste, H. (in press), 'Engagement and commitment: the role of affect in moral reasoning and moral responsibility', to be published (in German initially) in W. Edelstein and G. Nunner (eds.) (Title to be announced) (Suhrkamp Verlag 1986)

Wells, B. W. P., *Personality and heredity* (London: Longmans 1980)

Wells, C. G., 'Describing children's linguistic development at home and at school', *British Educational Research Journal,* **5** (1979), pp. 75–98

Wells, C. G., 'Some antecedents of early educational attainment', *British Journal of Sociology of Education,* **2** (1981a), pp. 181–200

Wells, C. G., 'Pre-school literacy related activities and success in school', in D. R. Olson (ed.), *The nature and consequences of literacy* (Cambridge: Cambridge UP 1981b)

Wells, C. G. *Language, learning and education* (Bristol: Centre for the study of language and communication 1982a)

Wells, C. G., 'Influences of the home on language development', in A. Davies (ed.), *Language and learning in school and home* (London: SSRC/Heinemann 1982b)

Wells, C. G. *Language development in the pre-school years* (Cambridge: Cambridge UP 1985)

West, D. J., *Delinquency: its roots, careers and prospects* (London: Heinemann 1982)

West, D. J., 'Delinquency', in M. Rutter and L. Hersov (eds.), *Child and adolescent psychiatry: modern approaches* (Oxford: Blackwell 1985)

Wetherford, M. J., and Cohen, L. B., 'Developmental changes in infant visual preferences for novelty and familiarity', *Child Development,* **44** (1973), pp. 416–24

Whiting, B. B. and Whiting, J. W. M., *Children of six cultures* (Cambridge, Mass.: Harvard UP 1975)

Whittaker, S., 'Memory development in 3 to 6 year olds: learning how to learn' (Unpublished PhD thesis, University of St Andrews 1983)

Wilkinson, A. *et al., Assessing language development* (Oxford: OUP 1980)

Willes, M. J., *Children into pupils: a study of language in early schooling* (London: Routledge & Kegan Paul 1983)

Wilson, E. O., *Sociobiology* (Cambridge, Mass.: Belknap/Harvard 1975)

Wilson, H. and Herbert, G. W., *Parents and children in the inner city* (London: Routledge & Kegan Paul 1978)

Wilson, J., 'Philosophical difficulties and "moral development"', in B. Munsey (ed.), *Moral development, moral education and Kohlberg* (Birmingham, Alabama: Religious Education Press 1980)

Wilson, R. S., 'The Louisville Twin Study: developmental synchronies in behaviour', *Child Development,* **54** (1983) pp. 298–316

Wimmer, H. 'Children's understanding of stories: assimilation by a general schema for actions of coordination of temporal relations?', in F. Wilkening, J. Becker and T. Trabasso (eds.), *Information integration by children* (Hillsdale, NJ: Erlbaum 1980)

Winnicott, D. W., *Collected Papers* (London: Tavistock 1958)

Witkin, H. A., *Cognitive styles in personal and cultural adaptation* (Worcester, Mass.: Clark Univ. Press 1977)

Witkin, H. A. and Goodenough, D. R., *Cognitive Styles: essence and origins* (New York: International Universities Press 1981)

Witkin, H. A., Goodenough, D. R. and Oltman, P. K., 'Psychological differentiation: current status', *Journal of Personality & Social Psychology,* **37** (1979), pp. 1127–45

Wolff, P. H., 'The natural history of crying and other vocalisations in early infancy', in B. M. Foss (ed.), *Determinants of infant behaviour,* vol. IV (London: Tavistock/Methuen 1966)

Wollheim, R. *Freud* (London: Fontana 1971)

Wood, D. J., 'Teaching the young child: some relationships between social interaction, language and thought', in D. R. Olson (ed.), *The social foundations of language and thought* (New York: Norton 1980)

Wood, D. J., *Working with underfives* (London: Grant McIntyre 1981)

Wood, D. J., Bruner, J. S. and Ross, G., 'The role of tutoring in problem solving', *Journal of Child Psychology and Psychiatry,* **17** (2) (1976), pp. 89–100

Yarrow, L. J. and Klein, R. P., 'Environmental discontinuity associated with transition from foster to adoptive homes', *International Journal of Behavioural Development,* **3** (1980), pp. 311–22

Yarrow, M. R. and Waxler, C. Z., 'Dimensions and correlates of prosocial behaviour in young children', *Child Development,* **47** (1976), pp. 118–25

Yawkey, T. D. and Pellegrini, A. D., *Child's play: developmental and applied* (Hillsdale, NJ: Erlbaum 1984)

Young, G. and Lewis, M., 'Effects of familiarity and maternal attention on infant peer relations', *Merrill-Palmer Quarterly,* **25** (1979), pp. 105–19

Yule, W. and Rutter, M., 'Reading and other learning difficulties', in M. Rutter and L. Hersov (eds.), *Child and adolescent psychiatry: modern approaches* (Oxford: Blackwell 1985)

Yussen, S. R. and Levy, V. M., 'Developmental changes in predicting one's own span of short-term memory', *Journal of Experimental Child Psychology,* **19** (1975), pp. 502–8

Zahn-Waxler, C., Radke-Yarrow, M. and King, R., 'Child rearing and children's prosocial initiations towards victims of distress', *Child Development,* **50** (1979), pp. 319–30

Zajonc, R. B. and Marcus, G. B., 'Birth order and intellectual development', *Psychological Review,* **82** (1975), pp. 74–88

Zingg, R. M., 'Feral man and extreme cases of isolation', *American Journal of Psychology,* **530** (1940), pp. 487–517

Zipes, J., *Fairytales and the art of subversion* (London: Heinemann 1983)

Author index

Subject index